D1452777

PERSPECTIVES ON SOUTHERN AFRICA

The House of Phalo

The House of Phalo

*A History of the Xhosa People
in the Days of Their
Independence*

J. B. Peires

UNIVERSITY OF CALIFORNIA PRESS
BERKELEY LOS ANGELES LONDON

For Mom and Dad

University of California Press
Berkeley and Los Angeles

University of California Press, Ltd.
London, England

© J. B. Peires 1981, 1982

First published in 1981 by Ravan Press (Pty) Ltd.
Johannesburg, South Africa

Grateful acknowledgement is made
to the Africana Museum, Johannesburg
for various reproductions which illustrate the author's text.

Library of Congress Cataloging in Publication Data

Peires, J. B. (Jeffrey B.)
  The house of Phalo.
  (Perspectives on Southern Africa; 32)
  Bibliography: p.
  Includes index.
  1. Xosa—History. I. Title. II. Series.
DT764.X6P44 1982   968'.004963 82-2624
ISBN 0-520-04663-3 AACR2

Contents

ABBREVIATIONS

The following refer to series in the Cape Archives, Cape Town:

Acc	Accessions
BK	British Kaffraria
BO	British Occupation (1795 – 1803)
CO	Colonial Office (ie Secretary to the Governor of the Cape)
GH	Government House (Dispatches from the Governor to the Secretary of State in London)
GR	Graaff-Reinet
LG	Lieutenant-Governor of the Eastern Cape
VC	Verbatim Copies (of original documents in other places)

Other abbreviations:

Abo Com	Report of the Select Committee on Aborigines, Parliamentary Paper 538 of 1836. (All other Parliamentary Papers are cited by number and year only.)
CFT	*Cape Frontier Times*
GTJ	*Grahams Town Journal*
MS	Manuscript in Cory Library, Grahamstown
RCC	*Records of the Cape Colony,* ed. G.M. Theal (London, 1897–1905)

Preface

This book is a history of the Xhosa people in the days of their independence. Despite its importance, there has been only one previous book on this subject, John Henderson Soga's *The South Eastern Bantu* published more than 50 years ago. Although *The South-Eastern Bantu* still demands attention and respect, Soga did not have access to the secret documents and private papers of persons living before 1850, and he possessed only a limited selection of printed books. Many of these were biased and prejudiced — for example with regard to the so-called Bantu migrations — and their effect on *The South-Eastern Bantu* was almost entirely negative. And so, great work though it undoubtedly is, the only existing history of the Xhosa suffers from serious flaws of omission and inaccuracy.

The House of Phalo is an attempt to write a complete and comprehensive account of Xhosa history. This is not to say that it is final or definitive, and I fully expect that many people who read this book will be dissatisfied with all or part of it. Some are going to say, this is not what we heard from our fathers. Others, perhaps, will say, this is not what we learnt in school. There is nothing strange in this. Just as no two people visiting a foreign country will form exactly the same opinion of it, so each person who approaches the past finds different aspects of it significant. No history book can recreate the past as it actually was: it can only record the impressions of a particular observer, and what an observer sees depends to a considerable extent on what sort of person he is.

This book is no exception. The section on chiefship would have been different if it had been written by someone who believed in the royalty of the blood; the section on Ntsikana would have been different if it had been written by someone who believed in revealed religion; the whole book would have been different if it had been written by a Xhosa. This is not therefore *the* history of the Xhosa — it is *a* history of the Xhosa, written by a particular individual. In self-defence, however, I should add that history is not a work of the imagination. Within this book, the reader should find some idea of the scope and dimensions of Xhosa history, and some glimpses of its major landmarks; and in the footnotes and bibliography he or she should find the guides and signposts needed for an independent journey.

A word or two is necessary by way of explanation concerning the structure of the book. Unlike many histories, this one is not purely chronological in sequence, but alternates narrative and thematic chapters. I felt that a generalised social and economic chapter describing the Xhosa way of life in the precolonial period would have created a false impression of stagnation, and that occasional paragraphs on social and economic change would lack coherence and interfere with the flow of the narrative. By allocating a separate chapter to each of geography, political structure, religion, economics and war, it has been possible to show more clearly the way in which these changed over time. I have tried to minimise the disruption by placing each thematic chapter at an appropriate point in the narrative; for example, the chapter on religion comes immediately after the Fifth Frontier War, in which the religious figures of Nxele and Ntsikana played a critical role. Each of the thematic chapters is complete in itself, and the narrative can be read straight through without reference to them, if the reader so prefers.

One of the great barriers to historical understanding is that the more distant the event, the harder it is to grasp, partly because our sources of information deteriorate and partly because the earliest times are least like our own. This poses an intractable problem for the historian: he must begin at the beginning, which is precisely the section that the reader finds most difficult and least rewarding. I regret that I have found no solution to this difficulty, except to suggest that those readers who are primarily interested in the blood and thunder of frontier conflict should skip or skim over the first four chapters, and save their concentration for chapter five onwards.

The House of Phalo ends in 1850, on the brink of the horrific decade in which Xhosa independence was finally lost. I had originally intended to include the War of Mlanjeni (1850 − 1853) and the great cattle-killing delusion (1856 − 1857), but have not done so for two reasons. First, this is the history of the life and achievement of the Xhosa people in precolonial times and I did not want to reduce the whole of it to the status of a prelude to the coming catastrophe. Second, the story of the 1850's deserves a book to itself, which I hope to provide at some future time.

Two notes on terminology: by 'Xhosa', I mean only those people who claim descent from an ancestor named Xhosa, that is the amaGcaleka and amaRharhabe of the present day. Other peoples usually classified as Xhosa-speaking, for instance the Thembu, Mpondo, Mpondomise, Bhele, Zizi, Hlubi and Bhaca, have long and proud histories of their own, and I can only hope that they receive attention in the near future. Second, some readers may be surprised and offended at the occasional appearance of the abusive word 'Kaffir' or 'Caffre' in this book, and they have a right to an explanation. Before 1850, the word 'Kaffir' was generally used by all whites, even sympathetic ones like 'Justus', to refer to the Xhosa. This certainly reflects an aspect of their mental attitude, because it was well known even then that the people referred to themselves as 'Xhosa' and objected to the use of 'Kaffir'. Their prejudices live on, however, since they used the term 'Kaffir' in their writings. No historian can alter a written document, no matter how much he might want to do so, and therefore, whenever my document says 'Kaffir' I must repeat it faithfully, much against my will.

With regard to pronunciation, 'c' represents the front click, 'x' the side click, and 'q' the top click. Readers who do not know these sounds would probably be best advised to think of each of them as equivalent to 'k'. The letter 'r' is the same as the Afrikaans 'g', or 'ch' in the Scots 'loch'. Except with 'sh', which is pronounced the same as in English, every 'h' is sounded, thus 'Phalo' is pronounced 'p-h-alo', and not 'f-alo'.

Many people have helped me during the five years and more that this book has been in preparation. Professor Rodney Davenport has been pushing me forward and clearing the road ahead ever since I was an undergraduate. Professor Wandile Kuse spent more than two years trying to teach me Xhosa. Professor Steven Feierman acted as my adviser for even longer, and I would especially like to thank him, Professor Jan Vansina and Dr David Henige for reading through the entire manuscript and making so many useful and constructive suggestions. Whatever they failed to salvage is, I am afraid, beyond redemption.

I would also like to thank everyone, Xhosa and others, who received me kindly during the period I did fieldwork, and particularly those who offered me hospitality over extended periods: Chief T. Sigcawu of Jujura, Mr. N. Qeqe of Shixini, Rev. H. Oosthuizen of Kentani and Mr. B. Kruger, formerly of Willowvale. Mr. Alcott Mpumelelo Blow acted as my assistant for most of the seven months, and whatever success I had in the field was largely due to his efforts. Messrs. R.G.S. Makalima, A. Ndude, M. Spekman, G. Thompson and S. Zotwana helped with the arduous task of transcribing and translating the tapes of the oral interviews. Michael Berning, Sandy Fold, Jackson Vena and Melanie Webb of the Cory Library, Grahamstown took a lot of time and trouble on my behalf, as did the staffs of the Government Archives and South African Library in Cape Town. The latter stages of my research were assisted by a grant from Rhodes University, and a generous contribution from the Anglo-American Corporation relieved me from my teaching duties and enabled me to complete this work. Mrs. L. Ranchod and Mrs. L. Corcoran typed the successive drafts of the manuscript. Mr. W.O. West of the Rhodes Cartographic Laboratory drew the maps. One of these follows prototype of Richard Elphick; I am grateful for his permission. Parts of Chapter V appeared in the *Journal of African History* (1979). The people at Ravan made everything easy for me — may they prosper in all their undertakings.

This book is a poor repayment for all the debts I have incurred while writing it. Obviously, no one mentioned above shares my responsibility for anything in it. The same applies to the many colleagues and friends who have helped me with discussions and suggestions. They are literally too numerous to be listed ·here, but I feel I must single out William Beinart and Cecil Manona: friends in need. *The House of Phalo* is dedicated to my parents, to whom I owe so much.

J.B. Peires

Grahamstown
March 1981

1. Land and People

1. AN AERIAL PHOTOGRAPH

The boundaries of the territory occupied by the Xhosa fluctuated considerably over time, but in the years between 1700 and 1850 they did not often extend west of the Sundays River or east of the Mbashe River, along the coastal strip which separates South Africa's inland plateau from the Indian Ocean.[1] It is an area of temperate grassland which yields crops such as maize, sorghum, tobacco and pumpkins but the shallow clay soils are far better suited to stock-farming than to intensive agriculture. Rain falls in a succession of summer thunderstorms between October and February, and the land is well drained by numerous rivers which run from the escarpment down to the sea. None of these is navigable for any distance, and the Xhosa have no taste for fish nor a tradition of seamanship. There are virtually no mineral deposits, except for a little ironstone around the Tyhume and Kei Rivers.

These general characteristics allow for considerable local variations. Xhosaland (emaXhoseni, lit. 'at the place where the Xhosa are') is most easily, if somewhat simplistically, conceived as comprising four adjacent belts running parallel to the coast. The northernmost of these, between the great mountains of the interior plateau such as the Drakensberg and a secondary tier of smaller ranges further south, was never permanently settled by the Xhosa. Apart from being especially cold in winter, it is covered almost exclusively by sourveld, which does not normally provide good year-round pasturage. The Xhosa used it occasionally for summer grazing, but for the most part they were content to leave it to the weaker Thembu nation and to surviving bands of San hunters who had nowhere else to go.

The overwhelming majority of Xhosa lived in the 'highlands',[2] the slopes of the smaller mountains such as the Winterberg and the Amatola, where innumerable streams and rivulets drain into the great rivers of Xhosaland, the Fish, the Keiskamma, the Buffalo and the Kei. These river basins contain the richest and deepest soils, and the mixed pasturage *(Valley Bushveld)* is composed of both sweetveld and sourveld.[3] This region also gets the highest rainfall, averaging 800 − 1 200 millimetres per year with some places such as Pirie in the Amatola getting as much as 2 000 millimetres.

The highlands eventually level out into a flatter and more open belt of *Eastern Province Thornveld* which provides poor grazing and little wood. The region is moreover badly watered owing to low rainfall and the lack of even small streams. Around 50 kilometres from the sea, the uplands drop sharply into the coastal lowlands, where the tertiary limestone outcrops permit somewhat better grazing *(Alexandria Forest* west of the Keiskamma; *Coastal Forest* east of it). A spate of smaller rivers − Kowie, Bira, Tsholomnqa, Kwelera, Qora, Nqabara and others − rise in the escarpment caused by the abrupt descent to the coast, thus creating a strip which is well-watered, but rugged in the extreme.

It was the water not the land which determined the pattern of human settlement.[4] Areas with many rivers and streams could accommodate many people and many different communities; a large land area drained by a single river was likely to be occupied by a single community only. Ideally, each chiefdom had its own river and each subchiefdom had its own tributary. The hinterland was no more than the appendage of the river, an undefined reservoir of pasturage and hunting-ground to which different communities had overlapping claims.[5] But there was no latitude for doubt in the matter of access to water. Only the people of the community and their cattle had the right to drink the water of their own particular stream.[6] Thus nearly all Xhosa place-names are the names of rivers, with a very few exceptions for mountains and lakes.[7]

It is difficult to estimate how many people occupied this vast area. As one early investigator pointed out, since the Xhosa were 'themselves unacquainted with their population, it is impossible for a stranger to know it.'[8] In 1800, the missionary Van der Kemp calculated an adult male population of 38 400 by counting the number of homesteads he passed between the 'centre' of Xhosaland and the sea, guessing that the area observed was equal to one-eightieth of the country, and assuming that it carried an 'average' share of the population.[9] Van der Kemp would probably have attained a higher 'average' if he had travelled to the mountains instead of to the sea, but, surprisingly, his contemporaries agreed that his figures were too high. Lichtenstein thought that it could not be greater than 30 000, including women and children, since Ngqika was unable to defeat the Xhosa west of the Fish, 'and the whole body of these did not consist of above two thousand, five hundred persons.'[10] Colonel Collins, who enumerated the number of fighting men per chief, arrived at a total of 6 580 all told, from which he estimated that the total population could not be more than 40 000.[11] It is not clear whether any of these estimates included the Xhosa east of the Kei, whom Collins assessed at 10 000 'souls'.[12] The first attempts at a methodical census were much later. The detailed census of 1848 taken immediately after the War of the Axe showed 64 009 Xhosa west of the Kei.[13] Maclean, one of the census-takers, subsequently wrote that 70 000 would have been more accurate and suggested quite arbitrarily that there were another 70 000 Xhosa east of the Kei.[14] In sum: none of the available population estimates is at all reliable. What there is seems to indicate that the Xhosa population in 1800 was well under 100 000 and possibly as low as 40 000, but that it stood at 100 000 or more in the year 1850.

2. A VIEW FROM THE RIDGE[15]

The Xhosa chose to live on the ridges intersecting the valleys of the hilly country where wood and water were most often found.[16] Their homesteads were built facing the rising sun and near the tops of the ridges, where they could be sheltered from the wind and drained by the downward slope. Most homesteads consisted of eight to fifteen beehive-shaped dwellings, a framework of branches plastered with clay and dung and thatched with long grass. The only opening was a low door, and the smoke from the hearth in the centre escaped through the roof. These dwellings were arranged in a semi-circle around a cattle-enclosure made of mimosa thorn-bushes. The 30 metres or so between the dwellings and the gate of the enclosure formed a yard (*inkundla*) where most of the social and formal activities of the people took place. Further down, between the homestead and the water, lay the gardens of maize, sweetcane, pumpkins and melons, likewise enclosed by thorn fences.

The homestead-head (*umninimzi*) was the senior male of his lineage in the homestead. He lived with his wife, his unmarried children, and possibly one or two impoverished relatives. Polygamy was the ideal but not necessarily the norm. Only a minority of commoners had more than one wife, though some chiefs had as many as 12.[17] Relationships between members of the homestead were strictly prescribed according to kinship: father's brother, eldest son, older brother, younger brother and all other positions were carefully distinguished both in terminology and in the rights and duties attached to each. Generally, the elder ranked above the younger and the men above the women.[18]

Elaborate rules of avoidance in speech and behaviour governed the relationships between men and women in areas where sexual tension might arise, for instance between father-in-law and daughter-in-law. Division of labour within the homestead went strictly according to sex and age. The men looked after the cattle and erected the permanent structures, the women cared for the gardens, prepared the meals and maintained the dwellings. Crafts were shared, with the men working in wood and iron as well as preparing the hides, and the women sewing, making pots and weaving baskets. A number of specialist ironworkers, leather-workers and woodcarvers took care of particularly difficult tasks.

The role of cattle in Xhosa life was well symbolised by the position of the cattle-enclosure at the centre of the homestead.[19] The meat and milk of the cattle provided the people with their staple food. Their slaughter and sacrifice was the principle means whereby the deceased forefathers were invoked and propitiated. Cattle were also the lynch-pin of Xhosa social structure. It was not simply that they served as a store of wealth and a means of exchange — spearheads, copper bangles and beads did too. But only cattle were exchangeable against women. Thus they represented not only the accumulated product of past labour, they also served as the key to all future production and re-production.[20] This has led some scholars to suggest that possession of cattle was the crucial variable which enabled some lineages to expand at the expense of others.[21] Above all, cattle were valued for their own sake. As Landdrost Alberti pointed out, a Xhosa's cattle 'is the foremost and practically the only subject of his care and occupation, in the possession of which he finds complete happiness.'[22]

The world of the homestead-head extended far beyond his homestead. Perhaps he was first and foremost aware that he was the subject of a chief who demanded tribute, extended protection and judged cases at law, but he was equally conscious of his independent links with other homestead-heads through ties of kin-ship and neighbourhood. The Xhosa were a patrilineal people who traced descent through the male line. Each Xhosa belonged to a lineage, that is to say a group of people who could trace their descent back to a specific forefather. He was also a member of a clan, that is, of a group of lineages who did not quite understand how they were related to each other, but who believed through their common clan-name and clan-praises that they shared a common ancestor.

Many, perhaps most, of a Xhosa's neighbours would be members of his clan but the exogamy rule ensured that he would certainly have neighbours who were not clansmen and clansmen who were not neighbours.[23] Duties to fellow-clansmen were not as clearly defined as duties to members of one's lineage, but if a stranger was discovered to be a fellow-clansmen, the obligation to give him help and hospitality was renewed a hundredfold. Very often the senior member of the dominant lineage in a particular locality served on the chief's council and represented the homestead-head's interests to the chief.[24] Somewhere perhaps there lived an old man who was commonly recognised as the head of the senior lineage of the clan. Under exceptional circumstances he might be called in to give advice on a point of ritual or to offer sacrifice to the clan's ancestors.[25] But apart from that, clans had no distinct corporate identity.

The ties of neighbourhood were very much stronger. Neighbours lived under the same chief, they shared the same pasturage, they suffered from the same droughts. Each neighbourhood had its wise men and its fools, its brave men and its cowards, its ironworkers, its diviners and (somewhere) its witches. A homestead-head would expect his neighbours to attend his feasts and his dances, and he would attend theirs in turn. Sometimes he would join them on visits to other neighbourhoods, where he would cheer on the local stick-fighters and racing-oxen. Social links were reinforced by economic ones. A homestead-head could not kill a beast or open a grain-pit every time his people were hungry, and even when he did so it was impossible for the homestead to consume all the meat and grain on its own.[26] The solution was to provide for the future by creating a network of obligations. White observers admired the willingness of the Xhosa to 'divide what they get amongst each other, be it ever so trifling' while they condemned an apparent inclination to waste and squander in time of plenty.[27] However, the two tendencies were perfectly complementary. A man gave as much as he could on one day in case he was hungry on another.

Cattle were pastured and herded together by the community as a whole, although they were milked and stalled individually. Hunting was largely a neighbourhood enterprise, although individuals did set snares for buck.[28] The hunt commenced with an appropriate communal ritual in which a young girl took the part of the game while the men played hunters.[29] To catch buck, half of the party acted as beaters and drove the animals towards the bush where the others were concealed. Co-operation was even more necessary in the hunting of the lion — one man acted as bait and threw himself on the ground covered with a shield — and the elephant, which had to be followed for days and kept encircled by fire. The Xhosa distinguished between short hunts returning the same day and great hunting parties, composed of many men accompanied by women carrying food, which might last several weeks. The main purpose of the hunt was to obtain rare skins (bluebuck, for instance) and ivory for armlets, but in time of famine game was an important supplement to the food supply.

Beyond the neighbourhood lay the wider world. Every homestead-head visited his chief's Great Place for reasons of law, war or politics; he might also travel to arrange a marriage, consult a diviner, trade for copper or cattle, or simply for the love of travelling. 'Their love of action is indeed such,' wrote one visitor, 'that they will occasionally take long journeys, in which they have all sorts of hardships to encounter, merely to visit some distant acquaintance, and not to be idle at home.'[29] Journeys were serious enterprises, possibly dangerous, and were carefully prepared for. Whereas travellers on short trips were apt to take a bag of dried maize kernels and trust to hospitality for the rest, those undertaking longer expeditions would be accompanied by pack-oxen carrying the milk-sacks and heavier baggage.[31]

Before leaving, the traveller would fortify himself with charms and herbs such as the iNyongwane (*dicoma anomola*) which would enable him to vomit up poisoned food the instant he received it.[32] For more visible dangers, he carried a bundle of sticks and spears. Well-trodden footpaths guided him through dense woods of mimosa trees, punctuated with yellowwood, erythrina, spekboom which the elephants ate, and sneezewood, the toughest of them all, which was hardened in fire to provide a substitute for iron. Emerging from the woods, he might pass through long stretches of open plain covered with long *qungu* ('Tambooki') grass, so high that it hid a man completely.[33] If a river was too full to cross at the ford, he might make a raft from reeds or simply hang onto the tail of his oxen.[34] As he went, he would doubtless recognise many of the sights and sounds of his place at home. The bush teemed with herds of buck, zebra and quagga. Occasionally the mighty elephant or the buffalo would appear. These the traveller saluted as chiefs. He recognised many of the birds and understood their cries, the dove calling 'I come from Xhosaland! I come from Xhosaland!' and the nightjar, 'I went and I went and I slipped!'[35] He watched particularly for the honeybird which might lead him to the nests of bees, and for the hammerheads and hornbills which would warn him of evil to come.[36] The blue-flowered plumbago and pelargonium warded off lightning and stopped up wounds. The aloe killed tapeworms, and the star-like *cluytia* cured anthrax in men and cattle.[37] Other plants cured the bites of spiders, cobras, adders and other inhabitants of the dense undergrowth. The Xhosa lived in an intensely personal environment. He was part of it and he felt at home in it.

By 1800 some adventurous Xhosa had travelled as far as Cape Town.[38] Conversely, African travellers from further afield had visited Xhosaland. Tsonga from Delagoa Bay reached Ngqika in 1805 in the course of a journey to find how far the land of the black people extended.[39] Tswana and northern Sotho likewise made their way south by the early nineteenth century.[40] The Xhosa thus had a fairly good idea of the continent in which they lived. The whites, they thought, originated on islands in the middle of the sea.[41]

3. SEASONS

The Xhosa reckoned time by the sky. A particular hour was indicated by pointing to the sun's position at that time.[42] Months were calculated according to the moon. The year began in June when the Pleiades *(iSilimela)* signalled the start of ploughing and ended with Canopus *(uCanzibe)* which pointed to the harvest.[42] The distant past was expressed as a series of 'significant events' *(iziganeko)*, according to which a man might fix his age — a battle, a comet, a drought, a disease, a great rain, the circumcision or death of a well-known chief.[44]

It was, of course, the agricultural cycle which was most closely bound to the passage of the year. When *Silimela* appeared, the wooden hoes appeared with it. By September, the flowering of the erythrina and the ripening of certain wild fruits announced that it was time to sow.[45] As the first rains of summer turned the sourveld green again the cows gave more milk, and milk remained the main source of food till January when the crops began to ripen, first the maize and the pumpkins, then the sweetcane and melons, and finally, by mid-April, the sorghum was harvested and the cattle turned loose in the stubble of the gardens.[46] Not all the grain would be consumed. Much of it would be stored in grain-pits, dug deep into the cattle-enclosures for the clear, cold, dry and hungry winters. Neighbours took it in turns to open their granaries and also to slaughter their cattle, the hides of which were now much thicker and warmer.[47] Winter was in fact a time of great sociability, as men wandered from place to place, eating of the newly roasted meat and drinking of the beer fermented from the sorghum of recently opened pits.[48]

From time to time, at least once in ten years, the rain failed and famine *(indlala)* set in. Rainmakers were usually summoned, and the odd showers which occasionally attended their ceremonies brought psychological as well as material relief.[49] Hornbills were captured and left in the dry river beds in the hope that the waters would rise up and sweep the evil omen away.[50] People called in their social obligations, and took cattle out on loan to replace those which had died. Herdsmen drove their herds to streams which were still running, even if it meant fighting with the local inhabitants. Whole communities might pack up and set off in search of a place which had escaped the drought.[51] But the situation seldom became so acute. Apart from hunting and eating the meat of cattle which had died, there was always famine food — berries, mimosa gum, onion-like roots, and the wild spinach which grew in the abandoned cattle-enclosures.[52] People slept a lot during droughts, even in the daytime.[53]

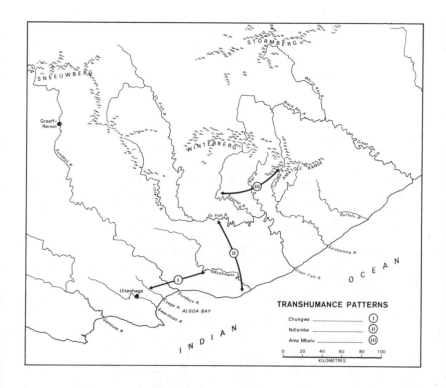

TRANSHUMANCE PATTERNS

Chungwa	_____	①
Ndlambe	_____	②
Ama Mbalu	_____	③

0   20   40   60   80   100
KILOMETRES

Cattle had a seasonal cycle too, one which extended in space as well as time. The basic problem which the Xhosa faced was the scarcity of really good mixed year-round pasturage. Sourveld, which predominated in the area, provided excellent grazing in summer but lost most of its nutritional value after about four months, so that an exclusive diet of it caused botulism and stiff-sickness. Sweetveld remained nutritious throughout the year but it was very fragile, and it was believed at the time that an excess caused consumption in cattle.[54] The ideal arrangement was to graze cattle on the sourveld in summer while resting the sweetveld, and to graze them on the sweetveld in winter when the nutritional value of the sourveld was at its lowest.

Since ideal solutions were not always available, certain techniques of pasture management were evolved. The long grass was burned from year to year to keep it short and sweet, and the sour grasses on the coast were judiciously overstocked for the same reason.[55] Chiefs or wealthier communities kept cattle-stations some distance from their residences at places where grazing was good, but the soil too poor for cultivation.[56] Trans-humance knew no boundaries. For instance, the Mbalu chief, Langa, was 'in the habit of moving away for a short time each year and then resuming his stay among the Christians.'[57] One traveller found the Mbalu chiefs west of the Fish River while their home-steads were maintained in perfect order east of it.[58] Nor was it only Colonial boundaries which were disregarded. Langa's son, Nqeno, a supporter of chief Ngqika, continued to send his herds across the Fish into the territory of Ngqika's rival, Ndlambe.[59] The Gqunukhwebe chief, Chungwa, alarmed the Colonial authorities every year by moving closer to Uitenhage, the seat of local administration. But the regularity of his movements between the Sundays/Zwartkops in summer and the Bushmans in winter indicates that he was only shifting his cattle between their summer and winter grazing. (See Table.)

'Bad grass' was the explanation usually given when the herds sickened and died. Xhosa medicine proceeded on the basis that the cattle had been poisoned, and since the indigenous diseases — anthrax, quarter-evil — were actually ingested through the mouth, the principle was not misleading.[60] The herb preparations administered produced results far in advance of European remedies of the time.[61] Sometimes cattle diseases spread to people. Anthrax, which was aggravated by the scarcity of salt, was the most common Xhosa sickness after tapeworm.[62] Human illnesses were treated by letting blood through cupping with a cow's horn or with purgatives to make the patient vomit up the 'poison'. Since most treatment was successful, failure was usually blamed on sorcery. But there were no indigenous remedies for the European diseases which first arrived with the smallpox in the mid-eighteenth century.[63]

Constant changes of pasturage did not mean that the Xhosa were nomads who wandered from place to place in search of better grazing-grounds. As we have seen, their transhumance patterns were regular, and they managed their pasture as well as they could. Observers commented on the attachment of each Xhosa community to its locality, and on their reluctance to move. Alberti's comment is typical: 'These villages are only abandoned under special circumstances; one is struck by the stability and assiduity, and the surrounding country is given over to agriculture.'[64] Changes in location were due not to ecological imperatives but to the evolution of the human life-cycle. When a young man grew up among the Xhosa, 'his father gives him an axe, and says: Go and extend the homestead, set up an outstation (that is, your own home).'[65] When an old man died, his homestead was shut up, his children were forbidden to go near it, and the materials of which it was composed were allowed to crumble into dust.[66] In this way, generation by generation, the people inched their way down the coast.[67]

TABLE
RECORDED RESIDENCES OF THE GQUNUKHWEBE CHIEF, CHUNGWA

YEAR	WINTER		SUMMER	
1792			Feb.	Tshaka & Chungwa on Bushmans[1]
	June	Tshaka trekking to Sundays[2]		
1797			Nov.	Chungwa at Kowie and Bushmans[3]
1798	April	Between Zwartkops and Van Stadens[4]	Sept.	Bucknas forest, near Bushmans[5]
1799	April	At Sundays[6]		?
1800	May/ June	Baviaans River[7]		
1801			Nov.	Zwartkops[8]
1802	Aug. ?	Bucknas[9]		
1807			Sept.	Chungwa at Koega: followers between Van Stadens and Gamtoos[10]
1808		?	Oct.	Langkloof[11]
1809		Somewhere east of Sundays[12]	Sept.	Arrives Sundays[12]
1810			Feb.	Chungwa has moved, but many of his people still at Sundays[13]
		Somewhere east of Sundays[14]	Oct.	West of Sundays[14]

SOURCES AND COMMENT

1.   Chiefs (presumably with main body) at Bushmans, some followers at Sundays (February being transitional part of season), J.S. Marais (1944), p 17.

2.   J.S. Marais (1944), p 18.

3.   J.S. Marais (1944), p 49.

4.   Bresler-Macartney, 27 April 1798, BO 73.

5.   Bresler-Macartney, 16 September 1798, BO 74.

6.   J.S. Marais (1944), p 106.

7.   J.S. Marais (1944), p 124. As Marais points out, this is far north of Chungwa's usual area. The probable reason is that, having just made peace with the British, Chungwa wished to keep as far west as possible, in accordance with their wishes, and changed his transhumance pattern from east-west to north-south. This hypothesis is strengthened by the fact that when Ndlambe resided in the area, he too followed a north-south pattern. (J. Cuyler — Caledon,

25 Dec. 1809, CO 2572; R. Collins (1809), p 50. Unfortunately there is not enough information on Ndlambe's movements to reconstruct his transhumance pattern.)

8.   J.S. Marais (1944), p 132. (From this time on, we find a shift in Chungwa's transhumance pattern, almost certainly due to the arrival of Ndlambe west of the Fish).

9.   J.S. Marais (1944), pp 142 − 3.

10.   This move far to the west is probably due to a 'great mortality' in his cattle at the Koega, his usual residence in the Sundays area. Cuyler − Barnard, 26 Sept. 1807, CO 2561; R. Collins (1809), p 53. Chungwa also complained to Cuyler about Ndlambe's presence in his area.

11.   D. Moodie (1840), 5:59.

12.   J. Cuyler − Colonial Secretary, 9 Dec. 1809, CO 2566. Chungwa told Cuyler that he could not stay at his old place because he had lost over 40 head of cattle there. It was at this time that the incident of the ox took place. See p 111.

13.   J. Cuyler − Alexander, 10 Feb. 1810, CO 2572. Chungwa moved ahead of his subjects (transitional part of season again) in order to please Cuyler.

14.   J. Cuyler − Colonial Secretary, 8 Jan. 1811, CO 2575. Chungwa made a pretence of moving early because of Cuyler's threats but soon sent a message saying he wished to return because wolves (hyenas) were destroying his cattle.

2. The Foundation of the Xhosa Kingdom

The Xhosa people today think of themselves as being the common descendants of a great hero named Xhosa who lived many hundreds of years ago. Some writers go so far as to assert that Xhosa was the son of Mnguni and the brother of Zulu and Swazi.[1] Such ideas are, at the very least, highly suspect. There is every reason to believe that the word 'Xhosa' is derived from the Khoi '//kosa', meaning 'angry men'.[2] It is not unusual for a people to adopt names invented by outsiders: Vete, the historian of the neighbouring Mpondomise, informs us that his people were named by the Thembu.[3] The belief that all culturally related peoples belong to a single genealogy derives more from the understandable wish to bring order into history than it does from history itself.

The earliest historical occurence specific to the Xhosa concerns the installation of the amaTshawe as the royal family of the Xhosa. The story of Tshawe is probably the best-known and most widely spread of all Xhosa traditions. The version given here is that of J.H. Soga in *The South-Eastern Bantu* the first complete history of the Xhosa ever written.[4]

1. THE STORY OF TSHAWE

Among his mother's people Tshawe was a favourite on account of his courage, and when he reached manhood was granted, in accordance with custom, a considerable number of retainers, who formed the nucleus of a tribe. After a time, probably desiring to distinguish himself, and considering himself sufficiently strong, he collected all his people and set out ostensibly to visit his father Nkosiyamntu, though he probably knew that his father w dead.[a] As he proceeded, numbers of broken men from c tribes joined him and he reached his father's place to find the heir, Cira, in power. For a time he settled down, no sufficient excuse presenting itself for the trial of strength which he contemplated with his elder brothers.

On a certain day a general hunt was proclaimed, and all sections of the tribe joined in. Tshawe was successful in killing a bluebuck antelope and, following the usual custom, the principal chief, Cira, required that a certain portion should be reserved for him. This Tshawe refused, on the plea that the animal was too small.[b] Cira replied that it was old, as it had horns. But Tshawe's refusal was final . . . (Cira) asked for the assistance of Jwara, chief of the Right-Hand House, and this was given[c] . . . During the course of the fighting which was going against Tshawe, he sent to the neighbouring tribe of Pondomises for assistance, and the clan ,of the AmaRudulu of the Imi-Haga section was sent.[d] These being fresh warriors and in numbers considerable gave the advantage to Tshawe, who completely overthrew his older brothers, and usurped the chieftainship of the Xhosas . . . Cira ignobly elected to stay under the usurper's rule, but his authority was gone. Jwara . . . went off with a certain following to seek a new home. He left behind him his son and heir, Mazaleni, who remained with Tshawe, and acted as spokesman. The ama-Cira are now broken and hold no position of authority in the Xhosa tribe.

---

a. The story of the return of the prodigal son/wrongfully dispossessed sibling is obviously a cliche disguising the conquest of the country by a new dynasty. Vansina cites no fewer than 25 African peoples among whom it is found (J. Vansina [1965], pp 74, 211). Several passages in the myth ('broken men from other tribes,' 'excuse . . . for trial of strength,' 'usurper's rule') make it quite clear that this is also the case here. The idea that the three main actors were in fact brothers should also be discarded. False genealogical affiliation is quite common among the Xhosa, being obvious in the attempts of the amaBamba (Interview with Mr. K. Billie, Mdantsane, 3 July 1975) and the amaNgqosini (J. Maclean [1858], p 171) clans to relate themselves to the amaTshawe. There is also a tendency to try and link all the Nguni nations in a single genealogy (for example, genealogy in Maclean; interview with A.M.S. Sityana, Alice, 11 Sept. 1975). Any genealogy which includes the name 'Xhosa' is clearly fictitious in part because there was never any such person (see G. Harinck [1969] p 152n). The names of Xhosa's 'son' and 'grandson', Malangana (One who follows) and Nkosiyamntu (Lord of Man), are further indications that they are mythical. Some amaTshawe even tell the story without indicating any relationship between Cira and Tshawe, as a straight story of conquest (for example, K.B. Manxiwa, Ntlabane Location, Willowvale District, 19 Nov. 1975).

b. This apparently frivolous argument, which Soga does not explain, is in fact the crux of the Tshawe justification for the usurpation. Cira, as the chief, was entitled to demand his portion of the bluebuck, but since the

Reduced to its essentials, the story of Tshawe tells how Cira and Jwara and their followers were conquered by Tshawe and his followers. This interpretation is explicitly stated in the following tradition:

> There were various nations *(izizwe)* who were distinct in their greatness and their kingship. These used to rule themselves over there, like the amaTipha, the amaNgwevu, the amaQocwa, the amaCete, the ama-Ngqosini and the amaNkabane. These nations stood alone and were ruling themselves long ago. They were abolished by fighting *(bagqugqis-wa ngokulwa)* by Tshawe, they were overcome so that they became one nation.[5]

The story of Tshawe's conquest is thus a tale of how Tshawe destroyed the independence of the various *izizwe* ('nations' or 'clans') then in existence.

These traditions present a particularly difficult problem in historical reconstruction. People today still think of themselves as descendants of the ancient amaTipha, or amaNgwevu or ama-Ngqosini who, in earlier days, acted as coherent political units, migrating, fighting battles, abandoning their chief and so on. But, just as all Xhosa people are not the biological descendants of a man named Xhosa, so members of a clan (as I shall translate

---

bluebuck was too small, there would not have been enough for the rest of the people to eat. By insisting on his royal prerogative at the expense of his people's well-being, Cira contravened the ethic of generosity and therefore merited deposition. Today the amaCira all agree that Cira was wrong to insist on his share.

c. Soga's assertion that the Jwara clan of the Xhosa is related to the Jwara clan of the Bhele (Mfengu) was disputed by my Jwara informants. Coincidence of names is not rare among the Nguni. For instance:

Xhoxho	—	son of Ngqika
Xhoxho	—	cousin of Mapassa, son of Bhurhu
Mapassa	—	son of Bhurhu
Mapassa	—	grandson of Tshatshu, son of Xhosa (Thembu)
Tshatshu	—	son of Xhoba (Thembu)
Tshatshu	—	son of Ciko (Ntinde)

d. As the result of the assistance, the Rudulu (who became known as ama-Ngwevu) were 'offered chiefship' by Tshawe. They refused, saying they would rather serve Tshawe. They accepted special status and were given their own 'ox', Qawuka, in other words, the right to act as chiefs without the equivalent rank. The head of the Qawuka became a powerful man in the chiefdom, though his position as most powerful commoner was later challenged by the heads of the Ndluntsha and Ntshinga. (Series of interviews with N. Qeqe, current head of the Qawuka, Shinxini Location, Willowvale District, Nov. 1975).

izizwe)[6] should not be thought of as blood relations or as biological descendants of the man after whom their clan was named. (Indeed, several clans — amaNgwevu, amaNtshilibe, amaMfene, isiThathu — are not named after people at all.)[7] The size and composition of each clan fluctuated over time. Clans assume that every lineage which shares its name and praises must be related, but since relationship need not be demonstrated it was easy for clans to expand through the incorporation of individuals or groups of alien origin. A case in point is that of Hermanus Matroos, hero of the Eighth Frontier War, who crossed the colonial frontier as a runaway slave and was admitted into the Jwara clan.[8] His descendants remain amaJwara to this day. It was possible for chiefs to confer membership of the royal clan *(ubuTshawe)* on deserving commoners, as was the case with the Gqunukhwebe chiefs.[9] Clans have been known to unite, as in the case of the Maya and Gqubulashe clans which fled to the Thembu king to join the Xhosa.[10] The isiThathu clan was formed by the amalgamation of three previously unrelated Khoisan groups.[11] We should thus bear in mind that the clans whose histories we are about to relate were not constant and immutable bodies, but that their composition was continually changing.[12]

Clans claim either Bantu or Khoisan origin. Some joined the Xhosa voluntarily by immigrating into land ruled over by the amaTshawe, namely the Maya and the Qocwa (Thembu), the Ntshilibe (Sotho), the Ngwevu (Mpondomise), the Giqwa (Khoi) and the Ngqosini (Khoi or Sotho).[13] There were also many individual immigrants belonging to clans located outside Xhosa-land. The Mfene and Vundle (originally Sotho, now found mainly in Thembuland), the Ntlane and Zangwa (Mpondo) and the Mpinga (Mpondomise) are all numerous among the Xhosa. All of these have traditions of migration which account for their origin and their arrival among the Xhosa. Other clans were incorporated involuntarily, when the territory they occupied was invaded by the expanding amaTshawe. Many of these were Khoisan: the Sukwini, Gqwashu, Nqarwane (Khoi); the Cete (Khoi or Bantu); and the isiThathu (mixed Khoi and San). Others obviously belong to this category through their claims of descent from Nkosiyam-ntu, 'father of Tshawe': the Cira, Jwara, Kwemnta and Qwambi. There is a residual category of clans which remember little or nothing of their history. This seems to be because they can no longer remember a time when they were independent and not subject to a Tshawe. No person who is not a Tshawe can be a chief among the Xhosa, and the word 'Tshawe' is used generally in the Xhosa language to mean 'royal person' — the British royal family, for example, are referred to as amaTshawe. The impossibility of articulating the concept of royalty without invoking the name of Tshawe was well demonstrated by one good informant, an umTipha, who said, in discussing the history of his clan, 'the amaTipha used to be great, together with the amaTshawe, their names were Bayeni and Tshewu', and it is said they lived where they were amaTshawe *(bakwangamaTshawe)* but we get lost with this *(silahlekwe apha)*.[14] Such clans, including the Bamba, Nkabane and Ntakwenda, are most probably formerly independent clans who were subjected by the amaTshawe.

The story of Tshawe cannot be dated. Archaeology has told us nothing definite yet.[15] Attempts have been made to date Tshawe's reign by multiplying the number of chiefs included in the genealogy by an estimate of the average number of years per reign,[16] but these cannot be accepted because the genealogy is certainly faulty and the length of the average reign varies greatly according to the chiefly lineage chosen.[17] The earliest documentary sources are the shipwreck narratives of the sixteenth century, which suggest small-scale political organisation but are too vague and unreliable to be of any value.[18] The first substantial account of Xhosaland was by the survivors of the *Stavenisse,* wrecked in 1686. George Theal identified a minor chief mentioned therein as the Xhosa king, Togu, a mistake which went unnoticed for more than seventy years.[19] In fact, the first definite date we have is 1736, by which time Phalo was ruling the Xhosa.[20] In seeking to date the reign of Tshawe, we can do no better than to work backwards from the reign of Phalo.

Since Phalo, a mature adult in 1736, was a posthumous child, we can place the death of his father, Tshiwo, no later than 1715. Both Tshiwo and Tshiwo's father, Ngconde, were rulers of some distinction, and it does not seem unreasonable to estimate their reigns at twenty years apiece, which would take the reign of Ngconde back to 1675.[21] This in itself is sheer speculation, but the names further back on the genealogy present difficulties which are even greater. We know nothing about Togu, Sikhomo and Ngcwangu apart from their names. It is possible that a number of names have been forgotten, but it is also possible that Togu, Sikhomo and Ngcwangu are not different people but praise-names of the same person.[22] It seems therefore safe to say that the story of Tshawe is set some time before 1675, but rash to say anything more than that.

Nor do we know where the reputed clash between the followers of Cira and Tshawe is supposed to have taken place. Only one of my informants — and a relatively unreliable one at that — even hazarded a guess ('Mpondoland').[23] What information there is points to an early association between the Xhosa and the

GENEALOGY 1

THE SUCCESSORS OF TSHAWE

Tshawe
|
Ngcwangu
|
Sikhomo
|
Togu
|
Ngconde
|
Tshiwo
|
Phalo
(Fl. 1736)

Mpondomise to their northeast. A lone Mpondomise tradition remembers the two together on the mysterious Dedesi River somewhere in the foothills of the Drakensberg.[24] The Rudulu who came to help the Tshawe are definitely related to the Majola royal clan of the Mpondomise, the name Sikhomo occurs on both the Xhosa and Mpondomise genealogies, and Togu, the name of a Xhosa king, is also the name of a Mpondomise clan.[25] Yet this evidence is not conclusive, and it seems better to confess our ignorance than to leap to an unwarranted conclusion.

Why was it the Tshawe who established their dominance, and not some other clan? A tradition recorded by Theal suggests that Tshawe introduced iron to the Xhosa.[26] Apart from the possibility that this might simply be the attribution of a useful commodity to a folk-hero, there is no evidence that superior knowledge of iron-making conferred political benefits among the southern Nguni. It certainly did not do so for the Qocwa or the Mfengu when they arrived among the Xhosa, or for the Khuma who introduced iron-smelting to the Thembu.[27] Did Tshawe have superior political skills? All we know is that 'numbers of broken men from other tribes joined him' and that the Rudulu came when he called. Did he benefit from a favourable ecological situation, or was he fighting to secure one? We do not even know where he came from. Speculation here seems entirely pointless.

The creation of the major political groupings of the southern Nguni area, the Xhosa, the Thembu, the Mpondo and the Mpondomise, resulted from the rise of particular descent groups, respectively the Tshawe, Hala, Nyawuza and Majola, to a position of dominance over their localities. The extension of their power was a slow process, beginning long before the more dramatic creation of the Zulu state in northern Nguniland and continuing right up to the Colonial conquest. Gradually, the small autonomous clans found themselves sucked into one or other of their more powerful neighbours. The Ngqosini, for example, were either Sotho or Khoi in origin. They were subjugated by the Xhosa after a fierce resistance, switched their allegiance to the Thembu king, and finally returned to being Xhosa again.[28] There were minor cultural differences among the larger polities, but clansmen who crossed national boundaries found it easy to adopt the fashions of their new home. Thus the Ngqosini took to red ochre when they came to live among the Xhosa, and the Zangwa (originally Mpondo) stopped scarifying their faces and started circumcising their children on their arrival in Xhosaland in the nineteenth century.[29] The clan composition of each polity thus fluctuated over time, a reminder that the Xhosa should not be seen as the descendants of a single eponymous ancestor named Xhosa, but as the subjects of the royal Tshawe clan.

The view that the Xhosa nation is heterogeneous in origin, rather than a genetically defined 'tribe' clearly distinct from its neighbours, and that it expanded and incorporated rather than migrated, has important implications with regard to the old problem of the western boundary of Xhosaland. European Colonists, keenly aware that they were intruders in the southern tip of Africa and that they had dispossessed the indigenous Khoisan inhabitants, were anxious to prove that the Xhosa had done much the same thing. Moodie, who proved to his own satisfaction that the 'Caffres' were east of the Keiskamma in 1775, felt that this showed that the Xhosa had as little right as the Colonists to the country west of the river since both invaders had displaced the original Khoi residents.[30] This argument fails to consider what became of the Khoi who were defeated by the Xhosa. The Gona, Dama and Hoengiqua were not expelled from their ancient homes or relegated to a condition of hereditary servitude on the basis of their skin colour. They became Xhosa with the full rights of any other Xhosa. The limits of Xhosadom were not ethnic or geographic, but political: all persons or groups who accepted the rule of the Tshawe thereby became Xhosa.

2. THE DYNAMICS OF XHOSA EXPANSION

The boundaries of Xhosaland expanded every generation with

the departure of the sons of the reigning chiefs to found new chiefdoms of their own. The Xhosa mark the transition from childhood to maturity by circumcision, and a close examination of the social circumstances surrounding the ritual reveals it to be the time when such new chiefdoms first took shape.[31]

At the age of ten or twelve, Xhosa boys were sent off to their parents' chief. They tended his cattle, and were instructed in the basic arts of war. When one of the chief's sons reached maturity, he was circumcised together with the male children who were then at the Great Place, and these became his first councillors. Councillors usually tried to have one of their sons circumcised with a high-ranking son of their chief, and the ceremony might even be delayed to permit the son of a particularly influential man to attain this honour. Among the Gcaleka, the different huts of the circumcision lodge were allocated with the political ranking of the councillors well in mind. The representative of the powerful Giqwa clan slept together with the chief, while that of the less prominent Nkabane clan slept in a different hut.[32] Thus the political unit of chief and councillors was reproduced every generation, and councillorship, like chiefship, became hereditary. Important chiefs had large numbers of commoners circumcised with them; one reliable figure reports nearly forty companions for a minor Gqunukhwebe chief. The first boy circumcised became the *isandla senkosi* (hand of the chief),[33] that is, his main assistant, while the others constituted the core of his council. The young chief's father usually gave his son an older councillor or two for advice and guidance, and, as time passed, the council would grow through the addition of outstanding individuals and the representatives of newly-incorporated local groups. But the age-mates circumcised with the chief were his personal followers, and they were supposed to remain loyal to him whatever direction his fortune might take.

After remaining in the circumcision lodge from the seed-time to the harvest, the novices washed off their white ochre and emerged for the great ceremony which marked their formal acceptance as adult males. Not the least important part of the festivities was *ukusoka*, the giving of gifts. All the young men received gifts of cattle, clothing, spears and so on, but the young chief received most of all. The herds of a chief were divided among the 'houses' of his various wives, each of which had its own particular earmark. Part of the herd belonging to his mother's house, already known as his 'inheritance' *(ilifa)*, was given to the young chief on his accession. In addition, he received *amawakhe*, or inaugural offerings from the chiefs and other visitors who attended the ceremony.[34] He married his first wife soon afterwards, and moved off with his age-mates to establish his own Great Place in virgin territory.[35] He would receive the balance of his inheritance when his father died, but he would never return to the deserted site of the old man's place, which would be guarded by royal grave-watchers.

Tensions between fathers and sons were, if anything, exaggerated in chiefly families. The chief kept a special dwelling of his own (the *intanyango*) at the back of his Great Place which his sons were forbidden to enter. If they wanted to speak to their father, they were compelled to kneel down at the entrance and put their heads through the opening.[36] Sons were liable to take the part of their mothers in domestic disputes.[37] Armed conflict between the generations was more likely in the case of a regency, as the well-known example of Ngqika and Ndlambe demonstates:

> Ngqika did not wait to be given his chiefship which had been kept with clean hands by his uncle, Ndlambe. He took it himself by force together with his councillors. Not waiting a day after he had come out of the circumcision lodge, he went to live with his age-mates at Mgqkwebe forest together with that body of choice children of councillors.[38]

The Great Wife was usually married late in life, and the Great Son was often still a child on the death of his father. This arrangement was probably due not only to the fears of the chief himself but to the influence of his age-mates whose sway would extend into the regency. Councils often survived as corporate bodies long after the death of the chief they had served: that of Khawuta outlived him by more than twenty years.[39]

The Xhosa explicitly recognised the danger of conflict between their chiefs, and deliberately relieved it by providing for the dispersion of young chiefs and their followers to territories of their own. 'You cannot have two bulls in one kraal', runs the proverb.[40] Not all chiefs used this safety valve. Some contested precedence, as we shall see: Mdange with Gwali, Ngqika with Hintsa. Others restrained themselves while young in the hope of future benefits. The descendants of Mdushane claim that Mhala usurped the Ndlambe chieftainship by staying home and 'creeping in' with their father.[41] On the other hand, not all chiefs' sons were equal to the duties of their position. The timid and unsuccessful settled down with their brothers, retaining only a few personal followers and the rank and privileges (for example, the right to be saluted) of chiefs.[42] Naturally, younger brothers gravitated towards full brothers of the same house but such a process was not inevitable. Nukwa, father of Gasela, was born of the same mother as Ndlambe, and the Dondashe of the same mother as Sandile.[43]

The dispersion of the young chiefs thus eased political tensions at the centre of the kingdom. It also extended the territory over which the Tshawe ruled, and assisted in the subordination of commoner clans. Concentrations of commoner clans were broken up as their members followed different chiefs to settle in new areas. The arrival of the young chief would increase the control of the Tshawe over that area, as he co-opted representatives of the local inhabitants onto his council. On the other hand, increasing decentralisation in an era of poor communications inevitably led to decreasing political cohesion. The process was a gradual one and the Xhosa who adopted it from preceding generations never stopped to weigh the advantages and disadvantages of what seemed to be the natural order of things.

3. THE XHOSA AND THE KHOISAN[44]

By the middle of the seventeenth century, the Xhosa had acquired a loose political ascendancy over most of the coastal Cape Khoi extending to the very fringes of the Cape Peninsula. Van Riebeeck, the first commander of the Dutch fort, was told that the king of the Inqua 'altogether the greatest and mightiest of the dirty Hottentot race' and 'the highest lord of the Hottentots', was 'one of the principal chiefs or captains of Chobona (the Xhosa)'.[45] Various other Khoi groups were described as 'willing subjects and friends of Chobona.'[46] The Xhosa seem to have acquired their influence by allying with particular Khoi chiefdoms against their local rivals. The best-documented case is that of the Chainouqua, who lived between the Breede and Zonderend Rivers in the southwestern Cape. The Chainouqua chief was given a young Khoi girl brought up among the Xhosa. (Van Riebeeck commented: '. . . it is a mark of great favour when any one gets a wife out of Chobona's house; it is thus he attaches these tribes to his interest.')[47] The Chainouqua were constantly visited by Xhosa and looked to them for military assistance in time of need.[48] In return, the Xhosa expected their Khoi allies to fight against Khoi groups such as the Hoengiqua who defied them and refused them tribute.[49]

Xhosa influence in the far west disappeared with the advance of the Dutch from the Cape of Good Hope. The Khoi disintegrated between the two. The Inqua kingdom of Hinsati, most powerful of all the Khoi rulers, fell to the Xhosa around 1700.[50] Hinsati made the mistake of giving refuge to the Xhosa king, Gwali, shortly after the latter was dethroned by his brother, Mdange, in the name of the 'true heir', Phalo. Mdange sent

C. Howen and J. Smies, *View of a Kaffir Settlement on the South Coast of Africa* (1810). Note especially the beehive-style dwellings, and the elaborate manner in which the horns of the cattle have been shaped.

NGQIKA CHIEFS

Ngqika

Maqoma

Sandile

Bhotomane
(*ImiDange*)

expeditions against Gwali and eventually even the refugees turned on their hosts. The Inqua were shattered and assimilated into the Xhosa nation as the Sukwini, Gqwashu and Nkarwane clans.[51]

The Xhosa advance into the country of the Khoi continued, and the next clear evidence we have of the destruction of a Khoi chiefdom occurs with the surrender of the Amatola Mountains to Rharhabe by the Khoi chieftainess, Hoho, some time after 1750.[52] Hoho's people cannot be identified by a Khoi name, but the traditions of the isiThathu clan relate that when Rharhabe crossed the Kei he found three men standing there, and he incorporated them into his chiefdom as the isiThathu clan, (Xh. *isithathu* means three).[53] The destruction of their political cohesion weakened the ability of the Khoi to withstand San raids. A Colonial expedition which passed through the area at about this time gave a vivid description of their plight:

> Those [Khoi] whom we met could not say what nation they belonged to, naming themselves according to the river where they lived or sometimes 'the Hottentots of the country'. All these Hottentots were at one time rich in cattle, but have lost them through the thieving of the Bushmen and in the wars they have fought among themselves and with the Caffers.[54]

The break-up of established Khoi political structures created a situation in which exceptional individuals were able to form short-lived chiefdoms of their own. A Colonial refugee named Ruiter (Kohla) was able to rally the remnants of the Hoengiqua, but during the reign of Khawuta (1778 — 1794) these were absorbed in the Xhosa kingdom as the Giqwa clan.[55] Other Khoi were able to associate themselves with Xhosa chiefdoms, especially the Ntinde and the Gqunukhwebe, on the basis of clientage.

> Near [the Xhosa] and with them mix the Gonaqua Hottentots. These the Caffers use as servants and in war time, they also serve them as soldiers; their clothes and lifestyles are precisely alike and they intermarry without differentiation.[56]

It is certain that a Khoi who entered Xhosa society did so on terms of distinct inferiority, but since this inferiority was expressed in economic terms and not in social or racial ones, it passed within the course of a generation. Khoi submission was not entirely voluntary however. Active resistance continued into the 1770s, and many Khoi sought the service of the Boers in preference to that of the Xhosa.[57]

The extent of interaction between Xhosa and Khoi is well

indicated by the influence of the Khoi and San languages on Xhosa. One sixth of all Xhosa words contain clicks.[58] Very few of these have Zulu cognates, which suggests that most of the linguistic changes took place after the Nguni settlement of the coastal region. Ever since Professor Maingard broached the idea in 1934, historians have tried to utilise loanwords as evidence for the social impact of the Khoi on Xhosa culture.[59] Maingard's observation that the Xhosa (and southern Bantu) root for cattle, -*komo*, is related to the Khoi root *goma-*, not to the common Bantu root, -*ombe*, has recently been revived by Ehret,[60] but Maingard's conclusion — that the Xhosa acquired their cattle from the Khoi — cannot be sustained. The -*ombe* root was recorded in Nguni by an early lexicographer, and still survives in the *hlonipha* (respect) language of Xhosa women.[61] The long-horned Sanga cattle of the Nguni are distinct in type from the 'Afrikaner' cattle of the Khoi.[62] The usage of the two societies regarding cattle were radically different; Xhosa women were rigorously excluded from the pastoral sphere, while Khoi women did the milking.[63] In any case, the borrowing of a word does not necessarily prove the borrowing of the object denoted by it — the Xhosa also borrowed their word for grass (*ingca*) from Khoi.[64] Maingard is on far safer ground when he points to the number of terms relating to the colours of cattle which the Xhosa derived from the Khoi. The inter-mingling and cross-breeding of Xhosa and Khoi herds must have greatly increased the number and type of cattle available to the Xhosa. Clearly, contact with the Khoi extended the resources available to the Xhosa and influenced them in the elaboration of social practices, even if it did not radically alter their way of life. We will find a similar pattern when we consider the interaction of Khoi and Xhosa with regard to religion (Chapter 5) and trade (Chapter 7).

The Xhosa were, at times, exceptionally brutal towards the San (*abaTwa*).[65] There was, however, a peaceful side to the relationship. San were renowned rainmakers and useful trading partners, exchanging ivory for cattle and dagga.[66] Intermarriage was rare, but not unknown.[67] San became tributary to Xhosa chiefs and according to one report, there were more San than Gona Khoi living among the Gcaleka.[68] At least one Xhosa clan, the isiThathu, was partly San in origin.[69] Conversely, Xhosa sometimes joined San bands.[70]

4. DISCERNIBLE DEVELOPMENTS FROM TSHAWE TO PHALO

The conventional genealogy gives three chiefs — Ngcwangu, Sikhomo and Togu — between Tshawe and Ngconde, the grand-father of Phalo. Nothing is remembered of these chiefs, except that they led 'migrations', and there is no telling how many names have been forgotten. With Ngconde, we are on slightly firmer ground and we may place his reign as sometime in the seventeenth century. S.E.K. Mqhayi saw Ngconde's reign as something of a landmark:

> During the period which preceded Ngconde, the practice was that the fellow possessing the greatest power became the great chief; but now the law was established on this subject.[71]

Even if this is not entirely reliable, the picture of warring chief-doms succeeded by a single royal lineage is compatible with the picture of historical development suggested above. Among the new clans which appeared in Xhosaland around the time of Ngconde were the Maya, a refugee branch of the Thembu royal clan and the Qocwa, a clan of skilled ironworkers and armourers.

Tshiwo, son of Ngconde, married the daughter of Ziko ('Gandowentshaba'), his father's brother. In order to preserve the exogamy rule, Ziko's descendants were separated from the Tshawe clan and formed into a clan of their own, the amaKwayi.[73] During the reign of Tshiwo some remnants of the commoner clans attempted to strengthen their position by forming an alliance called the amaNdluntsha ('people of the new house') under the leadership of the Nkabane clan. Being commoners, they could not aspire to a chiefship of their own, and so the alliance took the unusual form of constituting itself as the council to an imaginary queen named Noqazo. For more than 150 years, the Ndluntsha met in council in front of a pillar carefully arrayed in the clothes of a woman.[74]

Another important event was the invasion of the Ngqosini clan. Gaba, their leader, hoisted the elephant's tail at his Great Place to indicate he viewed himself as a chief.[75] Tshiwo was saved only by the intervention of a councillor named Khwane. A wide-spread oral tradition relates that Khwane had been the councillor entrusted with witchcraft executions, but that instead of doing his duty, he had hidden the condemned people in a forest where they had intermarried with the local Khoi. At the critical moment when Tshiwo was on the brink of defeat, Khwane led his secret army into battle and saved the day. Tshiwo rewarded him by appointing him a chief equal in rank to the amaTshawe. His people became known as the Gqunukhwebe, probably because of the large number of Gona Khoi in their ranks.[76]

3. Chiefs and Commoners

1. CHIEFS

The matrix of Xhosa political and social organisation was the homestead, at the head of which stood the homestead-head. The homestead-head was drawn into wider relationships partly through his membership of a patrilineage: his brothers, their father and his brothers, their grandfather and his brothers, and so on up four or five generations to the earliest ancestor remembered by all. The patrilineage was simply an extension in time and space of the father and his sons, and its members related to each other as fathers to sons, uncles to nephews, elder brothers to younger brothers, as the case might be.

The elevation of the amaTshawe to the position of royal clan did not significantly alter their existing concepts, which remained lineage-based. The chiefs referred to each other as 'elder brother' (umkhuluwa) or 'younger brother' (umninawa), according to their status, and the king was known as the inkosi enkhulu, meaning not only 'the big chief' but also 'the chief who is the eldest son'.[1]

The king was the head of the lineage, as the chief most closely related to Tshawe himself. It was he, or his representative, who installed a young chief by placing a necklace of red beads around his neck.[2] The rights of the other chiefs derived from the king.[3] This was expressed in a metaphor which provides a striking illustration of the way in which inter-chiefly relationships were conceptualised in domestic terms: the king 'allocates' (lawula, also, to share out portions from the pot at mealtimes) each chief his 'dish' (isitya) that is to say his chiefship. The king, as head of the lineage, was responsible for all matters which affected the lineage as a whole, such as the national first-fruits ceremony.[5] The other chiefs, his younger brothers, owed him respect and obedience in matters concerning the whole lineage. The king had the right to mobilise the entire nation for war, and the junior chiefs had to seek his sanction before they could go to war themselves.[6] He was the ultimate arbiter in all judicial and ritual disputes.[7] When two chiefs fell out, they were entitled to call on him for adjudication and, if necessary, physical enforcement of the sentence.[8] At marriage feasts, the councillor of the king was entitled to the right foreleg, even if the great Rharhabe chief himself required it.[9]

On the other hand, the position of the king as lineage head did not permit him to make unreasonable demands at the expense of his subordinates, or to interfere unwarrantedly in their domestic affairs. The 'dish' which the junior chiefs received contained the right to wear the royal insignia, to judge cases among their own people, and to receive the various forms of tribute due to a Great Place. They were entitled to defend these rights by force, if necessary. As Tshiwo told Khwane when he installed him as chief of the Gqunukhwebe, 'You may throw your spears against me myself if I wrong you.'[10]

It was beneath the dignity of the king to visit his juniors; they had to come to him. Hintsa was most taken aback at the suggestion that he should visit Grahamstown, and asked, 'Was the Governor in the Cape in the habit of visiting other people?'[11] On most occasions, chiefs did not meet personally, but communicated by means of trusted councillors. No chief would take an important step without first consulting the opinions of other chiefs, both senior and junior. This was true even of bitter rivals, unless they were engaged in active hostilities.[12] The king himself could not take a decision which would bind his junior chiefs, unless they were present and had discussed the matter.[13]

Given the imprecise character of these rights and obligations, the successful working of the system depended on two conditions, both of which obtained in the small-scale lineage, but which became increasingly absent among the amaTshawe with the passage of time. These were, first, constant contact between 'brothers', and second, the perpetual familiarity of circumstances, so that new contingencies could be judged with reference to old ones. Continuing migration and segmentation led to an increase in geographical and genealogical distance, and this considerably diminished the personal understanding and co-operation which were necessary to make up for structural deficiencies. Faced with new circumstances, like the European presence, the Xhosa political system, with no abstract norms as guidelines, no precedents to follow and no tradition of unconditional obedience to the king, was confounded. Some chiefs thought that the newcomers were a threat and should be met by joint action. Others saw personal political advantage, and could claim that their dealings with the Europeans fell within their domestic jurisdiction, as relations with the Khoi and the San had done.

The coherence of the Xhosa polity was also weakened by political competition between chiefs. Competition exists in all political systems, and the ascriptive nature of political offices derived through kinship inhibited but did not eliminate it. On the suface, the rules were clear enough: all sons of chiefs were chiefs, and they were ranked according to the rank of their mother. The heir to the chieftainship, known as the Great Son, was the son of the Great Wife, who was usually a Thembu. The bridewealth for the Great Wife was paid by all the people and her status was publicly proclaimed. The second-ranking wife was known as the Right-Hand Wife and her son was the Right-Hand Son. All the other wives were *amaqadi* — minor wives. The eldest son in each house ranked ahead of his younger full brothers. Yet despite the apparent clarity of the rules, it was possible to circumvent them. This was made easier by the fact that the Great Wife was often married late in life and that sons often died young through illness or war.

The political situation was at its most fluid after the death of a chief. The superior rank of the Great Wife could be challenged by a subsequent bride.[14] It might be alleged that the chief was not the real father of the Great Son,[15] or that he had disowned the heir-apparent's wife before his death.[16] A contender could be eliminated through a witchcraft accusation.[17] The longer a chief remained in office, the more secure his position became. He was at his most vulnerable at his accession, when his legitimacy could be challenged.[18] It was more difficult to depose him once he had been recognised, but even this was possible, and once accomplished, a reason could always be found. Chiefs have been deposed or superseded for being 'cruel', 'stingy' or even 'stupid'.[19] It is impossible to know to what extent such reasons were simply pretexts. Competition between chiefs could take the relatively peaceful form of enticing away one's rival's vassals, or it could result in open hostilities. Such contests were not part of the 'ideal' of inter-chiefly relationships, and informants stressed that they were simply domestic quarrels, qualitatively different from proper wars.

> Let me say, the chiefs were never at variance with each other except for a little misunderstanding at home (*amakhaya*) because they are people who were born chiefs of a single lineage (*umnombo*). I have never heard of a war where they fought greatly with each other. I have

only heard about Ngqika and Ndlambe over Thuthula, and things like that are simply domestic quarrels. They never had wars like when nations *(izizwe)* differ with each other, because they are chiefs of the same lineage.[20]

In oral societies even more than in literate ones, it is the victors who record the history, particularly if the losers become reconciled to their defeat. Genealogies, for instance, are not so much accurate chronicles of genetic relationships as indexes of relative political standing. Mdange, probably born a minor son, is today remembered as a Right-Hand Son. The upstart Mhala is regarded as the Great Son of Ndlambe.[21]

Political competition of this nature was by no means entirely negative in its effects. Given the ascribed nature of political office, it permitted the most capable chiefs to rise to the highest positions and reduced the likelihood of highly-born incompetents holding office too long. Moreover, competition between the major chiefs allowed junior chiefs and even ordinary councillors to hold the balance of power, thus reducing the chances of a Zulu-type despotism. But it endangered the nation as a whole, since it gave rise to the temptation for factions to call in outside help.

The military preponderance of the king was due to the fact that, in addition to those subjects directly under his control, he alone commanded the allegiance of the Great Councillors (Qawuka, Ndluntsha, and later, Ntshinga) and their armies. But even this was insufficient to guarantee him military superiority over ambitious junior chiefs, particularly after the rise of the amaRharhabe. In fact, the king rarely chose the path of military confrontation and tended to maintain his position through judicious interference in the quarrels of his subordinates.[22]

Every year the junior chiefs reaffirmed their loyalty to the king in the first-fruits ceremony, in which each of them awaited the king's word before tasting the harvest.[23] Junior chiefs were also supposed to send him messengers to keep him informed of important events, to consult him and to ask his permission.[24] He then sent them orders *(imiyolelo)*, although he could not expect to be obeyed if he was too arbitrary, or lacked the power to enforce his will where necessary.[25] The extent to which the king controlled his subordinates at any given time depended on circumstances and his own personality, but he was constantly a factor in Xhosa politics, and could be defied but never ignored. It should be remembered that absolute domination was no part of the Xhosa political ethic. The power of any chief was limited by what his subordinates were prepared to accept.

Moreover, the kingship possessed symbolic and emotional

associations which transcended its narrow political functions. The king was the 'very personification of government' and the symbol of national unity.[26] Even the great split which occurred after Rharhabe crossed the Kei did not entirely divide the Xhosa nation, for, as we will see, the Gcaleka kings continued to assert their superiority over all the Xhosa chiefs.[27] 'Chiefship,' said Chief Botomane, 'was allocated from this great side of Phalo and Hintsa and Gcaleka. It cannot stand without them, because it originated with them.'[28] Apart from Ngqika, none of the Rharhabe chiefs ever challenged this claim. They continued to consult the king in peace and in war. Mhala sent his Great Son, Makinana, to Sarhili, 'to grow up at the Great Place, and learn the art of chieftainship there.'[29] The shooting and mutilation of Hintsa in 1835 was a national calamity, even to those who had rejected his order to participate in the war.[30] Long after the creation of British Kaffraria had brought the Rharhabe chiefs under direct Colonial rule they continued to look to the king across the Kei. It was Sandile's loyalty which eventually drove him to fight and die in the last Frontier War:

> How can I sit still when Rhili fights? If Rhili fights and bursts and is overpowered, then I too am nothing. No longer will I be a chief. Where Rhili dies, there will I die, and where he wakes, there will I wake.[31]

2. COMMONERS

The shifting relationship between chiefs and commoners in pre-colonial Xhosa society was produced by the interplay of two distinct and antithetical principles. The first emphasised the homestead, and probably had its roots in the obscure period before Tshawe founded the Xhosa kingdom. The second emphasised royal domination and the inherent superiority of the amaTshawe to other people.

The homestead principle was exemplified in the authority of the homestead-head over his dependents. Just as the father organised the economic production of the homestead, protected it from its enemies, settled its domestic quarrels and communicated with the spirits of its dead, so the chief directed the economic, military, judicial and religious activities of the chiefdom as a whole. Most obviously and explicitly, he became known as the 'father' of his people, and they in turn became his 'children'. The chiefdom could be conceptualised as a homestead, thus *umzi kaPhalo* means both 'the homestead of Phalo' and 'the kingdom of Phalo'. The chief's subject addressed him as *'Mlondekhaya!'* —

'Protector of the home!' — and his place might be referred to
simply as 'the hearth'.[32] The double meaning of the verb
ukulawula ('to govern' and 'to dish up food') underpinned the
metaphor in which the practice of government was often
expressed.[33] Like a father, the chief provided refuge for culprits,
bridewealth for young men and assistance for all who needed it.

We shall probably never know whether the redistributive
homestead idiom reflected the real productive relationship
between clan-head and clansman before the time of Tshawe.
But it certainly differed from the ideology of chiefship/
commonerdom which was evident in the later Tshawe kingdom.
Royal ideology implied not redistribution but domination. It
sought to entrench and accentuate the distinction between chief
and commoner. Symbolically, the chief was thought of as a 'bull'
or an 'elephant' whereas commoners were referred to as 'dogs'
or 'black men'.[34] Each chief had a 'shadow' *(isithunzi)* which
set him above his subjects. He never spoke to them directly, but
his words were relayed to them through a 'spokesman'. His
decisions were regarded as infallible, and any mistakes would be
blamed on the 'bad advice' of his councillors.[35] Each chief was
saluted by a special praise-name, and commoners who accidentally
neglected to salute could be beaten.[36] No man could approach
the Great Place with his head covered, on pain of a fine.[37] No
commoner could raise his hand against 'a person of the blood'
(umntu wegazi) even when, as sometimes happened, the chief's
sons raided his herds or gardens.[38] A chief would not drink the
milk of his subjects' cattle.[39] The opposition between chiefs and
commoners was ritualised at the time of a chief's accession when
distinguished elderly commoners were allowed to rise and insult
the chief, apparently as a form of catharsis.[40]

The struggle between chiefs and commoners took the form of
a struggle for cattle. Because cattle were the primary means of
reproduction in a pastoral society, he who controlled the cattle
also controlled the men who depended on them. In this simple
fact was rooted the unity of politics and economics which is the
most striking feature of precolonial Xhosa society. 'Love your
cattle,' said Hintsa to his son, Sarhili. 'My people love me because
I love my cattle, therefore you must love your cattle as I have
done. If you have cattle, poor men will not pass by your place.
No, he will stop with you.'[41] Where transactions between chiefs
and commoners involved cattle, it is often impossible to
distinguish between the economic and the political elements since
cattle comprised wealth and influence at the same time. For the
purposes of exposition, economics and politics must be discussed
separately, but it is an artificial separation.

Among the Xhosa each homestead produced most of its own consumption requirements and each allocated its labour resources independently. The homestead-head decided what and when to plant, supervised the herding and milking of the cattle, and chose whether to hunt, trade or stay at home. Commodity production and trade were relatively undeveloped, and were usually undertaken to supplement rather than to replace the normal pursuits of the homestead-head. But even though most of the production took place within the homestead, the homestead was unable to guarantee its own reproduction in isolation from the chiefdom as a whole. Living in an uncertain environment, his existence punctuated by drought, disease and war, the homestead-head did not, could not, regard himself as an isolated economic entity. Independent as the homestead might appear in periods of prosperity, danger and disaster soon revealed the links which bound it to the chiefdom. If enemies swept off the cattle or if the rain declined to fall, it was the chiefdom as a whole which acted. The chief might raise a levy to pay a celebrated rainmaker,[42] he might lead the people to a new country;[43] or he might organise the men for hunting and raiding.[44] When misfortune struck an individual or when a young man lacked bride-wealth, the chief provided for him. And, as we have seen, even in times of peace and plenty a man often looked beyond his homestead to the neighbourhood.[45]

Above all, the chief participated in production through his role as *owner* of the land. It is important to differentiate between *ownership* and *possession*. In precolonial Xhosa society, the commoners *possessed* the means of production but they did not *own* them. The position was somewhat analogous to Western Europe in the Middle Ages, where a serf worked the land himself and directly appropriated the products of his labour although both land and produce were the property not of himself but of his lord. The fact of ownership did not give the lord the right to expropriate the serf at will, since the serf was hedged about by customary observances which protected him in the enjoyment of his possessions. As one witness told a colonial commission, ' . . . although it (land) was held in the name of the chief, he had no right to disturb me in my garden.'[46] On the other hand, ownership was no mere form of words, since it was precisely by virtue of such ownership that the lord was entitled to extract part of the serf's labour. In Xhosa society, ownership was vested in the chief:

In theory the [Xhosa] Government is a pure despotism. The [king] of the tribe is regarded as sole lord and proprietor of its lands, its people and their property. Many of the ordinary laws show this. The chief can assign a place of residence to any of his people within the limits of the tribal territory . . . The cattle of the tribe are, by a sort of fiction of their law, all considered to belong to the Chief. As his mode of securing retainers is by giving them hire stock from time to time, it is considered that all the cattle possessed by them have been derived either from those granted by himself, or from such as had been given in previous generations, by his ancestors, to their forefathers. Hence the punishment for great crimes is what they expressly call 'eating up' that is, the chief deprives the unfortunate culprit of the whole of his property which it is considered . . . he has a right to do; since in carrying off the cattle and other property of the offender he is only resuming his own. For crimes not deemed so serious the chief merely inflicts a penalty of a limited number of cattle: these all belong to him as the proper owner.*

The chief's rights of ownership were not vested in him as an individual — as was the case with the medieval European feudal lords — but in him as a representative of the state.[47] In pre-colonial Xhosa society, the dominant class did not merely control the state, they were actually indistinguishable from it.

The power of the state within Xhosa society was however very weak, partly because of the divisions among the chiefs, which we have already examined, and partly because of the absence of a state apparatus entirely dependent on the chief and divorced from the people. The state apparatus of a Xhosa chief was not a standing bureaucracy of named officers, but a variable and shifting aggregation of people, usually referred to as his *ibandla,* or following.[48]

Roughly, this consisted of all the people the chief could assemble at a given moment. These were usually drawn from two

---

*   W. Shaw (1860), p 437. Cf. Andrew Smith, 'Kaffir Notes': 'All the cattle possessed by every person in a tribe are considered as held by a sort of grant from the chief — who appears to be, in fact, the only real proprietor of the cattle in the hands of the people of his tribe.' See also J.W.D. Moodie (1835), 2: 242. For the distinction between 'possession' and 'ownership' see N. Poulantzas (1973) pp 26 — 27. Journal of the Resident Agent, Fort Peddie, 10 — 11 Jan. 1945, GH 14/1 gives a good illustration of the practical implication of this doctrine. Mhala had lent one of his subjects cattle and was continuing to collect instalments on the loan, although the last of his own cattle had long since been returned. Shepstone comments, 'From custom immemorial the receipt of those cattle in the first instance has entailed on his heirs and successors the arbitrary exactions above described to an unlimited extent, either in reference to time and amount.' He adds that he is now seeing it for the first time — a sign, perhaps, that the principle was more important than the practice.

categories, the 'milkers of the Great Place' (young men engaged in *busa* clientage, to be discussed below) and the more dependable of his councillors. It will be remembered that the chief's council was made up partly of his personal friends (for example, circumcision age-mates) and appointees, and partly of men who were influential in their own right. Men who were wealthy or who headed large lineages — and the two were usually associated — expected to be consulted on matters concerning themselves and their dependents. Unfortunately, we have no information with regard to the relation between a councillor and his people, although ties of kinship, clientship and neighbourhood were obviously important. We do know, however, that the chief relied on his councillors to execute his orders, collect his tribute and furnish him with warriors. We also know that on occasion people were prepared to follow their local leaders (as councillors were perceived, when viewed from the perspective of their own homes) against the chief himself.[49] The chiefs were therefore forced to treat their councillors with the deference appropriate to their strength.

Councillors were obliged to recognise the sovereignty of the chief over his own territory, and in order to transfer their allegiance they had to desert. In order to join his new chief as a man of substance rather than a destitute beggar, the deserter had to take elaborate steps to preserve his herds and his following. One tradition gives a graphic account of the escape of a councillor expecting to be charged with witchcraft.

> This man who was plotted against sent a young man to Ngqika's place: 'Here I am surrounded. I am going to be done to death.' And this was Ngqika's reply: 'Bring all of your belongings here. We will meet on the road with the army that I shall bring out to meet you.' The Qocwa left Ndlambe's place by night, in order to reach Ngqika's place . . . By the blessing of God, when Ndlambe's army appeared, he could already be seen with all his family, driving all his livestock, and there, suddenly, the Ngqika army in front of him.[50]

The councillors were at their most powerful during a succession dispute or a regency. It was more difficult for them to combine together against a mature and politically adept chief, but it was not impossible. Ngqika's attempt to acquire the inheritance of all commoners who died without heirs in the direct line was met by a threat of mass desertion, which apparently followed well-established precedents:

> Some kraals break up, and march towards the borders of the country and there they stay, keeping themselves ready to emigrate to another

country; they are successively followed by others, and this seldom
fails to have the effect wished for (of forcing the chief to retract).[51]

Although the councillors had no established assemblies or meeting-
places outside of the chief's Great Place, this did not preclude
informal consultation where necessary. W.K. Ntsikana gives some
idea of the manner by which this was done in his account of the
rebellion of Ngqika's councillors following his abduction of his
uncle's wife.

> Nontshinga, a councillor from the south of Ngqika's area, heard that
> Ngqika had taken his mother and made her his wife. He visited all
> around the place, saying, 'Why has Ngqika disgraced himself by doing
> this?' The thing was discussed, and it was concluded that he should
> be punished.[52]

So many people crossed over to Ngqika's opponents that their
number grew from around 2 500 in 1803 to over 10 000 in
1809.[53]

Desertion or the threat of desertion was the most common and
probably the most effective means of resistance open to
commoners. They also attempted, as far as possible, to keep out of
the chief's way. The area around a Great Place was very thinly
populated.[54] Some commoners attempted to evade the payment
of death dues by concealing the deaths of their relatives.[55] At
least one man killed his cattle rather than hand them over to the
chief.[56] Bolder spirits sought to recoup their losses by stealing
back their cattle.[57] There might even be an open resort to arms.
Backhouse reported that this happened almost every year among
the Ngqika, and that the chiefs were not always victorious.[58]

Chiefs were therefore constantly preoccupied with the problem
of maintaining the loyalty of their followers. Xhosa historians
usually explain the appeal of a particular chief in terms of his
personal qualities: bravery, wisdom, kindness, and so on. These
were, of course, important, but the attribute of generosity was the
most important of all. This is clearly demonstrated in the story of
Tshawe, where Cira loses his chiefship because he is so greedy that
he demands a small buck without horns.[59] According to another
tradition Nqeno replaced Thole as Great Son of Langa because his
mother cooked out of a big pot while Thole's mother cooked
out of a small one, which is another way of saying that Nqeno
provided for his people while Thole did not.[60] High-ranking sons
obviously found it easier to be generous. Since they received the
major share of the inheritance and the richest presents after
circumcision, they had more resources to give away. But birth and

inheritance were not the only factors: after all, Thole's mother cooked out of the small pot, even though she was the Great Wife. Xhosa history furnishes several instances of low-ranking chiefs acquiring prominence through skill and chance. Mhala, for instance, acquired the status of Ndlambe's Great Son although outranked by four living members of his lineage.[61] Tyhali, whose mother was a concubine, became the second most powerful son of his father, Ngqika.[62] Bhotomane was more influential than other, more senior Mdange chiefs.[63]

There is no evidence that these chiefs were more fortunate than their brothers in war, trade or ecological situation. Both Tyhali and Mhala were personal favourites of their respective fathers, but that does not seem to be the whole story either. The case of Mhala, though poorly documented, is better documented than the others, and suggests an alternative explanation. During the brief Colonial occupation of western Xhosaland in 1835 – 1836, Mhala showed himself infinitely more grasping, more implacable and more insistent on his dues from the commoners than any other Xhosa chief.[64] And yet a missionary who visited him at the height of his power in 1848 reported that he had no blankets of his own because he had given them all away.[65] This apparent anomaly can easily be resolved by narrowing the concept of generosity so as to emphasise its selectivity. It is more than probable that Mhala did not hand out his possessions indiscriminately, but that he distributed them to those whose support he required, namely the councillors. A councillor was both the adviser of his chief and the representative of his locality. A successful chief was one who made sure that his councillors put him first and their people second. This was done by judicious distribution of the fruits of office. Councillors who sat in the chief's court shared in the judicial fines, and councillors who accompanied the chief on his visits shared in the hospitality provided by unwilling hosts.[66]

The jealousy among councillors — the fact that the fall of one (perhaps through a witchcraft accusation) meant the enrichment of the others — also strengthened the position of the chiefs. Moreover, the chiefs did exhibit a certain degree of solidarity which limited the extent to which their internal squabbles damaged their common interests. The lives and persons of chiefs were held inviolable to commoners, even by enemy chiefs. Thus Chief Ndlambe once told his victorious army not to pursue his mortal rival Ngqika because, as he put it,'that is a chief, and you are only black men.'[67] Similarly, Thembu traditions relate that the Thembu commoner who killed Madikane, the invading Bhaca chief, dropped dead on the spot.[68] All chiefs exacted tribute, which meant that even if a commoner defected from a particular chief he could not escape subjection elsewhere. This was vividly demonstrated when Ngqika attempted to acquire the inheritance of all commoners who died without heirs in the direct line. Many commoners fled to other chiefs, only to find that these 'were equally interested with him (Ngqika) in the question of inheritance' and had adopted the same stance.[69]

The political position of the chief over and against the commoners was nevertheless a weak one. A chief was forced to compete with other chiefs for the allegiance of his subjects. For the execution of his orders he depended on the commoners themselves. The political weakness of the chief together with the role he played in production as owner of the land and cattle jointly determined the form in which surplus was appropriated, namely through tribute and judicial fines.

The right of the chiefs to levy tribute and judicial fines was not disputed by the commoners. Nor were the occasions on which they were to be levied. A commoner was reminded at his wedding to 'duly pay the tribute he owes to the king, and to his representative, the chief of the kraal.'[70] Thereafter he was supposed to pay 'an annual contribution of cattle . . . in proportion to his own riches', besides a portion of every beast slaughtered and every granary opened.[71] Certain products of the hunt — ivory, bluebuck skins, eland and buffalo breasts, blue-crane feathers — had to be handed over to the chief.[72] When a newcomer arrived in a chief's territory, he was asked to pay a fee for the right to settle on the chief's land, an important principle even when the fee itself was waived.[73] Special levies *(amaqola)* were raised for special occasions and emergencies, for instance the circumcision, inauguration and marriage of a chief, or the death of his cattle.[74] When a chief and his following toured the country, they expected an ox to be slaughtered in every homestead they visited.[75] Death dues were paid to the chief to 'compensate' him for the loss of his man, and these varied from chief to chief and time to time: on some occasions they were only partially enforced and on others not at all.[76] A man who declined to pay tribute might have his cattle confiscated and his house plundered.[77]

Judicial fines were not fixed in most cases, but depended largely on who it was that was being fined. 'Family and personal influence, and favouritism, have much to do with regulating the amount when the decision is given by the chiefs.'[78] Although belief in witchcraft was perfectly genuine, it is not an exaggeration to say that in some cases the witch-hunt was no more than an elaborate charade masking the expropriation of the accused's cattle. Whenever the chief or his children or his cattle fell ill, an opportunity presented itself to bring a charge of witchcraft against a commoner. The accused usually knew of the accusation in advance — he was sometimes officially warned by means of attaching a loop of the *ingximba* creeping vine to his doorpost — and acted accordingly.[79] The course of action which he chose depended on the extent of his support. He might flee for his life, leaving his cattle behind him. He might assemble his followers and fight his way to another chiefdom.[80] If he felt strong enough, he might even stay put and confront the diviner with fraud.[81] The man who could not persuade his own family to join him in flight must have been unpopular indeed![82] On the other hand, no man who commanded substantial support could be convicted by the diviner. One estimate placed the incidence of witchcraft executions as no more than one a year.[83]

In resisting the chief's demands, the commoners were simply trying to secure their independence of action, guarantee their subsistence, and hang on to the product of their labour. The aims of the chiefs are not, however, as clear. It has been suggested that one aim of appropriation among Nguni societies was to increase the level of consumption — even to the point of conspicuous consumption — and leisure time.[84] The Xhosa chiefs did, in fact, enjoy a higher standard of living than the commoners. Their houses were bigger and better.

> Surrounded by huts of greater magnitude and better construction than any we had yet seen, that of Tyali's rose superior, and bespoke its master the chief of chiefs. Its interior was ornamented by a double row of pillars of straight smooth wood, carefully selected, which supported the spherical roof; this being composed of compact materials bid defiance to the rain, and the whole being plastered, conveyed an idea of neatness which we did not expect to find.[85]

Other chiefs' houses were subdivided into apartments and could hold 30 – 40 people.[86] Not only did the chiefs have more cattle than their subjects, they also had cattle of greater quality and beauty, such as riding and racing oxen. Lichtenstein thought that these were 'kept only for pomp, and as a proof of their wealth'.[87] Chiefs also ate better than commoners. Most commoners ate meat only in winter and on special occasions, whereas the more powerful chiefs ate meat whenever they liked, and they got the best portions of it. They also received rare skins and delicacies from the hunt. They had more women and concubines than ordinary men. They had attendants at their disposal. Yet their standard of living was still so close to that of the commoners that less perceptive outside observers remained under the impression that there was no difference at all.[88] In this the Xhosa and their Thembu neighbours contrast sharply with the more stratified northern Nguni kingdoms where the chiefs and their women lived lives of conspicuous luxury and ease. This can be attributed to the greater control by the northern chiefs over the labour-power of their commoners.

Although tribute and judicial fines were the principal mode of appropriation, cattle-clientage was the most visible form of labour exploitation to be found among the Xhosa. The more common type, known as *busa*, was that of a single individual — for example, a young man in search of bride-wealth — attaching himself to the place of a wealthy person, usually a chief or important councillor. He would tend the cattle (hence the term 'milkers of the Great Place' for the young men who served the chief) and perform other services, and from time to time he would be given a calf, or perhaps a beast in recognition of some special achievement.[89] Alternatively, a man who had already established his own homestead but had lost his cattle through misfortune — for example, the victim of a drought, or a refugee — might be able to obtain cattle on extended loan, caring for them in return for a share of their natural increase.[90] The two forms of clientage did have one thing in common. Neither created a class of permanent dependents because in both cases clients resumed their independence as soon as they had acquired enough stock to do so. It would therefore be quite incorrect to think of the relationship between patron and client as the dominant contradiction in Xhosa society. The majority of people were neither patrons nor clients, although all, without exception, were chiefs or commoners. Since wealthy commoners acted as patrons and since most commoners were not clients of their chiefs, one cannot reduce the relationship between chief and commoner to that between patron and client. Moreover, clients tended to support their patrons, whereas the struggle between chiefs and commoners was a constant factor in Xhosa political life.

Among the Xhosa, clientage was never associated with inferior status or loss of personal freedom. Clients were too few in number to constitute a distinct social category of unfree dependents, and there were no visible external characteristics such as race or language which marked out a man as a client or a descendant of clients. This was true even of the Khoi, many of whom — as we noted earlier — passed through the condition of clientship in the process of becoming Xhosa.[91] Perhaps the easy terms of clientage around 1800 ('Such assistance is often rendered without any reward to the lender,' wrote Landdrost Alberti)[92] were partly due to the relative abundance of land and cattle: one could lend cattle without missing their value or begrudging the unlucky his independence. The sudden influx of Mfengu refugees from Natal after 1820, coming as it did shortly after the Colonists had appropriated some of the most fertile Xhosa lands, placed the entire social structure under severe strain and might have resulted in entirely new forms of clientage, had not other factors intervened. But that is a story which will.be dealt with later.[93]

The role of female labour in male-dominated societies has long been a matter of contention and cannot be fully dealt with here.[94] Nevertheless, since more than half of all Xhosa were women, it is impossible to conclude without some consideration of the subject, albeit brief and inadequate. Xhosa men consciously and explicitly valued the labour-power of women.[95] Old men who were no longer capable of desire married young women to secure their agricultural labour, and were quite prepared to tolerate infidelities.[96] Unlike some other African societies where women produced prestige goods which were appropriated by the male elders,[97] Xhosa women were disadvantaged precisely inasmuch as they were excluded from the privileged sphere of cattle. A woman could not slaughter or milk cattle, or even wash the milkpails.[98] She could not even walk through a herd of cattle in the company of other women. More important, she had no formal voice in the disposition of cattle as inheritance or bridewealth, or in the political and legal arenas where the role of cattle was crucial. In short, women remained jural minors subject to male control throughout their lives. On the other hand, they were not exploited in the Marxist sense because they were never deprived of the products of their labour. Women worked within the limits of their homestead and its garden, and what they produced was distributed and consumed in their presence. In return for their domestic and agricultural labour, they ate the meat and drank the milk of the cattle tended by the men, as well as benefiting from trade and the hunt.[99] If we distinguish between control and exploitation as different aspects of male domination, it is probably fair to say that Xhosa women were controlled but they were not exploited.

The ideology of royal domination never replaced the homely idiom of the family in Xhosa political discourse. The political position of the chief was too weak for the dominant ideology to take the form of a naked assertion of authority. The chiefs represented their interests as being the general interests of society as a whole, and this enabled them to govern with the active consent of the commoners.[100] They found this easy enough, not only because they controlled the state but also because they performed the necessary functions of the family head and could utilise precisely those expressions of the homestead principle which they had subverted. Thus, as we have seen, the chief acted as the 'father' of the people, 'dished up' for them, and so forth. We may add one more expression which we are now in a position to understand: the chief 'holds the land in trust' for his people. No specifically proprietary laws were required to enable the chiefs to appropriate their subjects' possessions. It was only necessary for them to enforce the laws incumbent on the commoners as subjects of the state which governed them.

3. OUTSIDERS

Social distance among the Xhosa was a function of kinship distance, geographical distance and political distance.[101] A man would naturally feel closer to someone who was a fellow clansman, who lived near him and was subject to the same chief, than he would to someone who was none of these things. The relative importance of these factors would probably vary with individuals — for instance, there can be no general rule concerning whether a man will feel closer to a neighbouring non-clansman than to a clansman living in another chiefdom. Social distance was important because it was strongly related to moral community.

> Although the rights of private property are regarded with great strictness in reference to the subjects of the same king or captain; yet [the Xhosa] consider themselves under no absolute restraints on the grounds of Justice to act in the same manner towards the subjects of any neighbouring king or captain ... [A Xhosa might say] 'If you need cattle, it is certainly not unfair to take them from the colonists; because they are another tribe of people'.[102]

People who lived entirely outside the range of Xhosa social relations were entirely outside the moral community; hostility was natural, and there was a general expectation that the strongest would prevail. Told of a clash between emigrant Xhosa and the Tswana, Ngqika commented that 'it was no harm to murder the Briquas; that they had fought with the Caffres and that the Caffres had got the better of them.'[103]

This state of hostility towards strangers was neither inevitable nor indefinite since it was always possible to reduce social distance. For the Xhosa, this was most satisfactorily done by the incorporation of the alien group into the Xhosa nation where it would become bound and protected by Xhosa law and customs. Nations that were not incorporated could, however, establish kinship links through marriage.

> The chiefs of the Gcaleka married the daughters of the Sotho and the daughters of the Thembu and the daughters of the Mpondo, and sent our own daughters there. You ask why we do that? We do that so that we should not quarrel, that we should not fight. Those great chiefs of nations would say, this is my nephew, the son of our girl, and they would not kill him. That was the way they ended the fighting between them.[104]

Conversely, to reject a marriage alliance was a deliberate political affront. Consider the reception by Sarhili of an embassy from his old enemy Faku:

> Fako's message to Rili was this: 'Rili I have sent you my daughter. I wish to form an alliance with some one. I am alone, exposed to the wolves.' On our arrival at Rili's great place we were left outside till late when an old woman put us in an out house. Rili was away. The next morning we were hungry and we took one of our oxen and killed it in Rili's kraal. Rili's men came in the kraal, seized the leg of meat and threw it outside the kraal and beat us with sticks . . . We then went into the hut and a man came to us from Rili to tell us to go away home, that Rili did not want a Fingo wife, would not have Fako's daughter, Rili wanted no Fetkani wife, and to be off.[105]

In most recorded Xhosa royal marriages, the Great Wife was a Thembu, from the nation with which the Xhosa were most often in contact. In Phalo's time, however, the Mpondo ranked above the Thembu.[106] Hintsa, who was at odds with both Thembu and Mpondo, took the daughter of his Bomvana ally for his Great Wife.

The most effective manner of establishing friendly relations, apart from marriage, was through the exchange of gifts. Chiefs expected gifts from Colonial officials, and slaughtered oxen and gave them elephant tusks as presents. These were not considered as commercial transactions, but as signs of respect and friendship. Ngqika was offended by the first gifts he received from the British authorities at the Cape, because he considered them 'trifles' and an insult to his dignity.[107] Colonel Henry Somerset's lavishness with presents and hospitality was greatly appreciated and remembered long afterwards.[108]

Gift exchange was complicated by its implications with regard to rank. Xhosa commoners offered Colonists counter-gifts and labour in return for 'presents' whereas chiefs expected tribute. On visiting Grahamstown Chief Mdushane refused to give a shop-keeper anything in return for his gifts, although he made it quite clear that he would not have refused his equal, the Landdrost.

'I have left my country,' he said, 'not to give but to receive presents.'[109] Exchanges of brides and goods were not in themselves sufficient to establish good relations, and in addition to affecting social relations, they reflected them. Thus brideexchange between Xhosa and Thembu could not always outweigh the other factors creating tension between the two polities. When the Thembu withheld a promised dowry, or when the Thembu king ill-treated his Xhosa bride,[110] these were indications that the Thembu were challenging the power of the Xhosa to avenge these insults. Similarly, exchange of goods did not in itself produce goodwill, since it was not only the exchange, but the spirit of the exchange which mattered. When a climate of distrust and profiteering on both sides dominated trade, hard bargaining was the order of the day, and cheating and theft permissible. Milk and food which were dispensed freely to travellers were sold to professional traders.[111]

The Xhosa succeeded in drawing most of their neighbours into a network of reciprocal social relations. They were not successful with the Colonial government or its white subjects who would not intermarry with them, would not share their wealth with them, would not even accept their common humanity.[112] Small wonder that the Xhosa perceived the Europeans as standing outside the moral community. Small wonder that the polite term *abantu abasemzini* (people of another house) was replaced in Xhosa popular usage by *amagwangqa* (pale beasts) or even *amaramncwa* (beasts of prey).[113]

4. From the Reign of Phalo to the Triumph of Ngqika (1700—1820)

1. THE REIGN OF PHALO (c 1715 — 1775)[1]

The reign of Tshiwo, father of Phalo, seems to have been a successful one, marked by the subjection of the Ngqosini clan and the creation of the Gqunukhwebe chiefdom. He died on a hunting trip in middle age and was survived by his brother, Mdange, and his son, Gwali, among others.[2] Tshiwo's acknowledged

GENEALOGY 2

THE ACCESSION OF PHALO

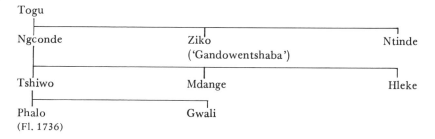

Great Wife had not yet borne him a son, and was sent back to her people. After Gwali had been ruling for some time, Mdange produced a child named Phalo whom he said was the son of Tshiwo. Gwali rejected the claim but was defeated by Mdange and fled to what is now Somerset East, where he was given land by the Khoi chief Hinsati. Mdange's army followed him and defeated Hinsati, destroying his chiefdom and incorporating his people into the Xhosa as the Sukwini, Gqwashu and Nqarwane clans.[3] When Phalo came of age, Mdange yielded the royal authority to him, and went to live west of the Kei, which he ruled in the name of the king.

Phalo remains a shadowy figure about whom almost nothing is known, except that he too crossed the Kei and settled on the Izeli, a tributary of the Buffalo River. In his own lifetime, he came to be overshadowed by his sons, Gcaleka and Rharhabe.[4] One of the most widely spread and best-known traditions in Xhosaland relates that Phalo was one day embarrassed by the simultaneous arrival at his Great Place of two bridal parties, one from the Mpondo king and one from the Thembu king. By choosing one girl as his Great Wife, he would offend the father of the other. A wise old man named Majeke solved the problem by saying, 'What is greater than the head of the chief? And what is stronger than his right hand? Let the one girl be the head wife, and the other the wife of the right hand.' Thus, according to tradition, was the division between Great House and Right-Hand House created.[5] The first commentators on Xhosa history correctly pointed out that so deeply ingrained an institution as the house system could hardly be an overnight innovation, but they then proceeded to dismiss the tradition altogether.[6] However, the tradition has an important function among Xhosa today: it explains how the Xhosa came to be divided between Gcaleka of the Transkei and the Rharhabe of the Ciskei. This split may be regarded as the most significant feature of Xhosa internal politics in the second half of the eighteenth century.

After Gcaleka had been circumcised, he and his retainers went to live in the Komgha district. It is said that one day he disappeared into the Ngxingxolo River. A beast was sacrificed to the river and Gcaleka eventually emerged. This mystical experience, known as *thwasa*, qualified Gcaleka as a diviner.[7] Another tradition refers to his incessant witchhunting. He was sickly, and 'was always killing people in the hope of improving his own health.'[8]

Leaving aside the question of the literal truth of these tales, it is clear that Gcaleka assumed greater magical powers than were usual for a Xhosa chief. This may have alarmed many of the people, but its political implications are perhaps more important. By increasing the scope of his power, Gcaleka endangered the autonomy of junior chiefs. Rharhabe, Gcaleka's brother and possibly already his rival, is believed to have said, 'It is all right if ordinary black people *thwasa* — they are afraid to smell out a chief. But now that a chief has *thwasa*'d, who will escape being smelt out?'[9]

When Gcaleka's councillors threw a corncob among Rharhabe's

men, the fighting began. Helped by the Ndluntsha, Gcaleka defeated and captured his brother. Eventually Rharhabe was released and crossed the Kei, settling at Amabele near present-day Stutterheim.[10] Near the drift where he crossed, he killed a buffalo, and sent the breast and foreleg to the Great Place as tribute.[11]

Phalo died in 1775 and Gcaleka survived him by only three years.[12] Khawuta (reigned 1778 – 1794) was a weak ruler, described by one of his subjects as 'only a shadow of his predecessor'.[13] He was completely unable to assert his authority over the other members of his father's lineage. One brother, Nqoko, 'grew out of Gcaleka's back' to overshadow both Khawuta and his Right-Hand brother, Velelo.[14] The king's uncle, Nxito, was a diviner and also a dissident.[15]

Khawuta appears to have attempted to meet the challenge by appointing dependent commoners to positions of authority usually held by amaTshawe. His appointees were, however, 'less widely respected among the people than the very children of other women'.[16] His greatest success was the absorption of a large Khoi clan, the Giqwa, who may well have been the Hoengiqua, formerly under Ruiter.[17] The Giqwa chief, Nqwiliso, was not subordinated to a Tshawe, but given his own ox, Ntshinga, and 'a large part of the country to control'.[18] This may have been to counterbalance the power of the Qawuka (Ngwevu) clan which had been given special status by Tshawe himself.[19] The heads of the Ntshinga and Qawuka became deadly rivals, each claiming to be the chief councillor of the king. As commoners, they could have no dynastic ambitions of their own, and competed to show loyalty to the king. Some of their followers were stationed near the Great Place, and were the king's most dependable soldiers in time of war. Because they opposed each other almost as a matter of policy, they became the rallying-point for the formation of internal factions. Competition between these factions cross-cut the natural opposition between junior chiefs and the king and thus eventually stabilised politics in the east. The ingenious nature of the compromises arrived at may be illustrated by the arrangements at circumcision, whereby the boy who was circumcised immediately before the chief and slept in the self-same circumcision lodge was always a Giqwa,[20] whereas the master of the circumcision lodge *(ikankatha),* who instructed the boys in the arts of manhood, was always a Ngwevu. However, Khawuta himself did not reap any of these benefits and during his reign the power of the king declined to its lowest level, leaving the Rharhabe free to build up their power in the west.

GENEALOGY 3

THE HOUSE OF PHALO

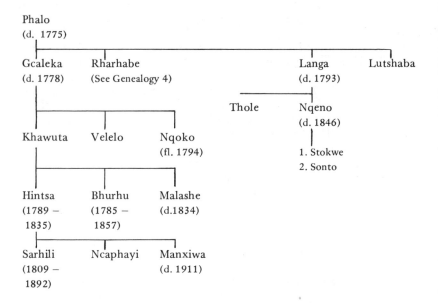

2.   THE RISE OF THE AMARHARHABE

West of the Kei, Rharhabe spearheaded the Xhosa drive against the Khoi and the San. Chieftainess Hoho was forced to cede her land in exchange for tobacco, dagga and dogs.[21] Rharhabe was also the terror of the San, killing even their small children and burning down their dwellings.[22] His advance was, however, opposed by the imiDange, who regarded themselves as Phalo's leading lieutenants in the west.

> Mdange refused to be under Rharhabe, saying 'I don't know this man. This is not my chief. My chief is Phalo, because Phalo is born of Tshi-wo, my elder brother, so I don't know this man, and I am not going to be under him.'[23]

On the other hand, his superiority was recognised by the Gwali, old enemies of the imiDange.[24] The Ntinde, formerly allies of the Gwali and still on bad terms with Phalo in 1752,[25] probably recognised him too. The other important chiefs in the west of Phalo's kingdom were the Gqunukhwebe (the followers of

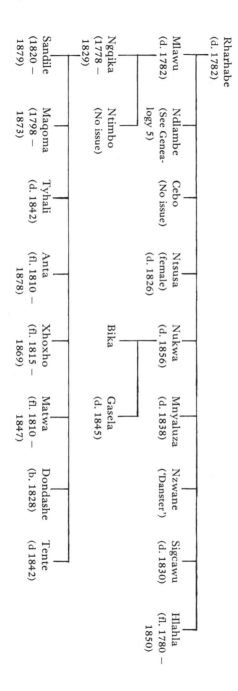

GENEALOGY 4

THE amaRHARHABE/NGQIKA

Khwane, whom Tshiwo had appointed a chief) and the Mbalu (the followers of Langa, brother of Gcaleka and Rharhabe). Neither of them was subject to Rharhabe.

Rharhabe took advantage of his brother's early death (1778) to attack Khawuta, Gcaleka's son and successor. So feared was he that a reported five to six hundred guards stood watch over the new king every night.[26] In the end, however, Rharhabe was driven off to the north, where his restless energies were diverted to the complicated internal politics of his Thembu neighbours. Both Rharhabe and his Great Son, Mlawu, died in battle against the Thembu. 'Today,' they cried, 'we have caught an old dog that has long destroyed our nation.'[27] Rharhabe's reputation stands high among his people, and it is therefore worth pointing out that great and ferocious a warrior as he was, his life ended on a note of defeat.[28] It was Rharhabe's son, Ndlambe, who was the real architect of Rharhabe greatness.

Ndlambe could not rule the amaRharhabe in his own name, since his deceased elder brother, Mlawu, had fathered two sons: Ntimbo, supported by the majority of the councillors, and Ngqika, supported by Ndlambe and his party. Both groups sought the support of the king, Khawuta. Ndlambe secured it, and ruled thereafter as regent for the young Ngqika.[29]

The power of Ndlambe was increased in the west at the expense of the other Xhosa chiefdoms. The imiDange were the first to go. Rharhabe had driven them across the Fish, killing their chief, Mahote. In their retreat, they intruded on the territory of the Boers of Agter Bruintjes Hoogte, who attacked them, together with the Gwali and the Ntinde who also happened to be west of the Fish, in what came to be known as the *First Frontier War* (1779 – 1781). Mahote's son, Jalamba, fell by a stratagem: he and some followers were shot picking up pieces of tobacco which had been strewn before them, apparently as a present. Jalamba's son, 'Dlodlu', was killed two years later, and the chiefship of the imiDange fell on the feckless Bangela, under whose rule the imiDange disintegrated.[30] Langa, chief of the Mbalu, pursued an independent course, but fought more often with Ndlambe than against him.[31] Ndlambe's chief rivals were the Gqunukhwebe under Tshaka and his son, Chungwa. Ndlambe defeated them three times, driving them deeper and deeper into the Colony, but they were able to recover from every defeat by recruiting Khoi from west of the Fish.[32] Ndlambe needed allies and, following the example of his father, sought them among the Boers of the Cape Colony.

In 1780, Rharhabe had proposed an alliance between himself and the Colony. In return for Boer assistance against the imiDange, whom he represented as rebel subjects, Rharhabe offered 'friendship and peace upon a permanent footing'. Local strongman Adriaan van Jaarsveld responded positively, but for some unknown reason, Rharhabe was unable to keep the appointment.[33] After at least two years soliciting, Ndlambe found a Boer ally in Barend Lindeque, a lieutenant in the Boer militia. They conducted a joint raid, but then the small Boer party lost their nerve and withdrew. Provoked by Boer intervention in their domestic politics, the Xhosa west of the Fish decided to teach them a lesson and drove them back beyond the Zwartkops River. This forced the Colonial authorities into action, and they sent out a strong commando (*Second Frontier War*, 1793). The hostile Xhosa attempted to retreat to Khawuta and safety, but Ndlambe cut them off at the Tsholomnqa River and defeated them crushingly, killing Tshaka and capturing Langa. Ndlambe offered to surrender Langa to the Landdrost of Graaff-Reinet who declined the offer, leaving the old chief to die in captivity. Chungwa, Tshaka's son, reached Khawuta, but shortly thereafter returned to 'his' country west of the Fish.[34]

As a result of this success, Ndlambe had become far and away the most powerful Xhosa chief in the west, but he was unable to build upon his triumph for shortly thereafter(1795), Ngqika, who owed him his chiefship, unexpectedly rebelled. According to the Ngqika, Ndlambe refused to surrender the regency. According to the Ndlambe, Ngqika launched a premeditated and unjustifiable attack after he had already been installed as chief.[35] The two versions are not incompatible; Ndlambe may have installed Ngqika as chief, but he continued to exercise the real power himself. Ngqika chafed at this restraint and decided to put a final end to the power of his uncle. Ndlambe appealed in vain to the Thembu and to his old allies, the Colony, but obtained help only from the Gcaleka regent (Khawuta had died in 1794). Once again Ngqika was successful. The Gcaleka were chased right across the Kei to the Jujura River in the present district of Willowvale, where peace was made.[36] From this time on, the king's Great Place was always situated east of the Kei. The exact terms of the peace are unknown, but shortly thereafter Ngqika began to represent himself as king of all the Xhosa. He made a costly slip, however, when the young king Hintsa succeeded in escaping from captivity. Ndlambe was taken prisoner, and remained at Ngqika's Great Place, allowed his wives and some cattle, but stripped of his power. Mnyaluza, Ndlambe's brother and chief lieutenant, crossed the Fish where he plagued Boer and Xhosa impartially.

Ngqika was only seventeen or eighteen. Gifted with considerable intelligence and with the imposing presence that

Ngqika

bespoke a great chief, he was ambitious and seems to have aimed at centralising the Xhosa under his leadership. But his early elevation and outstanding successes seem to have been ultimately detrimental, for to the end of his life he bore the character of a spoilt and greedy child. In his golden years, he pursued a policy calculated to concentrate power in his hands. He succeeded in reserving to himself the power of passing the death sentence. However, instead of using it he often substituted a fine in cattle, a measure that was far more profitable in buiding up a following. Private revenge for adultery was forbidden, which similarly added to chiefly jurisdiction and revenue.[37] Ngqika also extended the custom of *isizi* (death dues), so that instead of receiving one beast when a commoner died without heirs in the direct line, he received the entire estate. This measure was at first violently resisted but as other chiefs adopted it too, the commoners were left with no choice but to comply.[38] When the opportunity presented itself, Ngqika deposed councillors and brought their people directly under himself as well as taking over homesteads whose headships had fallen vacant.[39]

He is also credited with the introduction of the *ixhiba* ('grandfather house'). Ndlambe had placed the councillors of Mlawu (Ngqika's father) under his son, Mxhamli, in order to build up his power, as well as placing the councillors of his deceased Right-Hand brother, Cebo, under another son, Mdushane. Ngqika removed Mxhamli from office, and created a new institution, the *ixhiba*, by delegating the task of looking after one of his sons to the corporate body of councillors. This allowed them to express their ambitions through boosting their charge at the expense of his brothers, thereby assisting rather than obstructing the ruling chief. This institution was widely adopted by other chiefs since it resolved the structural conflict between the chief and his father's generation.[40]

Ngqika's quarrel with Ndlambe drew the support of the imiDange who were thus enabled to recognise the indisputable superiority of the amaRharhabe while revenging themselves on the man who had succeeded in bringing it about. He also appears to have successfully supported Nqeno, Langa's most capable son, against Thole, the legitimate heir, thus obtaining the allegiance of the Mbalu.[41] The Gqunukhwebe paid him tribute.[42] Other supporters included a number of autonomous Khoi[43] and a band of Boer adventurers led by Coenraad de Buys, known to the Xhosa as Khula ('the big one') because of his great height. Buys was living with Ngqika's mother and had promised him his fifteen year old daughter, but a more substantial reason for his influence was his access to Colonial gunpowder.[44] Ngqika was nobody's puppet however: he had defeated Ndlambe well before Buys's arrival , and he resisted the wilder anti-British schemes of the Boer refugees, who wanted to invade the Colony and install Buys as king.[45] In this, he followed the advice of the more experienced Ndlambe.

But Ngqika was not as strong as he thought he was, and in February 1800 Ndlambe and his brothers Sigcawu and Hlahla broke out of Ngqika's dominions to join Mnyaluza and the rest of his earlier supporters west of the Fish.[46] This was a turning point in that it drew the Cape Colony into the mainstream of Xhosa politics.

3. THE XHOSA AND THE COLONISTS (1775 – 1812)

Friction is endemic in frontier situations, and neither Xhosa nor Colonists were wholly innocent or wholly culpable.[47] The Boers feared the weight of Xhosa numbers and resented being pestered for presents or seeing their favourite pastures occupied by Xhosa herds.[48] On the other hand, the Xhosa had reason to complain of Boers who abused them physically, abducted their children, threatened them with firearms, and forced them to barter cattle for goods which they did not want.[49] Underlying specific grievances such as these was the clash of two pastoral peoples for land and cattle.

As we have seen, the political system of the Xhosa was geared towards indefinite expansion. Every bull had the right to his own enclosure, every chief had the right to his own territory. It was the fate of other people – San, Khoi, Thembu – to give way before the Xhosa and to accept their place in the Xhosa scheme of things. First contacts with Europeans did little to diminish the aggressive self-confidence of most Xhosa. They did not envy the Caucasoid features and Christian religion of which the Boers were so proud. They presumed Europeans wore peculiar clothes because they had feeble and sickly bodies.[50] They were surprised at many things white people did, 'but never think the white men are more wise or skilful than themselves, for they suppose they could do all that the white men do if they chose.'[51] Initial respect for guns and horses soon gave way to a shrewd appreciation of their ineffectiveness in dense bush.[52]

Consequently, the Xhosa saw no reason why Xhosa and European should not merge into a single society rather after the pattern of Xhosa and Khoi. They sought to include the Colony within their economic, political and social networks. They traded with the Boers as they did with other nations. Poor Xhosa wishing to acquire cattle worked for rich Boers as they would have done for rich Xhosa.[53] Politically, Xhosa chiefs saw the Boers as potential allies or enemies, and they offered to help them in turn against the San and the English.[54] Their chiefs assiduously cultivated Colonial officials by sending them presents and visiting them regularly. Ngqika hoped to marry Buys's daughter to cement the alliance between himself and the Dutch.[55] Xhosa were prepared to comply with reasonable Colonial usages (renting grazing land) and expected the Colonists to comply with theirs (giving tribute to chiefs).[56] Even Xhosa begging, the bane of the more nervous Boers, was no more than a replication among the Colonists of a process well-known amongst the Xhosa themselves.[57] Xhosa travelling in Xhosaland relied on the hospitality of perfect strangers, and were seldom disappointed. European travellers who commented approvingly on Xhosa hospitality probably never reflected that when the roles were reversed the hospitality was seldom willingly offered.

Whereas the self-confident Xhosa wanted an open frontier, the more vulnerable Colonial authorities wanted a boundary which was emphatically defined and closed. The problem was that both Xhosa and Colonists had conflicting claims to the rectangle of land, bounded in the east and north by the Fish River and in the west by the Bushmans River, that was known as the Zuurveld. The Colonial claim was based on an agreement made by Governor van Plettenburg with the Gwali chiefs in October 1778.[58] This claim has been justly criticised on two grounds. First the agreement with the Gwali chiefs was binding on no one but themselves. Second, the boundary intended by Van Plettenburg did not run along the entire Fish River, but along a more or less direct north-south line linking the upper Fish with the Bushmans and excluding the area between the Bushmans and the Fish, which does not seem to have been inhabited by the Colonists. Van Plettenburg's aide-de-camp, R.J. Gordon, was quite well aware of both these circumstances. He had visited the frontier area less than a year before the Van Plettenburg agreement, and had seen for himself that the territory of the powerful Gqunukhwebe chiefs stretched west of the Bushmans River.[59] Although Van Plettenburg made no attempt to visit the area or to speak to its rulers, subsequent governors took their stand on his treaty and concluded that since the Fish was the original boundary between the Colony and the Xhosa, any Xhosa found west of that river was an intruder who had no right to be there. The Xhosa claimed prior occupation as far west as the Sundays River, and supplemented their case with allegations that they had purchased the whole area twice, once from Ruiter and once from unnamed Company officials.[60]

Whereas the importance of the land question cannot be over-

GCALEKA CHIEFS

Hintsa

Sarhili

NDLAMBE

GQUNUKHWEBE

Mhala

Phato

F. I'ons. *Witchdoctor with Woman and Children.*

TWO CHRISTIAN CHIEFS

Khama

Dyani Tshatshu

stressed, it is possible that the importance of cattle raiding has been somewhat exaggerated. Theal and Cory, the old guard historians, thought that the Xhosa were inveterate thieves and that the peace of the frontier depended entirely on the steadfastness or otherwise of the Colonial authorities. S.D. Neumark, working within another set of preoccupations, also saw competition for cattle as the central issue, only his villains were not young Xhosa lusting after bride-wealth but Boer farmers attracted by the Cape Town meat market.[61]

In assessing these arguments one should bear two points in mind. First, cattle-reiving was usually less the object of war than the means of making it.[62] Competition for cattle played an important part in maintaining frontier tension, but as a factor it was more or less constant. A sharp increase in raiding was more often the consequence than the cause of a disturbed political situation. Second, the responsible authorities on both sides normally exerted themselves to keep the peace and to repress their

GENEALOGY 5

THE amaGQUNUKHWEBE

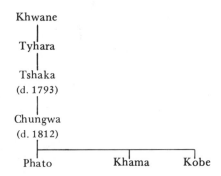

more unruly countrymen.[63]

The decision to go to war was a deliberate one, not undertaken in a fit of temper. For this reason it is hard to agree with the proposition that 'the number (of frontier wars) depends at what point raiding and retaliation may be termed war'.[64] Conventionally one distinguishes nine frontier wars, and it is significant that, with the exception of the hopelessly obscure *First Frontier War*, it is possible to isolate specific causes which go beyond general grievances to explain why a particular war happened at a particular time.

Most of the factors that shaped frontier relationships manifested themselves in the life of Chungwa, chief of the Gqunukhwebe from 1793 to 1812. In the 1780s, Chungwa and his father Tshaka were firmly established in the area between the Fish and Sundays. In essence, they wanted nothing more than a quiet life, and to placate the Colony they were quite willing to purchase the the land they occupied, or to rent it on the same terms as the Boers did. Certain Colonial officials appear to have pocketed their cattle without, of course, being able to give them anything in return for it.[65] The Gqunukhwebe also offered to help the Boers against the San in the north, a function which the Xhosa also performed for the Khoi. Because Ndlambe and his ally, Langa, had taken so many of their cattle, many Gqunukhwebe became herdsmen for the Boers.[66] Others took the easier path of theft. Xhosa cattle trampled Boer pastures and hungry Xhosa trapped 'Colonial' game for meat and skins. Being largely Khoi in composition, the Gqunukhwebe attracted slaves and Khoi servants. In retaliation, Boers started shooting Gqunukhwebe, and

Chungwa himself was locked in a treadmill and forced to turn it.[67]

Periodic meetings between Colonial officials and Tshaka and Chungwa prevented war until Lindeque's commando of 1793 provoked the Gqunukhwebe and Mbalu to settle old scores with the Colonists. The rise of Ndlambe to his east cut off Chungwa's retreat and forced him into a posture of defiance.[68] When requested to cross the Fish, he refused, adding that 'No landdrost knows how to make peace among the Caffers, and it is none of his business.'[69] To sustain his autonomy he forced the Mbalu chiefs Nqeno and Thole to stay with him by seizing their cattle.[70] War broke out again in 1799, when the British general Vandeleur attempted to drive Chungwa across the Fish *(Third Frontier War)*.[71] Chungwa was joined by rebel Khoi who feared that the British might abandon them to the Boers, their former masters. The combined forces were startlingly successful, one group of 150 men defeating a British force twice their strength in a night attack near the Sundays River.

In October 1799, Chungwa made a peace with Acting Governor Dundas, which allowed him to remain between the Bushmans and the Sundays Rivers, provided he did not molest the Colonists. Such an arrangement was exactly what he had been seeking all along, and he took care to maintain the peace, turning back a rebel Boer attack on the Colony.[72] When hostilities between Boer and Khoi flared up again in 1801, Chungwa did not join more opportunistic Xhosa chiefs in their attacks on the Boers, but gave shelter to the Khoi neutral, Klaas Stuurman.[73] Neutrality did not save him from a commando, or from being ordered to cross the Fish together with other more guilty chiefs.[74] Ngqika's implacable attitude reinforced his desire not to cross,[75] and the presence of Ndlambe pushed him yet deeper into the Colony. He clashed with Ndlambe, not only because the latter made sarcastic remarks about his 'large belly' and tried to force him to join in his war against Ngqika, but also because Ndlambe had taken over his old grazing land along the Bushmans River.[76] Chungwa's people were a familiar sight to the Colonists — who ascribed their 'roving', 'rambling' and 'strolling' to a desire to steal Colonial cattle — driving their herds from their winter pastures near the Bushmans to their summer pastures on the Sundays or even west of it.[77]

Chungwa did his best to stay on good terms with Major Cuyler, the Landdrost of Uitenhage, assuring him that he wished to 'live peaceably with the Dutchmen and the English'.[78] For Cuyler 'peace' meant Chungwa's withdrawal over the Fish, which the latter did not contemplate since it meant forfeiting his automony and, in his view, his birthright. He told Ndlambe that

he was in this part of the country before the Christians and as proof
asked me if I do not see as many of the remains of old Cafree's kraals as
the walls of old houses.[79]

He therefore continued his seasonal movements and, after one
indignant visit from Cuyler, sent the Landdrost an ox.[80] The
latter rejected it as a bribe, which, of course, it was not. It was a
'payment for grass'. Chungwa understood this to be the Boers'
custom. His gift was a recognition of Cuyler's authority and a sign
of peace. Cuyler's rejection was thus an *insult*, and the angry
Chungwa declared his intention to stay on anyway. The health of
his cattle demanded that transhumance should continue, and he
and his people returned the following summer with the excuse
that he wanted to be near the doctor.[81] The summer after that
(1811), he made a pretence of moving early, but soon sent a
message saying that he wanted to return as the 'wolves' (hyenas)
were destroying his cattle further east.[82] It was his last excuse,
for the following summer he was shot dead on his sickbed by
British troops expelling his people beyond the Fish.[83]

The career of Chungwa was parallelled in its earlier stages by
Langa and in its later ones by Ndlambe. His behaviour was the
product of motivations common to all the chiefs: the desire to
preserve his autonomy while maintaining his herds. He felt that
this could be done more easily under the Colony than under
Ngqika, and he did his best to remain on a friendly footing. The
Colonial authorities were not, however, prepared to accept the
inevitable inconveniences of coexistence, and finally closed
the frontier by the expulsion of 1812.

4. THE TRIUMPH OF NGQIKA 1800 – 1819

At the beginning of 1800 Ngqika was at the height of his power.
The regent, now in retreat across the Kei, was weak and not yet
fully in control of even the eastern chiefdoms. Ndlambe was under
his jurisdiction. The power of the imiDange and the Mbalu was
broken, and many of their chiefs had submitted to him. Chungwa
kept at a distance, but sent in tribute. Ngqika even dabbled in
Thembu politics.[84] Strong as he was internally, he could afford to
consider Buys's plan for the invasion of the Colony. But as his
power seeped from him and the number and strength of his
enemies grew, he was increasingly drawn into an alliance with the
Colony. He soon realised what it was they wanted to hear, and
told them willingly but untruthfully that he opposed cattle-raids
and was prepared to forgive his revolted subjects.[85] His main

object was to secure concrete military assistance as Ndlambe had done earlier.[86]

The chiefs west of the Fish, headed by Ndlambe, Mnyaluza and Chungwa, were in a weaker position, both numerically and strategically. They knew quite well that the Colony regarded the Fish as its boundary,[87] and many of them had taken advantage of the *Third Frontier War* to make up their herds at Boer expense. They were therefore quite ready to believe that the Colony was ready to help Ngqika against them, a fact which Ngqika exploited.[88] Moreover, they were divided among themselves. In their eagerness to remain at peace with the Colony, Ndlambe and Chungwa exerted themselves to repress cattle-raiding and even returned some deserted slaves and Khoi servants.[89] They began to barter with the Boers and to exchange their labour for cattle.[90]

In 1805, Ngqika poised himself for a decisive attack on Ndlambe, calling on the Colony and some Thembu for assistance. The Batavian Commissioner-General De Mist had set out to pay him a visit, and he attempted to inveigle De Mist into assistance, while giving his enemies the impression that such assistance was already promised. Mnyaluza deserted Ndlambe, while Chungwa got safely out of the way. But De Mist turned back as soon as he realised what was happening, and the attack never came off.[91] Ngqika wished to press ahead regardless, but, ironically, Ndlambe was saved by the Landdrost Alberti who did not want a Xhosa civil war west of the Fish.[92] At this point Ngqika made an error which even today his descendants consider reprehensible; he secured the abduction of the beautiful Thuthula, one of his uncle's wives.[93] It is hard to say whether this was a calculated insult designed to draw Ndlambe from his refuge or whether it was a purely personal matter, but it provoked a rebellion and Ndlambe seized the opportunity to inflict a crushing defeat on Ngqika and Mnyaluza. However, in the middle of the conflict, some important chiefs crossed back to Ngqika, thus denying Ndlambe a conclusive victory. Collins thought that this was because they shared Ngqika's ideas about death-duties, but it also seems likely that they feared Ndlambe as much as they did Ngqika, and that having taught the latter a lesson they were prepared to return to their old allegiance. They stood to gain more from a situation where they held the balance of power than from the destruction of the one chief and the domination of the other.

Hostilities were ended by an agreement whereby Ndlambe agreed to recognise Ngqika as his senior,[94] but Ndlambe and Chungwa remained west of the Fish, trying to maintain peace with the Colonists insofar as it was compatible with their pasturage requirements. In the same year that Chungwa attempted to present Cuyler with an ox, Ndlambe requested the Landdrost to be allowed to graze his cattle at Swartwater (further inland and much nearer the Boers) for three months so that they could get fat.[95] Cuyler turned down the request and when troops landed at Algoa Bay, Ndlambe withdrew his herds. The result was that many of his supporters left him and went over to Ngqika.[96]

Another problem for Ndlambe was that just as he sought autonomy from Ngqika, some of his own subordinates sought autonomy for themselves. Some chiefs of the imiDange named Habana, Galata, and Xasa migrated to the good grazing around the Zuurberg where they raided the Colonists. Ndlambe did what he could to bring them to heel but Xasa was able to evade him by hiding in the woods. Eventually, Xasa and Galata were forced to retreat across the Fish where they joined Ngqika (August 1811).[97] But Ndlambe was given no further opportunities of showing his good faith because the decision to expel him and Chungwa had already been taken. In December 1811, the Colonial Government mobilised its full military strength for the first time (Fourth Frontier War). British regular troops, backed by Boer militia, systematically and ruthlessly drove the Xhosa beyond the Fish.

In the meantime, the position of Ngqika had changed. During the period of his greatness, he had been treated by the Dutch authorities as an equal. He had offered to help them against the British in return for their help against Ndlambe.[98] Gifts were exchanged on a formal basis, and Ngqika was perfectly ready to reject them when he felt that his honour demanded it.[99] He drank 'wine with pleasure, but drank little'.[100] After the Thuthula debacle, he became a mendicant both politically and materially, begging the Colony for revenge on Ndlambe, and for clothes, cattle and brandy. In 1800, he had declared himself king of all the Xhosa; now he received with anxious satisfaction the Colony's assurance that they regarded him as the greatest chief.[101] His supporters were minor chiefs, men like Mnyaluza, Nqeno and Funa, who were not satisfied to be loyal subordinates. Their chief amusement was robbing the Boer farmers and they hid behind Ngqika because they realised he was best able to shield them. Inevitably therefore, the interests of Ngqika's two allies, the Colony and the minor chiefs, were incompatible.

Not surprisingly the 1812 expulsions caused an increase in cattle-raiding instead of eliminating it. Governor Lord Charles Somerset conferred with old frontier hands like Uitenhage Land-drost Cuyler and came up with what seemed a promising package. Well aware of Ngqika's weakness at home, Somerset offered him active military assistance in enforcing his will on his subordinates in return for his assistance in suppressing cattle-raiding. The Xhosa remember this offer as a succinct 'You protect me, and I'll protect you'.[102] The deal was proposed at the Kat River Conference (1817). Ngqika, who seems to have immediately appreciated the implications of the proposal, attempted to evade it. According to one eyewitness:

> Gaika said to the governor, 'There is my uncle and there are the other chiefs'. The governor then said, 'No, you must be responsible for all the cattle and the horses that are stolen.' The other chiefs then said to Gaika 'Say yes, that you will be responsible, for we see the man is getting angry,' for we had the cannon and artillerymen and soldiers and boors with loaded muskets standing about us.[103]

Ngqika was now put in the awkward position of being forced to chastise his Xhosa allies in order to satisfy the Colony. He temporized by sending back horses and making exaggerated professions of his loyalty. Meanwhile, he attempted to derive the maximum benefit out of his association with the Colony in terms of presents and by taking a share of stolen cattle, while blaming continuing deficiencies on Ndlambe.[104] Ndlambe did his best to make a separate peace with the Colony, three times sending emissaries and returning cattle, firearms, and even a British deserter.[105] Somerset and Cuyler, obstinately adhering to their preconceived notions of good Ngqika and bad Ndlambe, turned a deaf ear. Well might the amaNdlambe complain:

> We lived in peace. Some bad people stole, perhaps; but the nation was quiet – the chiefs were quiet. Gaika stole – his chiefs stole – his people stole. You sent him copper; you sent him beads; you sent him horses – on which he rode to steal more. To *us* you send only commandoes![106]

5. AMALINDE

Ndlambe's hand was strengthened by reconciliation with his son, Mdushane,[107] the rise of the great wardoctor, Nxele,[108] and the resurgence of the Great House east of the Kei.

The Gcaleka had gradually recovered from their internal divisions, from Khawuta's weakness, and from their defeat by Ngqika in 1795. Around 1805, Bhurhu, the Right-Hand son of Khawuta, declared, 'Let the people of different customs come together, and the houses of the Great Place stand close.' The resistance of dissidents led by Chief Nxito of the Tshayelo was

overcome.[109]   Bhurhu did not attempt to assert his own
autonomy, but threw his weight behind Khawuta's Great Son,
Hintsa, easily the most impressive figure in the whole history of
the descendants of Tshawe.[110] Two quotations will have to
suffice as some indication of his political style. The first comes
from his speech to his heir, Sarhili, at the latter's circumcision:

> Now hear! Love your cattle, My people love me because I love my
> cattle, therefore you must love your cattle, as I have done — if you have
> cattle, poor men will not pass by your place, no he will stop with you —
> you must respect the rich only — you must not despise the poor — see
> the reason why I have so many cattle. I love my cattle and my people
> love me. A man that is a coward, when he gives you council, you must
> hear that man, he will give you wise council. A bold man by his council
> will bring you into trouble . . . Take care of pride, when you go into the
> field to look at the cattle, and you see a piece of firewood, take it up,
> and carry it home and make fire — When a councillor asks you for
> cattle, give him some, though your cattle are pretty, because through
> this thing, your people will love you.[111]

Available records indicate that Hintsa was at the same time a
ruthless hounder of the rich and a generous benefactor of the
poor. This is not really paradoxical: it was the only way to be
both wealthy and popular. Hintsa's mode of proceeding and the
care which he took to preserve the outer niceties is admirably
illustrated by the following:

> In Hinza's territory, a Kaffer, whose possessions excited envy and
> dislike, was accused of keeping a witch, which though confined during
> the day, roamed about the country at night, and destroyed the cattle.
> On this plea he was seized and deprived of everything, half of the cattle
> being taken by Hinza, while the other half were distributed among the
> councillors . . . The missionary . . . said, 'You have plenty of cattle, why
> did you ruin the poor man?' When the chief turned to him with a
> peculiar smile, which marked that he was not deceived, and with a tone
> of mock seriousness said, 'Yes, but it is a shocking thing you know, to
> keep a witch wolf.'[112]

Further progress was made when Nqoko, chief of the amaMbede,
died, and Hintsa was able to back one of his sons, Mguntu, against
the other, Kalashe.[113] The autonomy of the powerful Ngqosini
clan was destroyed by the massacre of seventeen unsuspecting
Ngqosini councillors on a hunting expedition, and the degradation
of their chief to the position of headman under Hintsa's Right-
Hand son, Ncaphayi.[114] Thus by degrees the Great House re-

established its control over the Xhosa chiefdoms east of the Kei, and Bhurhu re-occupied Gcaleka's old territory west of the Kei.[112]

Hintsa now began to consider extending his authority over the westernmost chiefdoms, and the troubles of the Rharhabe seemed to invite intervention. Nor was he hard put to choose between Ndlambe, his father's old ally, and Ngqika, whom he had good reason to believe had nearly murdered him. Ndlambe was recognised as chief of the Rharhabe ('He was Hintsa's eyes') whereas Ngqika was not recognised at all ('He was there but he never reigned').[116] Hintsa is reported to have led the allied armies against Ngqika in person at the battle of Amalinde.[117]

Events soon precipitated a crisis. A Colonial commando seized the cattle of the minor chiefs, under the impression that they were supporters of Ndlambe.[118] They demanded that Ngqika join in an attack to recover them. He attempted to get the cattle back by negotiations, but in the meantime many of the imiDange joined Ndlambe's wardoctor, Nxele.[119] Ngqika demanded that Ndlambe hand Nxele over to him. Ndlambe refused, saying that Hintsa alone was king and that Ngqika was just a chief like himself (and therefore could not give him orders). Ngqika answered 'haughtily', 'I too am a king!'[120] But he knew too well the basis on which his kingship now rested and sent urgent appeals to the Colony for its promised aid. Ndlambe forced the issue by seizing the cattle of one of Ngqika's sub-chiefs, and Ngqika's councillors compelled the reluctant chief to attack. At the great battle of Amalinde (October 1818), Ngqika's forces were overwhelmed. Ndlambe and his followers sent an urgent message to the Colony 'declaring they were anxious to remain at peace with the Colony, but at the same time refusing to submit to Gaika, whom they had conquered.'[121] The appeal was ignored by the Colonial authorities, who believed that Ngqika was being punished because he had tried to repress cattle-raiding. The *Fifth Frontier War* commenced when Colonel Brereton attacked Ndlambe (December 1818), and took 23 000 cattle. The Xhosa swept into the Colony, attacking Grahamstown in broad daylight (22 April 1819).[122] Inevitably, British firepower was victorious, and by October the Xhosa had been defeated. Ngqika's ascendance over Ndlambe and Hintsa was now established — but at a cost to himself that he could hardly have anticipated.

5. Visions and Interpretations

1. EARLY INFLUENCES ON XHOSA RELIGION

It is impossible to trace the purely endogenous evolution of Xhosa religion. This is partly because oral traditions are notorious for their assertion of the immutability of customs[1] and partly because of the absence among the Xhosa of the type of elaborate religious ritual found elsewhere in Africa in which historical elements have been embedded.[2] One exception was the annual sacrifice to the Ngxingxolo River in celebration of Gcaleka's initiation, but this has now been discontinued. However, it seems probable that most of the important features of Xhosa religion are extensions of household worship, relating as they do to ancestor veneration or the life-cycle. Each household head was a religious practitioner in that he made the offerings and performed the beneficent magic which accompanied the daily business of living. With political enlargement of scale, certain tasks which affected the whole area and all of its resident kinship groups became the responsibility of the chief, the only father shared by all the people. These included responsibility for a successful harvest: (first-fruits ceremony), the bringing of rain and the national defence (the *ithola,* or wardoctor, was attached specifically to the chief).

Khoisan religious beliefs influenced Xhosa religion to a limited extent, but the central premises of the two religious complexes remained very different.[3] Whereas the Xhosa had only a very hazy conception of a High God and perceived good and evil forces in the relatively mundane terms of ancestors and witches,[4] the Khoi worshipped an anthropomorphised deity named Tsui//Goab, associated with the moon, and attributed evil to a rival being, associated with black sky and whirlwinds, known as //Gaunab.

The existence of witches on earth was recognised, and it was believed that when they died they became evil spirits. Ancestors were respected but they were largely disregarded in ritual and as active agents.

Since the basic ideas of Khoisan religion were not adopted by the Xhosa, its influence cannot be said to have been very profound despite the widespread borrowing of religious loanwords.[5] This is all the more remarkable considering the substantial proportion of Xhosa who were of Khoi origin. Typical practices definitely borrowed from the Khoisan include cutting off the tip of the little finger *(ingqiti)* and throwing stones on wayside cairns *(izivivane)*. These, however, were only charms to bring strength and good luck, and were devoid of deeper religious or social significance. Harinck's attractive hypothesis that the Khoi enjoyed high religious status among the Xhosa because they were the original occupants of the land is untenable in the absence of supporting evidence.[6] Harinck apparently based it on the fact that most rainmakers around 1805 were Khoi, but they were later superseded by the Mfengu, who had even less title to the land than the Xhosa. On the other hand, the indirect influence of Khoisan religion in preparing the way for Christianity through familiarising the Xhosa with analogues of God and the Devil may have been considerable.

2. CRISIS

Xhosa ascendancy on the frontier was suddenly broken as a result of the British decision to retain the Cape after 1806. In 1811, Governor Sir John Cradock ordered Lieutenant-Colonel Graham to expel all Xhosa living west of the Fish, urging 'the expediency of destroying the Kaffer kraals, laying waste their gardens and fields and in fact totally removing any object that could hold out to their chiefs an inducement to revisit the regained territory.'[7] Nothing loath, Graham determined 'to attack the savages in a way which I hope will leave a lasting impression on their memories.'[8]

The war which followed *(Fourth Frontier War* 1811 – 1812) was brief, but of unprecedented ferocity. The Xhosa chiefs' request to stay on until the summer crops were fully harvested was deliberately turned down. 'We chose the season of corn being on the ground,' Graham informed his ally Ngqika, 'in order ... that we might the more severely punish them for their many crimes by destroying it.'[9] Graham's adjutant recorded entries such as these in his journal: 'Friday 17th, two parties of 100 men each were sent to destroy gardens and burn huts and villages . . . Sunday 18th, 300 men went early to destroy gardens and huts, taking with them 600 oxen to trample down the covered vegetables in the gardens.'[10] After one particularly successful operation, Graham exulted: 'Hardly a trace of a Kaffir now remains. Almost all they saw were killed or wounded . . . '[11] The war was marked by atrocities on both sides, the Xhosa murdering Landdrost Stockenstrom during a parley, and British troops shooting the elderly Chungwa as he lay dying on his sickbed unable to move. The army found it difficult to distinguish women in the dense bush and many of them were shot.[12] When the expelled Xhosa attempted to re-enter the Colony, Cradock simply reiterated his previous orders. 'It is painful to express,' he wrote to the Commandant of the Frontier, 'that the Order must be to destroy and lay waste.'[13]

Total war was a new and shattering experience for the Xhosa. Wars between Xhosa chiefs or with their African and Khoi neighbours were rarely bloody.[14] The throwing assegaai was not a very effective weapon and was not usually used with intent to kill; the warriors concentrated their attention on trying to abduct the enemy's cattle and women. The purpose of war was not the destruction of productive resources, but their acquisition and absorption. The havoc wrought by the Colonial forces was not only cruel but incomprehensible. Instead of being subjected to the victors and incorporated into their society — a painful process, but one which they would have understood — the Xhosa were rejected and expelled, the already blurring division between the two cultures was revived and their irreconcilable differences were re-emphasised. For the first time the full extent of the Colony's immense technical and material resources was revealed. Moreover, the situation was not regarded as stable. Now that this foreign entity had crystallised as a threat there was no telling where it would all end. This feeling is well demonstrated in one of Nxele's harangues: 'There they come! They have crossed the Qagqiwa (Zwartkops) and they have crossed the Nqweba (Sundays); only one river more, the Nxuba (Fish) and then they will be in our land. What will become of you then?'[15] The Xhosa knew what had happened to the Khoi and feared a similar fate.

The expulsion created a set of problems which the chiefs were unable to solve. Thus in the years immediately following 1812, political leadership passed from the hands of chiefs into the hands of prophet-figures. This should not, however, be seen simply as a switch from the secular to the sacred or as a flight from reality. Historians have made much of Nxele's promise to turn bullets into water, but such a promise — if he made it at all — is unremarkable. Every wardoctor was credited with the ability to 'tie up' the enemy and nullify his weapons,[16] and if one believes that spears can be rendered harmless it requires no great leap of faith to believe the same of bullets. The peculiar attraction which Nxele and Ntsikana had for the Xhosa stemmed not from any unfathomable magical powers but from their capacity to provide rational answers to pressing and very real questions: Who were these white people? What did they want? What should be done about them?

Like most other African religions, Xhosa religion was logical enough, given the assumption that the unseen world was active in this one and exercised an important causal influence.[17] Health and fertility were accepted as the natural condition of things, and any deficiency was attributed to dereliction of duty or to the influence of malevolent persons. It was further assumed that the unseen world was comprehensible, that its forces behaved according to set patterns, and that it was therefore open to manipulation and control. This made religious practice an inseparable part of secular activity. On one level, it was a technique of getting things done and its practitioners, the diviners, were not metaphysicians but technicians who understood the mechanics of the unseen world. Rain magic and field magic were as essential to a good harvest as sowing and weeding. Similarly, correct observance of rituals was a prerequisite for success and happiness in everyday life.

It is important to note that this world-view did not rule out experimentation and hypothesis. For instance, in their persistent attempts to procure a secure supply of rain the Xhosa turned at different times to the Khoi and the missionaries to see if their cosmologies were more effective. Later there was also a school of thought that favoured the San and Mfengu because they came from the 'north' where the rain came from.[18] However, speculation was necessarily limited by the bounds of the world-view itself. Gcaleka, for instance, has been described as a sickly man, who was always killing people in the hope of making himself better.[19] The fact that his health did not improve did not show that disease is not caused by witches; it simply showed that the witch had not yet been caught.

Nxele and Ntsikana commenced their careers as diviners ('witch-doctors'). All diviners were (and still are) called to their office through a mystical experience characterised by what many Western psychologists would call hysterical symptoms, but which the Xhosa regard as marks of divine attention.[20] The signs of possession varied and might include nervous paroxysms, dreams, visions, association with familiars, and so on. Often these signs were ambivalent, so that it was not always clear whether the possessing spirits were good or evil, and a qualified diviner would be called in to decide what should be done. If the symptoms were acceptable and if the initiate could keep them under control, he would probably be admitted as a diviner; and if not, the offending spirits would be cast out. Relatively few initiated persons actually practised as diviners, and it would appear that the successful diviners were those who told their clients what the latter wanted to hear. The implications of this are important. It was not spiritual experience alone which qualified a person as a diviner. The initiate had to be recognised as such by established diviners, and his subsequent performances had to conform with the expectations of his public. The process of divination was not a one-way street through which the charismatic diviner led his passive flock, but a dialogue between diviner and clients where the course of action prescribed by the former was circumscribed by what the latter were prepared to accept.

Obviously, the traditional cosmology had no place for white men and no formula for dealing with the threat they posed. If a solution was to be found, it was surely somewhere among the new stock of concepts introduced by the Europeans. The Christian ideas most readily absorbed by the Xhosa were those concerning God, the Devil, the Creation and the Resurrection. Of these, the first two were familiar from Khoi religion. The third had a Xhosa equivalent, according to which man was created from a bed of reeds. But it was the idea of the Last Judgement and Resurrection which had the greatest impact, as it filled a gap in Xhosa belief. There had been no satisfactory explanation for death, which was regarded as a product of witchcraft and as the ultimate impurity. So great was the horror of death among the Xhosa that after the great smallpox epidemic of the late eighteenth century the fatally ill were not allowed to die in their homes, but were chased out into the bush. The relatives of the deceased had to undergo elaborate rites of purification before being allowed to re-enter the community.[21] The missionary message that the dead did not really die but would rise úp again was thus received with joyful misunderstanding:

> When . . . [the missionary, James Read] told them that woman and all mankind would rise again from the dead, it caused uncommon joy among the Caffres. They said they should like to see their grandfathers, and others whom they mentioned. Congo inquired when it would happen, and if it would be soon, but Mr Read could not gratify his wishes on that point.[22]

Some sort of religious synthesis was needed: a synthesis which was firmly rooted in the traditional world-view (which was still seen to work from day to day), but which was capable of explaining the presence of these strange people and suggesting a means of controlling them.

3. NXELE

Nxele grew up in the Cape Colony, son of a commoner who worked for a Boer farmer.[23] Here he picked up Dutch and, perhaps, that knowledge of Christianity and European ways which enabled him to mediate between two cultures. While still a young man he began to exhibit the hysterical symptoms associated with the initial calling of a diviner, but to an exaggerated degree. He lived in the woods and fields, refusing to eat any prepared food because it had become unclean through the 'sins' of the people.[24] After his circumcision he began to preach, saying 'Forsake witch-craft! Forsake blood!' This was unusual behaviour even for a diviner. Nxele was bound and a rope was tied round his neck, but a man named Qalanga, recognising that this was no ordinary madness, said, 'Take that rope off his neck and say *Camagu*.'[25] Nxele subsequently attributed this deliverance to the intervention of Christ.[26] He was taken to Ndlambe. Whether that chief was genuinely impressed or whether he simply felt that the madman might prove useful is difficult to say, but he allowed Nxele to set up his own Great Place and offered him cattle, which were refused.

These occurrences seem to have taken place shortly after the Xhosa were expelled across the Fish in 1812. This disaster did not cause Nxele to turn against the whites; if anything, it inspired him to seek the sources of their power. He spent much of his time in the new frontier outpost of Grahamstown, carefully observing the military and technical side of the behemoth, but evidently more interested in its magical underpinnings, represented in Grahamstown by Chaplain Vanderlingen, whom Nxele puzzled 'with metaphysical subtleties or mystical ravings'.[27] During this early phase his views seem to have been fairly orthodox. He preached against witchcraft, polygamy, adultery, incest, warfare and the racing of oxen. He spoke of God (*Mdalidiphu* — creator of the deep), his son Tayi, the Creation, the Fall, The Flood, the Passion and the Resurrection. His personal following increased slowly, but he had little impact on Xhosa society as a whole, and he complained to the missionary Read that the Xhosa would not listen to him. At this point in his career (1816), he viewed the missionaries as brothers in a common pursuit, and urged them to establish themselves in Xhosaland under his protection.[28]

The dynamic of Nxele's personal development and the dynamic of the historical situation in which he was placed made it impossible for him to co-operate with the European missionaries for very long. It was but a short step from proclaiming divine truth to associating himself with the divinity, particularly since Nxele knew that he was unique among the Xhosa. Already by 1816 he was calling himself the younger brother of Christ, although this should be interpreted in the classificatory rather than the literal sense. It became increasingly clear to him that orthodox Christianity as embodied by the missionaries would not accept him as an equal partner in the evangelisation of the Xhosa, much less believe in the divinity of his origins or the authenticity of his visions. In any event, his inclination was not to piecemeal conversion through individual persuasion, but rather to mass conversion through dramatic demonstration of his divine power. To this end, he levied a large number of cattle and summoned the people to Gompo Rock (near modern East London) to witness the resurrection of the dead from beneath the rock, and the damnation of the witches thither. Although the expected event did not materialise, Nxele's reputation was not substantially affected.[29] He now began to move away from Christianity with increasing rapidity. He began to use red ochre and to dance (*xhentsa*) in the manner of diviners. Previously a staunch adherent of monogamy, he now married two young San women. Whereas he had at first rejected gifts, he started to demand (*ruma*) the diviner's due of cattle.[30]

The political events of a wider world were also inexorably drawing Nxele into conflict with the Europeans. Desperate to end the cattle-reiving which the expulsion of the Xhosa had only aggravated, the Colonial Government concluded an agreement with their old ally, Ngqika (April 1817) (See above, p 61). This provoked the other chiefs into uniting against his pretensions. Nxele was a moving spirit in the coalition. Ndlambe was the old patron who had saved him from death, whereas Ngqika had sponsored a rival named Ntsikana. Ngqika was moreover an adulterous and incestuous sinner, through his marriage to Ndlambe's ex-wife, Thuthula.

Ngqika was overwhelmed at the great battle of Amalinde (October 1818), but with characteristic slyness he appealed to the Colonial authorities on the grounds that he was being punished for his attempts to halt thieving. Colonel Brereton, later famous for shooting down rioters in Bristol, swept into Xhosaland and carried off 23 000 cattle. For the Xhosa, it was a repetition of the expulsions of 1812. As a councillor of Nxele put it:

You sent a commando — you took our last cow — you left only a few calves which died for want, along with our children. You gave half the spoil to Gaika; half you kept yourselves. Without milk — our corn destroyed — we saw our wives and children perish — we saw that we must ourselves perish; we followed, therefore, the tracks of our cattle into the colony.[31]

These internal and external pressures fused the Christian, traditional and personal elements in Nxele's religious thinking into a comprehensive cosmological synthesis. He now saw the world as a battleground between Thixo, the God of the whites, and Mdalidiphu, the God of the blacks. The whites had killed the son of their God, who had punished them by expelling them from their own country into the sea whence they had now emerged in search of land. But Mdalidiphu was more powerful and would push the whites back. The correct way to worship God was not 'to sit and sing M'de-e, M'de-e all day and pray with their faces to the ground and their backs to the Almighty', as the missionaries taught, but to dance and to enjoy life and to make love, so that the black people would multiply and fill the earth.[32]

Nxele was now at the height of his power. Acting as the supreme wardoctor, he led the Xhosa armies in ravaging the Colony. In May 1819 he attacked Grahamstown in broad daylight, a fatal error which almost certainly cost him success. Three months later, he surrendered himself in the vain hope that this would end the British counter-offensive, and was imprisoned on Robben Island. In 1820 he and some companions overpowered the crew of a small boat and attempted to escape, but the overloaded craft capsized and he was drowned.

Many Xhosa refused to believe Nxele was dead and his personal possessions were preserved in expectation of his return.[33] And he did indeed return from time to time, but only in dreams and visions.[34] For a while his mantle passed to Mngqatsi, a rainmaker who lived near Pirie mission from about 1832 to 1842.[35] When the rain was late, Mngqatsi blamed the missionaries and urged the people to drive them away. He organised a provisions boycott of the missions, threatening those who disobeyed with lightning. He held rainmaking ceremonies on Sundays. But his inability to break the drought of 1842 discredited him as a fraud, whereas missionary powers were vindicated through the success of their irrigation works.

4. NTSIKANA

The revelation of Ntsikana, like that of Nxele, gradually emerged through a combination of personal evolution and external pressure.[36] But Ntsikana's thought developed in the opposite direction to Nxele's, towards Christianity rather than away from it. Until his religious visitation, Ntsikana was a locally respected but quite unremarkable homestead-head in Ndlambe's country. His initial experience was an hallucination at the gate of his cattle enclosure, where he saw a strange ray of light shining on his favourite ox, an animal with which he had a mystical and quite unChristian relationship.[37] Shortly thereafter he attended a dance, and a whirlwind sprang up whenever he tried to join in. Be that as it may, he certainly seems to have experienced a revulsion for traditional dancing. As he was returning home he felt an irresistible impulse directing him to plunge into a stream and wash off his red ochre. An insistent voice within him cried 'This thing which has entered me, it says "Let there be prayer! Let every thing bow the knee!"'[38] It should be emphasised that there was nothing Christian in this: Ntsikana had experienced a mystical vision and an urge to rid himself of impurity, all completely comprehensible in Xhosa religious terms. Ntsikana took himself and his vision to Ndlambe, but the latter politely declined his services in favour of the already established Nxele.[39]

Rejected by Ndlambe, Ntsikana turned to Ngqika and with his backing set up as Nxele's rival. Tradition recalls that his constant cry was 'Nxele has turned upside down! Why does he mislead the people?'[40] Directly or indirectly, he learnt something of Christianity from Joseph Williams, the missionary at Ngqika's Great Place, and this gave him the conceptual ammunition to attack his enemy:

> Nxele is wrong in saying that God is on earth: God is in the heavens. He is right in saying that there are two Gods, but they are not Tayi and Mdalidiphu, but Thixo and his son . . . He lies in saying the people must put away witchcraft, for what is witchcraft but (the badness of) the heart of man?[41]

'You only go to wash yourselves with sea-water at Gompo!'[42] he warned those who were hurrying off to the expected resurrection. He appealed to the chiefs, all members of the Tshawe royal clan, by pointing out the dangers of extending recognition to a commoner like Nxele:

> I am only like a candle. Those who are chiefs will remain chiefs because

they were given [the chiefship] by Him and only He can take it away; I
have not added anything to myself; I am just as I was, Nxele is wrong in
saying he should be saluted; he is not a chief.[43]

Ntsikana even went so far as to deny the impurity of incest, which
Ngqika had clearly committed through his liaison with Thuthula.

It is thus evident that Ntsikana's theology developed as a
reaction to Nxele. But he should not be dismissed as a mere
political opportunist. The basic idea expressed in his original
vision, 'Let every thing submit!', is also the central theme of his
magnificent hymn, which is still sung today. The image of God as
a shield of defence is repeated three times in the original version,
and the hymn continues:

> He is the one who brings together herds which oppose each other.
> He is the leader who has led us.
> He is the great blanket which we put on.[44]

The essence of Ntsikana's message, his answer to the problem of
stress, was complete submission to the will of God, where alone
peace and protection were to be found. Peace was a part of
Ntsikana's politics too. Just before the disaster of Amalinde he
warned the amaNgqika that he saw their heads 'devoured by ants'[45]
and tried unsuccessfully to restrain them from battle. This was in
direct contrast to Nxele, who threatened that they would become
'firewood and ants'. Nxele was a wardoctor and his cosmology
was one of battle between good and evil. Ntsikana was a man of
peace and submission, and his cosmology was one of peace and
submission.

Amalinde dates Ntsikana's emergence to before 1818. Thereafter he preached and composed hymns at home. Tradition has it
that when he felt death approaching (1821), he asked his family to
bury him in the ground in the Christian manner. When they
hesitated, he picked up a wooden spade, and turned the first sods.

The more obvious contrasts between Nxele and Ntsikana
should not obscure the essential similarity of their social
functions. Although adjectives like 'prophetic' come readily to the
pens of historians and Nxele has even been claimed for the
millennium,[46] they represent an adaptation within the traditional
religious framework of innovation and experimentation rather
than a radical break away from it. Their different revelations were
simply alternative permutations of the same stock of concepts,
deriving from the necessity of fusing Xhosa religion with
Christianity in order to formulate a new world-view capable of
comprehending the irruption of the Europeans. Their ultimate

conclusions evolved slowly, and they were elicited by the outside world rather than dictated to it. Nxele's nationalist theology emerged as a result of white hostility to his version of Christianity and to his patron, Ndlambe, whereas Ntsikana's pacifism was due to the political circumstances of his sponsor, Ngqika. Their popular impact depended less on their personal charisma than on the popular acceptability of their respective messages. Nxele's following among the Xhosa increased as he moved away from Christianity towards more comprehensible patterns of magical behaviour. Ntsikana's position was understood by very few, and he made very little impression even on Ngqika's people.

Nxele is supposed to have led 10 000 warriors against Grahamstown. Ntsikana's immediate influence was confined to his immediate circle. The spiritual heirs of Nxele from Mngqatsi through Mlanjeni to Nongqawuse, prophetess of the cattle-killing disaster, and beyond, found traditional techniques increasingly helpless against European power. By the turn of the century '*Kukuza kukaNxele*' (the return of Nxele) was the byword for a vain hope. At the same time the seed Ntsikana planted had flourished, through the efforts of men like Tiyo Soga, son of one of Ntsikana's converts, and Christianity was well and truly planted among the Xhosa as an African religion brought not by missionaries but by Ntsikana. Today the wheel has come full circle as young Xhosa turn towards the nationalism of Nxele rather than the humility of Ntsikana.

That the relative appeal of Nxele and Ntsikana has fluctuated over time should surprise no one. In their own day their attraction depended not on their charisma or their supernatural abilities but on their power to reinterpret a world which had suddenly become incomprehensible. They are giants because they transcend specifics to symbolise the opposite poles of Xhosa response to Christianity and the West: Nxele representing struggle and Ntsikana submission. Nxele died defiant to the end: Ntsikana dug his own grave. So exactly does their rivalry foreshadow the struggle for the Xhosa mind that the contest between the two would surely be taken for a myth if it were not known to be a reality.

5. MISSIONARIES

The cases of Nxele and Ntsikana show that some form of Christianity was not lacking in appeal for the Xhosa. It remains to consider the impact of formal Christianity brought by the missionaries. In the years before 1850, the initial optimism of the early period gave way to the pessimism and lack of success which led the missionary Bryce Ross to label the years 1838 – 1846 as 'the dreariest in the history of the Caffre missions'.[47] This was due to the fact that the traditional Xhosa world view received a new lease of life after the partial success of the 1834 – 1835 war.

A new religion could appeal only to those whose old world was irrevocably shattered and who wanted new tools to build a new one. This was true of the Mfengu, who supplied the missionaries with their first mass conversions, and it was to be true of many Xhosa after 1857, but it was not true of the Xhosa before 1850. Thus it was largely in vain that the missionaries, most of whom equated Christianity with European civilisation and behaviour, attempted to persuade the Xhosa to abandon trusted practices which they regarded as essential to their earthly prosperity and well-being in favour of a doctrine which was abstract and explicitly devoid of material benefits. The contrast appears clearly in the reaction of one old man who warned his neighbours that such useless speculation would ruin the Xhosa because 'their children would neglect the cattle'.[48] Another old man indicated the essential irrelevance of Christian doctrine to the Xhosa when he said that:

> He had gone once or twice [to hear the missionaries] but that he could not understand what they said, and he had therefore discontinued his visits, though he believed them to be a good kind of people who did him no harm.[49]

The missionaries' primary targets were some of the Xhosa's most treasured social institutions, and they met with a resounding snub. Their attack on 'witchcraft' was in fact an attack on witch-finding; for the Xhosa, this was like denying the existence of a disease and suggesting the elimination of the medical profession. Nor was there much prospect of persuading the Xhosa to abandon polygamy and bridewealth, the cement of all social relationships. Lacking a concept of 'sin', they could hardly share the missionaries' objections to dancing and nudity. Only on the question of rainmaking did the missionaries take up a comprehensible position: accused by the rainmakers of holding back the rain, they retaliated by laying the blame on the sins of the people, or on the rainmakers themselves.[50]

Christianity could not hope entirely to replace traditional religion, intimately bound up as the latter was with the family and with the life cycle of birth, maturity and death. This association with the irreducible social unit and the inevitable daily round transcended any possible political, social or economic vicissitude. Moreover, the Xhosa could see no reason why they should believe the new dispensation. 'How did those words get in the book you tell us about?' they asked, 'How did the first man who wrote them know them?'[51] Much of it seemed impossibly farfetched. A favourite remark of Xhosa sceptics was that if God was all-powerful and the Devil the author of all sin, God should simply convert the Devil and save everyone trouble.[52]

The chiefs agreed to receive the missionaries for a number of reasons, all of them secular. Political prestige, the provision of a regular channel of communication with the Colony, and fear of the consequences of a possible refusal all played their part.[53] But these benefits were offset by suspicions of the missionaries' secular motives. Some were viewed as spies (which, in a sense, they were) or, even worse, as part of a plot to destroy the Xhosa by drought and disease. Bhotomane once asked the missionary Kay:

> Can you tell me why it is that the Amakosae chiefs are dying so fast? S'Lhambi is dead; Dushani is dead; and now Gaika is dead. Enno is very ill, and I am also not well. Pray, what is it that is killing us all?[54]

More concretely, the mission stations were seen as an invasion of the sovereignty of the chiefs. The mission people considered themselves British citizens under the protection of the British Government. Since most of the people attracted to Christianity in the early years were misfits and refugees from Xhosa justice, it would not be surprising if the chiefs, like their Colonial counterparts, regarded the missions as refuges for criminals and good-for-nothings. The aggrieved Ngqika 'talked much upon the natural right which he had to do with his own people, and in his own country, according to his pleasure, without the interference of a foreign power,'[55] and occasionally used the missions as whipping boys for the frustrations of his dealings with the Colonial government.

It is hard to pin down the reasons why certain missionaries were more successful than others. Their political stance was naturally important. The extremely liberal Read was 'loved'[56] by the Xhosa, whereas the political activities of Thomson, official Government Agent among the amaNgqika, and Ayliff, who supported the Mfengu against the Xhosa, made them hated. But personal politics alone is insufficient as an explanation. Among the Wesleyans, for example, Shaw and Shepstone were far more successful than the more liberal Kay. Perhaps it was hard-headedness in secular matters which was the crucial asset. Maqoma wanted a missionary, but 'not a fool or a child' nor one who 'prayed more than one day in seven', which suggests that he knew missionaries who did not meet these requirements.[57] Shaw's popularity with the Gqunukhwebe is not surprising when one considers the fact that it was he who restored peace with the Colony after the 1818 – 1819 War, won them grazing-rights in the Ceded Territory, and started a trading store. His correspondence with the Wesleyan Missionary Society indicates that he was far less given to effusive sentiment than Kay or Shrewsbury.

The success of individual missionaries depended to a large extent on a political situation which was beyond their control. Shaw, whose people were not raided by commandos, did not have to face the same problems as the capable and liberal Ross, whose assistant was once asked: 'How many are these gospels that you preach? . . . We ask that because Somerset came and said "Stop doing evil," and yet he kills people every day.'[58] When the troops expelled Maqoma from the Kat River, the most Ross could do was ask them not to burn huts on the Sabbath, and even this was disregarded once his back was turned.[59] Dyani Tshatshu, the Christian chief, may be excused for asking, 'Why do not the missionaries first go to their own countrymen and convert them first?'[60]

The first missionary, J.T. Van der Kemp, was in a category of his own. His impact was due to his imposing presence, combined with the eccentricity that marked him out as no ordinary man. Dyani Tshatshu remembered that the first time he saw Van der Kemp, the latter had been 'on foot, without a hat, shoes or stockings'.[61] He ate Xhosa food and lived in Xhosa huts,[62] unlike the other missionaries who generally strove to combine personal comfort with beneficial example and live as European a life as possible. Van der Kemp's influence extended beyond his short stay in Xhosaland itself, for many Xhosa, including Ndlambe himself, came to visit him at his Khoi mission at Bethelsdorp.[63] His Christianity was mystical, based, like Ntsikana's, on a spiritual experience, and he attempted to communicate faith rather than doctrine or 'civilisation'. In this too, he differed from his successors.

The converts were mainly people who lived in Xhosaland, but were out of place there.[64] There were large numbers of women rejecting various oppressions, such as unwanted husbands, the levirate, and *upundlo*. Some were accused witches and others were disfigured – blind, albino, leprous, or just too old. Many were there because they had been overcome by the fear of death. A disproportionate number were Gona Khoi who had picked up the elements of Christianity as a living religion while servants in the Colony.[65] All of these were peripheral to Xhosa society, and their loss in no way endangered its cultural integrity. It was quite different in the case of more highly placed converts. Great pressure was applied to chiefs who inclined towards Christianity, and except for Khama and Dyani Tshatshu, they were successfully kept away from outright conversion. The Christianity of these two chiefs did not extend to their own families, much less to their followers.[66]

Attitudes towards Christianity must have been linked to attitudes towards Western culture as a whole, a subject about which little evidence has survived. Attitudes did vary, however, from the nonchalance observed by Campbell:

> When any of them have visited Cape Town, on their return they used to describe how the people dressed, how they washed their mouths, their houses etc., but never imitated or attempted to introduce any of their customs. They expressed surprise at many of the things which they saw, but never think the white men are more wise or skillful than themselves, for they suppose they could do all the white men do if they chose. They consider reading and writing as insignificant things of no use.[67]

to Ngqika's impassioned outburst to the missionary Williams:

> You have your manner to wash and decorate yourselves on the lord's day and I have mine the same in which I was born and that I shall follow. I have given over for a little to listen to your word but now I have done, for if I adopt your law I must surely overturn all my own and that I shall not do. I shall now begin to dance and praise my beast as much as I please, and I shall let all see who is the lord of this land.[68]

The most common attitude, however, was probably one of selective acceptance. As William Shaw remarked, when asking the secretary of the Wesleyan Missionary Society to perform the delicate task of requesting the 'benevolent ladies' of the society not to sew dresses for the poor savages, but just to send the cloth:

> The natives do not always admire the pattern of the made up articles ... strange as it may seem to you, they are not very easy to please.[69]

With Christianity, as with the rest of Western culture, the Xhosa were not passive recipients, but chose what they wanted and discarded the rest. They were prepared to accept certain Christian concepts and rituals — God, the Devil, the Creation and the Resurrection, Sunday services and the singing of hymns. But they were not happy with the pattern that the missionaries had made up for them.

6. From Ngqika's Peace to Maqoma's War

(1820–1835)

1. THE SUPREMACY OF NGQIKA IN THE WEST
(1820 – 1835)

After the Xhosa defeat at Grahamstown, the Colonial authorities launched follow-up operations against Ndlambe and Hintsa. They combed the territory between the Buffalo and the Kei, and Hintsa fled to the Mbashe.[1] Ngqika urged his colonial allies to attack the Xhosa king in his refuge, and would probably have succeeded but for the intervention of Landdrost Stockenstrom.[2] Meanwhile, Ngqika and Maqoma, his eldest son, drank, danced and showed off their martial skills for the amusement of their officer 'friends'.[3]

But Ngqika's victory was to prove hollow indeed, for at his next meeting with his friend and ally, Governor Somerset told him that he was appropriating some 4 000 square miles of Ngqika's own lands between the Kat and Keiskamma, 'as fine a portion of ground as is to be found in any part of the world,[4] for the purpose of establishing a neutral belt of territory as a buffer zone between the Xhosa and the Colony.[5] The thunderstruck Ngqika protested that it was his birthplace, but to no avail.[6] As an act of special clemency he was told that his people would be allowed to occupy the area between the Tyhume and the Keiskamma. Many Xhosa today believe that Ngqika sold the land in exchange for Colonial assistance and a bottle of brandy, but in fact Ngqika was as helpless before his terrible allies as Ndlambe and Hintsa had been. He is said to have remarked 'that though indebted to the English for his existence as a chief, yet when he looked upon the fine country taken from him, he could not but think his benefactors oppressive.'[7] The incident has given birth to a proverb: *omasiza mbulala* (they who came to help came to kill).[8] Ngqika denied making the concession,[9] but the Colonial authorities held it to be morally binding on the Xhosa. Moreover, they used it against chiefs such as Kobe of the Gqunukhwebe, who had never been subject to Ngqika and who was not present at the conference.

Having effectively subdued the hostile Xhosa chiefs, Somerset sowed the seeds of the next war by making enemies out of his friends. The Ndlambe and the Gqunukhwebe had been expelled from their territory in 1812. They had tried to recover it in 1819, and had been driven back still further. This effectively discouraged them from further military adventures and the chiefs who had taken leading parts in the 1818 — 1819 war were conciliatory, receiving missionaries well and checking the depredations of their subjects.[10] On the other hand, the Ngqika had as yet no first-hand knowledge of what it was like to be defeated by the British. The sons of Ngqika, now grown to maturity, were not compromised by their father's double-dealing and far from being under an obligation to the Colony they had a betrayal to avenge.

Not only did the Colony take Ngqika's land, it demanded that he perform the impossible by eliminating cattle-stealing. Ngqika had already experienced difficulties before 1819 because the principal cattle-raiders, the Mbalu and the imiDange,[11] were the basis of his political support. Naturally enough, the confiscation of the 'Ceded Territory' caused cattle-raiding to increase. Somerset found that despite all his exertions depredations had actually increased, and he could no longer ignore evidence of Ngqika's complicity. An attempt was made to force Ngqika to commit himself by making him execute a suspected thief in public. Ngqika's behaviour on this occasion shows something of the way in which he viewed his collaboration with the Colony. He had not scrupled to call in Colonial assistance, but he had always thought of the Colony as an equal and an ally, and not as a superior whom he served. When asked to execute a Xhosa for stealing from a white — an act that was perhaps injudicious, but not morally reprehensible — Ngqika repeatedly refused 'saying that the (thief) had never done him, or any other of his People injury, and he did not see why he should execute him.'[12] He was quite prepared to allow the Commandant of the Frontier to do what he wanted with the thief but he had never envisaged himself as the Colony's instrument among his own people. Eventually the Commandant got his way at gunpoint.

Ngqika viewed the Chumie mission station under the Reverend W.R. Thomson, who was soon known to be a Government Agent as well, as a further encroachment on his sovereignty. The return of some stolen horses by mission Xhosa confirmed his view that they were there as spies, and 274 head of cattle were swept off in reprisal. Maqoma, busy establishing himself as an autonomous chief, crossed west of the Tyhume and troubled the Boers on the Baviaans River.[13] Beset by criticism in other quarters, Somerset decided to take a hard line and ordered the Commandant of the Frontier to detain Ngqika if certain stolen cattle were not restored.[14] The operation was bungled and Ngqika escaped dressed as a woman (March 1822). For a short time, he hovered on the brink of playing a new role, that of Xhosa national leader. Raids on the Colony were stepped up, and he held meetings with other chiefs to plan revenge.[15]

But Ngqika was not the sort of man who was capable of saving his honour at the expense of his material and political well-being. Ndlambe, Mdushane and Kobe had proved at Amalinde that they were stronger than he was, and his allies Nqeno, Bhotomane and Ntsusa,[16] being equally aggressive and self-seeking, were by no means reliable. Maqoma's ability gave him such power and influence that he was more a threat than a support to his father, who was rather afraid of him.[17] The Colony may have betrayed him, but they were the only friends he had, and he used his reputed influence with them to its fullest extent. Although he did not dare appropriate Ndlambe's old territory, many of Ndlambe's former supporters came over to him.[18] He tried to impose his authority on the Gqunukhwebe,[19] and he interfered in the politics of the small Hleke chiefdom.[20] All of his major supporters gave him trouble, and the way in which he dealt with the amaNtsusa may be taken as illustrative of his tactics.

A military patrol was sent out after a group of Xhosa who had stolen some horses. Tyhali, Ngqika's son and right-hand man, was called in and 'traced' the spoor till it was lost. He then pointed out the Ntsusa as the culprits, complaining that they were the 'terror of the country' and the resort of all Xhosa 'who fell under the displeasure of their chiefs' (that is, Ngqika and his sub-ordinates). As a result a commando was sent out against the Ntsusa.[21] The device of accusing his enemies of depredations in order to instigate the Colony to send a commando against them was also tried against Nqeno.[22] When Maqoma roused Colonial anger by raiding certain Thembu, Ngqika urged the Colony to allow him no opportunity to make amends:

> Gaika has strongly urged to go at once to MacComo, without waiting to see whether he returns the Tambookie cattle and attack him, fire upon him and his people, and take his cattle, and then after that to reason with him.[23]

Ngqika was even able to use his status as friend of the English to threaten Hintsa with commandos.[24]

The opening of the Fort Willshire fair increased his power and his dependence on the Colony. The traveller Steedman has described his conduct on these occasions.

> When a bargain of any magnitude is concluded, the Chief is generally at hand to substantiate his claim, considering himself entitled to a certain portion of the profits as his tribute, in consequence of his territory having been made the scene of traffic. His retainers are therefore dispersed through-out the fair, to watch the various negotiations, and summon their chief at the close of any considerable bargain . . . Every look and movement of this arbitrary chieftain was narrowly scrutinised by the desponding group . . . their features clearly bespoke their secret rage, the loud expression of which was alone restrained by fear of the Chief.[25]

Part of Ngqika's income went into attracting talented young men to his Great Place. Their function was military rather than economic, and they were termed not *abasengi basekomkhulu* (milkers of the Great Place) but *amasoldati*, after the Dutch word for soldier.[26] Whatever was not distributed to his followers was spent on brandy. He purchased it,[27] danced for it,[28] sold his wives for it,[29] begged for it,[30] and ultimately died of it.[31] He would do nothing unless he was paid for it, and he even took to receiving his presents in private in order to avoid sharing them with his councillors.[32] His great good looks had not deserted him, and at fifty he still looked thirty[33] but in the last years of his life he was a despised drunkard who had lost the love and respect of his people.

The *de facto* ruler of Ngqika's people in his last degraded years was Tyhali, the son of a concubine. Described as a man who combined great shrewdness with 'the look of the utmost simplicity',[34] Tyhali aspired through his close association with his father to attain a position far above that to which his birth entitled him, and was a strong contender for the regency.[35] His rivalry with Maqoma obscured and probably protected Ngqika's disliked Thembu Great Wife, Suthu, and her lame son, Sandile, who resided together with two other younger sons, Anta and Matwa, at Burnshill mission. Ravaged by liquor and tuberculosis, Ngqika died in a welter of blood and witchcraft accusations (1829). While he danced himself into a state of collapse, his sons struggled for the succession.[36] It was indeed a macabre end to a reign which had commenced so auspiciously.

The Ndlambe were deeply divided among themselves, It appears that Ndlambe's heir was killed in his wars against the Colony.[37] In the chief's old age, many of his powers were exercised by

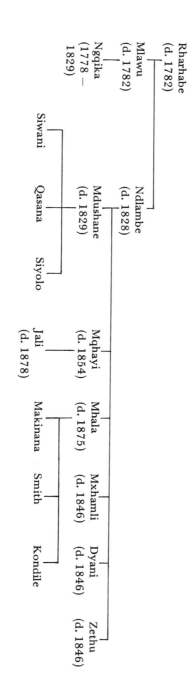

GENEALOGY 6
THE amaRHARHABE/NDLAMBE

Mdushane who was now reconciled with his father. Mdushane kept Ngqika in check, running an illegal trade to circumvent the latter's hold on the Fort Willshire fairs and shielding the Gqunukhwebe from his ambitions.[38] But when Mdushane died (May 1829) shortly after Ndlambe (February 1828), the chiefdom disintegrated.

Mdushane had quarrelled both with his Great Wife for giving him the venereal disease that was killing him, and with her son.[39] An assembly of the Ndlambe was held which proclaimed Mdushane's son, Qasana, chief of all the Ndlambe.[40] Qasana was placed under Mdushane's brother Mqhayi, a staunch supporter of peace with the Colony and of the Wesleyan mission at nearby Mount Coke. However, Mhala, another son of Ndlambe, had secured the support of the eastern Ndlambe, after disposing of yet another contender, Dyani, through a witchcraft accusation.[41] The situation was further complicated by a split between Mqhayi and Qasana, when the latter chose the belligerent side in the 1834 – 1835 war. Thus Ndlambe's people became divided among the amaNdlambe of Mhala, the imiQhayi (those western amaNdlambe who followed Mqhayi in supporting the Colony), and Qasana's imiDushane (which subsequently divided yet again).[42] On the other hand, the Ndlambe faction was strengthened by the accession of the amaNtsusa, now led by Gasela, son of Nukwa. These abandoned Ngqika and took up residence along the Kwelerha in alliance with Mhala, and with the approval of Hintsa.[43]

2. XHOSA RELATIONS WITH THE EAST

The Xhosa's nearest eastern neighbours were the Thembu.[44] Like the Xhosa, the Thembu were composed of a number of clans which had accepted the leadership of a royal clan. The Thembu royal clan, the Hala, had not however succeeded in imposing their control on the local level to anything approaching the extent attained by the Tshawe among the Xhosa. Some clans were entirely subordinate to the Hala, but others such as the Vundle, Gcina, Qwathi and others maintained their chiefship and their territorial integrity.

The Xhosa had fished in the troubled politics of their Thembu neighbours since the time of Tato (c. 1760).[45] Thembu chiefs were reluctant to take Xhosa wives because the Xhosa used the relationship to intervene in Thembu affairs.[46] The reign of Ndaba (c. 1775 – c. 1800) was especially disastrous.[47] He was forced to flee from his own subjects, taking refuge first with Gcaleka then

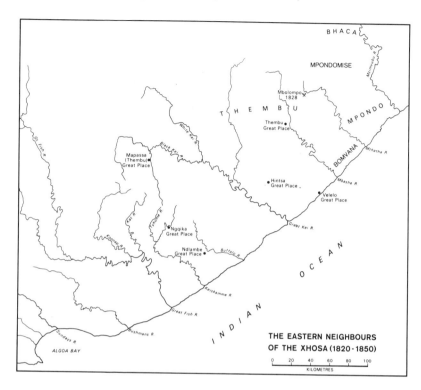

THE EASTERN NEIGHBOURS
OF THE XHOSA (1820-1850)

with Rharhabe. Eventually he fled Rharhabe in fear of his life, sparking off a series of wars which did not end with Rharhabe's death (1782). In 1788 one of the few foreigners to visit the Thembu reported that the Xhosa devastated Thembu homes, stole their cattle, and dragged them off to do heavy service.[48] Hintsa claimed some authority over the Thembu and enticed the Ntshilibe clan away from their allegiance to the Thembu king.[49] The Nqabe, an autonomous clan in Thembu territory, also seem to have been tributary to the Xhosa.[50] Ngqika was son-in-law to Tshatshu, a Hala chief junior in rank but almost superior in power to the Thembu king, and had pretensions to authority in Thembu-land through his mother, also a Thembu.[51] Ngubencuka, King of the Thembu (c. 1800 – 1830), brought some stability to his kingdom by defeating his subordinates and then reconciling them by making concessions with regard to tribute.[52] The Thembu resurgence did nothing to improve relations with the Xhosa, who disputed possession of the territory around the sources of the Kei.[53] War was avoided only by the need to join forces against the Mfecane invaders. Even so, co-operation was not easy. Hintsa failed to arrive for a rendezvous against the Bhaca, and when the two kings finally met during the campaign against Matiwane's Ngwane, neither opened his mouth for fear of speaking first.[54]

East of the Thembu were the Mpondo. The Nyawuza, royal clan of the Mpondo, were continually engaged in attempting to establish their domination over powerful local clans such as the Tshezi and the Khonjwayo, who had themselves succeeded in subordinating a number of smaller clans. Shortly after 1800, Ngqungqushe, the Mpondo King, allied himself with one Tshezi faction against a second known as the Bomvana, which was led by the chief Gambushe.[55] Gambushe proved too strong for the alliance and defeated them, killing Ngqungqushe. In the succession war which followed, Gambushe's candidate for the Mpondo kingship, Phakani, was defeated by Phakani's brother, Faku. Gambushe and Phakani fled to Hintsa. Gambushe's people became tributary to Hintsa and Gambushe's daughter, Nomsa, became Hintsa's Great Wife.

This is how matters stood when the Mfecane — the great wave of battles and migrations set in motion by the rise of Shaka and the Zulu state — struck the southern Nguni. The first invading group with whom the Xhosa had to contend were the Bhaca who moved so fast, according to tradition, that they ate their meat raw because they had no time to roast it.[56] After many vicissitudes, the Bhaca moved down into Thembuland where they attacked the Tshatshu and Gcina Thembu. The Xhosa, Thembu and Mpondomise combined forces and crushed the Bhaca, killing their leader, Madikane (1823 – 1825). The Bhaca and the Mpondo entered into an uneasy alliance and launched a joint attack on the Bomvana, but this was repulsed by Hintsa and Gambushe.

In 1827, the Ngwane chief, Matiwane, fearful of Mzilikazi and restless under Moshoeshoe, moved south over the Orange.[57] He raided cattle and tried to force the Thembu chiefs to pay tribute, but intended to settle down and therefore started to cultivate the ground. Matiwane's intentions were not fully understood, for Shaka was then at the height of his power and sending threatening messages to Ngubencuka and Hintsa, demanding their submission. They refused, mobilised their forces and asked the Colony for help. The Colonial authorities, alarmed at the prospect of thousands of Xhosa and Thembu refugees aggravating the frontier situation, decided that Shaka had to be turned back by persuasion or force.

W.B. Dundas, the Landdrost of Albany, was sent ahead with a small detachment to try persuasion, while Henry Somerset, the Commandant of the Frontier, followed with an army. As he proceeded, Dundas observed the destruction caused by the war between the Mpondo-Bhaca and Xhosa-Bomvana alliances, and the ravages caused by a Zulu attack on the Mpondo. When he arrived at Ngubencuka's Great Place and found the Ngwane in the neighbourhood, he mistakenly concluded that these were Zulu regiments and that they had caused the damage he had witnessed. His small party attacked an unsuspecting Ngwane division and drove it back.[58] He then returned, thinking he had repulsed the Zulu.

When the Ngwane attacked the Thembu to recover the cattle lost through Dundas, Ngubencuka sent a message to the Colonial army saying the Zulu had returned. Hintsa had been kept informed of proceedings by a party of councillors whom he had sent with Dundas, and, probably scenting plunder, joined up with Somerset to fight the Ngwane. At a pre-battle conference, Somerset introduced Hintsa and Ngubencuka, who were rivals of long standing and had never seen each other before. He told them to treat the enemy mercifully, and not to take revenge. The two kings hedged, probably feeling that there was no point in fighting the Ngwane unless they could benefit materially from their anticipated victory.[59] The Colonial army attacked the Ngwane at dawn and routed them with artillery (*Battle of Mbholompo,* 27 Aug. 1828). The Xhosa, Thembu and Mpondo gathered a good booty of women, children and cattle, much to the disgust of the British, who failed to appreciate that they had joined the attack for this very purpose. The battle was subsequently represented to the Xhosa as disinterested Colonial assistance in their time of need, and Hintsa's refusal to help the Colony against Maqoma was considered to be rank ingratitude.[60] In actual fact, the Colony had little call on Hintsa's gratitude. He had not taken the initiative in attacking the Ngwane and certainly had no reason to feel threatened by them.

Shortly after Mbholompo, Hintsa and Ngubencuka fell out over the division of the spoils.[61] Hintsa's Bomvana allies attacked two of Ngubencuka's subordinates,[62] and the Thembu moved further north, virtually abandoning the coast. War was prevented by the missionaries and the veiled threat of Colonial intervention. Ngubencuka died in 1830, leaving Vadana regent for his minor heir, Mtirara. There were then three main political groupings among the southern Nguni. In the west were the Xhosa, who were allied with the Bomvana and close to the Tshatshu Thembu.[63] In the east were the Mpondo allied with the Bhaca. In the middle were the weak and isolated Thembu, increasingly looking towards the Colony as their only salvation.

Matiwane's prestige, already strained by previous defeats, did not survive Mbholompo, and many of his followers stayed among the Thembu and the Xhosa where they swelled the ranks of other refugees to form the people known collectively as Mfengu (from the verb *ukumfenguza*, 'to wander about seeking service'). The most important of these peoples were the Bhele, the Hlubi, the Zizi and the Ntlangwini. Their subsequent relationship with the Xhosa has inevitably distorted accounts of their initial reception, but the Xhosa tradition relating to it seems to sum up the situation. According to the tradition, the Xhosa gave the Mfengu food, but the food was on the Xhosa side of the fire and the Mfengu had to pass their hands through the flames in order to reach it.[64] Like the Gona and the Thembu, the Mfengu had to pass through a period of servitude and social inferiority in order to lose their previous identity and emerge full Xhosa.

The Mfengu were initially well received by the Xhosa chiefs, who always welcomed the accession of new followers.[65] When Hintsa discovered that the Bhele had hidden their chief, Mabandla, he pointed out 'that he was not in the habit of killing people who sought refuge in his country'.[66] He singled out Njokweni, a noted diviner, for special favour.[67] The young chiefs, Matomela and Mhlambiso, ate food from the same dish as his son, Rhili.[68] Mfengu chiefs sat on his council and participated in all important discussions.[69] Mfengu who arrived destitute and without cattle were distributed among Hintsa's people in the usual manner of *busa* clients. Hintsa told his people to take good care of the Mfengu and he offered them redress in his courts, but he warned them that in the last resort they had to fend for themselves: 'Were you not men in your own country? Were there no forests with sticks on the Tugela? These Xhosa have bodies just the same as you. When they hit you, hit them back.'[70]

The Mfengu were not as isolated and leaderless as the Khoi had been, and were not prepared to forego their national identity. The availability of iron hoes in their homeland had accustomed them to agriculture, and they became assiduous cultivators. They cultivated tobacco for sale, and went into the Colony-interior trade on their own account.[71] They acquired cattle over and above the natural increase which was normal for *busa* clients, and they hid them in forests and gulleys, out of sight of their employers. Meanwhile, ordinary Xhosa, suddenly elevated in status by their acquisition of clients, indulged in the prerogatives of the rich and extracted what they could from the Mfengu. But the Mfengu were less willing to bear tributes and exactions such as *upundlo* when these were demanded of them by aliens. They turned towards the only alternative source of power available to them — the Cape Colony, represented in Hintsa's country by the mission station at Butterworth. The missionary Ayliff refused to hand over a Mfengu who had roused Hintsa's anger, although he was demanded by the

king in person. This incident was widely reported among the
Mfengu.[72] Moreover, the 'Great Word' offered more than material
salvation to the Mfengu. The old had led them to a life of
wandering and misery; the new one seemed to offer them peace
and prosperity.

3. THE ROAD TO WAR (1829 – 1835)

The drought of 1829 scorched the country from the Baviaans
River well within the Colony to the Kei and beyond. One of the
few areas to be spared was the well-watered basin of the upper
Fish River, drained by the Kat, Mankazana and other tributaries.
Although this formed part of the Ceded Territory which neither
was supposed to occupy, both Boers and Xhosa drove their
herds into it. 'There is not a blade of grass anywhere else, and the
distress . . . is beyond anything I can possibly express,' wrote
Colonel Henry Somerset. 'The portion of land allocated to the
several Caffre tribes is already very confined.'[73]. In the middle of
the drought (May 1829), the Colonial authorities saw fit to expel
Maqoma on the grounds that he had unjustifiably attacked certain
chiefs of the Tshatshu Thembu.

At the time of the Bhaca incursions of 1823 – 1825, the
Tshatshu under chief Bawana had entered Maqoma's territory as
refugees and were allotted land. Galela, the Gcina chief, then took
up arms against Bawana. Maqoma entered the fighting, with the
result that a number of Thembu fled into the Colony. The Colonial
authorities were alarmed by the prospect of refugees, and angry
with Maqoma for attacking people who had never done the
Colony any harm. It is probable that they had long wanted an
excuse to get rid of him.[74] Maqoma maintained that he was only
supporting the legitimate chief, Bawana, against the rebel,
Galela.[75]

Behind the personalities of the affair lay a more important
principle. In the words of one informant, 'Maqoma wanted to
make those Thembu Xhosa.'[76] The Thembu had settled on
Maqoma's land, and Maqoma wanted to reduce them to political
subservience. He could have had no reason to anticipate that the
Colonial authorities would penalise him for what he did to his own
people on his own territory. Since he had foregone opportunities
to increase his prestige at the expense of the Colony, it was not
unreasonable that he should find an outlet for his political and
military skills elsewhere.

After Maqoma was expelled, his old territories were given to
Khoi and 'Bastards' who formed what became known as the

Kat River Settlement. Governor Cole confirmed the expulsion and reminded the chiefs that they only occupied land in the Ceded Territory at His Majesty's pleasure. Cole's account of the meeting relates only what he told the chiefs; presumably he ignored whatever they said to him.[77] The missionary Ross 'met with nothing but abuse' when he tried to present the Xhosa case.[78] There was a general belief among the Colonists that cattle-raiding could be stopped altogether, if the authorities used enough gun. Cole believed this and was harsher than his liberal predecessor, Bourke. His military secretary, Colonel Wade, believed it too, and when he became acting Governor he was even harsher than Cole had been. During Wade's short term of office (1833), Maqoma and Tyhali were expelled from their last grazing grounds beyond the Tyhume, at the time of another terrible drought, to land where 'there was not a morsel of grass . . . it was as bare as a parade.'[79] Commandant Henry Somerset, who understood the importance of the land question,[80] allowed Maqoma back for a time, but his permission was overridden by the Governor and the Xhosa were expelled once more. The Xhosa thought that the Europeans were making fun of them and in sheer frustration drove their cattle into the green corn.[81]

The Xhosa drew their own conclusions from these policies. Colonial policy was rationalised to them on two grounds: Ngqika's cession in 1819 and the continuance of cattle-raiding. Neither reason appeared particularly valid. The Kat River valley was their birthright and Ngqika had never fought against the Colony.

> The time when Gaika assisted the English, then we put our assegais away from the English, and T'Slambie's people had weapons, and were the enemies of the English; but we were friends of the English; that was a most difficult thing.

> Gaika was a great friend of the white people. And they murder his children after he is dead.[82]

There can also be little doubt that the chiefs exerted themselves to the utmost to repress thefts, considering the ease with which two or three individuals could steal the loosely-guarded Colonial cattle. Maqoma even kept the receipts for the Colonial cattle he sent back.[83] He pointed out that magistrates were not punished when Colonial wrongdoers escaped.[84] On the occasion of the 1833 expulsion:

> He absolutely stated 'I will allow you to inquire at Fort Willshire whether or not I have not sent in horses and cattle re-captured from

other Caffres, which had been stolen from the Colony.'[85]

The reasons for his removal were not explained to Maqoma. According to the officer who delivered the news:

> He distinctly said, which we found out afterwards to be the case, that he could not make out the cause of his removal, and asked me if I would tell him; and I really could not; I had heard nothing; no cause was ever assigned to me for the removal.[86]

The ordinary Xhosa were as puzzled and angry as their chiefs. One Xhosa called out to the military force conducting the 1829 expulsions,

> and asked us, why were we burning his house? and it seemed to be difficult to make a reply: there was a general silence.[87]

Feeling that the cattle question was a mere pretext, the Xhosa concluded that the real object of the Colony was the appropriation of their land. Maqoma visited the other chiefs, saying that this was but the 'prelude to other measures, which would not only endanger their independence, but lead to a complete subjugation of their country.'[88] The chiefs, including Hintsa, often raised the question with sympathetic whites 'apparently thinking it was part of a general system of taking their country away from them.'[89] According to chief Bhotomane:

> Macomo's heart was very sore about the land; the subject always set him on fire; he fought in hopes of getting it back.[90]

Although the loss of their land was the primary cause of Xhosa discontent, there were others too. One of these was the reprisal system enforced by military patrols known as commandos.[91] The reprisal system permitted the commando to follow the spoor of stolen cattle to the nearest homestead to demand restitution there, and to take Xhosa cattle in lieu of missing Colonial cattle. The system was open to numerous abuses. Farmers whose cattle had strayed through negligence or who simply wanted more cattle could 'trace' a spoor to the nearest homestead and secure cattle out of all proportion to their losses. At best, the system made the innocent suffer for the guilty. These aspects were strongly criticised by the more liberal Europeans, but there were others that alarmed the Xhosa even more.[92] As far as they were concerned, commando raids were random and unpredictable. Since commandos were anxious that 'thieves' should not be forewarned in time to flee but should be caught with their spoil, they marched at night and attacked at dawn by charging the suspected homestead and firing at random.[93] Innocent homesteads were not given the opportunity to prove their innocence, or guilty ones to give up the stolen property. One of Nqeno's sons was killed as he came out of his hut to see what the matter was.[94] The most famous mistake of all was the 'blundering commando' of 1825, which twice attacked the wrong homestead, while allowing the suspects to escape.[95] Small wonder that the Xhosa fled at the passage of a commando, even one not meant for them.[96] The coming and going of patrols, even those intended for purely defensive purposes, kept the Xhosa in a perpetual state of alarm. Tyhali asked, 'Shall I never have peace in my own country? Am I to be teased this way, day after day?'[97]

The Xhosa knew that the whites despised them and they resented it. They acknowledged that European technology was superior to their own, but felt that as individuals they were equal to any Colonist they had met.[98] This resentment was particularly acute in the case of the chiefs. They were conscious of the difference between themselves and the common 'black people' and set great store by it.[99] They expected the whites to respect these differences too. Ngqika once broke off a negotiation because a group of Boers asked him to return some cattle, and told Land-drost Alberti that he was prepared to deal with him as an equal but would not allow himself to be messed on by dogs.[100] Ndlambe and Mdushane expected tribute from the Colonists.[101] In practice, the chiefs were prepared to accept leading Colonial officials as their equals, but Ngqika probably expressed a general feeling when he told the Landdrost of Graaff-Reinet that the latter was his inferior because he was not born a chief.[102]

On their side, the Colonists felt that all whites were superior to all Xhosa, and even Philipps, one of the more liberal of the settlers, thought Ngqika's remark about the Landdrost of Graaff-Reinet was a piece of 'impudence'.[105] Consequently, the chiefs were persistently subjected to indignities. When they went to Fort Willshire, they were often kept waiting, subjected to insults by junior officers, or lodged in premises which they felt suitable only for commoners.[104] They liked Colonel Somerset because he 'always treated them like chiefs,'[105] gave them presents, accommodated them in his house and invited them to his balls.[106] Although at least three chiefs tried, none of them was ever able to marry a white woman.[107] They also resented the fact that they were not trusted to come and go as they pleased. Maqoma once told a meeting of Kat River Khoi,

> I see no Englishman in the Kat River, there are none in Grahamstown, and where are they? I have got them all in Caffreland, with their wives and children, living in safety and enjoying every protection: and yet I am accounted a rascal and a vagabond, and am obliged to come here by stealth.[108]

Hours later he was removed from a tea-party with the Reverend Read, by a sergeant who added the crowning humiliation of offering him liquor in front of the missionary.[109]

Not only the dignity of the chiefs, but their very existence was endangered. In traditional warfare, the life of a chief was regarded as sacrosanct.[110] The Colonists had no such inhibitions. Chungwa was shot dead while sick.[111] Ndlambe was hunted, as he bitterly remarked, like a springbok.[112] An attempt was made to seize Ngqika's person. Nqeno's son was shot around 1825. In 1830 a commando shot Sigcawu, Ndlambe's brother, and seized 'Magugu', another chief.[113] The news caused great indignation throughout Xhosaland.

> At this distance [eighty or ninety miles] from the scene of action, the most exaggerated and romantic stories obtain full credence . . . The king himself [Hintsa], upon whom reports of an inflammable nature are daily pouring is of course greatly unhinged; and moves about with suspicious caution . . . The circumstances of a *chief* having been taken *captive* seemed to arouse the ire of the nation, and everyone became enraged while speaking about it.[114]

Compensation, which might have made all the difference to Xhosa feelings, was never offered. Thus it was that the wounding of Tyhali's brother, Xhoxho, who was defiantly pasturing the chief's cattle in forbidden territory, provoked the War of 1834 – 1835. Pro-Colonial writers have made much of the slightness of the wound, and taken it as evidence that the attack on the Colony was premeditated, but there can be little doubt that the indignation was genuine. Xhoxho was wounded in the head; in intention, he was dead.[115] The reaction of the people was spontaneous:

> Every Caffre who saw Xoxo's wound went back to his hut, took his assegay, and shield, and set out to fight, and said 'It is better that we die than be treated thus . . . Life is no use to us if they shoot our chiefs.'[116]

The chiefs themselves were more conciliatory, and Tyhali sent a curious letter to Commandant Somerset, saying 'You must today use your power, and cause me to pay for my people's folly,' implying that he could no longer restrain his followers and that only a strong show of force by the Colony could prevent a full-scale war.[117] The Xhosa rushed into the Colony to avenge their chiefs, their lands, their losses at the hands of the commandos. Their initial successes forced the initially reluctant chiefs to throw themselves wholeheartedly into the fray. The *Sixth Frontier War* had begun.

This frontier war was primarily a Ngqika war, but it involved all the Xhosa. Hintsa was consulted and approved.[118] He was in touch with the frontier Xhosa and aware of their difficulties. Chiefs were being shot, their cattle seized, their lands appropriated. He must have felt that he was next in line.[119] Moreover, these chiefs were his relatives, members of the clan of which he was the head.

> Several of Hintsa's chiefs stood up, as if by one accord and declared it
> to be their duty to stand by Gaika's children to the last; that they were
> orphans of the Caffre nation, and under the protection of Hintsa.[120]

He was urged on by Mnyaluza, the old frontier warrior who had fled to him in 1819.[121] Lochenberg, an old Graaff-Reinet rebel, had been his trusted adviser until his death in 1829.[122] In 1833 more anti-British Boers under Louis Tregardt had settled in his country. They supplied him with firearms, and became close advisers.[123] More concretely, the presence of traders and missionaries in his country had undermined his authority and encouraged the Mfengu. He himself remained inactive, but many of his men entered the Colony, and his country became a refuge for captured cattle.[124]

A few chiefs refused to enter the war. Mqhayi and Dyani Tshatshu did so out of conviction, and were deserted by all but their immediate associates. The Gqunukhwebe chiefs were more successful in retaining their followers. They were motivated partly by their belief that the Colony was militarily invincible,[125] and partly through the influence of their missionaries, who, since the time of William Shaw (1823 – 1830), had been instrumental in winning them minor concessions. Although they turned a blind eye to those of their subjects who entered the Colony and received cattle for safe-keeping, Phato and Khama betrayed the norm of lineage co-operation by remaining at peace. Only the protection of the Colonial Government saved them from the wrath of their brother chiefs in the years following the war.[126]

7. Exchanges and Innovations

not unlike Most whites?!

1. 'AN ENTHUSIASTIC PROPENSITY FOR BUSINESS'

'There is an enthusiastic propensity for business amongst these Kaffirs,' wrote Landdrost Alberti in 1810, 'the cause for which appears to be due less to a desire to satisfy certain of their needs, than greed and enrichment.'[1] Indeed, the distinctive feature of early Xhosa trade was that it was directed not so much towards supplying subsistence deficiencies but towards the acquisition of greater wealth.[2] The major items sought by the Xhosa in trade were cattle, copper, iron and beads. All of these functioned in the Xhosa economy as money equivalents, that is they were exchangeable for each other and for goods and services. The acquisition of cattle in trade should be seen primarily in terms of wealth and prestige, since the Xhosa were never so short of cattle that they were unable to lead their preferred way of life. Copper and beads had no use-value as such, but were worn as ladies of other cultures wore precious stones. Iron had a use-value, but it also served as a currency in the form of spears.[3] Although its use-value gave it a stability which other currencies lacked,[4] it is significant that when trade with the whites began iron goods were not much in demand compared with beads. A further indicator of the lack of interest shown in subsistence articles was the absence of a trade in salt, despite its uneven distribution in the area.[5]

Since trading cattle for beads or copper was trading one form of currency for another, Xhosa trade was not primarily the exchange of one use-value for another use-value but a form of financial speculation. Individual transactions are comprehensible only as part of a series. A would sell cattle to B in exchange for beads and then make a profit by selling the beads to C for more cattle

The cattle had the value

than the beads initially cost him. C could attempt to make a profit by selling the beads to D for more cattle than he had paid B. In this way, it was possible for a string of beads to move from Delagoa Bay to Xhosaland, or from Xhosaland to Natal.[6] Theoretically, there should be no losers in such a series of transactions as the value of the beads depended not on their intrinsic value, but on their value in terms of cattle, which in turn depended on their rarity. The great danger in speculation of this kind was the possibility that there might be a glut in supply which would cause the exchange-value of one trade-item to fall relative to the others. A trader who had visited both the Xhosa and the Tswana commented how much greater the trade of the latter (consisting mainly of use-values) was.[7] Paradoxically, the success of Xhosa trade depended on the low level being maintained.

In their trade with the east, the Xhosa received iron from the

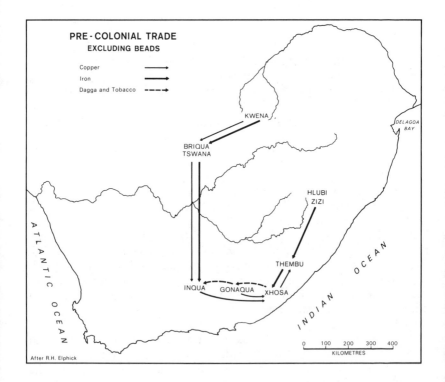

PRE-COLONIAL TRADE
EXCLUDING BEADS

Copper

Iron

Dagga and Tobacco

KWENA

DELAGOA BAY

BRIQUA
TSWANA

HLUBI
ZIZI

ATLANTIC OCEAN

THEMBU

OCEAN

INQUA   GONAQUA   XHOSA

INDIAN

0   100   200   300   400
KILOMETRES

After R.H. Elphick

Thembu which probably originated among the Zizi and Hlubi of Natal, who are known to have supplied the Tlokwa with iron goods.[8] Beads of Portuguese origin circulated in Xhosaland, which the people conceived to be the natural produce of 'Imbo' (the East) country.[9] By 1816 they had a tolerably clear picture of Delagoa Bay, without knowing the names of all the peoples who lay between it and them.[10] From the Mpondo they received bluebuck-skins, rare shells and shark-skin (for field medicine).[11] In return they supplied cattle and copper.[12]

Xhosa trade with the northwest goes back to the seventeenth century. Here they acted not only as middlemen but also as producers. They were the southern end of a trade network in which the Kwena supplied the Tlhaping (known to the Xhosa as the 'Briqua' or 'goat people') with iron and copper, and other Tswana traded the iron and copper to the Inqua Koi for cattle, and the Inqua traded it to the Xhosa in exchange for tobacco and hemp.[13] The Xhosa would then trade some of the copper east to the Thembu and the Mpondo. There is a later recorded instance of Xhosa trading honey to Khoi in exchange for small stock,[14] and there must have been many small-scale exchanges of this kind. One report states that parties of Khoi travelled to the Xhosa every year to trade copper and beads for dagga at a designated time and place.[15] If correct, this is the only reported case of a regular market in precolonial times.

Xhosa tobacco was specially cultivated for the Khoi trade.[16] It must have acquired a substantial reputation, since some northern Sotho visited Xhosaland in 1823 with the intention of opening a trade there.[17]

There was also a trade in ivory, which was fashioned into rings worn on the left arm. In principle, whenever an elephant was killed the tusks became the property of the chief, who awarded them as marks of distinction.[18] In practice, however, there was some circulation of ivory as a trade commodity. The San killed elephants for meat, then traded the tusks for Xhosa dagga and cattle.[19] Xhosa used to accompany Boers on their shooting expeditions, bringing their cattle along to exchange them for ivory.[20] Coenraad de Buys commenced his career in Xhosaland by shooting elephants and selling the ivory to the Xhosa.[21] Van der Kemp reported a going rate of five armrings to a young heifer in 1800.[22] One informant thought that the chief traded part of his ivory tribute, although never within his own chiefdom.[23]

The Xhosa economy was neither static nor subsistence-orientated. That there was no lack of innovation is demonstrated by the introduction of new crops such as maize (eighteenth century), production for the market, and trade with other peoples. This does not mean, however, that on the eve of their involvement in the European economy the Xhosa were on the brink of major economic changes. In order to increase their wealth, they by-passed the sphere of production and entered into a trade which was largely speculative. The goods obtained in these exchanges were utilised not as consumption or capital goods, but as cattle equivalents or as a direct means for the acquisition of more cattle. Consequently, exchange did not lead to the internal diversification of the economy.

2. COMMODITY TRADE BETWEEN XHOSA AND COLONISTS

Trade between the Boers and the Xhosa began in the early eighteenth century. Since this was illegal as far as the Colonial Government was concerned we have little written record of it. The first known trading party recorded its presence only by virtue of the fact that some of its men were killed by Xhosa who wanted to take the iron from their wagons.[24] Significantly, the survivors met another trading-party heading east while they were returning.[25] If the asking price of ivory is anything to go by, there was already a substantial trade by 1752,[26] and by 1770 there was a well-beaten wagon-road to Xhosaland.[27] Copper, iron and beads from the Colony were exchanged for cattle and ivory from Xhosaland. Though the evidence does not permit us to be certain it seems that the Boers were elephant hunters rather than ivory traders. In all probability, the pattern reported by Sparrman in 1779 was typical. A Boer gave a chief a present in exchange for permission to hunt in his country, and the chief gave him guides to show him where the elephants were to be found.[28]

The Xhosa chiefs were far more interested in the cattle trade, and competed with each other for potential trading partners from the Colony.[29] Certain Boers kept trade goods, and were visited by Xhosa wishing to trade cattle.[30] Naturally, disputes arose, and Xhosa who trusted the Boers were sometimes forced to trade cattle for less than their value in beads.[31] It is unlikely that similar things did not happen when Boers trusted the Xhosa.

It is possible to see in this early trade the beginnings of either a pleasing interaction, or of dependence and underdevelopment.[32] Initially however, the trade seemed profitable to both sides. Certainly the Xhosa were neither dupes nor unwilling participants. Beads were a source of profit to the Xhosa, and at least one Boer was turned back 'from the want of articles suited to barter'.[33]

Ndlambe, Chungwa and others explicitly stated that with all its disadvantages they approved of the trade and wanted it to continue.[34] The Dutch East India Company government at the Cape feared that trade quarrels might result in war, and therefore tried to prohibit trade at some times, but must have encouraged it at others since the Xhosa were regarded as one of the two chief emergency suppliers of meat in times of shortfall at Cape Town.[35]

The British take-over of the Cape in 1806 produced no immediate major changes.[36] There were concerted efforts to expel Xhosa and Gona Khoi servants in 1807 and 1809, and Governor Cradock meant his Zuurveld clearance of 1812 to be the beginning of a strict system of non-intercourse.[37] The arrival of the British settlers of 1820 was accompanied by a reiteration of official policy, but the settlers soon proved that the lack of a national stock-farming tradition was no barrier to undertaking the economic enterprises for which the country was most obviously suited. The illegal cattle and ivory trade was soon in full swing. Contacts were made between soldiers and Xhosa during the 1818 – 1819 Frontier War, and these were kept up by discharged soldiers turned settlers, especially those at the short-lived quasimilitary settlement of Fredricksburg.[38] Warned by their settler trading partners of the movements of military patrols, Xhosa slipped across the river. One settler entertained his Xhosa guests with sugared beer and sent his English servant to dig red ochre for them. They were accommodated for days at a time and hidden from the Landdrost's men. The settlers were hesitant about entrusting themselves to the Xhosa but after the initial risk was taken, regular visits followed. They were received with honour by the chiefs themselves, and traded ivory and cattle for beads, buttons and probably liquor. The Gqunukhwebe chief, Kobe, built a special hut for their accommodation. But because the trade was not friendly exchange but directed towards profit,[39] suspicion remained on both sides. In at least three cases, the partners fell out and settlers were killed by distrustful Xhosa.[40] Settlers also faced danger from their competitors. One unfortunate party was betrayed to the authorities by a Khoi who was in the illicit ivory trade on the Landdrost's behalf.[41] Ngqika, who benefited from a monopoly of the official trade, tried to kill a settler who was trading with his chief political and economic rival, Mdushane.[42] Meanwhile the Colonial Government, faced with its inability to stop illegal trade and with the impending economic collapse of the British settlement at Albany, attempted to cure both evils by instituting an official fair. The idea of fairs had been well received by Xhosa chiefs on a previous occasion,[43] but no concrete action had been taken until it was decided to have a trial run at certain clay-pits on the Fish River, which had been the prime source of red ochre, an essential element of Xhosa dress before the expulsion of the Xhosa over the Keiskamma in 1819.[44] The Xhosa chiefs Nqeno and Bhotomane responded enthusiastically, but were greatly disappointed to find that only red ochre was available for barter. As a result, only two small tusks of ivory were said to be available, and more barter was done illegally on the side with settlers than at the official fair itself. When beads and buttons were allowed at the next clay-pits fair, the response was staggering: the same people who had previously managed no more than two small tusks now produced 434 pounds of ivory.

This insistence on beads and the lack of interest in red ochre shows that the Xhosa were not motivated by a simple desire to decorate themselves but by the intention of profiting on the initial transaction. One missionary pointed out that the Xhosa 'were unwilling to give anything in exchange for ornaments, even of a more durable nature,' and that they were 'not easily captivated with show and glitter.'[45] Beads and buttons were insisted on because they were convertible into the only form of wealth that interested the Xhosa — cattle. For the beads received for a single hide they could get a living beast further inland.[46] For the Xhosa this was no barter, but a money exchange. They were selling their cattle dear, and replacing them with cattle bought cheaply elsewhere. Another reason why beads and buttons were demanded was that they enabled profit to be shared among several participants in an enterprise, as for instance the several men who killed an elephant.[47]

In 1824, the Colonial Government opened the trade to the Colonists at a regular fair held at Fort Willshire near Ngqika's country. Strict regulations were proclaimed to provide for the orderly conduct of the fair.[48] There was also regulation of the goods to be offered for sale. Naturally, liquor and firearms were forbidden, and although beads and buttons were perforce allowed, each transaction also had to contain a 'useful' item from a list which included iron pots, tinder boxes, blankets, and cloth. It is perhaps not too cynical to suggest that part of the righteous indignation against beads derived from the fact that, whereas the useful items were manufactured in Sheffield or Manchester, the most highly prized beads had to be imported from Italy.[49] The Xhosa resisted the useful items ('No father will think of giving away his daughter for a suit of clothes'),[50] but responded eagerly to the fair. The first seven months drew 50 441 pounds of ivory, 16 800 pounds of gum, about 15 000 hides and 137 trading licences.[51] Xhosa from as far as the eastern side of the Kei and Thembuland attended the fairs, which seem to have attracted some two or three thousand at a time.[52] So great did competition between the settler traders become that the cost of trade goods went up at the wholesale end while the selling price went down. 'The Xhosa,' wrote one observer, 'are now become so knowing and the competition among the Buyers so great that the full value is obtained by them.'[53] Andrew Smith thought that they got 'rather more than half' the real value of their ivory.[54]

In a few years, the selling price of Xhosa cattle doubled.[55] The settlers attempted to remedy the situation by manipulating the market regulations, according to which the Xhosa were allowed to cross the Keiskamma River at 10 o'clock and to stay until 4 o'clock in the afternoon. Transactions were arranged by the Xhosa placing the sale goods in front of them and the settlers passing among them making them offers which were accepted or refused. Given a large number of buyers and sufficient time for business, the Xhosa were able to exploit competition between buyers to get the best price for their produce. But with the passage of time, a cartel of big traders came to dominate the settler end of the market. They shortened the time available for trading by refusing to commence at the official opening time.[56] They also took steps to have the number of fairs per week reduced.[57]

Xhosa traders were affected in two ways. First, it was difficult and at times dangerous for them to cross the river with their produce, and this must have been an incentive to get their business completed on the same day. Second, they had to pay for their food and accommodation,[58] and the price of foodstuffs is known to have more than tripled on the Xhosa side in the neighbourhood of the fairs.[59] Every day spent at the fair thus diminished the profit of the transaction. Nor was this the only disadvantage of the fair. Ngqika was present at every fair and used to exact tribute on all sales of ivory: he used his own power and his status as a friend of the British to manhandle and tax subjects of other chiefs, including those of Hintsa.[60] Moreover, local stocks of ivory were becoming exhausted and the ivory had to come from a greater distance. Thus, on the Xhosa side, costs were rising at the same time that prices were falling. Futhermore, the bead market on the Xhosa side was constantly fluctuating. Settler traders, who were unloading beads onto the market much faster than Xhosa traders could disperse them, blamed the Xhosa for the fickleness of their taste without realising that they themselves were responsible for it. Since settler traders were sometimes reduced to bankruptcy by sudden changes in the bead market, it is probable that this also occurred among the more under-capitalised Xhosa traders.

It is therefore not surprising that the Fort Willshire fairs suddenly began to decline.[61] The Colonial authorities realised that

Ngqika was partly to blame, and tried the experiment of opening another fair at Ngqushwa ('Clusie') River near Gqunukhwebe territory.[62] This also failed after a brief initial success. It was not in elephant country[63] and since it was never held on a regular basis, it was impossible for the more distant peoples, who were now the chief suppliers of ivory, to attend.

In 1830, the Colonial Government abandoned the fairs and allowed the traders to penetrate the interior.[64] They soon spread as far as Mpondoland, establishing regular stations at which they resided for months at a time. This process was accelerated by the big traders, who set up poor settlers in business as their agents. The settler trading network soon eliminated the Xhosa traders by virtue of its more efficient wagon transport and its control over the supply of trade goods. Above all, once the supply of beads was made general throughout Nguni territory their resale value was destroyed. The demand for beads thus dropped from £4 576 in 1825 to £287 in 1831,[65] and was largely replaced by a demand for British manufactures, primarily blankets and iron pots.

The quarrels and disputes inevitable in trade were aggravated by the bad character of many traders.[66] Many of them cheated the Xhosa systematically and extorted compensation for alleged thefts. Most never learned more of the Xhosa language than a few commands and swearwords. Whereas the more careful kept on good terms with the local chief, others relied on their firearms and threats of Colonial retribution.[67] More important than such irritations was the implication for the Xhosa of their increasing dependence on the Colony. The barter of hides for blankets, equivalent to the exchange of local clothing for imported ready-mades, is a classic example of the process. Hintsa was acutely aware of the dangers involved:

> In speaking of the trade he said that now their cattle were all sold and also their skins, so they would now have no means of getting what they wanted. He was anxious that there should be introduced cows and that the Caffres would be glad to change oxen for them (one for one).[68]

In other words, Hintsa was quite prepared to import productive resources (cows) and export finished products (oxen) but perceived the danger of draining his country of its natural wealth. Indeed the health of the trade depended largely on the poverty of Xhosa-land. When the season was favourable, fewer cattle were slaughtered and fewer hides came onto the market.[69] Hintsa was equally apprehensive of the threat traders posed to Xhosa national sovereignty.[71] He ostentatiously seized the goods of traders resident in his country to show them that they were not exempt from the obligations of his other subjects. 'Tell them that I took (these goods),' he said on one occasion, 'you need not hide it, for they have taken my country from me.'[71]

It is not surprising therefore that the widespread killing of traders was a notable feature of the 1834 – 1835 war. Altogether the war was a great setback for the frontier trade, which declined from over £30 000 a year in the early 1830s to well under £20 000 a year thereafter.[72] Traders were more strictly vetted and licensed by Colonial and Xhosa authorities, so that their numbers dropped from more than a hundred to about thirty.[73] There was not a single resident trader in the whole of Ndlambe country.[74]

The most significant development after 1835 was the expansion of agricultural production. The demand for mimosa gum boomed with the discovery of the American market, and for the first time maize and sorghum were purchased for consumption within the Colony.[75] Traders sent their wagons from homestead to homestead collecting corn, and ships called at Mazeppa Bay in Sarhili's country. Colonial horses ate Xhosa barley and Xhosa oat hay.[76] Another crop which flourished was 'that poisonous herb "Dacha" which inebriates and ruins the constitution of the Hottentots in the Colony'.[77] Of course, it should be remembered that the Xhosa were spending the proceeds on consumption goods — blankets, cotton rugs, soldiers' greatcoats, hats, hand-kerchiefs and so on.[78] And they were sometimes selling rather more grain than they could really spare over winter.[79] Neverthe-less it is in this period that we see the genesis of that class of peasant producer which was to become so important later in the century.[80]

3. THE TRADE IN LABOUR

The trade in labour across the Colonial frontier eventually engen-dered an entirely new class of permanent labourers whose labour was directly exploited by their employers and who lost the means to pursue any alternative existence. No such class existed in precolonial Xhosa society. The wealth of Xhosa chiefs derived not from exploitation of commoner labour but from the appropriation of cattle and other products of labour by means of tribute and judicial fines. *Busa* clients were directly exploited but they did not form a permanent class.[81] Outsiders suffered in their transition to membership of the community, as the Khoi and Mfengu discovered.[82] But even outsiders possessed their own homesteads and enjoyed equal rights to water and pasturage. If there was a class of permanent dependent labourers in Xhosaland, it was the Xhosa women.

Xhosa servants were reported among the Boers as early as 1777.[83] Some of these were kidnapped as children or taken as prisoners of war, but most engaged voluntarily.[84] Men were employed as herdsmen and women as domestic servants or garden workers. They usually served a year at a time and were paid in beads, iron and brass wire. These were preferred to direct payment in cattle, because they enabled the Xhosa to buy a greater number of cattle in Xhosaland. Xhosa workers were occasionally beaten or cheated out of their wages, but Boer excesses were checked by the ease with which they could desert, carrying off cattle with them. For those Xhosa who returned home after they had earned the cattle they required, white employment was nothing more than a slightly exotic form of *busa* clientage. But there were others who stayed on permanently with the Boers, or returned regularly to the same employers after short spells on vacation in Xhosaland.

By 1811 there is evidence of Xhosa working continuously in the Colony for 15 to 20 years, and by 1839 of two full generations of Xhosa born and brought up on white farms.[85] Here we see the beginnings of a permanent class of wage labourers. One can only speculate as to why some Xhosa chose to treat the Boers as temporary patrons and why some chose to remain with them. The most likely explanation is that the latter had become dependent on European goods not readily available in Xhosaland. European liquor — the 'tot system' was apparently functioning in the eastern Cape by 1809[86] — is one obvious possibility.

The early Colonial governments opposed the use of Xhosa labour as politically disruptive, and made successive attempts to expel all Xhosa across the Fish, but the urgent need of the Colonists for Xhosa labour ensured that these were uniformly unsuccessful.[87] The arrival of the British settlers in 1820 did little to change frontier attitudes towards black labourers. In fact, indications are that they picked up local attitudes rather quickly:

> They called 'morrow, morrow.' He brought them to the tents. When my mother motioned them to sit down, and then we saw they were all women with long sticks in their hands. We gave them a lot of Settler's bread i.e. hard biscuit. It was not long before a lot of men arrived from our neighbours, and made all the old women prisoners. They then searched the clay pits and found a lot more. They were all taken to Grahamstown and we were given to understand were hired out to farmers.[88]

Eventually the labour crisis resulting from the collapse of settler indentures combined with the irresistible influx of Mfecane refugees forced the Colonial authorities to reformulate their policies.[89] Ordinance 49 of 1828 provided for the employment of 'native foreigners' on a contractual basis.[90] The overwhelming majority of workers registered in this way were Xhosa.[91] The terms of the contracts — normally one cow or its equivalent for a year's labour — suggest that most of the Xhosa were still temporary clients rather than permanent labourers.[92] They preferred short contracts of a year; indeed some went back as soon as they could without waiting for their contracts to expire.[93] They continued to send home the stock they earned.[94] But alongside temporary migration of this kind, a new form of labour relationship was developing. Xhosa and other blacks began to squat on white farms as labour tenants.

> This place ware Faku live on belonged to Mr Mark Cockroft but Faku was not to have aney more then four or five to live with him but at this place we found six men besides women and children all without passes and thear wifes and Children: sum of the men had two and three wifes. Theas Kaffers had upwords of hundred head of verey fine Cattle ... the Kraal was more then a mile from the main Kraal ware Faku was liveing.[95]

Sheepfarmers were so desperate for labour that they were prepared to tolerate Xhosa workers bringing their families and their cattle with them. The Xhosa for their part were driven into the Colony by the increasing destitution of Xhosaland in the wake of the 1834 — 1835 war.[96] Not only had they lost their grazing rights in the Zuurveld and the Kat River valley but they had to accommodate the Mfengu and other refugees from the Mfecane.[97] At some point in the 1830s — it is impossible to be exact — Xhosaland became unable to provide for its population. In 1841, a Xhosa declared he had entered the Colony because 'a man without property was not able to live in Kaffirland.'[98] It is significant that one of the attractions of the Colony was that it was still possible to trap wild buck without too much difficulty.[99]

Once the Xhosa settled in the Colony, their history merged with that of the incipient working class. Xhosa chiefs began to express opinions on Colonial matters. Tyhali, for instance, 'asked how it happened that the prisoners confined in our trunk, and at hard labour in our streets, were all Hottentots and black people.'[100] Like other Colonial blacks, Xhosa workers were stoned, lashed with whips and hit over the head by their employers.[101] Like them, they learned to demand higher wages and appeal to the law.[102] Many evaded passes and contracts altogether and worked as porters and casual labourers.[103] From the 1830s, the black quarter or 'location' — sited on communal waste or old burying grounds — became a familiar feature of the eastern Cape country town. The first faction fight erupted between Xhosa and Mfengu in Grahamstown in 1841, and the first race riot between black and white in Richmond in 1849.[104]

But as long as they still had an independent subsistence base in Xhosaland, the Xhosa as a people could not be forced onto the labour market, whatever the fate of some individuals. They could still opt out when wages were too low.[105] Before 1846 proletarianisation was still partial, temporary and to a certain extent voluntary. The *War of the Axe* changed all that.

4. COMMERCE AND CHRISTIANITY

The social impact of trade between the Xhosa and the Colony did not stop at the frontier but leaped right over it to become internalised within Xhosa society. The dynamic which stimulated the production of commodities for the Colonial market within Xhosaland and created a demand for new commodities from the other side was powerfully abetted by the Colonial authorities in their desire 'to transform the Kaffirs from a thieving nation into a commercial one'.[106] Recognising the essential unity and self-sufficiency of Xhosa society, they realised that any disturbance of the 'national torpor'[107] of Xhosaland, particularly one which would stimulate the Xhosa to emulate west European civilisation, would be conducive to the pacification and Christianisation of the people. The missionaries had a key role to play in this process. In the pitiful communities of misfits and refugees collected at their stations they had a social laboratory in which to show the Xhosa the image of their own future.

The production of commodities for the market (dagga, tobacco) and the use of certain forms of money (cattle, spears) were important features of precolonial Xhosa society. Such commodity productions and money exchanges had not disrupted existing social relationships — if anything they had reinforced them by bringing more cattle into Xhosaland. The new spirit of commodity production, however, succeeded in weakening existing social relationships by elevating the market principle to the centre of society.

Physical labour became a moral virtue rather than a simple necessity and indolence became a sin. The saintly Van der Kemp incurred the wrath of the Colonial authorities by refusing to associate conversion to Christianity with hard labour, but, with the notable exception of his colleague James Read, his fellow missionaries did not follow his example. The difference between missionaries and Africans with regard to the religious relevance of work is well illustrated by the following exchange between Ayliff and one of his converts:

'You mynheer are a missionary to our souls — you have nothing to do with working . . . ' I took up the Bible and said, This Book says 'six days shall thou labour' and 'if a man will not work neither shall he eat.'[108]

'Work' in a missionary context implicitly excluded anything to do with cattle. Cattle were seen as a means of subsistence which enabled the people to live in idleness except for the occasional diversions of fighting and raiding. Real work was agricultural work and the missionaries encouraged the men to undertake it by paying them themselves at the beginning and securing them contracts for forage and other produce.[109] Since the fields were traditionally the women's domain, the diversion of substantial numbers of men to agricultural labour implied a significant reorientation of values. When a man joined a mission station and began to work in the fields, he left behind forever the old world of cattle and the Great Place, where he was henceforth the object of pity and scorn. He committed himself to a new world in which material affluence conceived in European terms became the main indicator of social prestige.

Of the various artificially induced wants, clothing was first in both time and importance.[110] The missionaries on their stations and the whites in their towns demanded that the Xhosa be 'decently' attired. In many respects European clothing was indeed warmer and more comfortable, and, once the trade had become fully established, it was easier to exchange a hide than to engage in the laborious process of dressing it, piercing it and sewing up.[111] Iron pots and iron axes were obviously superior to clay pots and hardened wood. The taste of salt and sugar was not easily given up once acquired. Moreover, the essence of new consumption requirements was that they could never be fully satisfied, as there was always some new attraction: by 1845 Colonists were complaining that Xhosa were wearing 'coats, knee-breeches, and silk-stockings, umbrellas and parasols'.[112] Paradoxically, even the purchase of capital goods, such as ploughs and wagons, tied the Xhosa to the Colonial economy. The whole package was integrated by the use of colonial money.[113] As long as the Xhosa confined themselves to beads and buttons, they could at least maintain their independence. One could not buy European goods with beads and buttons. But the collapse of the bead currency in 1829 finally set the seal on their economic subordination. It is hard to fault the judgement of an oral historian, Mwezeni Mnyanda:

> The white man has always wanted this land. For this, he pulled out sugar, he pulled out liquor, and he pulled out buttons without holes (money).[114]

Soga, son of Jotello and councillor to Ngqika and Tyhali, was the herald of the new age. Significantly, he had started off as a spearmaker, one of the few economic specialists operating within the precolonial economy.[115] When already a mature man he was converted to Christianity by Ntsikana himself. Although Soga never deserted his old loyalties, he was more inclined than his fellows to listen to the missionaries. He was the first Xhosa to irrigate his land and the first to grow maize and sorghum for the market. Smith gave him a plough and he used it to increase his yield. To the joy of the missionaries, who viewed the communal ethos as 'hostile to the temporal and spiritual improvement of the race',[116]

> Soga had moral courage enough to break through this bad custom as well as some others; he would not allow the other Caffres to work for him without wages, and when they came to beg of him, he told them, that he paid them for their work, and they must pay him for his corn. In case he slaughtered an ox, he also sold its flesh, and refused to give it away, according to the common custom of his nation.[117]

On the opposite side, Tyhali, Soga's chief, set his face against economic innovation. 'Tyhali is a Kaffir,' he said, 'a son of Gachabie, and he is not going to spoil his oxen with ploughing while he has plenty of wives to till the ground for him.' And, in refusing money, he added, 'I don't want a cow that I can put in my pocket but one that can walk on its legs.'[118]

8. A Break of Sorts
(1835—1846)

1. THE DEATH OF HINTSA

Hintsa, king of the Xhosa, was consulted by Maqoma and Tyhali before they went to war, and he sanctioned the invasion.[1] He was motivated partly by the way the traders and missionaries had undermined his authority in his own country and partly by his responsibility as head of the nation and of the Tshawe royal house. 'The English have killed some of his relations who are captains,' he told his principal diviner, 'and these his relations had no guilt with the English.'[2] A number of chiefs, old Mnyaluza at their head, entered the Colony and the Rharhabe were allowed to drive captured Colonial cattle into Hintsa's country for safekeeping. Hintsa adopted an official position of studied neutrality. As the war proceeded, it became clear that the Gcaleka were not as adept at Colonial warfare as the Rharhabe and that their bodies 'lay scattered like stones' across the Kei.[4]

When Maqoma and Tyhali retired to mountainous regions inaccessible to wagons and artillery, Governor D'Urban and Colonel Smith turned towards the easier target of Hintsa's country. Demanding that Hintsa order the surrender of the Rharhabe chiefs and compensate the bereaved settlers to the extent of 50 000 cattle and 1 000 horses, the British army advanced to Hintsa's old Great Place on the Gcuwa River. On 29 April 1835, having received assurances of his personal safety, Hintsa entered the British camp. He said he would have come earlier, 'but he was dissuaded from it by some of his council, who said we should only kill him. He showed no appearance of fear.'[5] Hintsa was never to leave the camp alive. To begin with, however, he was treated well, being fed soup, biscuits, potatoes and coffee with sugar. One of the more perceptive settlers commented, 'During the whole

of the time he has been overwhelmed with presents, at the same
time that he was kept a prisoner. Reminded one very much of the
tickling of a trout.'[6] It was not to be long before D'Urban tore
away even the pretence of friendship.

Missionary Ayliff's actions at Butterworth had kept alive the
flame of Mfengu discontent that might otherwise have died of
sheer hopelessness.[7] By giving refuge to individual Mfengu, he
held out the possibility of a country where the entire nation
might find asylum. The outbreak of war east of the Kei brought
matters to a head. Though he still admitted their chiefs to his
councils, Hintsa was aware that the Mfengu were potentially
disloyal and ordered them to join him at his new capital in the
north. He was particularly angry with the Bhele chief,
Nkwenkwezi, for carrying Ayliff's messages and said 'we regarded
Mr. Ayliff more than him.' This was true. The Mfengu refused to
move, sending Hintsa a bloody spear as a sign of defiance.[8] At the
same time, Mfengu clients scattered among the Gcaleka as herdsmen broke out in spontaneous rebellion. The great Mfengu leader,
Veldman Bikitsha, has left a detailed account:

> No one said to them 'go,' no one said 'that this or that has happened'
> but there was a rising and a moving in every village and a taking up by
> the Mfengu of their goods and their families, and a gathering together
> of their cattle and every Mfengu took that which was before him and
> did not wait for that which was not in sight. Were his cattle away at the
> cattle posts he did not delay to go for them. Were his master's cattle
> under his hand he did not hesitate to carry them off . . . When morning
> dawned the valleys that surround the mission station at Gcuwa (Butter-
> worth) were black with a mass of cattle and people.[9]

Butterworth mission was the only conceivable meeting place for
the dispersed and leaderless people. Ayliff himself had fled but
kept in touch from the safety of Thembuland, acting as a channel
of communication with the Governor and repeatedly urging
the Mfengu to meet the British army when it crossed the Kei, and
ask to be received as British subjects.[10] This they did, a fateful
decision which was to weigh heavily on them thereafter. They had
only a vague conception of the land of the whites, but were led
to believe that they would be helped to re-establish their
community as it had existed on the Tugela before the time of
Shaka.[11] But their expectations of the future did not coincide
with the plans of their benefactors. D'Urban planned to settle
them as buffers in the agriculturally inferior Fort Peddie area
where they would guard against the entry of the Xhosa to the Fish
River bush and would 'besides afford to the Colonists a supply of

excellent hired servants'.[12] For the moment, however, the Mfengu saw the British as liberators and flocked to join their army.

Naturally, the Xhosa resisted the attempts of their former herdsmen to depart with their cattle. As the fighting became more bitter and widespread, reports reached the D'Urban camp that the Xhosa were massacreing the Mfengu. Presumably forgetting that only five days previously he had given Hintsa full assurances for his personal safety, D'Urban threatened to hang the king from the nearest tree unless he stopped the 'carnage'. Hintsa gave the necessary order, thus permitting the Mfengu to take off 22 000 cattle without further molestation. His retinue was forcibly disarmed and his guard strengthened. Realising his true position for perhaps the first time, the king became very uneasy. This Smith interpreted as sulkiness, and with his usual condescending insensitivity he tried to cheer him up 'by singing and playing the fool for them',[13] as if it lightened the burden of Hintsa's confinement to be treated like a child. Hintsa bore the painful charade with a good grace, but Bhuru refused. 'I have not got two faces or two hearts,' he said.[14] Smith thought Bhuru 'a vulgar sort of fellow compared to Hintsa'.[15] But although he played along with Smith, Hintsa was not prepared to save his life by betraying his nation. Commanded to order the surrender of Maqoma and Tyhali, he sent secret messages warning them that he was a prisoner. Commanded to raise a ransom of 25 000 cattle and 500 horses for his release, he sent secret messages ordering that the cattle be driven further on. 'What have the cattle done that you want them?' he asked Smith. 'Why must I see my subjects deprived of them?'[16]

As the column marched along above the Nqabara River, Hintsa made a dash for freedom. He was pulled off his horse, shot through the back and through the leg. Desperately he scrambled down the river bank and collapsed into the water-course. A scout named George Southey, coming up fast behind him, blew off the top of his head. Then some soldiers cut off his ears as keepsakes to show around the military camps. Others tried to dig out his teeth with bayonets. Thus died Hintsa, king of the Xhosa, for trusting the honour of a British Governor.* That it was D'Urban who

---

*   It seems pointless to analyse in detail the smokescreen erected by D'Urban's apologists, which involves questions like whether Hintsa volunteered to remain hostage for 25 000 cattle, or whether Hintsa threatened George Southey's life with a spear. Suffice it to say that the private correspondence of at least three apologists conflicts with their public statements. See: Acc. 519 (5) (D'Urban papers), J. Alexander-B. D'Urban, 3 Oct. 1837; Original Field Diary of Caesar Andrews, S.A. Library, Cape Town, pp 95 –97; J. Bisset in CO 48/165, ZP 1/1/88,

referred to Hintsa as a 'treacherous, ungrateful and cunning savage, whom no obligations could bind' is, beyond all belief, true.[17] How much D'Urban owed to Hintsa's naive good faith appears from a letter he subsequently wrote to Smith: 'It was a fortunate circumstance, Hintsa's coming in, and so putting an end, most seasonably for us, to a sort of warfare . . . which, in our secret mind, we confessed our inability to have prosecuted further.'[18]

The Rharhabe surrendered on better terms than D'Urban intended to give them. 'The most humane Governor the Cape ever had'[19] had concocted a weighty scheme for the settlement of the frontier. Not for him the piecemeal tinkering with the boundary which had characterised Somerset's grab of the Ceded Territory. D'Urban boldly planned to boot all Xhosa across the Kei, except for a few proven collaborators, and fill their 'fertile well watered, sufficiently wooded'[20] country with Colonists in need of compensation for their war losses.[21] He was unable to impose this solution for the simple reason that the Xhosa were not yet beaten. A few exploratory forays into the Amatola mountains were sufficient to demonstrate that Maqoma and Tyhali could not be dug out without many more troops than Smith possessed.[22] The amaNdlambe near the coast were hardly troubled by the few posts and patrols in their country and emerged from the war virtually unscathed.[23] By June 1835, Smith was complaining that his horses lacked forage, his Boer volunteers had all gone home, and his Khoi conscripts were insubordinate.[24] Even were his ranks somewhat increased, he would need 100 000 men to keep the Xhosa across the Kei.[25] Sir Benjamin was forced to allow the Xhosa a little land in their old country. When this offer was rejected, he conceded that he would have to allow them territory adequate to their numbers.[26] His pique was somewhat mollified by the thought that there would still be enough land left over for European 'occupations and speculations'[27] and that the Xhosa had agreed to come under the

---

p 481, Q. A. Harington (1977), p 481. The inquest into Hintsa's death was stage-managed by Smith (See Acc. 519 (4), H. Smith-D'Urban, 1 Aug. 1836) and contains several Kafkaesque passages, such as the following:
'Did you see those ears? — I did see ears, but I do not know if they were Hintsa's.
In whose possession were those ears? — I cannot say, they were lying on the ground.
Were they shown as curiosities about the camp? — Not to me.'
Evidence of R. Daniels, *Minutes of the Proceedings of the Court of Inquiry . . . on the fate of the Caffer chief Hintsa.* (Cape Town, 1837), p 170.

British flag in order to retain their land. The chiefs were not beaten but they were tired of war, and on 17 September 1835 they concluded a peace.

What the Xhosa understood by agreeing to come under the British Government is not clear. Maqoma said, 'We place ourselves under the Governor's feet; but we wish to be his children, his soldiers, we will assuredly fight for him whenever he wishes, and his enemies shall be our enemies also.'[28] It appears from this that they envisaged their submission as entailing nothing worse than becoming intact and autonomous tributaries of the British crown, and that they set more store on that clause of the treaty which said, 'English laws do not apply . . . to, or interfere with, the domestic and internal regulations of their tribes and families, nor with their customs' than on the one which ordered them 'to live in submission to the general laws of the Colony.'[29] Later they were to complain that it was the British who had sued for peace,[30] and that they had been deceived into making peace under false pretences.[31] This can only refer to an unofficial but fully authorised delegation of Wesleyan missionaries who, with D'Urban's concurrence, deliberately misled the Xhosa into thinking that the Governor would be generous.[32]

To Harry Smith's febrile mind the Province of Queen Adelaide (as the territory between the Keiskamma and the Kei was now called) was to be a sort of infernal machine for civilising the Xhosa.[33] Commander of the new province under martial law, Smith had expressed his attitude towards his new subjects as follows: 'I view them as irreclaimable savages . . . whose extermination would be a blessing; although if circumstances hereafter identify me with them, my study and exertions should be for their information, improvement and consequent happiness.'[34] According to Smith's conception, the chiefs were to become magistrates, administering English law.[35] They were to live off salaries rather than fines, and their decisions were to be subject to reversal by higher authority. Commoners, freed from the 'oppression' of their chiefs, would ally with the benevolent British administration. Smith would flood the country with missionaries, schools of industry, trade in money, and so on until the final triumph of European civilisation. There was, however, one important provision: 'That this conclusion, however, should eventually work itself out, it is necessary that they be not startled at the outset, or their eyes opened to the future consequence of the process, until, by its advancing force, when they do, at length, discover all its influence, they shall have no longer any power to be effectually restive.'[36]

The chiefs' eyes were, however, wide open from the outset.

They could hardly forget that military posts had been erected all over their country and that their activities were supervised by Resident Agents. Smith fondly believed that he had adopted Xhosa idiom and tradition when he referred to himself as the *inkosinkulu* (Great Chief), or when he called the seizure of Xhosa cattle 'eating-up' (*ukudla*), or when he played childish games with his gold-knobbed stick, or when he made the chiefs prostrate themselves before him.[37] The chiefs bore it all stoically, but 'the forced smiles which play on their features ... are exchanged for bitterness and scorn when the chiefs return to their people. Macomo has often turned into ridicule the fine speeches that were delivered, and the imposing scenes which were displayed.'[38] In the short term they found it expedient to play on Smith's vanity while the all-important land allocation was proceeding.

D'Urban was still hoping to find land for settlers in Adelaide, believing as he did that since the Xhosa notoriously used land wastefully they would take up much less space if properly located. The census revealed, however, that there were over 55 000 Ngqika, which forced Smith to grant them a lot more land than he had anticipated.[39] Maqoma even managed to flatter his way back to the Ceded Territory. Further east, Smith tried to get the Ndlambe to occupy the west bank of the Kei at the expense of Bhuru and his people. In this he was partly motivated by a desire to drive a wedge between the Rharhabe and the Gcaleka. But Bhuru's people just kept on coming back, claiming they were Mhala's people now.[40] Indeed, all over Queen Adelaide Province, Xhosa were returning to their homes, whether or not these were situated in Smith's new settler towns or near his military posts.[41] The soldiers were kept busy burning huts — 2 700 in one week[42] — but found it hard to enforce residence in the prescribed locations.

Smith attempted to distract the attention of the chiefs by setting them at each others' throats. Maqoma and Gasela showed some interest, but not enough to matter.[43] Tyhali ('a vacillating fellow,' 'an ignorant fellow,' 'always a forward fellow')[44] and Mhala[45] were steadfast in their opposition. As the inevitable clashes mounted over the rights of chiefs to fine their people and execute witches, at least one Resident Agent cautioned 'against giving the chiefs too much trouble'.[46] The chiefs thought of moving north over the Orange or east across the Kei, but the people were loath to leave their lands to the invaders.[47] And so, despite the destruction of the last war and the difficulty of remobilising under the eyes of the soldiers, the Xhosa had no alternative but to prepare again for war. The depredation rate soared in spite of the troops.[48] There were rumours of war in January, in March, in May and in July.[49] Agent Stretch later maintained that had Queen Adelaide lasted much longer, the chiefs would have executed a plan they had devised 'to fall, on a favourable opportunity upon King William's Town (the capital), to put every white person to death.'[50]

Queen Adelaide Province was a seething volcano, but it retreated from the brink of eruption. As a man, Lord Glenelg was revolted by the circumstances surrounding the death of Hintsa. As His Majesty's Secretary of State for the Colonies, he was not prepared to sanction the annexation of a new province which, however economically beneficial to the settlers, would only involve the Crown in unlimited military expense. He therefore ordered D'Urban to abandon Queen Adelaide.[51] This was a wise and humane action, but in retrospect it seems almost a pity that the failure of D'Urban's system was never made more manifest through a Xhosa uprising. For the settlers were thereby enabled to call for its return throughout the decade which followed.

2. SARHILI'S EARLY YEARS

Sarhili, Hintsa's Great Son, was 26 years old at the time of his father's death. Although nobody challenged his right to the succession, his authority was very far from established. Sarhili had been estranged from his father because Hintsa had quarrelled with his mother and sent her back to her own people. Indeed Sarhili's circumcision was delayed until the councillors managed to prevail on the king to allow his Great Wife to return to prepare food for her son during his seclusion.[52] At the final ceremony, Hintsa addressed Sarhili as follows: 'Today you are circumcised, but we don't know you because you have always been a wanderer – the son of a captain should always sit by his father and mother, and by his father's councillors to hear and ask, but you don't know the place of your father.'[53] Less than a year later, Sarhili was suddenly and unexpectedly the king of the Xhosa. He found that most of Hintsa's power had devolved not on him, but on his father's Great Councillors, Kwaza (Gxabagxaba) of the Ntshinga and Runeyi, military head of the Qawuka.[54]

The ceremonies associated with the induction of the new king were never properly performed and the section of the people under Runeyi's influence refused to contribute towards the accession gift.[55] As late as 1877, Sarhili was still trying to under-cut the influence of the Great Councillors by having himself officially installed. His most senior relatives were of little help. Bhuru, who had served Hintsa well in similar circumstances, was preoccupied with recovering his land on the west bank of the

Kei.[56] Gxaba, son of Velelo, who ruled about one third of the Gcaleka, used the opportunity to increase his independence. Asking for his own missionary in 1837, he emphasised that he informed the Great Place what he did, he did not ask its permission.[57] Sarhili was forced to rely on rainmakers and diviners, but their powers were found wanting under pressure, and he had at least two of them killed.[58] The few reports received from Sarhili's country at this time all stress the weakness of the king and the power of his councillors.[59]

Sarhili knew that he would never command respect as long as he lived in his father's place among his father's cattle without having won a place or cattle for himself.[60] He did not find it easy to do so. At first he sought his victories against the Sotho, but he failed even where lesser chiefs had succeeded.[61] After having suffered further setbacks against Faku on his eastern border,[62] he turned his attention to the region of the upper Kei, which had previously been the subject of contention between Hintsa and Ngubencuka. The Thembu had taken possession of it during the *Sixth Frontier War* in the name of assisting the British Government.[63] In 1839, Sarhili announced he was returning to the White Kei. 'It was my father's, it is mine,' he declared. 'My father lived there. I wish to do so.'[64] But the Thembu, led by the aggressive Mtirara and pushed westward by the Mpondo-Bhaca alliance, refused to give way. They had, moreover, recruited a formidable ally in the person of Myeki, the chief of the Mpondomise. After a year of raids and skirmishes the Gcaleka retreated to the coastal regions, utterly defeated.[65] The Mpondomise had killed the very dogs in their homesteads and milked their captured cattle before their helpless eyes.[66] Sarhili's fortunes had sunk to their lowest depths. The expeditions against the Thembu which were to have brought him glory had proved anything but triumphant.[67]

But by July 1843, the Gcaleka were ready to try again, and this time they were successful.[68] In January 1844, an attacking Thembu army led by Myeki and Tyopo, chief of the Gcina, was routed with a reputed loss of 500 men, including four of Myeki's sons. Many Thembu fled across the Orange and the whole of Thembuland was at Sarhili's mercy.[69] Mtirara was in no position to resist any further — 'They stared eyelash to eyelash' wrote a Thembu historian, 'but they never came to blows' — so he paid Sarhili a large compensation and conceded the issue.[70] Sarhili was finally able to establish his own capital, and he did so at Hohita, in the heart of the disputed territory.

Part of the Gcaleka success was due to their skilful use of firearms and horses.[71] The first time they had tried to use these, the firing had frightened the horses and the riders had been thrown,[72] but in time they mastered the new armaments. It was firearms too, which turned back the Mpondo, when they marched to join the Colonial forces during the *War of the Axe*.[74]

When war broke out in 1846, Sarhili knew where he stood. 'Where is my father?' he asked his councillors. 'He is dead. He died by the hands of these people. He was killed at his own house. He died without fighting . . . Today we all fight.'[74] Sarhili opened his country as a refuge to Rharhabe cattle and warriors during the long war of attrition. 'A hiding-place for his great men; Phato and Sandile' was added to his praises.[75] Sarhili remained resolutely stoical in the face of the forces sent after the Colonial cattle. 'I am almost inclined to think that the abelungee are merely seeking an occasion to quarrel with me, in order that thay may send me after my father who was killed by them without the shadow of guilt being proved against him,' he told them. 'If this surmise of mine really be correct, then of course nothing I can possibly say will have any effect, and so I must patiently wait the result.'[76] Stockenstrom withdrew without pressing the issue.

The creation of British Kaffraria in 1847 finally sealed the division of the Xhosa kingdom between the Gcaleka and the Rharhabe.[77] But paradoxically, even as the Xhosa king lost the vestiges of his political authority over the western Xhosa, so his moral and emotional power over them grew. As the Rharhabe became increasingly enmeshed in the cultural and material toils of the European world, so too did they increasingly look backward with longing towards Hohita, where the great python was firmly settled in as the very self and personification of everything which was Xhosa.

3. THE ROAD TO THE NORTH

Just as the Boers, obstructed in their expansion eastward, eventually turned the Xhosa flank by heading north, so there were times when some Xhosa thought there might be salvation from the troubles of the frontier across the Orange River. Small parties of Xhosa had strayed off in that direction as early as the eighteenth century, and by 1820 a Xhosa community was firmly established in the Kareeberg mountains, an isolated and relatively well-watered redoubt near modern Carnarvon, which proved a way-station for further penetration into the far north-west.[78]

One chief of note to take the northern escape route was Nzwane, son of Rharhabe, better known by his later name of Danster.[79] He and his followers began by working in the Colony until each man had acquired cattle and a gun. Around 1805 they moved north of the Orange where they lived the lives of frontiersmen, more raiders and hunters than cattle-keepers, more Griqua than Xhosa. Some episodes of Nzwane's life have come down to us, tinged with blood and treachery: how he won his nickname, *Umgagi* (the taker-by-surprise, the creep-mouse), by stealing back his cattle from Jonker Afrikaner and how he turned the tables on his troublesome Khoi neighbours by wiping them out at a beer-drink.[80] It was Nzwane who gave Moshoeshoe his first gun, receiving in return his land at 'Danster's Nek'. Other Xhosa started out with Nzwane, but they could not adapt to the demands of the new life and they returned.[81] Nzwane did not completely cut himself off from his origin and remained in touch with his brother Mnyaluza.

Mnyaluza, son of Rharhabe, fled from Ngqika to Hintsa after the Frontier War of 1818 — 1819. He had always been well-disposed towards the Boers and had offered to help them in the abortive Slachters Nek rebellion against the English.[82] Possibly he had known Louis Tregardt, who had been farming on the Tarka at the time, and was the first Voortrekker to leave the Colony. In 1834 Tregardt settled under Hintsa and near Mnyaluza on the upper Kei.[83] Tregardt probably ran guns to the Xhosa; Mnyaluza certainly joined in the war of 1834 — 1835.[84] In any event when the British army crossed the Kei in April 1835, the partners decided it was time to leave. Tyhali sent men up after them. They brought back messages reminiscent of a happier, more open frontier:

> These Boers abused the English very much, said 'We have no powder yet, but we shall have; tell your chiefs to come to us; the English will seize them as they have done others before and will make servants of the whole of you. Do not trust the English.' The [Xhosa] said 'We cannot go back now, it is too late; our chiefs are over, and so are our cattle. Umyalousie is to cross three more rivers; we then come to a large bush where we are to live, Boers and all together. Louis Trichard and Umjaloosie are our chiefs: we cannot come back.'[85]

Several of Mhala's people joined Mnyaluza. As the weight of Queen Adelaide Province pressed more heavily on them, the thoughts of other border Xhosa turned northwards. Tyhali went up to the Orange 'to get his cattle', as he told Smith, and to have a look around. Maqoma also thought of going.[86] But their followers refused; the north was a strange country, far from their native places, where one had to live like a Griqua to survive.

The retrocession of Queen Adelaide Province killed the

TWO KINDS OF LABOUR

F. I'ons. *Preparing a Caross.*

T. Baines. *Kaffirs Leaving the Colony for their native seat, with all their acquired property.*

Lord Charles Somerset

Sir Andries Stockenstrom

Sir Benjamin D'Urban

Sir Harry Smith

incentive to proceed north, but an even greater discouragement was still to come. It was learned that Mnyaluza and his followers had been overwhelmed by Moshoeshoe's Sotho in a great night attack and that most of them had perished including the old chief himself.[87] Tyhali was supposed to lead the Xhosa to revenge the death of Rharhabe's son, but when the expedition did set off it was under the unlikely leadership of Gasela and some lesser Ndlambe chiefs. It was widely believed that they would be defeated, and Gasela was already given up for lost when he returned with a large number of cattle and captives. This raised his prestige to such an extent that he vied with Mhala for the leadership of the amaNdlambe.[88]

Despite this happy ending, the Xhosa remained mindful of Mnyaluza's death and continued to regard the Sotho as madmen who ate horses and people. But the idea of the road to the north did not entirely disappear. Sarhili felt its attraction as late as 1850 and went as far as seeking a rapprochement with Moshoeshoe.[89]

4. THE TREATY SYSTEM AND ITS ENEMIES

The treaty system which regulated relations between the Xhosa and the Colony from 1836 to 1846 was essentially the conception of one man, Andries Stockenstrom.[90] Formerly Landdrost of Graaff-Reinet and Commissioner-General for the Eastern Districts, he surfaced in London in 1836 as a star witness for the humanitarians on the Aborigines Commission. Curiously blind on the land issue,[91] Stockenstrom hammered home his contention that the 1834 – 1835 war had resulted from the inevitable abuses of the commando system. Impressed by his liberal protestations and his long experience of frontier administration, the Colonial Secretary appointed him to the lucrative position of Lieutenant-Governor for the Eastern Districts.

Stockenstrom's system was based on two fundamental propositions.[92] The first was that the Xhosa chiefs were sovereign rulers who could be dealt with in accordance with signed treaties regulated through Diplomatic Agents. The second was that the problem of cattle theft could only be solved within the Colony itself, and not across the border in Xhosaland. Stockenstrom maintained that cattle theft originated with negligent herding by the farmers. When cattle strayed or were eaten by wild animals, it was easy for the careless farmer to exact exaggerated compensation from the Xhosa.[93] Even where the robberies were genuine, these might have been prevented by more herdsmen, better armed. Stockenstrom was adamant that 'preventive measures on the part of the Colonists alone can secure their property, and this must be insisted upon in defiance of all remonstrance.'⁹⁴ He therefore sought to force the farmers into guarding their cattle more efficiently. For stolen cattle to be reclaimable under treaty, the farmer had to swear that they had been properly guarded by armed herdsmen and properly secured at night. The pursuit had to be commenced immediately and the spoor had to be taken all the way to the border. If cattle were stolen despite these precautions, the farmer might either seek them himself in Xhosaland with the assistance of a Xhosa official appointed by the chief to watch the drifts, or apply to the Diplomatic Agent for redress through the chief. In this way Stockenstrom hoped to end the indiscriminate seizure of cattle as 'compensation' which had been a mark of the old commando system. Above all, the onus was on the farmers to prevent theft rather than on the chiefs to catch the criminals. 'The frontier farmers should remember that they got *good* land *cheap*,' wrote Stockenstrom, 'and they should not complain of having to protect their flocks, as they knew they would have to do.'⁹⁵

The treaty system failed as, in the end, it was bound to do. One reason was that the British government was too stingy to police the frontier effectively and too short-sighted to see that this would inevitably lead to the far greater expense of a full-scale war. This point has been brought home by Galbraith in *Reluctant Empire* and there is no need to labour it here. It seems more useful to pick out two further issues which have hitherto been neglected.

The precautions insisted on by Stockenstrom might not sound unreasonable, but they could not be accommodated within the economic framework of settler agriculture. As Lieutenant-Governor Hare put it, 'It is idle to say why do the farmers not properly guard their cattle, the thing I say is impossible in this country, where servants are not to be had.'⁹⁶ It was precisely in the question of cattle-herdsmen that domestic and foreign policy became inextricably fused.

For the successful prosecution of commercial agriculture in the Albany district an abundance of cheap labour was required. During the 1830s, this simply did not exist. Indeed, the situation grew more acute as the transition from cattle to woolled sheep proceeded.⁹⁷ For woolled sheep need to be sheared as well as herded, and their fleeces need to be periodically washed. Most farm labour was obtained by allowing 'native foreigners' to squat on farms as labour-tenants.⁹⁸ The arrival of loyal Mfengu after the 1834 — 1835 war had destroyed the remaining inhibitions of white farmers concerning the enemy within the gates and finally shattered the frail capacity of Ordinance 49 to regulate the inflow of black labour. Many Xhosa, impelled by the loss of their cattle during the war, passed themselves off as Mfengu and joined the stream.[99] By 1842, there was an estimated 6 000 'native foreigners' in Albany district (30 percent of the total population) and these formed 'the principal labourers on the farms as well as in the town and villages'.[100] Agent Stretch commented that African dwellings on settler farms were 'so numerous as scarcely to distinguish the Colony from Caffraria'.[101] It is clear from the ineffectualness of government attempts to remove them that the landowners connived at the squatters' presence.[102] It is even more clear that they were beyond the control of the farmers and that they were responsible for a high proportion of the thefts blamed on the Xhosa across the border.[103] Employing certain Xhosa as labourers and recouping some of their costs from those who retained their independence might seem unduly devious, but the time was not yet ripe for the more simple solution of depriving the nation of its land and its labour simultaneously. The Xhosa were still too strong.

The interrelationship between internal and external policy is again demonstrated by the question of armed herdsmen. One of the first of Stockenstrom's regulations to come under attack was that herdsmen should be armed with guns. The Colonists argued that this put herdsmen at grievous risk as it increased the temptation for the Xhosa to murder them. Such solicitude for the well-being of their herdsmen sits oddly with other settler attitudes towards their labourers. Surely, if one's herdsmen are being murdered, it seems more logical to double their numbers and their armaments than to disarm them altogether. In any case, only three herdsmen were murdered in the two years before the regulation was abolished.[104] Fortunately for the historian, a farmer named Thomas Robson was less circumspect than the worthy gentlemen who drafted official petitions. 'We will not arm people of this class,' he declared, pointing out that the sympathies of the herdsmen lay with the Xhosa and that, since they earned only two pence or three pence a day, they could earn more by stealing the cattle and selling the gun 'than by a whole year's service' with the farmers.[105]

It is a commonplace of settler historiography to represent the Colonists as innocent victims of official bungling. This view sadly underestimates the dynamic of expansion generated within the Colony, which was incompatible with the assumption of the treaty system that the Colonists would remain satisfied with the territory west of the Fish. The British settlers of 1820 were products of the age of mercantile capitalism. Numbed at first by the unfamiliar conditions of a strange country and by the autocratic government of Lord Charles Somerset, they took some time to find their feet. Somerset's fall was accompanied by changes which brought the Cape more into line with the new era.[106]

The transformation of the administration, the currency and the judiciary were part of this process. So was the freeing of labour under Ordinance 50 and of trade which, as we have already noted, penetrated Xhosaland after 1829. But the change which had the most significance for the frontier relations was that which related to land. When the British settlement came of age, it produced a demand for land which was quite unlike anything which had gone before. Although it would be wrong to view the Boers as simple subsistence farmers, they were not possessed by the spirit of accumulation to the same degree as their British counterparts. Those goods which the Boer produced and could not use he exchanged for goods he used but could not produce.[107] He did not invest money for the sole purpose of obtaining more money at the end of the transaction.[108] He looked on land not as a commodity to be bought and sold, but as a natural resource. This attitude was reflected in the loan-plan system of tenure which Boer economic habits had forced on the Dutch East India Company: first the Boer found a piece of land to use and then he set about registering his claim;[109] land could be transferred from Boer to Boer at a price, but there could be no claims to unoccupied land.

When the settlers arrived, they were provided with land on perpetual quitrent, which was the main form of tenure at the Cape from 1813 to 1844. Under this system the government retained nominal ownership, but the settler was provided with a title which he could 'transfer', that is to say sell. The speculative potential of the system was soon demonstrated by those settlers who left their locations but managed to hang on to their titles.[110] Godlonton, of the *Grahams Town Journal,* himself not free from the odour of speculation, had cause to remark that the 'mere adventurer who never expended one farthing or devoted one day to the improvement of the soil has not only received his title but turned it into solid cash and for aught we know − and the assumption is more than vague conjecture − may now be craving more at the hands of a too credulous government.'[111]

The possibility of reselling land obtained for next to nothing created an unquenchable thirst for new grants.[112] The rapid growth of a commercial wool industry at a time when improved surveying techniques were speeding up the measurement and distribution of available plots led to a rapid rise in land values.[113] The war of 1834 − 1835 was a setback for the farming community but only a minor and temporary one. As Arthur

Webb, the historian of settler agriculture, has pertinently observed, 'the Xhosa had not invaded the bank balances of these farmers.'[114] If anything, the war did the farmers a favour by encouraging them to switch to the more lucrative sheep. The years of the treaty system were not years of fear and poverty for the frontier farmers, but years of increasing wealth and prosperity. To quote Webb again, 'The greatest problem which faced the frontier community on the eve of the Seventh Frontier War was not a question of survival in the face of the Xhosa threat, but rather a question of finding markets for their expanded production.'[115]

It was also a problem of finding new pastures for the sheep. The plots in Albany were small and becoming increasingly expensive. No wonder that right in the middle of the war, T.H. Bowker found time to muse, 'The appearance of the country is very fine. It will make excellent sheep farms. Kaffir corn fields in every valley . . . Far too good for such a race of runaways as the Kaffirs.'[116] T.C. White, a leading sheep farmer, was an influential member of Smith's entourage. The Colonists felt that the Xhosa were too lazy to exploit their land properly and, in any case, they had plenty more in their rear. The reason they had crowded so close on the Colonial border was that they had come there to steal.[117] John Mitford Bowker was a man of vision:

> The day was when our plains were covered with tens of thousands of springboks; they are gone now, and who regrets it? Their place is occupied with tens of thousands of merino . . . I begin to think that he too [the Xhosa] must give place, and why not? Is it just that a few thousands of ruthless worthless savages are to sit like a nightmare upon a land that would support millions of civilised men happily?[118]

The beauty of the D'Urban system was that it offered the settlers the prospect of vast stretches of this beautiful country virtually free as compensation for war losses. Over 400 requests for grants in the new province were received, some from as far away as Cape Town, and there was every expectation that they would be acceded to.[119] And then Glenelg dropped his bombshell.

The merchant community of Grahamstown also showed a keen interest in frontier affairs. Bluff Thomas Stubbs, no negrophile, hinted darkly that 'the people on this frontier liked a Caffer War better than peace . . . I could if I wished enumerate a great many who owe their present positions (to) the Caffer Wars.'[120] Nor was he alone in voicing this suspicion. Unfortunately few contemporaries were prepared to risk libel suits by mentioning names, but certainly these included William Cock, James Howse and George Wood, all Methodists and members of the circle around the *Grahams Town Journal*.[121] Significantly, many of Grahamstown's merchants put their profits into sheep farming.[122] Few Colonists entirely escaped a slice of the large disbursements — £154 000 in the *Sixth Frontier War* and over ten times that amount in the *Seventh*[123] — called forth from the Imperial War Chest. Apart from direct military contracts (forage, wagon hire, for instance), almost all benefited from the general price rise due to increased demand, and this included the price of land.[124]

One need not deduce from this that a conspiracy of Grahamstown merchants deliberately fomented war. The *Sixth Frontier War* was a heavy blow to the Xhosa trade in which many of them were deeply involved, apart from being a source of personal danger.[125] But although they did not want war, they did want as large a military establishment as possible to protect their sheep and their trading agents, to push up the value of their landed property, and to spend vast sums of money while in town. The D'Urban system opened up delightful vistas of Xhosa kept endlessly in their places by endless martial law. Hence the continual calls for strengthening the frontier defences, calls substantiated by continual allegations that one or the other of the Xhosa chiefs was contemplating an attack on the Colony.[126] The Xhosa were of course, aware of this warmongering and it made them edgy in their turn. Agent Stretch thought that war scares were deliberately started.[127] This may seem far-fetched, but one should not forget the case of Governor Somerset who made use of a similar rumour to secure a command for his son.[128]

Nor were the settlers politically powerless. They made their feelings perfectly clear through public meetings, through petitions and remonstrances, and through their connections in Britain. They had broken Somerset and now they set out to break Stockenstrom. Leading the pack was the redoubtable 'Moral Bob' Godlonton, editor of the *Grahams Town Journal*. From issue to issue he blasted the treaty system and called for a return to the good old days of the benevolent Sir Benjamin D'Urban. Godlonton did not confine his politics to the editorials and the correspondence columns but they permeated the very news itself. Occasional cases of detectable misrepresentation seem to reveal only the tip of the iceberg.[129] Through its energy and persistence, and through its ability to capitalise on the mistakes of its opponents, the *Journal* made a case of appealing simplicity: since the Xhosa not the Colonists were the thieves, the Xhosa not the Colonists were to blame. If the farmers could not observe the treaty, then it was the treaty not the farmers which had to go. Occasionally the *Journal* added a little cant to the effect that the D'Urban system was more effective in 'civilising' the Xhosa. But the settlers' concern for the welfare of the Xhosa had not prevented them from applauding the good Sir Benjamin's attempts to throw the whole lot over the Kei. The *Grahams Town Journal* was not politically naive. It did not simply seek better protection for the farmer. It sought a return to the Province of Queen Adelaide. And it succeeded in creating a climate of opinion which ensured it got what it wanted.

The settlers found a ready ally in Sir Benjamin D'Urban. The portly veteran of the Peninsular War refused to accept the rejection of his martial exploits, and was confident that his aristocratic connections would bring about the reversal of Glenelg's decision. These connections were in fact good enough to interest King William IV in the fate of a province named after his queen and a capital named after himself. To mollify his monarch's ruffled feelings, Glenelg gave D'Urban the opportunity of submitting one final report to justify his proceedings.[130] D'Urban grasped the opportunity but in a most unexpected way. He simply delayed sending off his reply for a full year. This placed Stockenstrom in an impossible position. He was not allowed to implement his own plans until he had final instructions from the Colonial Secretary, and the Colonial Secretary could not send his final instructions until he had heard from D'Urban. As Lieutenant-Governor, protocol did not permit Stockenstrom to communicate with the Colonial Secretary except through the Governor. This meant that Stockenstrom had been in the Colony for over 12 months before Glenelg heard a word from him.

Fortunately for Stockenstrom, D'Urban overplayed his hand. Without giving Stockenstrom any notice of his intentions, the Governor lifted martial law in Queen Adelaide the day after the new Lieutenant-Governor left for the frontier. It is hard to say whether he acted out of spite or calculation but, as he knew quite well that Queen Adelaide's Province was unworkable except under martial law, D'Urban's action can only be explained in terms of a wish that Stockenstrom's arrival be greeted by scenes of slaughter and pillage.[131] The move backfired very badly. Sir Benjamin's most devoted appointees could not but agree that he had destroyed the entire basis of government, and that, will he nil he, Stockenstrom must make new arrangements at his own discretion. The Xhosa chiefs and people realised that good things were about to happen and were at pains to behave correctly.[132] Stockenstrom met the chiefs in September (1836), promised immediately that the posts would be withdrawn, and by December, the treaties were formally concluded.

Stockenstrom had weathered the first storm, but from the beginning he was sinking slowly. The settlers were not prepared to revolutionise their labour relations to conform to Stockenstrom's regulations and they were not prepared to abandon the fair fields of Adelaide. Their self-interest was fuelled by monumental indignation that the man who had destroyed them at the Aborigines Commission should be their Lieutenant-Governor. Stockenstrom was arrogant enough to withstand public vilification, but he could not tolerate subversion in the civil service charged with executing his policies. With the exceptions of Hougham Hudson, the Agent-General, and Stretch, the Ngqika Agent, the officials on the eastern frontier were D'Urban supporters to a man. When it came to Stockenstrom's attention that the Civil Commissioner of Albany was assiduously spreading a rumour that he had once shot a Xhosa in cold blood, he sued for libel — and lost.[133]

This was too much for the incoming Governor, Sir George Napier. Sir George was in favour of the treaty system, but he thought it would be possible to win the settlers to its support. He saw Stockenstrom's personal unpopularity as an insuperable obstacle and managed to fob him off with a baronetcy (1839).[134] Napier and his loyal subordinate, Lieutenant-Governor Hare, were contemptuous of the Grahamstown claque and fully aware of the 'longing of the (settlers) after the lands of the Kaffirs'.[135] They were fully committed to the treaty system if only because they perceived that it could not be replaced except by war.[136] But they made the cardinal error of assessing it solely according to its success in securing the return of stolen cattle. The essence of Stockenstrom's plan was that the farmers themselves should be forced to prevent the thefts in the first instance. Napier entirely overlooked this, amending the treaties in 1840 by withdrawing the requirement that herdsmen should be armed and by allowing any person who could show 'good and sufficient reason' to cross the boundary in search of stolen cattle.[137]

Even worse, Napier became bemused by an anomaly much beloved of the *Grahams Town Journal*, namely that it was possible for cattle to be stolen but not reclaimable under the treaties. A careless farmer who failed to obey Stockenstrom's regulations had no redress, even if he could actually see his very beasts grazing across the river in Xhosaland. Napier permitted the publication of a so-called 'not reclaimable list' of cattle stolen, but not reclaimable under treaty.[138] Regardless of the fact that the Xhosa scrupulously returned or paid compensation for all cattle reclaimable under treaty,[139] the non-reclaimable list was soon established as the only true indicator of the success of the entire system. This opened the door to precisely those abuses which Stockenstrom had deliberately framed his regulations to prevent. After 1839, the chiefs were presented with the irreclaimable list at quarterly meetings with the Lieutenant-Governor, a list which they had no means of checking and which they knew on occasion to be demonstrably false. Stretch called this 'a debt against Caffreland which increased according to the inclination of reporters for the press'.[140] Tyhali pointed out that 'there are many Englishmen who kiss the book, and then speak what is not the truth'.[141] Maqoma remarked, 'Our people steal oxen and cows, but the government steals with the pen'.[142] Conversely, Napier concluded that the treaties were unjustly hard on the Colonists, but he declined to press the issue and returned in 1844 with the boast that 'no shot was fired during his term of office'.[143] His successor was neither so tolerant, nor so fortunate.

5. TSILI STEALS AN AXE

The Xhosa chiefs were rather pleased to see 'Old Stock' and his treaties, except the collaborators, who had good reason to fear that they would be 'cut to pieces'.[144] As the operations of the sytem unfolded, they discovered a few minor grievances. They had difficulty obtaining their own cattle when they were stolen by settlers or other Colonial subjects.[145] Kat River Field-Cornet Piet Camphor and other frontier officials harassed them unnecessarily.[146] Above all, they still hankered after the Kat River Valley which they had lost before 1834.[147] But they were less concerned with the imperfections of the system than with the blatant efforts of certain Colonists and officials to undermine it. They were pleased that they were no longer held responsible for thefts by a government which could not even control its own illicit firearms trade.[148] They reiterated that thieves should be caught and punished in the Colony not in Xhosaland, and pointed out that they had not complained when a son of the great Mdushane was shot dead on Colonial territory.[149] But they saw clearly that there was more to the problem than robbery pure and simple. 'War is a bad thing,' declared Maqoma, 'and it cannot come because there are thieves in the world.'[150] The Xhosa did not trust the Colonial government. When Napier despatched troops against the Natal Boers in 1842, the Xhosa thought he was going to attack them in the rear. When smallpox hit Xhosaland in the same year, they believed it was engineered by the Government which was thus 'secretly destroying them.'[151] But not all their suspicions were equally unwarranted. Bhotomane was not far wrong when he said that although some officials

do not desire the blood of the Caffers to moisten their fields, nor to drink milk of the Caffers cattle. Others smell the grass and waters of Cafferland, and therefore they regard not their own peace, but would drive us into the bush with our women and children.[152]

Sandile called H.H. Dugmore, the Wesleyan missionary, 'a man who came to teach the truth to Caffers: but he does not know the truth himself. Such men from the Colony speak lightly of war: they delight in the grass and water of Caffraria and make strings of lies to secure it.'[153] Thus whatever reservations the chiefs may have had about Stockenstrom and his treaties, they viewed them as a 'great wall' protecting the Xhosa from the rapacity of the Colony. When they heard that Stockenstrom was gone they expected the worst. It was rumoured that the commando system was to be reintroduced and the chiefs prepared to resist the first patrols.[154] Bhotomane and Nqeno drove oxen down to the river to exchange them for guns.[155] They defended Agent Stretch, the last lone pillar of the Stockenstrom system, asserting that they would not accept another agent in his place.[156] 'It would appear that Government had determined to remove from them those persons whom they most liked,' Tyhali said.[157] To Stockenstrom himself, they sent messages. 'We earnestly beg of him to remain . . . things are every day becoming better . . . our friend must not leave us.'[158] Even five years after Stockenstrom's fall, Maqoma declared, 'I will hold by Stockenstrom's word until I die and my people put me in my grave. If the treaties are forced from us, nothing can preserve us from war.'[159] The Xhosa did not speak lightly of war. They knew what it meant. Determined to stand by the treaties, they swallowed Napier's modifications as they had swallowed Stockenstrom's departure. But when Sir Peregrine Maitland tore up the treaties in 1844, and substituted a new one of his own they could swallow no more.

Although the expansionist drive of the Colony was in itself sufficient to ensure the destruction of the treaty system at some point, the particular time and circumstances under which this eventually occurred were shaped in Xhosaland itself. Despite the hue and cry of the *Grahams Town Journal*, the treaty system was working fairly well until 1842.[160] The initial breakdown was undoubtedly due to the severe drought of that year, which not only killed large numbers of cattle but also destroyed the following year's crops. Many Xhosa were reduced to a diet of bark and gum.[161] 1842 was also the year of a major war scare, sparked off by the inclination of Siyolo, the fiery Mdushane chief, to help the Natal Boers against the British.[162] The *Grahams Town Journal* frantically attempted to implicate the new Ngqika Paramount, Sandile, who replied with apparent truth, 'Instead of the Caffres wishing to fight we are dying of starvation.'[163] Droughts and war scares were not unusual on the frontier. In fact, the Agent-General expected depredations on the Colonists to increase in the hungry months of May and June.[164] But 1842 was further distinguished by two events which wrecked the political equilibrium of the western Xhosa: the death of Tyhali and the defection of Phato.

On 1 May 1842, Tyhali, son of Ngqika, died.[165] He had contracted tuberculosis about six years previously and had been dying slowly ever since. By April, it was clear that he could not live much longer. Tyhali appreciated that he was dying of natural causes, but as the end approached he remembered that Suthu, the mother of Sandile, had given him lumps of sugar. This was enough for the Mfengu diviner in attendance to charge her with witchcraft, and she might well have been executed had it not been for the prompt intervention of the Colonial authorities reciprocating Suthu's good offices during the previous war. It was generally believed that the campaign against Suthu was orchestrated by Maqoma, who hoped thereafter to declare Sandile an idiot and himself the head of the house of Ngqika.[166] Tyhali himself had suspected as much two weeks before his death. 'I am a dying man,' he said. 'Maqoma wishes, when I am dead, to eat up my people, and destroy Gaika's house.'[167] Such a process, had it been carried through, would not have been new in Xhosaland. Mhala, chief of the amaNdlambe, had attained his position in such a manner. So had Tyhali himself.[168] Witchcraft accusation was one of the mechanisms whereby Xhosa society guarded against the dangers of the hereditary principle and allowed the strongest and most capable to rise to the top. Colonial intervention on Suthu's behalf, humanely intended as it was, was probably a mistake. Maqoma possessed the ability and strength of personality to pull himself and his people together, but now he fell apart in total frustration. He spent even more time in Fort Beaufort, drinking with his officer friends and neglecting the concerns of his people.[169]

Colonial officials of the time often remarked that the chiefs were losing power over their people, partly because of the widespread availability of illegal firearms. These observations are borne out by phenomena which can only be described as the beginnings of banditry. The chiefs themselves referred to the 'great number' of Xhosa who had taken up 'their abode in the thickets of the Kat, Koonap and Fish Rivers, over whom we have no control, and who are not subject to our laws.'[170] Flitting between the uncharted jurisdiction of the Colony, the Kat River Settlement and Xhosaland, sometimes robbers, sometimes homestead-heads, alternating in political allegiances but always loyal to themselves, numbers of Xhosa took up their residences on the fringes of society. The most famous of these was Hermanus (Ngxukumeshe) who led the Khoi revolt on the Kat River in 1851. But there were many others, such as Sende ('Caffre Jack'), robber, interpreter and spy, and the notorious jailbreaker Xegwana alias Klaas, the 'Rob Roy of Kaffirland'.[171]

Even within Xhosaland, the chiefs had to be careful with their people. As early as 1838, Hare admitted that Maqoma and Tyhali 'have amongst their people many desperate subjects over whom they have but little control, and both chiefs are afraid of them.'[172] The death of Tyhali aggravated this situation. More reliable and consistent than the brilliant but volatile Maqoma, Tyhali was never tempted to follow European ways or to become popular with Europeans. By the same token, he was the one chief who could repress cattle-raiding. When he died, his senior sons, Feni and Oba, were still minors. His people soon shrugged off the rule of the ineffectual Xhoxho and nominal leadership passed to his widows. In reality, his followers were leaderless.

Sandile desperately attempted to impose his leadership on a deteriorating situation. He has been described as vacillating and weak minded but this is not a fair estimate. Born with a withered leg by an unpopular mother, Sandile grew painfully to manhood under the shadow of his domineering older brothers. Indeed, all his life Maqoma despised Sandile for his deficiencies and hated him for his superior rank.[173] It is clear from his recorded speeches that Sandile was no fool. Moreover his policy was determined in consultation with his brother Anta and councillor Tyhala, who lived with him near Burns Hill mission. Sandile was acutely conscious of his status and aware that he lacked chiefly presence and that many did not respect him. He was therefore very anxious to assert himself to win popular approval. He also wanted very badly to establish good relations with his white neighbours. It was unfortunate that these impulses, reasonable in themselves, were so contradictory in practice. Sandile's very eagerness to be friends with the Colonial Government led him to approve measures which Xhosa public opinion later forced him to repudiate. Thus Sandile agreed to a joint attack with Colonial forces on Tola, one of the 'numerous petty chiefs who have been gaining strength since Tyali's death, and prevailing against his (Sandile's) authority.'[174] Alarmed by the dangerous precedent of inviting British troops into their country, the other chiefs assisted Tola to escape. Sandile rapidly backtracked, denied he had ever agreed to troops entering Xhosaland, and vented a little of his frustration on Theophilus Shepstone, the officious young agent at Fort Peddie.[175] This incident severely damaged Sandile's credit with both his people and the Colonial Government.

Stockenstrom had undone Queen Adelaide's Province, but he found himself unable to undo D'Urban's decision to settle the Mfengu west of the Kei. He correctly regarded the Mfengu 'as a stumbling-block in the settlement of the frontier'.[176] Originally D'Urban had planned to settle the Mfengu in the Ceded Territory as a human buffer against the Xhosa. Even under his amended scheme, they were left in possession of the fertile valleys of the Tyhume and the Gaga. When this area was returned to Maqoma and Tyhali, all Mfengu not willing to accept the rule of the Xhosa chiefs were bundled into the 'uninhabited and worse than useless' thornveld area around the military post of Fort Peddie.[177] Some were moved into the even more unhealthy district of the Tsitsikamma forest, where many of their cattle died.[178] Even this was not enough to satisfy the Xhosa. They regarded the Mfengu as thieves and traitors, 'dogs, fattening before their eyes upon the flocks of a chief whose memory they hold so dear'.[179] They were well aware that the Mfengu would fight against them if called on to do so; and that in terms of the treaty the British were committed to aiding the Mfengu.[180] They were well aware that this might mean that the Mfengu would regain the Xhosa lands they had held during the short life of Queen Adelaide's Province.[181] The continuing tension expressed itself in mutual petty cattle raids and murders,[182] culminating in an attack by Siyolo's people on the Mfengu at the very gates of Fort Peddie (1837).[183] The Mfengu chief Mhlambiso was stabbed at the side of the Resident Agent. The Xhosa attitude on such occasions was well expressed by Nqeno's people when they gathered shouting, 'Where were the fellows with big holes in their ears, for they were tired of their complaints (to the Government) and would dispatch them.'[184]

Of all the Xhosa chiefs, Phato of the Gqunukhwebe suffered most from the Mfengu presence. Conspicuously loyal to the British during the war, he had brought the wrath of the other chiefs down on his own head. The ill-feeling was kept alive by his refusal to return the cattle which Nqeno had sent to him for safe-keeping.[185] Constantly threatened with vengeance, Phato had welcomed the Mfengu into his territory (which included Fort Peddie), probably seeing them as an accretion of strength.[186] But after the affair of Nqeno's cattle was settled (1839), cracks began to appear. Although Phato was well-disposed towards the Europeans and their culture, tried to send his Great Son to a school in the Colony, attended church politely, and made suitable speeches on appropriate occasions, he never became a Christian. His younger brother, Khama, however, became a sincere convert, greatly embarrassing Phato by his refusal to accept a second wife, even a Thembu royal.[187] Worse still was that Khama, aided and abetted by his missionary, was moving from autonomy to independence. Fighting broke out between the two over an incident connected with the smallpox epidemic (1842).[188] With the blessing of Agent Theophilus Shepstone, the son of his missionary, Khama took his people off to a new country further north.[189] To add injury to insult, Shepstone and Hare decided that half the territory vacated by Khama should go to the Mfengu and not to Phato, the senior Gqunukhwebe chief.[190] This was not the sort of support Phato had anticipated when he first invited the Mfengu to stay with him. Fighting broke out between Phato's men and Mfengu attempting to settle in Khama's country.[191] Young Shepstone was playing the Mfengu chief in a way that boded ill for his future subjects in Natal and Phato decided that he had to go. After several threats on Shepstone's life, an unfortunate German missionary who happened to be riding in Shepstone's wagon led by Shepstone's servant was murdered.[192] Shepstone left rather hurriedly, and an uneasy peace settled over Fort Peddie.

Another example of the capacity of the British to divide the Xhosa among themselves occurred further east. Gasela, swollen with Sotho spoil, was challenging the leadership of Mhala in Ndlambe country. When a honeybird entered Mhala's hut and alighted on his throwing-spear, Mhala's diviner indicated that it was sent by Gasela to announce that he, Gasela, would reign alone.[193] Since Mhala was immeasurably more powerful, Gasela decided that he needed the patronage of the Colonial Government.[194] He easily succeeded in persuading Shepstone that he was a progressive chief. The Berlin missionaries, who knew him rather better, compared him to Herod.[195] When the fighting started, the Colonial authorities extended their protection to Gasela, a flagrant breach of the treaties. Mhala's protests ('Gasela is a man under my feet') were simply ignored (1843).

When Sir Peregrine Maitland arrived in the Colony as Governor (1844), the treaty system was under severe stress. Sandile's inability to exercise effective leadership and resentment against Colonial intervention in Xhosa affairs kept the depredation rate high. Thoroughly disgusted with the treaties, Napier was concerned only to hang on long enough to leave with his reputation intact. And yet the situation was not as bad as it appeared on the surface. The smallpox epidemic was past. The long drought had ended. It was only a matter of time before Sandile acquired the years and experience to assert his authority. The Xhosa chiefs and their people were determined to preserve the peace and the treaty system. It is true that Shepstone had turned the situation around Fort Peddie into a festering sore and that the *Grahams Town Journal* was still baying for a return to the Province of Queen Adelaide. But with even a modicum of patience and good sense, the new Governor could have prevented a war.

Unfortunately, Sir Peregrine's self-assurance was matched only by his ignorance. Having absorbed the opinions of the *Grahams Town Journal* he started from the premise that savage barbarians like the Xhosa could not be conciliated but could be frightened into obedience. Catching hold of some chance phrases from Lieutenant-Governor Hare, he concluded that all the trouble was caused by a small and definable group known as the 'young bloods' or the 'war party' who should be quickly put down.[196] When Maitland arrived on the frontier he met immediately with Shepstone and the Wesleyan missionaries, suddenly skipped his meeting with the amaNgqika, and presented his new treaties at Fort Peddie without prior discussion with the chiefs.[197] When Sandile offered to meet him there, Maitland replied that 'When Sandile was required by his Excellency he would send for him' and prided himself that he had made the amaNgqika sensible of his displeasure. He most certainly had. Sandile replied pointedly that 'From the message I received last night that his Excellency had no desire to see me I have not confidence to enable me to assure my people that peace exists in the country.'[198] Maqoma was more sarcastic: 'I cannot comprehend what has been thrown over my body that makes me so offensive in the eyes of the Government.'[199]

When Maitland did finally see the Ngqika chiefs, it was under the swords of 400 dragoons. His new treaties did not actually open up new lands for white settlement, but in every other way they destroyed the old Stockenstrom system. Forts were to be built, and troops stationed in the Ceded Territory. Farmers could follow up stolen cattle at any time. If the animals could not be found, 'equivalent' compensation would be demanded. A tribunal was created to hear the appeals of settlers against chiefs and agents. Missions and Christian converts were placed beyond the jurisdiction of the chiefs and Xhosa law. The chiefs agreed to everything except the last two articles, and prepared for war. Maitland took personal charge of the frontier from the safety of Cape Town. Even Lieutenant-Governor Hare could see disaster looming and tendered his resignation. Time was running out too quickly for it ever to become effective.

Shortly before Maitland hit the frontier, Hare had occupied part of the Ceded Territory in reprisal for the murder of a farmer named De Lange and established a military post there.[200] This was a final blow to the waning confidence of the Xhosa in

Stockenstrom's successors. With troops in the Ceded Territory and drunken soldiers jesting about occupying it permanently,[201] the Xhosa became increasingly convinced that their land was at stake. Harking back as far as the erection of Fort Willshire, they concluded that 'the land is the object aimed at, and that, in a conflict for it, they must all stand or fall together.'[202] Military patrols from the new post were threatened by armed Xhosa.[203] Roads to Fort Beaufort and Stretch's Residency were blocked up with stones and bushes. Fortuitously, the irregularity of the water supply at the established military post led the military authorities to ask if it could be moved.[204] Sandile, eager to please, acceded to a request which he should have refused. When the surveyors set up their tent east of the Ceded Territory, in Xhosaland itself, Xhosa indignation caused Sandile not only to revoke his earlier permission but also to demand the removal of posts and patrols in the Ceded Territory. Hare withdrew the surveyors but not the existing post. As tension mounted, many Xhosa stocked up with blankets, bridles, flints and knives, and moved off into the mountains. As in 1834, the chiefs began to seize trade goods in their territories and some traders were killed.

It was in this atmosphere that a certain Tsili was caught stealing an axe from Mr Holliday of Fort Beaufort.[205] His friends staged a daring rescue, only to find that Tsili had been handcuffed to a Khoi fellow-prisoner. Non-plussed, they hacked off the unfortunate man's hand and he died of his wound. Hare demanded the 'murderers' and Sandile refused. The war which followed takes its name from this dramatic little incident. But it would have been more appropriate to call it 'The War of the Waters' or 'The War of the Boundary', which is what the Xhosa originally called it.[206] For the war was not fought over the theft of axes, or the theft of cattle, or the theft of anything else. It was fought over the land, like the wars which had gone before it.

9. Fire and Sword

1. FIGHTING TECHNIQUES OF A HEROIC AGE[1]

Among the Xhosa, every healthy adult male was also a warrior. As a boy, he would learn to fight with sticks, to thrust, to parry, to throw at passing birds. As he grew older, he would exchange his sticks for the different types of spear.[2] Most important of these was the *intshuntshe,* or throwing spear, with its long shaft which quivered and vibrated when properly thrown thus adding to its power of penetration. It was not however possible to throw very accurately even from a distance of fifty yards,[3] and so the warrior carried his spears in a bundle of seven or eight. The last spear was never thrown, but was retained in case the order *'Phakathi!'* (Get inside!) was given. Then the shaft of the spear might be broken off, or a special striking spear with a wickedly serrated edge might be produced. For defence, the warrior carried a long oval shield, covering perhaps two-thirds of the body.

The order *'Phakathi!'* was not given often. Young chiefs and their age-mates, newly emerged from the circumcision lodge, usually tried to mark their coming-of-age by a daring exploit.[4] But this did not usually amount to much more than a cattle raid on one's neighbours or traditional rivals; as we have seen, it was one of the chief mechanisms whereby the Xhosa kingdom expanded. Raids and counter-raids were frequent, but wars were relatively rare. Official representatives *(amazakuzaku)* were sent on diplomatic missions to talk things over first.[5] These would usually be important councillors, sons or junior brothers, but never the chief himself. If the enemy seemed particularly dangerous or untrustworthy, women would be sent. A missionary who witnessed the protracted struggle between Hintsa and the Thembu king Ngubencuka wrote:

Between the period of receiving and avenging any wrong ... days
and weeks, and sometimes months, are spent in conferring upon all the
different bearings of the case ... Messengers are sent backward and
forward, to ascertain why or wherefore such steps have been taken, or
upon what grounds hostilities are contemplated.[6]

Thus if a youthful raid led to loss of life, or if herdsmen clashed
over the right to water their cattle at a particular river, or if
a chief objected to the way his daughter was treated by her
husband, this did not in itself lead to war. An unfortunate incident
could always be smoothed over by the payment of compensation
and the exchange of presents. Only when the insult was deliberate
(as when Gcaleka's men tossed a corn-cob into a meeting at
Rharhabe's Great Place)[7] or when the payment was derisory (as
when the Thembu presented Rharhabe with inadequate bride-
wealth),[8] or when the enemy overtly claimed sovereignty over the
land (as when the Ngqosini chief, Gaba, hoisted the elephant's tail
in Xhosa territory)[9] did it become necessary to go to war.
Hostilities were always preceded by a formal declaration.

Once war was declared, the king (or the chief, if the struggle
was one between two chiefs of the same nation) ordered his
followers to muster at the Great Place by sending personal
messages to his subordinate chiefs. The people were alerted by the
women who passed the *ixwili,* a sharp cry like that of a wild dog,
from ridge to ridge.[10] The men seized their weapons and set off
for the Great Place without knowing why they were called. Any
who stayed behind were liable to have their property confiscated.[11] At the Great Place the warriors would eat of the
specially-slaughtered cattle, and would dance and sing and learn
the causes of the dispute. Here too they would be doctored and
organised into battle order.

The Xhosa believed that magic affected every human activity
but most particularly war. Every chief had his wardoctor *(ithola*
or *igogo).* The very greatest, Nxele or Mlanjeni, defy generalisation
— their methods were entirely their own. Others were rainmakers
or the sons of wardoctors. The first task was to make the warriors
fierce *(ukuhlupeza)* by giving them a medicine derived from fierce
animals such as the poison of a snake or the gall of a bull.[12] It was
believed that the power of a wild animal passed to the man who
killed it, and so great hunters wore the claw of a leopard, or a
piece of lion-skin, or an ivory armlet where possible. After this,
protective medicines were prepared. These were either swallowed
or rubbed into incisions made in the body. The ingredients usually
included the plumbago, used in peacetime for warding off thieves
and lightning, and the pelargonium, otherwise used for dressing

cuts and sores. And finally since charms could hardly benefit anybody tainted with evil, the warriors were purified by bathing in a river previously prepared with purifying medicines. The war-doctor might also impose further ritual prohibitions, for example on sexual intercourse, to keep the army pure.[13]

Desperate situations called for extraordinary remedies. These usually involved sending for special charms from a distant place, perhaps from Myeki or Mhlontlo, the Mpondomise chiefs who were generally acknowledged as the greatest specialists in war medicine.[14] On another occasion, a man who had killed a python sacrificed himself at the Great Place so that his power could pass to Sarhili, the head of the nation.[15] Nor did the doctoring stop when the army left the Great Place. The wardoctor attempted to 'tie up' the enemy to prevent them passing over a particular spot. Or he might be able to bring down a thick mist or even render the army invisible, thus enabling it to escape out of dangerous situations.[16] It was also necessary to keep a sharp look-out for birds of ill omen such as the robin or the vulture or the hammerhead.[17] On the battlefield, it was advisable to rip open the stomach of the killed and release their pent-up spirits, lest they wreak terrible revenge on the slayers.[18]

The army marched from the Great Place in no particular order, accompanied by its slaughter cattle and often enough, by its women.[19] But when it drew up for battle every man had his place. The vanguard usually consisted of the youngest warriors, the ingqukuva or buds, followed by the older men. The most distinguished warriors wore crane feathers awarded to them by the chief.[20] The chief himself commanded the rear, which Soga calls the 'reserve' but which was more like an extended royal bodyguard and went by the name of *amafanenkosi* − those who die with the chief. Its main function was to urge the army forward and to prevent their flight. Not the chief but his sons led the fighting divisions. Thus three of Ndlambe's senior sons died in the battle of Grahamstown.[21] The chief directed the battle by shouting orders and sending messengers to the various divisions. Cowardice, however, was greatly despised and the chief was supposed to be there.[22] Indeed Alberti thought that the outcome of the battle depended on the behaviour of the chief as the warriors would not be willing to fight for a coward.[23] However, the chief was excused if he was old and sick, or if there were special circumstances. Mhala, for instance, was very nearly killed in the battle of the Gwangqa and when the following war broke out his councillors demanded that a commoner replace him at the head of the army.[24]

Once the battle commenced, the army divided into three:

a centre flanked by two wings *(amaphiko)* on either side.[25] The basic tactic in Xhosa warfare was the attempt to outflank the enemy with the object of either encircling him or else capturing his cattle. There were many possible variations on this theme as the different divisions of the armies manoeuvred to gain position, to counteract the movements of the enemy and to lend support where required. Occasionally a brilliant new tactic would swing the victory. This was the case at the great battle of Amalinde. When Ngqika's army charged forward, Ndlambe's young warriors deliberately fell back, and the amaNgqika, following up, exposed their flanks to Ndlambe's veterans.[26] By and large the battle was over as soon as one side broke and fled, leaving the victors to seize as many cattle as they could.

Because battles were largely fought over questions of political supremacy and because victory was easily computed in terms of cattle captured, precolonial wars among the southern Nguni tended to be relatively bloodless.[27] The wars of the Mfecane, in which people like the Bhaca fought for the sustenance of life itself were appreciably bloodier. It is remarkable that only three important Xhosa chiefs — Rharhabe, Mlawu and Tshaka of the Gqunukhwebe — died in battle against their neighbours, and the first two were fighting the Qwathi who had recently come down from the far interior.[28] Even the mortal enemies, Ngqika and Ndlambe, spared each other when they had the opportunity to do otherwise.[29] War did not lead to the destruction of productive resources. At the very worst, the huts of the defeated were burnt, but they were neither killed nor expelled.[30] The spirit of Xhosa warfare was expressed in the custom whereby the victors returned a portion of their spoil to the vanquished on the principle that 'we must not let even our enemies die with hunger'.[31] The San were killed without mercy, but then they were regarded as animals rather than people.[32]

One cannot conclude without remarking on the part played by war in Xhosa national culture. Idioms and phrases associated with war were carried over into peacetime, thus *umdabazo,* 'the action of grabbing one's weapons and hastening off for war', became used to denote any sort of rushed departure.[33] The deeds of heroes and the shame of cowards were enshrined in praise-names which remained attached to the individuals who had earned them. The assemblage of warriors at the Great Place was a scene of feasting, singing and dancing. Individuals did not dance before the army to exalt themselves as the Zulu did, but all the men danced together, as they had done in the circumcision lodge.[34] Songs and war-cries were composed and sung.[35] War-cries were brief and onomatopaeic — *'Tsi-ha-ha izikhali* (weapons) *kaRharhabe',* for instance. Songs were usually variations and repetitions on a single theme. Often proper names were interchangeable, so that topical references could be made. Hence, Reverend Solilo describes the *igwatyu,* or national song, as 'a song to strengthen cowards. When it is heard, it mentions cowards by name, so that tomorrow he will be too embarrassed to run away.'[36] When the armies arrived on the scene of battle, the chief would deliver a final exhortation and the warriors would respond by shouting, by singing, and by striking their shields with their spears.[37] The battle itself was punctuated by war-cries, praises, exhortations and the bellowing of the warriors.

Even in the bitter fighting of the later frontier wars, the Xhosa attempted to express themselves in war, to personalise it, to communicate with the enemy through it. Secure on mountainous heights or behind rocks and bushes, they shouted at the white men, reproaching ('He called out to us . . . and asked why we were burning his house?')[38] or taunting ('They yoused sum vere busif langwage,' wrote an aggrieved and semi-literate Jeremiah Goldswain, 'and said that we ware afraid of them.')[39] The insults were not purely gratuitous: the Xhosa were hoping to draw the Europeans into the bush. But there was more to the challenges than this. In some way, it seems, it was important to the Xhosa to show that they were truly men. Even their most implacable enemies came to respect their bravery. Captain Alexander, Governor D'Urban's aide-de-camp, wrote: 'If one of them (Xhosa) was surrounded by a hundred foes, at first he would crouch to conceal himself like a cat; but if concealment was no longer possible, he would stand up like a man and throw his last assegaai.'[40] On one occasion at least this concern with bravery cost the Xhosa dearly. When the Ndlambe decided to enter the *War of the Axe,* Mxhamli challenged Mhala to cross an open plain by day. Mhala refused. 'I am the wildcat (Mbodla — Mhala's praise-name),' he said, 'a thing that walks by night.'[41] Mxhamli called Mhala a coward, but the wildcat was right. The British cavalry caught the Ndlambe in broad daylight and about 500 Xhosa perished on the plains of the Gwangqa.

Many features of precolonial Xhosa warfare were shared with other Nguni peoples, including several usually attributed to Zulu innovation, such as the short stabbing-spear and the conventional battle strategy (Xhosa, centre plus wings, equals Zulu, chest plus horns). The Zulu elaborated these strategies and tactics to a far higher degree than the Xhosa ever did, but the Xhosa had a distinct military genius of their own which should not be under-estimated. This consisted not in refining traditional fighting methods but in knowing when to abandon them.

2. THE FIRST FIVE FRONTIER WARS (1779 – 1819)

Very few substantial accounts survive of the military operations undertaken during the *First* (1779 – 1781), *Second* (1793) and *Third* (1799 – 1802) *Frontier Wars.*[42] Enough remains however to outline those features of these early conflicts which seem significant in the light of subsequent developments.

It may be remembered that the *First Frontier War* began when some of the minor chiefs crossed the Fish River in retreat from Rharhabe and Ndlambe.[43] The Boer commandos, spurred on by the prospect of booty, carried all before them. The Xhosa burnt farmhouses and abducted Khoi servants, but had no real answer to the power of the gun or the mobility of the horse. It seems unlikely that they were ever conclusively expelled across the Fish, but if they were they soon returned. It says little for Boer military strength that the minor chiefs feared Ndlambe more than they feared the Europeans. They were becoming less fearful of firearms, and when Barend Lindeque unwisely joined Ndlambe in his attack on Tshaka and Langa the latter exacted a bloody revenge on the Colony. They did not stand and fight, however, and, retreating a little too far in the face of Maynier's weak commando, they were shattered by Ndlambe's forces *(Second Frontier War).*[44] *The* Boers were lucky to patch up a peace and once again the Xhosa settled down west of the Fish.

Their hold on the disputed area was further strengthened as a result of the *Third Frontier War.*[45] In 1799 the new British administration tried to nudge Chungwa out of the Zuurveld. The Gqunukhwebe chief was joined by his fellow-Xhosa and rebellious Khoi. The Boers could not face men mounted and armed like themselves. They were 'terrified at even a single shot from a Hottentot'.[46] The Boers had been starved of gunpowder as the result of an unsuccessful republican insurrection, and when a combined force of Xhosa and Khoi defeated a commando twice its size, they took flight.[47] Apart from General Vandeleur's besieged encampment at Algoa Bay, not a single European remained east of the Gamtoos. The Xhosa and Khoi penetrated into the Tsitsikamma forest, throwing the district of Swellendam into confusion. Governor Dundas was pleased to conclude a peace which implicitly recognised Chungwa's right to reside west of the Fish. In 1802 the Boer hero, Tjaart van der Walt, organised a 'General Commando' but he was soon shot dead and Dundas concluded another peace on similar terms.

As early as the *First Frontier War,* it is possible to see the Xhosa developing those tactical skills which they were to perfect in the weary years of warfare which lay ahead. Most important of these was the discovery of natural cover — hills, rocks, kloofs, woods, bushes and the darkness of the night — as a protection against overwhelming force. Xhosa occasionally concealed themselves in the bush during their internal wars,[48] but, as we have seen, the predominant mode of fighting was the formal battle. As early as the *First Frontier War* we find that the Xhosa made little open resistance to the commandos sent against them but they 'came out of the woods in great numbers, and called out to us, that as soon as it was dark, they would retake their cattle'.[49] On another occasion Commandant van Jaarsveld lamented that 'from the number of the forests (he) could kill very few'.[50] Maynier, who led the 1793 commando, concluded that it was impossible to drive the Xhosa out because of 'the immense woods and dens which offer a safe retreat to them'.[51] In 1799, General Vandeleur found it impossible to catch up with the Xhosa and warned his dragoons that they should not risk themselves 'too near the bushes, but rather, by retreating to seduce (the Xhosa) into the plain'.[52] Nor were the Xhosa entirely dependent on the natural features of the country. On one occasion in the *Third Frontier War,* they blocked up the road with trees and bushes and while the Boers were trying to remove these, the Xhosa crept up behind and cut them off.[53] Nothing is known about how the 150 Xhosa and Khoi defeated the 300 Boers at the Sundays River, except that the attack was made at night. Bushes and kloofs were also used to conceal the Xhosa cattle, the warriors subsisting mainly on game.[54] Other features characteristic of later Xhosa warfare which appeared early on were the use of spies and signal fires, and the tactic of harassing the enemy's rearguard.[55]

The most successful offensives were not directed against the enemy's troops but against his homes. Like the Xhosa, the Boer commandos were a mobilised citizenry. They were reluctant to spend too long chasing fruitlessly after inaccessible Xhosa when their own houses and stock-kraals were exposed to attack. The more secure Boers nearer Cape Town were at all times noticeably reluctant to lend a helping hand and so the Boers, enthusiastic pillagers though they were, were unable to sustain long campaigns. The Xhosa were also successful in neutralising the clumsy Boer musket with the short stabbing-spear. In 1781 Van Jaarsveld reported that the Xhosa tried to get close in among his men so that they could not shoot for fear of hitting each other.[56] In 1799 Barrow observed that the Xhosa had 'perceived how much greater advantage was a short weapon to a muscular arm, than a long missile spear, whose slow motion through the air makes it easily to be avoided'.[57] A party of 20 British soldiers lost 16 of their number when the Xhosa jumped on them from behind the bushes and attacked them with the blades of their spears. But even with the assistance of the Khoi, the Xhosa were helpless against a properly fortified post as they found when they attacked Vandeleur's isolated post at Algoa Bay.[58]

It is hard to quantify bloodshed but straight from their inception, the *Frontier Wars* appear to have been appreciably more savage than the internal wars of the Xhosa among themselves. This is well symbolised by Van Jaarsveld's celebrated tobacco trick in the *First Frontier War,* when he shot down a group of Xhosa as they were scrambling for some pieces of tobacco he had thrown to them.[59] Even Professor van der Merwe is prepared to admit Boer atrocities, and these appear to have included some against women.[60] The Xhosa burnt many Boer houses and they did not always spare the women either.[61] And yet, because the primary object of both sets of fighters was the acquisition of cattle and servants,[62] the damage was minimised. There are occasional indications that the Xhosa did not perceive the Frontier Wars as being totally different from the others in which they fought. On one occasion, for instance, they released a captured party of Boers after coming to an agreement 'that the boors should return home and not further molest them; upon which the Caffres restored to them their arms and bid them depart.'[63] The Boers, for their part, took prisoners and at least considered returning part of the cattle they captured.[64] Occasionally a grim note was sounded, as when the Colonial Landdrosts warned the Xhosa chiefs that if they did not leave the Colony 'they should expect to be shot dead with all their people'.[65] But exaggerated threats were all a part of war, and the Xhosa, flushed as they were with victory, could hardly have believed that the whites were truly serious.

Thus the *Fourth Frontier War* (1811 – 1812) must have come as an enormous shock. For the first time, the Colonial government (now securely in British hands) was prepared to commit sufficient force to systematically sweep the Xhosa from the Zuurveld. Lieutenant-Colonel Graham made sure that his rear was well secured by a chain of posts and guarded by parties of armed Colonists. Four columns of Boers and regular troops pushed forward ready to expel the Xhosa with 'Mildness, Explanation and Persuasion ... in the First Instance' and 'forcible measures' in the last. 'You will be pleased to give orders to the officers and detachment under your immediate command,' wrote Graham to a subordinate, 'to fire on [any Xhosa not retreating with the main body] at all times during the night, and if they don't submit and deliver up their arms during the day also.'[66] Pathetically, Ndlambe and Chungwa tried to maintain the old heroism in the face of this cold-blooded professionalism. Their forces were mustered, they drew up in battle array, some wore crane feathers, Ndlambe exhorted his men. 'This country is mine! (stamping his feet violently on the ground), I won it in war, and shall maintain it.'[67] But when the British troops opened fire, the warriors were forced to retreat to the woods. There they lay on the defensive till the Colonial forces hounded them out bush by bush.

The *Fifth Frontier War* (1818 — 1819), which was partly a result of such policies, began as a punitive expedition against Ndlambe.[68] Unable to catch the old chief, Colonel Brereton whipped off some 23 000 Xhosa cattle and returned home thinking that that was the end of the affair. It was only the beginning. The Xhosa invaded the Colony, catching the authorities completely unprepared; indeed it took them some time to realise that Ndlambe regarded Brereton's commando as an unprovoked act of war. The Xhosa concentrated their attention on capturing Colonial cattle and attacking small patrols. The fate of a certain Captain Gethin indicates the sort of tactics they used.[69] Gethin's patrol fired at what they thought was a lone Xhosa, and before they could reload the main body of Xhosa surged out of a wood, killing Gethin and two companions. The Xhosa had also learned that firearms did not work so well in wet weather and made good use of the opportunities thus afforded.[70] The Colonists were helpless against so widely dispersed and numerous an enemy, but by this time they were too well entrenched to flee, as they had done in 1799. After about two months the Xhosa withdrew and the Colonial authorities, still slowly gathering their forces, thought they had retired to enjoy their plunder. Far from it. Nxele was planning an attack on the eye of the octopus, Grahamstown itself.

The *Battle of Grahamstown* (1819) was the only setpiece battle fought between the British and the Xhosa before 1850.[71] It was the only occasion on which the Xhosa attempted to adapt their traditional battle order to the exigencies of the new warfare. That the campaign was to some extent conceived in traditional terms is evident from the exhortations of Nxele to his army and from the fact that the army was accompanied by women and children. Nxele's promise to the army that he had doctored them against bullets has to be seen in this context. His battle plan, however, rested on more secure foundations. Nxele had spent a great deal of time in Grahamstown before the war, chatting to the officers and observing the fortifications.

Even before the battle began he succeeded in tempting part of the garrison out of town by means of a diversion. The Xhosa army, six thousand strong and divided into three columns, drew up behind a hill overlooking the town to wait for nightfall and make its final dispositions. However, the garrison came to know of its presence and when the British commander was seen observing its position, Nxele decided to attack immediately. In doing so he lost the essential cover of darkness and gained nothing in the way of surprise: the troops were waiting for him. They were drawn up in a hollow square and their artillery was ready. The Xhosa charged down the hill, two columns making for the square, the third moving out towards the barracks in the flanking movement so characteristic of traditional warfare. As they ran they broke up into little knots of warriors, rendering the cannon initially ineffective. They got within thirty yards or so of the soldiers, their spears broken off for close combat, but they could not sustain their momentum in the face of the steady fire of disciplined troops. Khoi marksmen picked off the Xhosa leaders, but what really halted the charge was the nature of the weapons which they faced.

> While kneeling and ducking in front of the troops, the right hand was always raised with the assegaai but their fear of looking at the fire prevented them from throwing as often or as correctly as they otherwise would have done. On seeing a flash they immediately placed the left arm with the kaross (bullock's hide) before their eyes.[72]

The artillery began to take effect too, and when the soldiers charged the Xhosa fled. The wounded crawled away, trying to stop up the bullet holes with tufts of grass, and many of them died in the waters of the Kowie ditch, which Grahamstown Xhosa still call *egazini* — 'the place of blood'.

Thus checked, the Xhosa fled towards the Kei.[73] They made no attempt to stand, even in the Fish River bush. When the troops were finally ready to take the offensive some two months later the mounted commandos found little to shoot but women and children.[74] The regular forces toiling behind them found it difficult to drag the cannon across the rivers and difficult to keep their powder dry. This was the shape of things to come. When Nxele surrendered himself, a sacrifice for his people, the Colonial authorities gladly called off the war, and the soldiers returned home.

The first five *Frontier Wars* were far more restricted in scope and duration than those which followed. They were sporadic actions punctuated by lengthy intervals rather than sustained and continuous campaigns. Even the War of 1811 — 1812, the most concentrated of the five, was little more than two sharp movements: two months to chase the Ndlambe and Gqunukhwebe across the Fish and a little less than that to rout the imiDange out of the Zuurberg. Moreover, the wars involved only a small proportion of the total population. Ndlambe entered only towards the end of the *Third* and Ngqika and the Gcaleka were not directly affected at all. Since Ngqika held the mountains, the wars were fought largely in the flatter and more open territory where the Ndlambe and Gqunukhwebe lived.

Xhosa victories in the *Second* and *Third* Wars kept the land question in abeyance, and even the loss of the Zuurveld produced more political than economic inconvenience. Many of Ndlambe's followers settled down under Ngqika or Hintsa,[75] and the normal processes of mutual aid must have done the rest. The point at which deprivation of territory became truly acute was reached only when Somerset appropriated the Ceded Territory from Ngqika in 1819. This ultimately produced the long and bitter wars of 1834 − 1835 and 1846 − 1847: *That of Hintsa* and *That of the Axe*.

3. *THAT OF HINTSA*

When Lord Charles Somerset forced Ngqika to cede the land between the Fish and the Keiskamma, he lit a long fuse which finally exploded in the War of 1834 − 1835, a war which burst beyond all previous constraints and charted new depths of slaughter and destruction. It involved all the Xhosa, with a few minor exceptions, and it raged unabated for a full nine months.[76] Militarily, it was noteworthy above all for the whole new assemblage of tactics which the Xhosa had developed to counter the type of warfare which the Europeans had introduced in 1811 − 1812 and 1818 − 1819. The *Battle of Grahamstown* demonstrated once and for all the futility of continuing with even a modified form of traditional warfare. The Xhosa now systematically employed the range of tactics derived from cattle-raiding and the early wars, but greatly refined and elaborated them.

The *Sixth Frontier War* began in December 1834, when the Xhosa swept into the Colony forcing the settlers to abandon virtually the whole country east of Algoa Bay, saving only the towns of Grahamstown and Fort Beaufort. Farmhouses were besieged and burnt, colonists were killed, and thousands of cattle were carried off. In February 1835, the Colonial forces went over to the offensive. After clearing the Xhosa out of the woody valleys of the Fish and the Kowie Rivers, Colonel Harry Smith made a preliminary attempt to clear Maqoma and Tyhali out of the Amatola mountains. When he realised that this would not be easy, he embarked on the more spectacular campaign across the Kei which led to the tragic death of Hintsa. On his return (May 1835), the war entered its final phase, that of attrition. D'Urban declared the territory west of the Kei to be the Province of Queen Adelaide but failed to make any headway against its inhabitants. The chiefs made peace — they never surrendered — on terms far better than D'Urban wanted to give them, and even then only because they were deceived into doing so.

The war was exceptional in that it was deliberately commenced by the Xhosa. After obtaining Hintsa's sanction, Maqoma and Tyhali co-ordinated their actions with the other Xhosa chiefs. They confidently expected the assistance of the Khoi settlers of the Kat River and the Khoi garrisons of Forts Beaufort and Willshire. And even though the ordinary Xhosa thought that they were going to sweep the English into the sea,[77] the chiefs' aims were more precise and realistic. These were embodied in a remarkable statement dictated by Tyhali just two weeks after the invasion, when the Xhosa were carrying all before them and the fall of Grahamstown was still a very real possibility.[78] The statement was very much in the customary tradition of declaring war and contained fourteen specific counts of grievance. The Xhosa demanded the return of all land east of the Fish River and full compensation for the wounding of Xhoxho. Any cattle captured in the Colony were to be regarded as legitimate payment for the wrongs they had suffered. The war would stop as soon as the negotiations began. Tyhali concluded: 'Today is now peace and they all wish to live in peace with the English; they shall now hold up from fighting until they obtain an answer.'

The Xhosa aim, therefore, was not war to the death, but a limited war undertaken to force a negotiated settlement of their grievances. Although they certainly underestimated the prejudice which prevented the settlers even considering submission to 'savages',[79] their military expectations were not unduly inflated. They hoped to take Grahamstown by night: Nqeno was to lead off with a diversion, while the united forces poured in from all other sides. They knew they could never hold the town, but they thought they could destroy it.[80] However, the Khoi garrisons did not rise as expected, and Grahamstown was left alone. For the rest, the Xhosa waged what was even then called a guerrilla war.[81] They had meditated on the defeat of 1819 and had braced themselves for another war during the great scare of 1829. As early as 1830, the basic tactics of the *Sixth Frontier War* were clearly conceived. The Xhosa told missionary Young that 'they shall not all come in a body as before but they will divide themselves into separate parties, and each party must have their own route appointed them, and in this way they say they can avoid our troops, and come upon the settlers and the Boers before they can have time to collect themselves together.'[82] And so they did. The Colony found itself faced not with a single enemy to be shattered by overwhelming firepower, but with innumerable small detachments which it was unable to pin down.

On the offensive, the Xhosa adopted a suitable variant of their staple outflanking tactic. Instead of facing the enemy army, they shadowed it until a small party became detached from the main body. Then, deploying their forces with amazing speed, they encircled and cut it off. Consider the following action in the Fish River bush, involving a Colonial patrol of 20 men:

> Less than half an hour from (the patrol's) first appearance, the enemy was seen issuing in considerable force from all the paths and defiles on the opposite side of the river, and, descending rapidly from the heights, began to cross the river at various points. The number at this moment, in sight, might amount from one thousand to fifteen hundred... From the moment that the enemy first issued from the bush until they all but succeeded in hemming in the party occupied a space of only ten minutes. Captain Harries ... withdrew the remainder of his men from the camp. They had to make their way with considerable difficulty through bodies of the enemy, who were fast closing in, under cover of a dry ravine, lined with detaching clumps of bush.[83]

Eight soldiers were killed before the patrol reached base. There were other even more successful ambushes which left no survivors to give full descriptions. Such was the case with Baillie's party, thirty men strong, who were trapped in the Amatola and killed when their ammunition ran out. 'You are like a mouse in a calabash,' shouted the Xhosa to one such Colonial detachment, 'you have got into it, but you cannot get out.'[84] Since the enemy were wary of such situations, the Xhosa introduced the further refinement of the decoy. Typically, a few captured cattle appearing to be strays would be seen on the brow of a hill.[85] A small patrol would come out after it, and find itself surrounded. At the height of the Xhosa offensive, many cattle were not driven away at all but deliberately kept near the farms while their captors hid in the bush.[86] On other occasions, small parties of Xhosa would themselves act as bait to draw the enemy into a trap. Taunts and insults were an important part of the baiting. Goldswain recorded the Xhosa shouting to his patrol 'to cum up and they wad fight with us', while T.H. Bowker wrote that the Xhosa 'are in high spirits and call to the boers to come out and "fight in the dark" — call them "old maids", cowards etc: they call themselves "men" and keep crying to each other, "drive on my cows".'[87]

When on the defensive, the Ngqika were able to fall back into their own impregnable fortress, the Amatola mountains, described by the *Grahams Town Journal* with the practised eye of an enemy:

> It is in fact one of nature's labyrinths. Its sides are bold and precipitous; it is split and intersected by ravines; it is broken by masses of rock, and it is clothed with noble forest trees ... altitude is considerable and they are thickly belted, and in some parts covered with thick bush. Masses of craggy rock here and there rise perpendicularly amidst these thickets, and in other parts the sides of the mountain are deeply scored by kloofs, or rocky gullies covered by rank vegetation.[88]

Hide cloak wrapped tightly about him, hide shoes protecting his feet, the Xhosa warrior sped lightly through rocks and bushes along paths invisible to the British soldier. Driving their cattle into the innermost recesses of the Amatola, the children of Ngqika held the mountains against all comers for the duration of the war. They appeared on the summits of the hills, they staged ambushes in the steep defiles, they hung onto the enemy's rearguard with unbelievable tenacity. They fought with guns if they had them, but more often with spears, and sometimes even with stones and wooden spades.[89] In the more open country near the coast, the Ndlambe shielded themselves behind herds of cattle which they drove down upon the enemy and his horses and his wagons.[90] In the *War of the Axe,* the Gqunukhwebe showed what could be done with the river beds of lower Albany. Using the banks as parapets, they exposed only their heads while their enemies' entire bodies were visible. They were able to hide for long periods under water, their nostrils emerging under cover of the reeds at the river's edge. Otherwise, they hid in trees, in antbear holes, and in caves though these last had the disadvantage of being completely indefensible once discovered.[91] In their ventures inside Colonial territory, the Xhosa forces were guided and assisted by those who had worked there as labourers and servants.[92]

When the Xhosa gathered for an attack, the chiefs directed the onslaught. Thus Mhala, Nqeno, Gasela and Bhotomane were all present at the Ndlambe attack on Fort Wellington in 1835.[93] In 1846, Dilima, Phato's Great Son, led the assault on Fort Peddie and Maqoma that on the Mankazana post.[94] Mhala narrowly escaped death on the Gwangqa; his brothers Mxhamli and Zethu ('Heart of Stone') were killed.[95] As in precolonial times, the chiefs remained at the rear. Dilima directed the attack on Fort Peddie mounted on a horse – the defenders could see him sending his messengers to the different detachments as the battle proceeded.[96] Maqoma watched his men from a hill overlooking the post.[97] They still urged the men forward. The Ndlambe chiefs beat them on with sticks and Maqoma threatened them with death.[98]

But important as their role remained in these formal actions, the chiefs played little part in the guerrilla war. They did not cross into the Colony, although their sons did, and they did not face the invasion of their strongholds. Indeed, there was necessarily little that the chiefs could do in guerrilla actions. One Xhosa-speaking European remarked that the Xhosa 'fight only when they please and obey orders only when they like them'.[99] Or as Hintsa's son Manxiwa told George Cory many years later, 'We do as we like in war. Orders are given, but when the battle has begun each man does as he likes – according to his madness.'[100]

Nevertheless, even during the guerrilla phases, the small Xhosa bands were not entirely isolated from each other. They knew the movements of their fellows and their enemies through a network of spies and signals. The work of the Xhosa spy *(intlola)* involved not only reconnaissance, but also communication and even assassination. Spies were specially doctored and some, who rode horses and spoke Afrikaans, tried to pass themselves off as Khoi.[101] Many of them were women, who took advantage of the immunity granted by both sides.[102] It was close observation which alerted the different Xhosa bands when a small Colonial party split off from the rest. For communication further afield, the Xhosa made use of signal fires.[103] When the enemy troops moved forward, the spies watching would light a fire. The Xhosa further off would answer the signallers with a fire of their own, which would itself act as a signal to Xhosa at an even greater distance. There were no smoke signals as such, but the different Xhosa groups were nevertheless able to interpret each other's intentions. 'Whenever our patrols appeared,' wrote Captain Alexander, 'the usual Kafir signals were made on the most commanding points, which enabled them, with the knowledge they had of the different paths intersecting the forests with which this part of the country abounds, to meet at any particular point.'[104]

Inasmuch as the Colonial authorities had any military answer to the guerrilla tactics of the Xhosa, it was the recruitment of auxiliaries with the same skills. The British forces were admittedly useless in the bush,[105] and the much-vaunted Boers were little better. 'I have always believed what was said of Boers as to their courage,' wrote one soldier, 'but now I know better. There is I assure you nothing equal to the Tots (Khoi) they will run in the direction a shot is fired in spite of precipices thorny bushes or in fact anything.'[106] From the middle of 1835, the authorities were also able to call on the Mfengu for assistance.[107] Neither trained in nor trusted with firearms, they were allocated the leading roles on the offensive and the most exposed ones on the defensive. The whites found it difficult to distinguish between Xhosa and Mfengu, and on at least one appalling occasion a detachment of fleeing Boers nearly wiped out their Mfengu allies who were standing their ground.[108] Ironically, it was left to a Xhosa enemy to deliver an appropriate judgement on the significance of the Mfengu contribution: 'They did not think much of [the cannons] as they killed so few, while the Fingoes killed so many.'[109]

4.   *THAT OF THE AXE*

The *Seventh Frontier War* began with a pre-emptive strike by the Colony on the Xhosa.[110] Maitland and Hare thought that a quick and powerful blow would settle Sandile and the so-called war party, but the gerontocratic warriors proved themselves incapable of delivering it. Heavily encumbered with wagons, artillery and supplies, the very first British column to enter the Amatola was overwhelmed and its wagon train captured. Phato and his well-armed Gqunukhwebe entered the war on hearing the news, and the initiative passed entirely to the Xhosa. 'I have to relate more of what the Kafirs have done, and of the preparations which are being made on our part to oppose them, than of actual operations carried on against them' wrote Maitland glumly.[111] The Ngqika and Mapassa's Thembu penetrated the district of Graaff-Reinet and settled down in the Addo bush at the headwaters of the Sundays River. The Gqunukhwebe stormed through the long-lost territory of their ancestor Chungwa and threatened Port Elizabeth. Another wagon train fell on the road to Fort Peddie, and the cautious Mhala finally committed himself to the struggle. Maitland attempted to carry the war into Xhosa territory by landing troops at Waterloo Bay, but this timid counter-offensive stuck in the mud with his pack-oxen.[112]

The tide began to turn at the end of May when the Ndlambe were crushed at the *Battle of the Gwangqa* after they had disregarded the wildcat's advice to walk by night.[113] Some five hundred Xhosa perished when the cavalry charged down the open plain. Stockenstrom, now a baronet, led an advance into Sarhili's country and wisely forestalled a repeat of Hintsa's tragedy by

C. Michell. *Departure of the Fingoes.*

TWO KINDS OF WARFARE

F. l'ons. *Chiefs and Councillors overlooking British troops.* Set in the Amatola mountains, this picture gives a clear indication of the terrain on which the Xhosa preferred to fight.

Sir H. Darell. *Charge on the Gwanga, Cape of Good Hope, on 8 June 1846.* Caught on the open plain, the Xhosa were completely unable to defend themselves against cavalry. Nearly 500 perished.

tacitly permitting the king to give refuge to the Rharhabe and the cattle they had captured.[114] But despite these successes, the Colonial army was on the brink of disintegration. Stockenstrom resigned when Maitland disapproved of his peace with Sarhili, and the Boer volunteers, unwilling to serve under anybody else, went home with him. With notable exceptions, the English settlers refused to do anything beyond guarding their property and robbing the commissariat.[115] The Khoi soldiers were conscripts and did not have such options, but they were openly mutinous at the Government's failure to provide adequately for their wives and children at home.[116] The problems faced by the British regular troops are well illustrated by Colonel Somerset's experiences during his disastrous campaign against Phato in January 1847.[117] To begin with, it rained for ten out of thirteen days. Then dysentery broke out among the soldiers and glanders among the horses. The troops never managed to engage the Xhosa at all, except for one small patrol of seven men who fell for a cattle decoy and were killed when their amunition ran out. Most of their time was spent pursuing cattle which they sighted but could not catch. Eventually, they seized 9 000 head from the neutral Gcaleka and returned home, but not before losing another three men drowned in the crossing of the Kei.

By September 1846, the British troops were forced to withdraw even from Waterloo Bay. The Xhosa had burnt all the grass, and the horses and oxen were dying of starvation. After four months of war, the *Grahams Town Journal* was compelled to report that that there was not a single Colonial soldier in Xhosaland proper, east of the Keiskamma River.[118] And yet it was precisely at this time, precisely when the Colonial army was virtually prostrated and utterly unable to prosecute the war any further, that the Xhosa sent in to ask for terms of peace. They were told that only an unconditional surrender would be accepted. They were told that the Colonial Government intended to annex all the land west of the Kei. But they gave themselves up anyway, Maqoma on 26 October and Sandile, after a prolonged truce, on 17 December. Indeed, this was the second time that the Xhosa had pulled back from the brink of victory. The first had been towards the end of May. Even before the *Battle of the Gwangqa,* at the very time that Mhala was entering the war and the Colony lay helpless before them, the Ngqika chiefs lit signal fires on the peaks of the Amatola and called their advance parties home.[119] Why?

It should not be forgotten that the *War of the Axe* was a war which had been forced on the Xhosa by the greed and prejudice of the settlers and their press, a war which they had striven desperately to avoid. When Hare's soldiers were poised to invade their country, they swore they would not fire the first shot.[120] The men who captured the wagon train were hardly as responsible for the war as the men who had sent the wagons and the cannons and the soldiers into Xhosaland in the first place. From the beginning of the war, Sandile never ceased to send in messages of peace.[121] And when the chiefs gave themselves up towards the end of 1846, they viewed it as a unilateral peace rather than as a defeat. The Xhosa did not surrender, they simply refused to fight. Sandile's attitude is characteristic: 'As many people have been killed on both sides, we had better, he says, drop the war, and cultivate the fields. He says he will return to his place and cultivate his gardens; the soldiers may come and kill him, but he will not fight any more.'[122] The chiefs told their people that the peace was one of victory, 'that the British troops were beaten and had given up the contest . . . that all was now peace, and that the Kafirs were to return and cultivate their gardens as before.'[123]

The Xhosa decided to make peace when they were still in a militarily strong position but the emphasis on the cultivation of gardens gave them away. Quite simply, they were starving. Their cattle had been driven to places of safety even before the war began and the Colonial forces had deliberately destroyed their stores of corn. Governor Maitland, who had proved himself as pathetically incompetent in war as he had been in peace, was not slow to claim the credit. He informed the Colonial Secretary,

> Their crops are absolutely in our power. We have captured some of their cattle and more have perished through the fugitive life which they have been compelled to lead, in a time too of severe drought. Their hordes of corn . . . have been taken by our coloured patrols; and the sowing season has been passing by unemployed owing to the scouring of the country by the troops. Great scarcity among them has been the result; many of them are much wasted, and the women have extremely suffered the horrors of famine.[124]

Indeed, the soldiers were forced to post guards to prevent starving women rushing into the very camps to carry away the army's discarded carrion and offal.[125] Moreover, the Xhosa faced not only the immediate problem of the destruction of their existing food supplies, they also faced the prospect of famine in the coming year. In war as in peace, the rhythm of Xhosa life was dictated by the seasons.[126] Better to fight in summer when the harvest was in and the nights were warm than in the cold and hungry winter months. The Xhosa offensive of 1834 took place in the December of a particularly fruitful year. The Colonial offensive of 1846 began in April after a lean and drought-stricken year. Sowing should have started in June, and September was the last month from which a good harvest could reasonably be expected. And so the Xhosa laid down their arms in September 1846 as they had done eleven years previously in September 1835.

On close examination, it is clear that victory in the *War of the Axe* turned almost exclusively on the question of provisions and supplies. The Xhosa themselves recognised this well before the war when they decided to make the great lumbering baggage wagons of the enemy their principal targets.[127] 'Pack oxen stuck in the mud!' became a metaphor for an enemy well and truly trapped. They even threatened the settlers that they would make them eat their own dogs.[128] The capture of that first wagon train at Burns Hill in the very commencement of the war fully vindicated the policy.[129] The convoy consisted of 125 heavily laden wagons, each drawn by 24 oxen. There was an advance guard and a rear guard but no defence along the line of wagons as they toiled up the steep slopes of the Amatola. The Xhosa waited until half the wagons were past and then struck the middle of the train, driving off as many oxen as they could and killing the rest. The troops up front could not turn the foremost wagons around, and were themselves forced into the bush by the need to by-pass the stranded wagons in the middle. Among the dead was Captain Bambrick, 7th Dragoon Guards, whose skull was sent to Myeki, dreaded war-magician chief of the Mpondomise. All in all, it was a famous victory, and was repeated the following month in the bush approaching Fort Peddie.

When the Colonial forces entered their country, the Xhosa concentrated on the supplies rather than the soldiers. Vast tracts of country between the Keiskamma and the Kei turned black when the Xhosa fired the pasturage in an attempt to starve the draught oxen.[130] At night they prevented the tired soldiers from sleeping by firing long shots into the camps and setting the surrounding grass alight. Maitland testified to the efficacy of these tactics shortly before they drove him from Xhosaland: 'The cavalry was paralysed and the baggage scarcely able to crawl along, while the wily robbers were constantly eluding our grasp, doubling around us through the jungles, and inflicting on us petty annoyances and losses, trifling in detail, but harassing by repetition.'[131]

The Xhosa knew what they were doing. 'The white man is now tired', they said hopefully.[132] But all expectation was in vain. The Colonial authorities sourly envied the mobility and dexterity of the Xhosa 'who carry no commissariat',[133] but ultimately it was the clumsy and vulnerable wagons that ensured the victory of the Colonial army.[134] The Xhosa could outstay the

Boers, who were farmers like themselves and had families and herds of their own,[135] but not the badly led and ludicrously dressed *amajoni* ('Johnnies') who had no option but to fight on.

Behind the Colonial army stood the inexhaustible resources of the British Empire, which might dismiss its Governors and begrudge its expenses but which would not, in the last resort, allow itself to be defeated.[136] Towards the end of 1847 when Phato's men were eating their shields,[137] the *Grahams Town Journal* was able to note with satisfaction that 'everything is now in a state of preparedness for the expected resumption of hostilities. Immense supplies, both of munitions of war and food, have been quietly moved to convenient depots along the line.'[138] The Xhosa, on the other hand, operated under the most severe of logistical constraints. Glutted at the start on his chief's oxen, the Xhosa warrior became progressively hungrier as the days went on. He might carry with him a bag of honeycombs or dried maize kernels, but otherwise he was dependent on what he could find.[139] There was little time to milk, let alone roast, captured cattle, and this must have been one reason why Xhosa offensives came to an end after about a month in the Colony. When fighting on the defensive the Xhosa usually relied on their women, who remained in occupation of huts and gardens and carried provisions to the bushes at night. But when the Colonial forces systematically burnt their houses, destroyed their crops, dug up their grain pits and frightened off their women, they were helpless. The *War of the Axe* was won on the hearth, not on the battlefield.

Maitland was completely perplexed by the Xhosa policy of passive resistance. 'They will not go from the country which we require them to evacuate, nor will they fight for it. They will stay and sow and reap, and merely avoid us when we enter to eject them,' he reported.[140] The frontier press was even angrier. 'They do not admit they are a conquered people,' wrote the *Grahams Town Journal.*[141] Even worse from the settler point of view, they showed no sign of moving to make room for white farms.[142] Maitland, keen to salvage something of his tarnished reputation, was prepared to let the Xhosa off with a gesture of submission. They were required to register individually as British subjects and to give up their weapons.[143] The Xhosa swore the required oaths, gave up a few spears and fewer guns, and attempted to return to their normal occupations. As far as the Government was concerned they were annexed to the Crown; as for themselves, they pretended nothing much had changed. Phato, Toyise and some other Ndlambe chiefs never submitted, doubling backwards and forwards across the Kei faster than the troops sent after them.

But this open resistance did not worry the Colonial Government nearly as much as the far more numerous Ngqika, who continued to insist that they were at peace without admitting that they had ever been defeated. Sandile refused to reopen discussions with the new Governor, Pottinger, saying that he had already made peace and there was nothing more to talk about. Asked if he would submit to a new land allocation, he replied that 'his possessions were too narrow before the war, and would not admit of being more circumscribed now'.[144] Pottinger did nothing until he had received all the reinforcements and supplies that he needed and then he seized on the theft of a few goats to make an example of Sandile. In vain did Sandile tell his people 'not to listen to any messages from the Colony, but to proceed with their ordinary occupations'.[145] Pottinger had learnt from Maitland's mistakes and, ignoring the Xhosa themselves, his troops made straight for the houses, the cattle, and the grain-pits. Four-square behind him, the settler press thundered:

> Let the war be made against Kafir huts and gardens. Let all these be burned down and destroyed. Let there be no ploughing, sowing or reaping. Or, if you cannot conveniently, or without bloodshed prevent the cultivation of the ground, take care to destroy the enemy's crops before they are ripe, and shoot all who resist. Shoot their cattle too wherever you see any. Tell them that the time has come for the white man to show his mastery over them.[146]

Surgeon Hall, who normally had little sympathy for the Xhosa, was moved to comment: 'This system of cattle-stealing and hut-burning is a disgrace to the age we live in . . . Seymour has a weakness for burning Kafir huts. In the course of these expeditions of destruction the miserable women and children have been found dying of starvation and it is stated that the 91st Patrol the other day shot some of these wretched objects to put them out of their misery!'[147] Sandile made the mistake of trusting to the honour of a British officer and was seized during negotiations, like Hintsa before him.[148] Without any further prospect of help from a fellow chief, Phato surrendered after 18 months of determined resistance.

One final aspect of the *War of the Axe* remains to be noted.[149] It was the first war in which the Xhosa made extensive use of firearms. As we have seen, the Xhosa were always ready to adapt their methods of warfare, and this was true of armaments as well as tactics. They abandoned the use of the shield as soon as they found it hindered mobility and was useless against bullets.[150] They soon became excellent horsemen, and if they never fought on horseback, it was because horses were a hindrance rather than a help in their bushy mountain fastnesses. They said, 'you cannot fight on horseback, and if you have to run away, the horses are in the way.'[151] However, the potential value of firearms was perceived right from the beginning. The major problems, of course, were supply and training. In the early wars, they were forced to rely on Khoi deserters but by 1819 the capture of arms and ammunition had become a principal part of their strategy.[152] In 1835, the Xhosa were already using firearms in significant numbers and by 1846 they had become a central feature of Xhosa warfare. Whereas the Zulus' obstinate adherence to their conventional tactics severely limited the utility of those firearms which they did possess, the Xhosa, fighting as they did from among bushes and rocks, maximised the effect of old-fashioned weapons which would have been completely useless in the open.[153] It was bullets rather than spears which brought down the wagon train at Burns Hill.

But well as they utilised the firearms available, these were still woefully deficient in quantity and quality. Despite occasional help from politically motivated Boers such as Coenraad de Buys and Louis Tregardt the clandestine arms trade was essentially a settler business. After 1835 small-time smugglers such as Mahoney and Brown[154] gave way to more substantial suppliers. It was common knowledge in Grahamstown that a good percentage of its inhabitants from wealthy merchants like James Howse and Mark Norden to butchers like Frederick Lee were engaged in the trade.[155] Many of them were land-grabbing *Grahams Town Journal*-lining men, or as Governor Napier aptly observed, 'the very persons most clamorous against the Kafir nation.'[156] The returns were lucrative. A gun costing 10 rix dollars (about 15 shillings) could fetch an ox worth five times as much; 30 bullets might buy a cow.[157] Perhaps one reason why the authorities never cracked down on the trade was that it never remotely jeopardised Colonial superiority. Colonial writers all agreed that Xhosa fire was relatively ineffective: they fired from the hip not the shoulder, they used too much powder, they did not take proper aim, they missed from fifty yards, and so on.[158] Such difficulties were largely the consequence of supply problems. Arms and ammunition were far too costly to be wasted on hunting, never mind on practice.[159]

In time of war supply problems became even more acute. The Xhosa were forced to improvise bullets from whatever came to hand: zinc or pewter stripped from the roofs of raided farmhouses, spoons, chain links, the legs of iron pots.[160] A raid on the Lovedale Mission Press produced balls made from the printing type and wadding made from the Bibles.[161] Even worse than the problem of obtaining firearms was the quality of the goods supplied. Not even the most hardened European smuggler would have sold the Xhosa anything better than the so-called Kaffir trade guns, which were specially imported for the purpose.[162] As one informant put it, 'They get the new fashion, they sell us the old fashion.'[163] By 1846, the new fashion consisted of the double-barrelled carbine introduced probably in the early 1830s and the percussion cap lock, introduced between 1838 and 1842.[164] These innovations increased the rate of fire by something like three to one, and reduced the possibilities of a misfire from 40 percent to four percent.[165] The Xhosa were left with the old single-barrel flintlock muskets, and singularly poor ones at that. When, on occasion, one of these did successfully go off, it was only at the risk of the barrel blowing up in the user's face. The considerable recoil of these weapons was much increased by the coarse black-grained powder that was sold with them. The results of such a grotesque mismatch of technology can easily be imagined. Colonel Bisset described one incident in a well-known passage:

> One fellow . . . stood not ten yards from me to reload and I was doing the same on horseback, loading both barrels against his one, but watching for the time when he would prime, for I saw he had a flint-lock musket . . . the fellow put up his gun and snapped it in my face. I did not give him a second chance, for had it been *fine* powder the pan would have filled, and I should not have been here to tell the tale.[166]

Private Adams, who nearly died in a Xhosa ambush, thought they would have been better off using spears than their 'old flintguns'.[167] And even if Xhosa firearms had been a great deal better than they were, they would never have approached the capacity to solve their most critical military problem, that is, their total inability to capture a properly fortified military position. The *Grahams Town Journal* was not far wrong when it wrote that 'A [stone-walled] fortress like Fort Peddie is absolutely impregnable to any army not having artillery — that to fire upon it with musketry only would be of as little avail as shooting at Table Mountain with a pop-gun, and that 100 men might hold it against all Kafirland.'[168]

In spite of everything, the Xhosa managed to adopt tactics which largely neutralised the superior firepower of their enemies. First exposed to the gun in the 1770s when it was still a weapon of very limited effectiveness, the frontier Xhosa learned to cope both psychologically and tactically with the continuing improvements in weapons technology to the point where a bemused Governor Maitland attributed the Burns Hill disaster to the Xhosa's 'persevering courage in facing artillery'.[169] The Xhosa were defeated less by firearms than by the infinitely greater logistic resources of the Colony.

5. 'THE LAND HAS DIED.'

It was above all the women who suffered in the attrition of the frontier wars.[170] Both the Xhosa and the Colonists attempted to avoid harming the civil population although there were exceptions on both sides.[171] Xhosa women played a vital part in the war effort by providing their men with food and information.[172] They occasionally hid fugitives and ammunition, and they carried messages from the chiefs to the officers.[173] When the Colonial forces attacked Nqeno's Great Place in 1835, his daughter put on his leopard-skin robe and was severely wounded while drawing the fire away from her father.[174] But even though Xhosa women and children were rarely intentionally molested by the soldiers, the impersonal forces of hunger and exposure affected them more severely than the men since they were less capable of foraging for themselves. It is impossible to calculate how many women and children perished in this way.

Some sort of estimates exist for the number of men killed in the war of 1835. In the first fine flush of victory, D'Urban claimed 4 000 Xhosa dead to fewer than 100 on the Colonial side, and what is more, 'there have been taken from them also, besides the conquest and alienation of their country, about 60 000 head of cattle, almost all their goats, their habitations everywhere else destroyed, and their gardens and corn-fields laid waste,' he added triumphantly.[175] Later, sensing a hostile reaction, D'Urban's apologist, the Reverend W. Boyce, lowered the official estimate of the killed to 1 400.[176] Later still, William Southey, brother to the killer of Hintsa, produced a figure of less than 800 in a macabre letter headed 'How many Kaffirs have been killed?'[177] Southey seems to have been methodical but later correspondence demonstrated that his estimate of 107 killed at the *Battle of the Gwangqa* was far too low. One incalculable affecting the estimates was that the Xhosa carried away their wounded, often at great personal risk.[178] In the end, Southey raised his total for the *Gwangqa* to 471, more than four times his original number.[179] In the light of this, Boyce's second figure of 1 400 killed is probably the minimum possible estimate. When one considers that the Rharhabe population at the time was well under 100 000 and that civilian deaths were not taken into account, there can be little doubt that at least two percent of the total population died and that a figure of five percent is well within the bounds of possibility.

Mortality in the drought-stricken and prolonged *War of the Axe* must have been even higher. The *Gwangqa* alone claimed 500 victims. One reason for the high death rate was that few prisoners were taken on either side. As early as 1810, Alberti contrasted the exchange of prisoners which characterised traditional Nguni warfare with the frontier wars in which no Colonist would 'spare the life of a Kaffir whom they could reach with a bullet'.[180] This attitude did not change with the passage of time. Bisset commented that many of the settler volunteers, 'smarting from the ruin of hearths and homes . . . had no idea of taking prisoners'.[181] On the *Gwangqa,* at least 471 Xhosa were killed but only three prisoners taken. One of these was later shot in cold blood by the dragoon whom Bisset had deputed to take care of him.[182]

D'Urban's figure of 60 000 cattle captured seems enormous but it was only the tip of the iceberg of cattle actually lost by the Xhosa. Many were killed as provisions by the Colonial troops and by the Xhosa themselves. Even when — as in the *War of the Axe* — the Xhosa managed to drive their cattle to neutral territory, numberless hundreds, especially calves, died from exposure and from the disruption of their routine of rest and pasturage. Despite their nimbleness, many cattle slipped on the narrow ledges of the Amatola and plunged down the steep kloofs; others were killed by frantic goading, as their herders attempted to hurry them ahead of the advancing soldiers.[183] And even those cattle which were ultimately deposited across the Kei were not always returned by the neutrals who had taken care of them. The few Colonial cattle captured and retained after the war must have been poor compensation for losses such as these.

Their houses burnt, their crops destroyed, their cattle dead, many of the Xhosa who succeeded in surviving the war were utterly ruined. The network of mutual aid which normally carried individuals through bad times was sadly impaired, for most men found their neighbours as destitute as themselves. As a result, many Xhosa were forced to seek work in the Colony which had destroyed them. After the War of 1834 — 1835, Agent Stretch reported that, owing to the 'unprecedented distress at this moment existing from starvation', many Xhosa were entering the Colony to seek a livelihood, 'pass or no pass'.[184] One such Xhosa described his situation: 'He had lost his cattle in the war . . . They beg corn from Hintsa's country, and they eat herbs and roots.'[185]

When an even greater desolation followed the *War of the Axe,* perhaps half the total Ngqika population prepared to enter the Colony.[186] As we shall see, Sir Harry Smith was only too ready to receive them.

The defeat of the Xhosa in the long drawn-out Frontier Wars has often been ascribed to their internal divisions. This seems an undue exaggeration. The Xhosa king and the Gcaleka remained officially neutral but they helped the Rharhabe in the vital aspects of supply and refuge. The Gqunukhwebe chiefs defected in 1834 — 1835, but many of their men participated in the war regardless. In any case, the Xhosa never suffered from a shortage of manpower and those Gcaleka who did participate were helpless because of their inexperience of frontier warfare. Arguably, the only occasion on which Xhosa disunity had serious military effects was towards the end of 1847, when the other chiefs abandoned Sandile to Pottinger.[187] Moreover, inasmuch as a decentralised political leadership resulted in a decentralised army, it may have served the Xhosa better than the highly centralised Zulu monarchy with its large but conservative and inflexible army.

The squabbling and sometimes unprepossessing Xhosa chiefs might lack the heroic stature of a Shaka, a Dingane or a Cetshwayo. The capture of the Burns Hill wagon train might pale before the victory of Isandlhwana. The scattered and sporadic attacks of dispersed Xhosa war-bands might not capture the imagination to the same extent as the mass onrush of the Zulu army. And yet, it does not seem too much to say that the Xhosa knew something about frontier warfare which the Zulu never quite understood. The Zulu learned little from four defeats in 1839. They continued to think that the best way to deal with firearms was to keep on coming. Even those guns which they did possess were not fully exploited. The Xhosa through their long exposure to European methods of making war learned how to face firearms and how to use them to the best advantage. They adopted tactics which neutralised the massive technological superiority of their opponents, and if they were defeated in the end, it was not on the battlefield but on the home front. *Ilizwe lifile* — the land has died — is the Xhosa way of saying 'War has broken out'. In the Frontier Wars, the expression ceased to be a metaphor, and became no more than the literal truth.

10. The Beginning of the End

1. TWILIGHT

As this history has proceeded, so the balance of the narrative has increasingly shifted towards the inter-relationship of the Xhosa and the Cape Colony. In part, this distortion results from the weight of the available evidence. But not entirely. The dynamic of Xhosa history and the shape of Xhosa society was slowly but stubbornly twisted and reoriented as the Xhosa people were progressively sucked into the vortex of advancing European colonialism. It is sad that our sources do not permit us to write very much about the marriage of Sandile to his Great Wife, or to describe in detail the joys of the great harvest of 1844. But by the 1840s even a happy occasion could be no more than a respite and a diversion for a people who were becoming increasingly enmeshed in the web being spun around them. It seems only fitting to conclude with an analysis of the changes wrought in Xhosa society during 50 years of unremitting struggle.

In 1800 the Xhosa nation was expanding, aggressive and self-confident. Its outriding chiefdoms lay on the Sundays, the Mbashe and the sources of the Kei. Voluntarily or involuntarily, individually or collectively, the people of the surrounding nations — Thembu, Sotho and Khoi — were adding their strength to that of the Xhosa kingdom. In the shade of the house of Phalo, every man had a ridge for his homestead and a stream for his cattle. When his sons left home after circumcision, they never feared that they would fail to find land and water of their own. Every summer the people drove their cattle to the green mountain sourveld and every winter they ate of the game which abounded in the dense bush. There were disasters in plenty but losses could easily be recouped with the help of neighbours and affines who did not

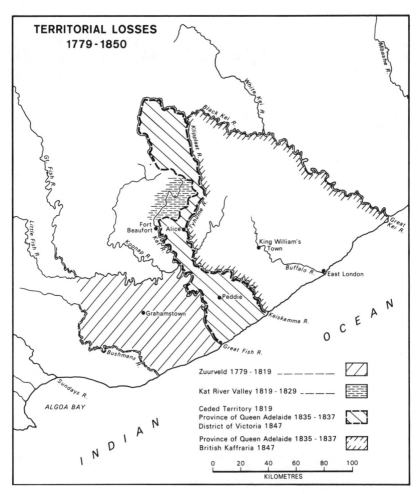

TERRITORIAL LOSSES
1779-1850

Zuurveld 1779 - 1819 _ _ _ _ _ _

Kat River Valley 1819 - 1829 _ _ _ _ _

Ceded Territory 1819
Province of Queen Adelaide 1835 - 1837
District of Victoria 1847

Province of Queen Adelaide 1835 - 1837
British Kaffraria 1847

0   20   40   60   80   100
KILOMETRES

demand too much in return.

By 1847 things were very different. The Xhosa kingdom had shrunk, and in shrinking it had lost vast tracts of its most fertile territory. The Xhosa were driven across the Fish in 1812, out of the Kat River valley in 1829, and right past the Keiskamma in 1847. None of the land which they still held west of the Kei was really secure. No longer did the sons of chiefs found new chiefdoms in virgin territory. No longer did the summer pastures guarantee the health and well-being of the people's cattle. The more powerful of the chiefs' sons set up permanently in the summer grazing;[1] the less powerful stayed at home as a terror to

the community.[2] In the old days, when a man died his homestead
was burnt and vacated; such marks of fear and respect now
became impossible, and the new cattle-enclosure was built back
to back with the old one. Dwellings clustered closer together, and
not everyone lived near a river.[3] The game was all shot out;[4] the
grazing patterns were all disrupted; a drought became an
irreversible calamity. It is no coincidence that the first great cattle
epizootic — lungsickness — followed hard on the yet greater land
losses of 1850 — 1853.[5]

'The appearance of the country is very fine. It will make
excellent sheep farms.'[6] Holden Bowker's words proved sadly
prophetic. Moreover, in losing the Ceded Territory, the Xhosa lost
much more than their land. Deprived of their means of
subsistence, many of them were forced into labouring for the very
men who had supplanted them. Many Xhosa had worked for the
farmers in the days before 1800, many had been happy, many had
stayed on. More however had preferred to take their wages and go
home. Indeed the very standard of working conditions on the
farms depended on the worker having the option of leaving at his
own discretion.[7] This option became increasingly eroded with the
passage of time, not so much because of direct coercive measures
on the Colonial side of the border — although these too were
shortly to appear — but because a smaller Xhosaland was
increasingly unable to support its population. As early as 1841 a
Xhosa was reported as saying that a man without cattle could no
longer find a living in his own country.[8] The large numbers of
'native foreigners' squatting on white farms testify that he was not
alone. How much more catastrophic were the confiscations of
1847! Even within Xhosaland itself many Xhosa were, however
unconsciously, working for the white man; growing him forage in
order to buy his textiles.[9]

There were also major changes on the political front. The
Colonial carrot proved as effective as the Colonial stick. Ngqika
sold his country after 1818, Phato stayed out of the War of
1834 — 1835, Maqoma retired early in 1846. Some minor chiefs —
Khama, Mqhayi, perhaps Dyani Tshatshu — defected altogether.
This was an entirely new phenomenon. It was not of course
unusual for a chief to step out of line in the precolonial Xhosa
kingdom, but it was unusual for the political system to remain
in a state of permanent disequilibrium. When Mdange and Phalo
defeated Gwali around 1700, Phalo became the heir and Gwali the
somewhat errant Right-Hand Son; when Mhala smelled out Dyani
Ndlambe, he replaced him as the Great Son; and so on.[10]

It was not unprecedented that Ngqika should rise up against
Hintsa, or that Phato should refuse to join his brother chiefs in

the War of 1834 — 1835. What *was* unprecedented was that these actions were not followed by their logical consequences. The pretensions of Ngqika would have been crushed at Amalinde and the treachery of Phato would have been punished after the rctroccssion of Queen Adelaide's Province had the Colonial authorities not stepped in to protect their clients. Deprived of the means of disciplining its recalcitrants, the kingdom was inevitably bound for political fragmentation.

At the same time that Colonial intervention encouraged the petty rivalries of the various chiefs, it also healed the breach between chiefs and commoners. Whatever their differences, both chiefs and commoners were united in their need to preserve the social order against the European intrusion that was destroying them all. Harry Smith thought he could win the commoners to his side by protecting their interests at the expense of the chiefs, but the people saw more clearly where their real interests lay.[11] The age of resistance was also the heroic age of the chiefs. Ndlambe and Chungwa, Hintsa and Sarhili, Maqoma, Tyhali and Sandile may have had their faults but they did not sell out. They stood up for their people and deserve a salute.

The struggle against the Colony did much to bring chiefs and commoners together, but it also created new cleavages which were to have lasting consequences. Most obvious was the difference between resisters and collaborators. Among the latter one can number chiefs like Khama and Mqhayi, and the host of nameless individuals who acted as informers and joined the Kaffir Police (founded 1835).[12] As significant was the growth of a 'school community' within and without the mission stations, a community which saw European culture and technology as desirable acquisitions. Their most important member, Soga, lived outside the mission and fought against the Europeans in wartime. Nevertheless, his adoption of the market and the plough was more subversive of the old way of life than the activities of any single Colonial spy. Even as new social divisions were springing up within the Xhosa nation, new social alliances were being formed between landless and threatened Xhosa and their Khoi counterparts.[13] The more the Xhosa nation became part of a wider South Africa the less important did its ethnic specificity become.

Ideological confusion went hand in hand with economic erosion and political disruption. Secure in the wisdom of his diviners and the mastery of his destiny, the Xhosa had looked forward to the future with confidence. Traditional usages were tested and established, some were quietly added and others quietly dropped, and there was every reason to expect that what had worked in the past would work in the future. Good management would lead to good fortune and if all dangers could not be warded off they could at least be explained. But the pale animals from across the sea disordered a universe in which they had no place, and the Xhosa had to think again. Those who followed Ntsikana thought they saw their initial gamble well rewarded, as their material wealth increased and their white patrons remained on the winning side. For those Xhosa who were not prepared to pay the social costs of isolation, alienation and dependence, life was harder. Their response was a more self-conscious assertion of their traditional values, a tendency to say, with Tyhali, 'I am a Xhosa' and to reject all things alien.[14] Even though Nxele had disappeared there was still the possibility that he might return,[15] there were still the efforts of men like Mngqatsi to pick up where he left off, there were still the visions of those who tried to persuade others of the truth of their dreams. The number of such men increased as the forties turned into the fifties building up to the one great revelation which was to destroy them all.

2. BRITISH KAFFRARIA 1847 – 1850

Sir Harry Smith returned to South Africa in December 1847, his overwhelming arrogance further bloated by victory in India and by the favour of Wellington. Convinced that his genius would solve the frontier dilemma which had baffled his predecessors, he ordered a return to the D'Urban system which he had administered in the days of the Province of Queen Adelaide. Indulgent biographers have treated his histrionic behaviour — simulated rages, blowing up ammunition wagons, symbolic maces of war and peace — as if it was all good clean swashbuckling fun.[16] But to an exhausted Xhosa nation, drained by two years of war, it was more like rubbing the salt of unnecessary humiliation into the gaping wounds of defeat. Perhaps nothing in the entire history of the frontier, not even the death of Hintsa, is as sickening as the repeated demands of Smith that the Xhosa chiefs kiss his feet.[17] This they did, literally under the guns of the British army. Once only was Smith crushed: in a verbal exchange with Dyani Tshatshu which is worth recording as an exercise in the comparative dignity of the British governor and the Xhosa chief:

SMITH: Fool! you dared join with the Kafirs against the power of the Queen. Have you anything to say to the Lord Bishop for the further-ance of education among your countrymen?

DYANI TSHATSHU: The Lord Bishop is a great and wise man, and the

Great Chief has already remarked that I am a fool. How, therefore can I
give any advice upon this subject?[18]

When Maqoma, who had consistently opposed war in 1846,
offered Smith his hand, the Governor ordered him to the floor.
Tradition has it that as he lay prostrated before the jeering
spectators, Smith's foot on his neck, Maqoma said, 'You are a dog,
so you act like a dog. This thing was not sent by Victoria, who
knows I am of royal blood as she is.'[19]

Even the personal indignities inflicted by Smith pale into
insignificance beside the system of government erected by him in
British Kaffraria. Behind Smith's fantastical language and
behaviour lurked the more conventional ideas of early Victorian
imperialism. Few of his European contemporaries would have
thought his objectives in British Kaffraria anything but laudable:

> Your land shall be marked out and marks placed that you may all
> know it. It shall be divided into counties, towns and villages, bearing
> English names. You shall all learn to speak English at the schools
> which I shall establish for you . . . You may no longer be naked and
> wicked barbarians, which you will ever be unless you labour and
> become industrious. You shall be taught to plough; and the Commissary
> shall buy of you. You shall have traders, and you must teach your
> people to bring gum, timber, hides etc. to sell, that you may learn the
> art of money, and buy for yourselves. You must learn that it is money
> that makes people rich by work, and help me to make roads. I will pay
> you. You tell me many of your youths desire to go into the colony as
> servants, they shall be allowed to do so.[20]

In the event Smith achieved relatively little with regard to
commerce and education and these remained in the hands of the
traders and missionaries. But in the matters of land and labour,
the alpha and the omega of Colonial greed, he made giant steps.

The land between the Fish and the Keiskamma, which the
Xhosa had held on sufferance since Ngqika allegedly ceded it to
Lord Charles Somerset in 1819, was annexed to the Colony as the
new district of Victoria.[21] Part of this was given to the Mfengu
and to an abortive Khoi settlement on the Beka; the rest was sold
off to Europeans to raise revenue for Smith's disastrous schemes in
other parts of the sub-continent. The triumph of the land
speculators and the *Grahams Town Journal* was complete. Three
military villages of discharged soldiers were established in the
foothills of the Amatola. They soon proved their fitness for the
great work of civilisation by desecrating the grave of Tyhali and
seizing Xhosa cattle which dared to wander back to their old

pastures.[22] Across the Tyhume, the Xhosa watched their precious cows and calves 'dying without resource within the sight of extensive pasture ranges, of which the infatuation of war has forever deprived them.'[23] For the first time, large numbers of men turned to agriculture, even though the rocky slopes of the Amatola were covered with boulders, and many of them had not even an ox left to plough with.

The territory between the Keiskamma and the Kei, now known as British Kaffraria, was not annexed to the Colony but was directly administered on behalf of Great Britain by High Commissioner Smith. As Kirk has aptly remarked, 'annexation to Britain . . . appeared as a mere device to permit military rule of Kaffraria unrestrained by British law.'[24] Smith's officers exercised arbitrary justice at their own discretion. Punishment was by fine (British Kaffraria's only source of revenue, apart from trading licences) and floggings of up to a hundred lashes. Apart from the new towns of King Williams Town and East London and a small area around each of the military posts, the whole territory was occupied by the Xhosa. It was divided up into counties and each of the chief's places was given a fanciful English name. Thus Sandile ruled from York and Phato from Bedford, while Mhala was turned into an academic and took his seat in Cambridge. A detailed census was taken, the land was surveyed and the new rulers debated the best means of taxation.[25] The Xhosa observed these proceedings in alarm and despair. The protest of Sandile foreshadows generations of struggle against beacons, trusts and betterment schemes: 'The whole of Kafirland is dotted over with the habitations of the white man, and with the surveyors' flags . . . he might die, but it should never be said he died in peaceable time — for it should be universally known that he died in the ranks fighting for the land of the Rharhabes.'[26]

Henry Calderwood, a missionary turned Government official, was the first to see that the devastation of the *War of the Axe* could be turned to good account in solving the Colonists' chronic labour shortage. 'There is indeed great suffering now in Caffreland,' he wrote optimistically, 'and the opportunity should not be lost of scattering the people far into the Colony where they can find food and be useful.' One hundred and seventy Xhosa, of whom only 58 were men, accompanied his letter into the Colony. Calderwood apologised for all the women and children, but he pointed out that 'the women will be as useful as the men . . . and many of the children will soon be useful.'[27] The flow of labour was greatly accelerated by a scheme, allegedly requested by the Xhosa themselves, whereby 'Kaffir youths' were indentured for three years' servitude in distant parts of the Colony.[28]

This horrible device cut two ways. On the one hand there was an enormous demand in the western Cape for the labour of little children aged between eight and ten years, as enthusiastic letters from farmers desirous of helping to civilise the Xhosa testify.[29] On the other hand, it was possible to apply regulations governing the apprenticeship of 'youths' to adults as well. The silence of records on this point is understandable, given Magistrate Edye's warning to Commissioner Maclean to describe all Xhosa as 'youths' in official dispatches.[30]

Ordinance 49 of 1828 had given Xhosa passes to seek work, thus enabling them to squat on white farms and to change employers with relative ease.[31] Under Ordinance 3 of 1848, which repealed some sections of the old regulations as 'repugnant', the Xhosa were firmly indentured to particular employers before they even entered the Colony, without necessarily specifying the wages they would be paid.[32] Numbers of destitute Xhosa who entered the Colony to seek work on their own terms found themselves unwittingly engaged to strange masters in distant places.[33] There also seems to have been an increase in the fining and flogging of Xhosa work-seekers who failed to comply with the official regulations.[34] Curiously enough — since the Xhosa had supposedly asked for the apprenticeship scheme — Xhosa parents showed a 'distinct aversion' to commit their children to hard labour far away.[35] The official response was that parents who were reluctant to part with their children should simply be sent to work alongside them.[36] That so many went is a testament to the starvation of the Xhosa, newly resettled in their remaining possessions. It was estimated at the time that quite as many amaNgqika left their homeland as remained within it.[37]

None was more assiduous in channeling Xhosa labour to the Colonial interior than the newly appointed Assistant Commissioner to the Ngqika, Charles Brownlee. It took him only three or four days to find 180 servants for the arid and unpleasant district of Beaufort West, and he felt that if whole families were wanted, he could easily find another three to four hundred Xhosa to be sent off in lots of sixty to one hundred. He appended only one word of warning: applications should all be made before the end of November when the harvest came in. After that the people would not be hungry enough to go out and work.[38]

In August 1850, Commissioner Maclean sat down to report an unusual but doubtless quite trivial incident which had occurred in his jurisdiction.

> I have the honour to report that Umlanjeni a Kaffir of Umkai's Tribe and location has lately revived the witchdoctoring craft, and great

numbers have attended his meetings from all ⌐   ⌐d; in
consequence of which I ordered him to a⌐   also his
father 'Kala' (at whose kraal Umlanjeni ┠   ⌐ witchcraft
poles). Both parties failed to appe⌐   ⌐ered the 2nd
division police to apprehend them   ⌐o head of cattle
for their disturbance.[39]

For the Xhosa, British Kaffraria was a monster which swallowed
them up, tore them from their children, and squeezed them off
their land onto the labour market. Weary and despondent, they
determined to make a final stand.

Appendices

1. ORAL TRADITION

There are three types of Xhosa oral tradition directly related to history: genealogies *(iminombo)*, praises *(izibongo)* and tales *(amabali,* singular *ibali).*

The genealogy is today the most highly esteemed and politically relevant of these. For the chief it is the essential proof, and the only necessary proof, of his chiefship. It is still the crucial index of seniority. All chiefs can recite their genealogies even if only very incompletely, and most have a more detailed written one readily available.[1] For the historian who already has the names this emphasis on genealogies is counter-productive since, in many cases, it satisfies the need Xhosa feel for historical knowledge without preserving much information. Both clans and chiefs have *praises.* Clan praises, usually consisting of only one word, are still in universal use. When one Xhosa tells another the name of his clan, the latter will probably respond with a clan-praise (For instance, 'I am an umNgwevu' 'Ah! Tshangisa!'). The praises have historical roots. For instance, 'Hlomla', one of the praises of the Cira clan, refers to the famous incident in which Cira demanded a bluebuck from Tshawe.[2] Unfortunately, very few Xhosa can explain any of their clan-praises, the usual explanations being that the praise is the name of 'some old chief or other'.[3] It should, however, be standard practice for historical field-workers to obtain clan praises and, where available, explanations from their informants.

The character of Xhosa praise-poetry has changed considerably, from being primarily memorised and therefore fixed, to being primarily improvised.[4] Fortunately, many of the old praise-poems were collected and published by W.B. Rubusana.[5] But they are difficult to use as historical sources because of the obscurity of most of the allusions.[6] Most of the more comprehensible lines are either simple metaphors or stereotypes. Praise-poetry was far from sycophantic, but criticism was usually implicit[7] — damning with faint praise being a typical technique — and is therefore completely lost through the subsequent obscurity of the allusions. Occasional details are illuminating, such as the following from the praises of Rharhabe:

> He dresses himself in short garments
> but they suit him well
> Because he says the big ones hide his knees.

The point is that Rharhabe was restless and liked freedom to move about.[8]

Valuable as such details are to descriptive history, they do not contribute substantially to the sort of interpretative general history with which we are here concerned. Praise-poetry's greatest asset is its ability to provide the reader with the 'feel' of the period, but it is best read as it stands rather than in prose paraphrases.

The most important historical vehicle in Xhosa oral tradition is the *ibali,* or tale.[9] *Amabali* may be remembered because they explain how certain present circumstances came to exist. The story of Tshawe, for instance, tells how the amaTshawe came to be the royal house, and the story of Phalo's two brides explains the rise of the Right-Hand house. They may be purely local, dealing with circumstances of interest to the particular group which relates them, such as histories of particular chiefs or clans. Others may be remembered for their entertainment value. These include stories concerning the origins of the *War of the Axe* and the *War of Ngayechibi* (the *Ninth Frontier War*), the cattle-killing disaster and the death of Hintsa. Each tale is a separate unit, and they are not thought of as a sequence over time. It is up to the genealogy to take care of chronology.

The *amabali* are free in form, and their transmission is random in that there was no institutionalised means of making certain that they were remembered.[10] They were communicated, like all other necessary general knowledge, at court, round the fires, and in the circumcision schools. Inasmuch as chiefs and important councillors took care to instruct the sons who would succeed them, there was some assurance that a body of historical information would accumulate, and that it would be passed down. Despite this, it may readily be seen that there was plenty of scope for distortion and loss of traditions through failure of memory.

Since oral cultures usually lack the means of fixing the memory of the past, they are able to avoid being confronted with its difference from the present. This results in a tendency to bring the past into line with the present and to believe that things have always been as they are, a tendency which is exemplified in the presumption that custom is immutable. This influences what is remembered: the more socially relevant the tradition, the more people are likely to know it, and the longer it remains so, the longer they are likely to remember it.[11] The way it is remembered is also influenced. The more widely remembered the tradition and the further back in time it goes, the more mythical and non-specific it becomes. It is far better to view such myths metaphorically, as summaries or interpretations of past events, than literally, as straightforward narrations of events that actually occurred.

Distortion also occurs for political reasons. Even when political behaviour appears to adhere to a stringent set of rules, there is usually considerable room for flexibility and manoeuvring.[12] Irregular seizures of power, for instance, can often find some justification. As the event recedes into the past and the victor becomes even better established, the circumstances fade and only the justification survives. The dispossessed groups may retain an independent recollection of events but this is likely to disappear as soon as they accept the situation. Often, however, the tradition makes use of 'cliches' to cloak the ambiguities, and these supply clues to the historian: twins, for example, may indicate a succession dispute, and the return of a prodigal/formerly wronged son may indicate an invasion.[13] Oral genealogies, particularly those which place members of the same generation in ranking order, therefore tend to be chronicles of successes and failures rather than simple family histories. Political distortion is not confined to quarrels, as, for instance, when peripheral individuals or groups claim or receive genealogical affiliations which enhance their prestige.

These forms of distortion are common to most oral traditions, and Xhosa traditions are particularly subject to them because of their relatively loose form and method of transmission. For the same reasons, they are also liable to distortion through transposition of setting, aetiological error, lack of time depth, telescoping and contamination from written sources. Although the episodes and plot of a tale cannot be changed without destroying its coherence, the setting ('the time and place in which the tale unfolds, and the names of the persons who appear in it')[14] is not an integral part of the tale, and can easily be forgotten or mistaken. It was not uncommon to find an informant who remembered a story perfectly, but was not sure of the names of the heroes. Sometimes it seemed to be simply a question of putting the most appropriate chief into the vacant slot. Among the Gcaleka, for instance, any tale dealing with the high classical periods will usually be attributed to Sarhili, and one dealing with the very earliest period to Phalo or Gcaleka. Aetiology ('inference from the present')[15] occurs at all levels, from major institutions, like the Right-Hand house, to specific details, as in the case of one Gcaleka informant living in the Willowvale District who said that Ndlambe was living in the Idutywa district at the time of the abduction of Thuthula whereas in fact the amaNdlambe only arrived in Idutywa after 1857.[16] Aetiology is closely related to lack of time depth. The personal characteristics of the last chiefs of the classical period: Sarhili, Sandile, Maqoma, Mhala, Siwani, Phato, Khama, are remembered to some extent, whereas Hintsa, Ngqika, Ndlambe, Mdushane and Chungwa are little more than names. Even so, it is the later life of the former chiefs which is most clearly remembered. Many traditions concerning the *War of Ngayechibi* survive, but none at all concerning such dramatic incidents as Sandile's detention under false pretences in 1847, or the murder in error of James Brownlee in 1851. Oba and Anta, ferocious fighters in the *Eighth Frontier War,* are remembered as men of peace because they did not fight in the *Ninth.*[17] Sometimes this factor combines with transposability of setting to produce an apparent falsehood.[18] Telescoping, the reduction of several events to a single story, is frequent. The rivalry between Ngqika and Ndlambe, for example, is boiled down exclusively to the abduction of Thuthula, and the deeper issues are forgotten. Transposition of setting and telescoping joined up in the case of an informant who, having combined the stories of Nongqawuse and the 1885 famine, which she had lived through as a girl, believed that she had experienced the famine which followed the cattle-killing.[19]

Another problem is contamination from written sources since most informants have had some schooling. The best known oral historians in Xhosaland, Chief E. Botomane and N.C. Melane, prided themselves on their ability to cite dates, and were respected for this by other Xhosa. Several other informants possessed copies of Rubusana's *Zemk' iinkomo Magwalandini,* or W.G. Bennie's *Imibengo.* Mqhayi's *Ityala lamaWele* has been so far absorbed into the national consciousness that its contents were cited as oral tradition both by illiterates and by schoolchildren acquainted only with the abridged schools edition.

It is very apparent that Xhosa oral tradition has declined considerably in the twentieth century. The reasons are not hard to find. Unlike folktales, whose undying appeal is lodged in the fantasies of the unconscious and which still flourish in Xhosaland,[20] history is closely tied to the external world. The world of the traditions is very unreal to the Xhosa today, and difficult for them to visualise. Chiefs approximate more to the local bureaucracy than to the fighting leaders of a hundred years ago, and the presence of the white West permeates even the remotest corner of Xhosaland, so that it is impossible to imagine a time when all Xhosa wore red ochre and managed their affairs independently. Today the men go out into the cities and the mines, and when they return, the conversation revolves around jobs, employers and machinery, and the exploits related to these, and not around the heroes of an epoch now irrevocably dead. Alternative entertainments have taken their toll, primarily in the towns, but that is where most Xhosa men spend the greater part of their lives, leaving the children in the rural areas to be brought up by women, who do not know *amabali*.

Oral education is commonly regarded as a poor second to school education, even among the illiterate. Two examples should demonstrate this point. I was at a beer-drink with one of my best informants, who was acknowledged locally as an expert on history and custom, when he was approached for his opinion on a tricky point of marriage custom. While he was giving it, a third man interrupted, saying, 'Well, that's your opinion, but will the magistrate agree with you?' The neighbour then left to find someone who knew the official ruling on the subject.[21] On another occasion, I was interviewing Nongqawuse's great-nephew, a man whose mother had actually known the prophetess personally. In the middle of the interview, his sister walked in and told him he was talking nonsense. She knew the *true* story of Nongqawuse from her English school reader, and proceeded to recite it to me — in English![22] Chiefs now seek secretaries who are literate and speak the official languages. These are often complete outsiders, and it is they who are responsible for official business, which includes the history of chiefdom. Once this has been written down, it is considered to be 'known', and there is no functional need for history beyond it.

On the other hand, oral tradition will never entirely disappear. There are about 15 basic *amabali* in Xhosa,[23] and any reasonably well-informed Xhosa will know at least ten of them, and probably one or two more about his clan or his chief.

Ironically enough, one reason why Xhosa oral traditions have yielded relatively little new is that we already know so much from written sources. Because of our greater ignorance, Thembu oral traditions would probably furnish much more new information though they are probably no better preserved than those of the Xhosa.

2. XHOSA HISTORICAL WRITING

The first Xhosa newspaper, *Ikhwezi* (The Morning Star) (1844 – 1845) published the first historical writing in the Xhosa language.[24] It was both appropriate and significant that the subject was Ntsikana and the publisher was the Glasgow Missionary Society. The Christian missions created the literate class who first committed Xhosa traditions to paper and they continued to exert a dominant influence over the Xhosa written word for a long time thereafter. In the beginning this was a matter of conviction rather than coercion. Men such as John Knox Bokwe, the biographer of Ntsikana, William Kobe Ntsikana, son of the great man, W.W. Gqoba, who composed an 850-line didactic poem on the subject of paganism versus Christianity, and Isaac Wauchope, author of *The Natives and their Missionaries,* were convinced Christians. They were also keenly interested in preserving their cultural heritage and ephemeral mission newspapers such as *Indaba* (1862 – 1865) and *Isigidimi samaXhosa* (1870 – 1888) carried the occasional historical article.[25]

W.B. Rubusana (1858 – 1936) moved one step beyond the fold. Although a Congregationalist minister by profession, Rubusana's public life and published writings show few traces of his mission background. He played a leading part in Cape Parliamentary politics and ran his own newspaper, *Izwi la Bantu* (1897 – 1909) with the financial assistance of the Cape Progressive Party. The few surviving copies of *Izwi* testify to Rubusana's enduring interest in Xhosa history, an interest immortalised in *Zemk' iinkomo Magwalandini,* the massive 580-page anthology of praise-poems, histories and other cultural items which he had privately printed in London in 1906. Rubusana was more an editor than a writer, and it was left to S.E.K. Mqhayi, who once worked for him on *Izwi,* to carry his work to its logical conclusion.

Although there were always a number of Xhosa newspapers which occasionally published historical articles — apart from *Izwi*, there was Jabavu's rival *Imvo Zabantsundu,* the Chamber of Mines' *Umteteli waBantu* and the Argus group's Umtata-based

Umthunywa — one single press monopolised book publication in Xhosa.[26] In the beginning, the Lovedale Press willingly published secular works such as Mqhayi's masterpiece, *Ityala lamaWele* (1914). But from about 1930, just when Xhosa literature was coming into full flower, the press fell into the hands of the Reverend R.H.W. Shepherd. Shepherd's twenty-year reign of terror at Lovedale is a classic example of the vulnerability of vernacular literature to its financial sponsors. Shepherd had at least the virtue of being frank. His *Lovedale and Literature for the Bantu* (1945) is a more damning indictment of his own policies than anything an enemy might devise. 'The mass of the vernacular literature . . . emanates from missionary presses, and naturally such literature has sought to fulfil the aims of missionary societies,' he wrote.[27] Shepherd refused to print anything he disagreed with, even if the authors were prepared to pay for it themselves. He was thus indirectly responsible for the loss of three manuscripts by S.E.K. Mqhayi besides a number of works by lesser authors. Bowdlerisation of earthy and political references forced the survivors into a bland and inoffensive tone and content.

After Shepherd, the missionaries were replaced by the National Party's Bantu Education regimen. Although this effectively broke the monopoly of Lovedale, it reinforced the tendency of Xhosa writers to aim for the school textbook market and further narrowed the limits of acceptable historical interpretation. Xhosa-language history retained a tenuous hold in the newspapers, particularly in the years (c 1955 — 1965) when S.M. Burns-Ncamashe was contributing to *Imvo* under the pen-name of Sogwali kaNtaba. Ncamashe, widely regarded as Mqhayi's successor, has never written the major Xhosa history of which he is undoubtedly capable. Like so many other Xhosa historians, he has preferred the form of the newspaper article. He himself has observed that 'a book is only a book, it cannot be asked questions because it does not know how to reply'.[28] The written word is to some extent inimical to an oral political culture which depends on ambiguity, flexibility, and the possibility of forgetting old quarrels and changing sides and opinions. Newspaper articles are thus much closer than books to the form and spirit of the traditional Xhosa *ibali*.

This section would be incomplete without brief consideration of two outstanding Xhosa historians, S.E.K. Mqhayi and J.H. Soga.

Samuel Edward Krune Mqhayi (1875 — 1945) is generally acknowledged as the dominant figure in Xhosa literature.[29] Six years of his childhood were spent in Kentani district among the diehard Ngqika who were expelled from the Ciskei for their part in the last *Frontier War* (1878 — 1879). His further experiences as journalist, teacher and praise-singer added to his historical knowledge, and his horizons were further broadened by Justus's fiery polemic, *The Wrongs of the Caffre Nation* (1837). Mqhayi's favourite medium was the short biography, in which the life of the hero served as a vehicle for comments on past history and present politics. Many of these appeared in Xhosa newspapers such as *Umteteli waBantu*, and others were written for Lovedale's *Stewart Xhosa Reader* series. The fullest surviving exposition of Mqhayi's historical views may be found in *Ityala IamaWele*. This develops two preoccupations which were to recur throughout his work. Mqhayi was primarily concerned to establish that the history of the Xhosa was equal to that of any other nation.

> Among all these nations, the Xhosa have never obtained even a small share of their portion. Tshaka founded the Zulu kingdom with his stabbing-spear, his heroism, and the young men of his nation, in the time of Hintsa ... the very Hintsa who already possessed a kingdom which, with its outposts, began at the Mbashe and extended to the Gamtoos river and the mountains of Somerset East. Mshweshwe founded the kingdom of LuSuthu with his understanding and his wisdom and the wise old men of his nation, and he nursed it as a nursing mother nurses her baby; but he was the same age as Maqoma ... and the land of Mshweshwe was not greater than that of Maqoma, his age-mate among the Xhosa.[30]

As a practising Christian, Mqhayi was also concerned to counter the missionary view that Xhosa traditional ways were 'pagan' and therefore incompatible with Chritianity. In *Ityala lamaWele* he shows that witchcraft and divination were important features of the Old Testament. His lost manuscript, 'Ukwaluko', made the same point with regard to circumcision. The body of *Ityala lamaWele* is a tribute to the traditional Xhosa judicial process.

Secondly, Mqhayi was concerned to refute the image of the Xhosa presented in South African school textbooks. Some passages, such as a chapter on the death of Hintsa, were taken directly from the writings of Justus. Others came from Mqhayi himself:

> On the questions of boundaries; the white man made an agreement with the first person he met — counting for nothing. Then they come with this case against people who knew nothing about such agreements. The white man was preparing for war, for fighting against innocent people.[31]

He was equally scathing about the old canard of cattle theft. He pointed out that when the whites first came to South Africa, 'they were very poor, they had no cattle, they had nothing'. How could the blacks be accused of stealing the cattle of the whites when all the cattle had belonged to the blacks in the first place? Such arguments and others relative to the Xhosa-Mfengu division upset Shepherd and the Lovedale Press. They refused to publish Mqhayi's biography of Rubusana because it contained remarks on the origins of frontier wars, on the cattle-killing disaster, and on other 'irrelevant matters'.[32] The full edition of *Ityala IamaWele* was phased out in favour of a schools' edition untainted by the offensive passages. But Mqhayi could not be killed off so easily. Even after the printed word was lost, the burning questions lingered on, and the deletions from *Ityala LamaWele* are preserved in oral traditions ascribed by a younger generation to 'things we heard from our grandfathers'.

John Henderson Soga (1859 −1941) was the son of the great Xhosa essayist and churchman, Tiyo Soga (1829 − 1871), by a Scottish mother, and he was himself educated in Scotland.[33] To the knowledge he inherited from his councillor forefathers,[34] he added that obtained from the companions of Sarhili's last exile in Bomvanaland, where he served as a missionary for many years. Like his father, Soga was a composer of hymns and a translator of religious writings but he is best remembered as an historian. Soga was unable to persuade the Lovedale Press to publish his life work, *Abe-Nguni Aba-Mbo Nama-Lala* which he completed in 1926,[35] and the manuscript might well have disappeared had the editorial board of *Bantu Studies* not heard of it and commissioned the author to translate it for them. The translation appeared in 1930 under the name of *The South-Eastern Bantu.* The original remains unpublished. Lovedale did, however, bring out Soga's other major work, *The Ama-Xosa: Life and Customs,* which he wrote in English.

Soga wrote history after European models and the great virtue of *The South-Eastern Bantu* is its completeness and its logical arrangement. Unlike other Xhosa historians who produced fragments or, at best, biographies, Soga provided a solid frame of reference for all his successors, beginning at the beginning and ending at the end. He travelled widely to fill in gaps in his knowledge, visiting most of the Xhosa chiefs and recording many traditions and genealogies now forgotten.

Along with the virtues of his European contemporaries, Soga absorbed many of their defects. The Hamites wander in and out of his early chapters and his respect for printed authorities led him to make some rather spectacular mistakes in dating.[36] His desire to write a definitive general history inclined him to dismiss information which conflicted with his opinions, and to pass off his own rationalisations as traditions.[37] At times he combined a number of oral testimonies into a single version; at others he relied too heavily on a particular informant.[38] He was more concerned with prescribing the correct version than in telling the story and hence, even in Xhosa, Soga's history lacks the vigour and detail of Mqhayi, Gqoba, W.K. Ntsikana and other early writers. This seems however, a small price to pay for the structure and order which Soga brought to the history of the Xhosa.

3. EUROPEAN SOURCES

Much has been written about the Xhosa by European travellers, government officials, missionaries, settlers and politicians. Most of the more substantial early accounts contain an attempt at Xhosa history, and later European contemporaries wrote about current events that have since become history. It would be impossible to discuss such a mass of material here, and the reader is referred to the footnotes and the bibliography.

Early South African historical writing grew out of contemporary politics. John Centlivres Chase, who was one of the authors of the first history of the Cape, was a prominent associate of Godlonton, whose opinions are reflected in his book.[39] Theal, even at his most liberal, thought Godlonton's polemical history of the War of 1834 − 1835 was a 'thoroughly reliable history'.[40] Thus the early histories tended to exhibit the biases of their early source material.

It is worth noting that even at this early stage, interest was shown in Xhosa oral traditions. Theal, who taught at Lovedale and was Government Agent with Oba's Ngcangatelo during the *Ninth Frontier War,* 'applied to various antiquaries throughout Kaffirland', and even interviewed Sarhili.[41] His chapter 'History of the Xhosa tribe before 1800' is excellent as far as it goes.[42] It is a pity that no notes from these interviews have survived. Cory did a series of whirlwind interviews which are preserved in the Cory Library, Grahamstown, and are extremely valuable despite Cory's habit of asking leading questions and emphasising factual issues. An ambitious attempt was made in 1904 −1905 by J.M. Orpen to synthesise documentary and oral evidence into an authoritative history of the Africans of South Africa. He was too old to under-take the research himself, and government officials among the Xhosa responded very poorly, although valuable accounts of the Mfengu and Bhaca were obtained.[43]

The mighty edifices of Theal and Cory have fixed the predatory barbarian image of the Xhosa in the school-books till now. The liberal historians of the twentieth century, although sympathetic to the Xhosa, still concentrated on the Colonists.[44] Instead of rapacious Xhosa depriving peace-loving Colonists of their cattle, they tended to depict rapacious Colonists depriving peace-loving Xhosa of their land. But even on this view, the Xhosa were more acted against than acting.

The revolution in African historiography, heralded by the appearance of the *Journal of African History* in 1960 and Vansina's *De la tradition orale* in 1961, made its presence felt in South Africa by the appearance in 1969 of the first volume of the *Oxford History of South Africa.*[45] The Xhosa also featured, though not prominently, in two follow-up collections, *African Societies in Southern Africa* (1969)[46] and *Beyond the Cape Frontier* (1974).[47] For the first time, an attempt was made to write the history of South Africa with at least some Africans cast centre stage. However, as regards the Xhosa specifically, despite some useful insights, what was written was too brief and too general. Moreover, none of these used vernacular sources, whether written or oral.[48]

APPENDIX I B
FIELDWORK METHODS

Fieldwork lasted about five months, spread over a seven-month period from August 1975 to March 1976. Two months were spent in the Ciskei, and three in the Transkei, primarily in Kentani and Willowvale districts. Every known Xhosa chiefdom, including those not officially recognised, was visited, and information concerning it was obtained from the persons the chief judged best qualified to give it. This was the only practical method of covering such a large area within the limited time available. Not only was it the only way in which many informants could have been located, but the knowledge that the occasion was official diminished their very natural fears and suspicions.

Informants who demonstrated considerable knowledge at these official meetings were visited privately in their homes afterwards.

This, in a large measure, compensated for the deficiencies inherent in group testimonies. It may be urged that my time would have been better spent in fewer chiefdoms, acquiring knowledge in greater depth. However, the poor time depth of the traditions and the paucity of really good informants considerably limited the amount of information available in any one place. Moreover, relatively few traditions deal with Xhosa history as such; most deal with the histories of individual chiefs and chiefdoms, and to have omitted any of these would have been to invite rather lopsided history. Although it is virtually certain that I did not collect all the available information, I am convinced that what remains is not of a nature or a quality substantially to affect the conclusions of what is, after all, a general history. It is my sincere hope that eventually local histories will be written, preferably by the people themselves, which will supplement and correct this one.

Names of informants were also solicited from government officials, teachers, clergymen, traders and passers-by. I found the same names recurring over and over again, and it was indeed these men who supplied me with the bulk of my information.

Clan histories, the importance of which cannot be over-emphasised, were harder to locate than chiefly histories, though informants spoke more readily about their clans than on any other subject. The method adopted was to ask good informants who had been contacted for the purpose of giving a chiefly history to give the history of their clan. Towards the end of the field-work period, an attempt was made to seek out representatives of clans concerning which I had not yet found any information. It is in the field of clan histories that new information is most likely to turn up. Local histories were few and far between, because of the large-scale movements of population in the nineteenth century resulting from the rewarding of 'loyal' Xhosa and the displacement of 'rebellious' ones. I visited the scenes of several notable events, such as the battle of Amalinde and Nongqawuse's vision, only to find that the forefathers of the local people had come into the area after the event had taken place. Enquiries were also made on economic, social and religious topics, but although these were useful for the elucidation of present practices, some of which also operated in the past, they were fairly unsuccessful as regards past practices now discontinued.

I can read Xhosa, and speak and understand it to a limited extent, but found it necessary to employ an assistant to interpret and to set informants at ease. I was, however, able to check on the accuracy of the interpretation and to follow the drift of the conversation without interrupting it. My apparent inability to speak Xhosa was useful inasmuch as the people would speak freely when my assistant left the room, thus enabling me to gauge the nature of my reception. I would speak Xhosa to informants whom I knew well, and found that their attempts to assist me did much to improve personal relationships.

I recorded most of my interviews but found that even informants who trusted me were relieved to see the tape recorder switched off. I got some of my best information in casual conversation over tea when the 'official interview' was over. Most of this was written up later in notebooks kept for the purpose, and copies of these and the tapes will be deposited in the Cory Library for historical research, Rhodes University, Grahamstown.

APPENDIX I C
LIST OF PRINCIPAL INFORMANTS

All the men listed below have received some formal education, and all have spent three or more years at work in the urban areas. This list excludes those whose competence was limited to their own chief or clan. It was in conversation with the following men that my own ideas on Xhosa political organisation (Chapters II and III) were developed and clarified. Birth dates were given to me in some cases, and in others were deduced from important events (such as the Rinderpest Epidemic of 1897) which occurred at the time of their birth.

1. CHIEF ENGLAND BOTOMANE (b. 1892) (Clan: Tshawe). Universally considered as the greatest oral authority. His father was a diplomatic representative of Sarhili. When I met him, his powers were rapidly failing — between my first and second visits, he lost his eyesight and was relieved of his administrative duties. He died in 1977. Former residence: Ramntswana Location, Kentani District.

2. CHIEF S.M. BURNS-NCAMASHE (b. 1920) (Tshawe). See Appendix I A. Residence: Gwali Tribal Authority, Victoria East District.

3. JAMES KEPE (b. 1892) (Ntlane). Councillor to the iTsonyana

chiefdom, and local expert on ritual and history. Very little education and no knowledge of English or written sources. Friend of Chief Botomane, who lived fairly close. Residence: Thuthura Location, Kentani District.

4.   MBODHLELA MAKI (b. 1922) (Giqwa). Descendant of Feni, son of Maki. See J.H. Soga (1930), p 147. Residence: Shixini Location, Willowvale District.

5.   FRANK MATANGA (b. 1917) (?) Councillor of Chief Phato (Gqunukhwebe). Brought up on a farm in Adelaide District. Heard the traditions from his father. Good understanding of English. Residence: Mdantsane.

6.   NONHO CYRIL MELANE (b. 1903) (Ngqosini). His grandfather was a warrior of Sarhili. He became interested in history at a very early age, and deliberately sought out old men who could give him information. Well read. He died in 1980. Former residence: Qwaninga Location, Willowvale District.

7.   MWEZENI MNYANDA (b. ?) (Tshawe). Praise-singer to Chief Mcotama, the senior Gcaleka chief in Kentani District. Blind. Residence: Mcotama Location, Kentani District.

8.   CHIEF FRANK MPANGELE (b. ?) (Tshawe). Brought up in Kentani District. When I interviewed him, he was guardian to the heir-apparent of the late Rharhabe Paramount Mxolisi Sandile and chief of Mgwali Location, Stutterheim District. He has since been expelled from the Ciskei by the homelands authorities and is currently (1980) attached to the Gcaleka Paramount, Xolilizwe Sigcawu, Nqadu Great Place, Willowvale District.

9.   STANFORD NDAMASE (b. 1918) (Ngqosini). Claims to be heir of the last Ngqosini chief, reduced to headman by Hintsa. Ndamase is not really an historian in that he does not recite traditions, but has considerable knowledge and gives perceptive answers to questions. Residence: Shixini Location, Willowvale District.

10. HUGH MASON NIKANI (b. 1920) (Tshawe). His father was head of the amaNtinde in Kentani District, and a close associate of the late Paramount Velile Sandile. This position has now lapsed. Nikani qualified *(thwasa)* as a diviner, but is now an ordained minister of the Order of Ethiopia. Well educated and speaks extremely good English, but derives his information from oral sources. Residence: Thamarha Location, King Williams Town District, and Kentani.

11. WILSON NKABI (b. ?) (isiThathu). Councillor and Secretary to the Gasela chiefdom for many years. Speaks some English. Residence: Bulembo Location, King Williams Town District.

12. NDAWANGQOLA QEQE (b. 1912) (Ngwevu). Ritual head of all Iqawuka (amaNgwevu). His father was circumcision guardian of the late Gcaleka Paramount, Ngangomhlaba. None of his considerable body of information came from written sources, and he knew no dates. Was carefully instructed by his father so that he could fill the position of chief councillor to the Paramount. This position has now lapsed. Residence: Shixini Location, Willowvale District.

13. DANIEL RUNEYI (b. 1912) (Ngwevu). Relation of Qeqe. Educated and understands English. Runeyi was the only informant whose *amabali* were geared towards a political understanding of events. For instance, he gave a fairly long and detailed account of the origins of War of 1834 − 1835. Residence: Shixini Location, Willowvale District.

APPENDIX I D
LIST OF BASIC AMABALI

Every well-informed Xhosa knows eight or more of the following *amabali*. These satisfy his need to know about the past of his people. In addition, each will probably know a story or two about his chiefs and his clan.

1. The battle between Cira and Tshawe.

2. The arrival of the two bridal parties, which resulted in the formation of the Right-Hand House.

3. The *thwasa* of Gcaleka in the Ngxingxolo River.

4. The quarrel between Ngqika and Ndlambe:
   (a) the abduction of Thuthula.
   (b) Ngqika seeks help from the whites.

5. Ntsikana:

(a) his conversion.
(b) Ntsikana prophesies the arrival of the whites and the Mfengu.

6. The origin of the amaGqunukhwebe.

7. The death of Hintsa and the mutilation of his body.

8. The arrival of the Mfengu (the story about the food and the fire).

9. The origin of the *War of the Axe.*

10. The cattle-killing.

11. The *War of Nongxakazelo* (1875) between the Xhosa and the Thembu because of the Thembu Paramount's ill-treatment of his wife, Sarhili's daughter.

12. The *War of Ngayechibi (Ninth Frontier War):*
(a) The fight at the beer-drink.
(b) The flight of Sarhili across the Mbashe River.

APPENDIX I E
TWO SAMPLE TRADITIONS

These traditions are given as recited, without interruption. Interpolations are indicated by brackets.

1. A CHIEFLY TRADITION: INTERVIEW WITH CHIEF F. MPANGELE, MGWALI LOCATION, STUTTERHEIM DISTRICT, 26 AUGUST 1975

Tshiwo was the Great Son of Ngconde. While he was dying, Tshiwo left the affairs of the kingdom in the hands of Mdange. There were four men: there were Tshiwo, who was the chief, followed by Gwali, followed by Hleke, followed by Mdange.

These last two were twins. So when Tshiwo died, he left three younger brothers Hleke, Mdange and Gwali; and he left the affairs of the kingdom in charge of Mdange, so that he should be chief and guard the nation. Tshiwo had already married the mother of Phalo, but she was a young woman and the nation did not know that she was pregnant. It is the custom among the Xhosa that if a man dies and his wife has not yet had a child, she should be taken to her parents' home, since she is still small and it is not necessary that she should wear skins and put on black and mourn the husband. For this reason, that woman was taken home to her people, even though she was already pregnant with Phalo. When she arrived at her people this was reported to Mdange. Mdange was often troubled by Hleke and Gwali because they were older; apparently they were jealous. He often used to say to them: 'Just wait, and I will get you the 'phalo' of Tshiwo.' Among the Xhosa it is said that when a man has pains in the stomach, that it is called a 'phalo'.

One day, Mdange returned and said 'People of our home, that queen who went away, it appears that she already had a child in her stomach; it is now born, it is a girl!' And so the councillors carried on as usual, thinking it was a girl. But he (Mdange) knew that it was not a girl — he hid that child so that he should not be killed by jealous people. And so this 'girl' grew up, time passed and eventually the time arrived for the 'girl' to come to the court for the *intonjane* (female initiation ceremony). Gwali said: 'bring her, so we can see her.' And so, my friend, the 'girl' came to the court. When she arrived, Gwali looked at her and he saw that this did not look like a girl. He took his *ikrwane* (a type of small spear) and lifted up the skirt — and a man not a woman appeared! Then Gwali said 'Mdange! Why have you tricked me? You told me that it was a girl but it is a boy!' Then, says the history, fighting began among the Xhosa, it was fought, there on the other side of the Mthatha River. As a result of that war, the Xhosa came to Gcuwa (Butterworth), there where the site of Phalo's homestead is. On that account, many nations crossed — the amaHleke, amaNtinde, amaGqunukhwebe and amaGwali — they were chased out by Mdange, fighting because they had been cheated by Mdange who had hidden the fact that their older brother had given birth to a male. That was the first war among the Xhosa.

2. A CLAN TRADITION: INTERVIEW WITH M. KANTOLO, KANTOLO LOCATION, KENTANI DISTRICT, 27 OCTOBER 1975

What is the origin of the amaQocwa? They started off in Swaziland. They came from there and travelled until they arrived here among the Xhosa. When they came out from Swaziland, the chief here was Ndlambe, and they were under the Chief Ndlambe. They served him well and it seems they were great councillors. The majority of the councillors became jealous of this thing that the Qocwa was the foremost councillor at the Great Place, and very many of these councillors made a plot. They concocted a plan to drive away this Qocwa, he who was already the head of the councillors of the Great Place. It happened that there was a cattle disease and the cattle were dying. Now, there was a well-known diviner at another place. Those councillors chose a young man, and told him to go to the diviner and explain the whole thing, that the cattle were dying at the Great Place, and that when we come for a divination, the diviner must smell out the bald-headed man of the amaQocwa for killing the cattle of the Great Place. Because it is just as if he is killing those cattle, for he is attempting to kill the chief so that he may be chief here. The diviner agreed because he was bribed. When the young man returned he said 'Well, we have reached an agreement with the diviner.' 'Well then, everything's in order.' The councillors spoke to the chief: 'Chief, you are losing all of your cattle from dying. The cause of it should be divined.' The chief: 'Well, councillors it's up to you.' Then that diviner divined, and indeed, he spoke according to the wishes of the councillors. He smelt out the bald man who was the great councillor at (Ndlambe's) home. (The councillors) saw that (the Qocwa) should be surrounded, and killed, and his cattle captured because he was very rich. A certain man gave away the secret to that man of the amaQocwa: 'You are plotted against, and on such-and-such a day you will be harmed.' He said that Chief Ndlambe had already agreed that the thing should be done and said 'These cattle of mine are dying on account of this man.' This man who was plotted against sent a young man to Ngqika's place: 'Here I am surrounded. I am going to be done to death.' And this was Ngqika's reply: 'Bring all of your belongings here. We will meet on the road with the army that I shall bring out to meet you.' The Qocwa left Ndlambe's place by night, in order to reach Ngqika's place. In the morning, it was said: 'Tyhini! In that homestead, the doors are not open, nothing is coming out, nothing is happening, there are no cattle, there is nothing at all!' They followed the tracks of the cattle's hoofmarks. There, they were seen, going out, and the Ndlambe army already armed on their trail. By the blessing of God, when Ndlambe's army appeared, he could already be seen with all his family, driving all his livestock, and there, suddenly, the Ngqika army in front of him. Ndlambe saw them: 'Tyhini! That army is big. There is nothing we can do to catch up with that man.' Ndlambe returned and went back. That Qocwa was taken to the amaNgqika, and thrown in among them. That is how we became amaNgqika.

APPENDIX II
CLAN HISTORIES

The praises of most of these clans may be found in D.D.T. Jabavu (1952).

1. amaBAMBA: The only Bamba tradition of origin that I was able to trace was the spurious one of K. Billie (Interviewed Mdantsane, 3 July 1975), which sought to link the amaBamba to Tshiwo. Billie was a friend of the late S.T. Bokwe, son of J.K. Bokwe, who was an umBamba, and may have got the story from him. The amaBamba formed part of the amaNdluntsha. See also J.H. Soga (1930), p 115.

2. amaCETE: Possibly Khoi or Sotho in origin. See D.D.T. Jabavu (1952), pp 19 — 20; 'Sogwali kaNtaba', 'EzobuRarabe Jikelele', *Imvo Zabantsundu*, 16 September 1961.

3. amaCIRA: Dominant clan among the Xhosa until the rise of the amaTshawe. See Chapter II(1).

4   amaGIQWA: Khoi, probably the 'Hoengiqua' of the early travellers. Became important councillors of the Gcaleka Kings under the title of iNTSHINGA. See Chapter IV (2).

5. amaGQWASHU: Khoi, related to the amaSukwini, with whom they do not intermarry.

6. amaGQUBULASHE: Thembu. See under amaMAYA.

7. amaJWARA: According to Soga and Wm. Kekale (MS 172c, Grey Collection, South African Public Library, Cape Town), the amaJwara were present at the time of the war between Cira and Tshawe. See Chapter II (1).

8. amaKWAYI: Originally, a lineage of the amaTshawe, descended from Chief Ngconde, they were established in order to permit intermarriage between Tshiwo and the daughter of Ziko, founder of the lineage. This appears to have had political connotations. See Chapter II (4).

9. amaKWEMNTA: A Xhosa clan, supposedly present at the time of the battle between Cira and Tshawe. According to Soga, they do not intermarry with the amaCira, but none of my informants confirmed this. See J.H. Soga (1930), pp 283 — 284).

10. amaMAYA: The amaMaya were originally a rebellious lineage of the amaHala, the royal clan of the Thembu. They do not intermarry with the amaHala. They were accompanied in their flight to the Xhosa by the amaGqubulashe, who are now incorporated with them, and the amaQocwa, who are now established as a full independent clan. See Chapter II (4).

11. amaMFENE: Some amaMfene consider that the clan was always Xhosa in origin (Interview with G. Vitsha, Debe Marhele Location, Middledrift District, 15 August 1975). Others think that they are Thembu. M. Damoyi, (interviewed Ncikizele Location, Kentani District, 16 January 1976), said that there were many amaMfene among the Thembu but non-Mfene authorities consider them to be Sotho because of their totemic clan-name ('Mfene' means 'baboon') D.D.T. Jabavu (1952), p 22; J.H. Soga (n.d.) p 19.

12. amaNDLUNTSHA: See amaNKABANE.

13. amaNGQOSINI: The amaNgqosini at one time challenged the amaTshawe for domination in the area. (Chapter II [4]). They appear to have alternated between joining the Xhosa and joining the Thembu. Eventually, Hintsa caught them by surprise, and made their chief headman under his Right-Hand Son, Ncaphayi (Chapter IV (4)). The Ngqosini claim to

be Sotho in origin, but their name is not totemic, and there is a click in it. (This is the argument of R. Cakata (umTipa), Xobo Location, Idutywa District, interviewed 5 December 1975). They are therefore perhaps Khoi. The Ngqosini are also identified as Khoi in A. Kropf (1889), p 4.

14. amaNGWEVU: Of Mpondomise origin, they helped the amaTshawe against the amaCira, and were rewarded with high status among the councillors, under the title of iQAWUKA. See Chapter II (1).

15. amaNKABANE: The amaNkabane were one of the first Xhosa clans, and became the dominant element in the amaNdluntsha grouping of commoner clans. See Chapter II (4).

16. amaNQARWANE: Khoi clan absorbed by the amaGqwashu and amaSukwini.

17. amaNTAKWENDA: Xhosa clan which does not trace its links back to the Cira-Tshawe conflict. Apparently, they were incorporated by Rharhabe after he had left Gcaleka and Phalo. Interview with MacGregor Moya, Kentani Village, 17 December 1975.

18. amaNTSHILIBE: Sotho immigrants, who passed from independent chiefship among the Thembu to councillorship among the Xhosa. See J.H. Soga (1930), pp 290 − 294; M. Mbutuma, 'Ibali labaTembu' MS, Cory Library, Grahamstown.

19. iQAWUKA: See amaNGWEVU.

20. amaQOCWA: Clan reputed for their skill in ironworking. See amaMAYA.

21. amaQWAMBI: Xhosa clan, reputedly present at time of battle between Cira and Tshawe. J.H. Soga (1930), pp 283 − 284.

22. amaSUKWINI: Khoi clan, possibly the royal clan of Hinsati's Khoi kingdom, which was conquered by Mdange. See Chapter IV (1). Sukwini was the general and Great Councillor of Hinsati, and Chwama (now a praise-name of the amaSukwini) was Hinsati's son. A. Kropf (1889), p 8.

23. isiTHATHU: A mixed Khoi-San clan, descended from three men living west of the Kei on the arrival of Rharhabe. Interview with W. Nkabi, Bulembo Location, King Williams Town District, 24 August 1975.

24. amaTIPHA: Apparently an indigenous Xhosa clan. See Chapter II (1). D.D.T. Jabavu (1952), p 21, classifies them as Thembu.

25. amaTSHAWE: The royal clan of the Xhosa.

Footnotes

CHAPTER 1

1. The following is derived mainly from maps supplied by the Government Printer, Pretoria, and from contemporary descriptions, of which the most detailed are I. Stocker, 'Report upon Kaffraria', March 1820, in G.M. Theal, *Records of the Cape Colony*, 36 volumes (London, 1897 — 1905) (hereafter *RCC*), XIII, pp 32 — 81, and J. Brownlee-C. Bird, 26 August 1822, CO 163. An abridged version of the latter forms part of J. Brownlee (1827). Of the others, H. Dugmore (1858), pp 1 — 8 and W. Shaw (1860), pp 398 — 404, are especially vivid.

2. 'Highlands', 'uplands' and 'lowlands' are not indigenous expressions, but were coined by Rev. Dugmore.

3. Terminology and description of grass characteristics are taken from J.P.H. Acocks (1975).

4. The village settlement pattern has been diagrammatically represented by R. Derricourt, 'Settlement in the Transkei and Ciskei before the Mfecane', in C. Saunders and R. Derricourt (1974). Derricourt's discussion is weakened by his failure to situate his model in a local context. His diagram on p 67 correctly places his local community on both sides of the river, but that on p 68 contradictorily places larger political units ('tribal clusters') on different sides of the same river. Cf 'Tyali was also told he might remain on the Gaga (river), of course he understood such a word to mean both banks of the same.' W. Chalmers-C.L. Stretch, 21 November 1835. Quoted U. Long (1947), p 82.

5. H. Dugmore (1858), pp 8 — 9; S. Kay (1833), p 102.

6. For example, T.H. Bowker (1970), p 121. See also Cory interviews 112 (Maseti) and 125 (Yekele Vuyana), Cory Library, Grahamstown.

7. W. Shaw (1860), pp 376 — 377. Cf A. Kropf and R. Godfrey (1915), pp 497 — 508.

8. R. Collins (1809), p 42. See also ibid., p 50.

9. J.T. van der Kemp (1804), p 435.
10. H. Lichtenstein (1812 — 1815), 1:347. Lichtenstein's estimate was probably based on conversations with Van der Kemp and Alberti, who had every cause and opportunity to be well-informed on the subject.
11. R. Collins (1809), pp 42, 47, 50 — 51, 54.
12. R. Collins (1809), p 42.
13. The 1848 census, preserved in its entirety as CO 6155 and summarised in tabular form in J. Maclean (1858), was an ambitious attempt by the first rulers of British Kaffraria to record every person, horse and bovine in their new domain. It is remarkable for its precision and method (for example, it differentiates between girls, unmarried women, married women and widows). It seems, however, impossible to place too great a reliance upon it, since it was taken in the aftermath of a devastating war, when perhaps 50 percent of the male population were seeking work elsewhere (see Chapter X [2]) and large numbers of cattle had been lost. I would like to thank Jack Lewis, who is preparing a full analysis of the 1848 census, for discussions on the subject.
14. J. Maclean (1858), p 144.
15. The Xhosa and other southern Nguni peoples have been the subjects — perhaps the victims — of a substantial ethnography. What follows is necessarily selective. The most comprehensive work in English devoted specifically to the Xhosa is J.H. Soga (n.d.). Of the early accounts, L. Albert (1810) is quite outstanding. T.B. Soga (n.d.) and A. Kropf (1889) are not readily accessible, but full of useful information. Of the many works on related peoples, the best and most detailed is M. Hunter (1961) on the Mpondo. The fullest bibliography is in E.M. Shaw and N.J. van Warmelo (1972).
16. Most of the primary sources relating to the siting of homesteads and the construction of dwellings, granaries and cattle-enclosures are reprinted in E.M. Shaw and N. van Warmelo (1972).
17. J. Brownlee (1827), p 206; H. Lichtenstein (1812 — 1825), 1:322; L. Alberti (1810), p 68; J. van der Kemp (1804), p 439.
18. Chiefs were an important exception. See Chapter II.
19. One major problem on which evidence is lacking concerns the number of cattle possessed by the average homestead. On the one hand, one sees frequent references to 'thousands' of Xhosa cattle, while other indications point to each homestead owning relatively few cattle. These are (a) that so few Xhosa married more than one wife, although the bridewealth was usually no more than ten cattle (See sources cited in note 17 above); (b) that Xhosa were prepared to work a full year for a single head. See, for example, evidence of H. Hallbeck, Imperial Blue Book 538 of 1836 (hereafter *Abo Com*), p 338. One possible solution to the problem may be that some Xhosa possessed very many more cattle than others. According to J. Lewis (see note 13 above), the average homestead in the Ndlambe district averaged less than ten cattle

per homestead, but within each locality there was at least one homestead with considerably more, say between eighty and a hundred
cattle.

20. This interpretation follows that of J.J. Guy (1978), p 105.

21. J.J. Guy (1978), p 105; M. Wilson (1969c), pp 78 − 79. It is not clear
    how far one can push this argument. Could it be said, for example, that
    a lineage living in a favourable bioclimatic region will become more
    powerful than its neighbours because its cattle increase more rapidly?
    Dr Guy hints that this could be one explanation for the rise of the Zulu
    kingdom. Yet one must consider (a) that a favourable ecological situa-
    tion may attract invaders before it strengthens indigenes; (b) that an
    increase in cattle may lead to nothing more than an increase in bride
    price.

22. L. Alberti (1810), p 54.

23. This point has been forcefully argued by Professor Wilson in M. Wilson
    (1969a), pp 116 − 118.

24. See Chapter III (2).

25. Interviews with S. Ndamase and N. Qeqe, Shixini Location, Willowvale
    District, October 1975. Mr Ndamase and Mr Qeqe are respectively
    heads of the Ngqosini and Ngwevu clans.

26. Cf. M. Godelier (1977), p 41.

27. On Xhosa generosity, see I. Stocker, *RCC*, XIII, p 52; L. Alberti, (1810)
    pp 78 − 79; H. Lichtenstein (1812 − 1815), 1: 336. For Xhosa lavish-
    ness in time of plenty, see newspaper reports during the bountiful year
    of 1844, for example *Cape Frontier Times*, 23 May 1844.

28. For descriptions of Xhosa hunts, see L. Alberti (1810), pp 74 − 77;
    I. Stocker, *RCC*, XIII, pp 54 − 55; Lichtenstein; J.H. Soga (n.d.),
    pp 376 − 378; T.B. Soga (n.d.), pp 150 − 154; S. Kay (1833), pp 134
    − 138.

29. L. Alberti (1810), p 74, says one of the hunters plays the animal, but
    T.B. Soga, who gives the most detailed account of the ceremony,
    insists it is a girl. J.H. Soga says it is usually a girl, but sometimes a boy.

30. H. Lichtenstein (1812 − 1815), 1:333.

31. For instance, the Ndlambe chiefs travelling to a conference in 1824.
    W. Shaw (1860), pp 368 − 369; Interview with D. Mapakhati and
    M. Gobeni, Jujura Location, Willowvale District, 21 November 1975.

32. A. Smith of St. Cyrus (1895), p 65.

33. H. Dugmore (1858), p 7.

34. J. Campbell (1815), pp 367, 370.

35. A. Kropf and R. Godfrey (1915), pp 59, 73 − 74.

36. J.H. Soga (n.d.), pp 198 − 199; J. Campbell (1815), p 371.

37. A. Smith of St. Cyrus (1895), pp 56, 81, 105; J.H. Soga (n.d.), p 207.

38. H. Lichtenstein (1812 − 1815), 1: 268; J. Campbell (1815), p 367.

39. L. Alberti (1810), p 9.

40. J. Brownlee (1827), p 219; T. Philipps (1960), pp 179 − 182.

41. J. Campbell (1815), p 372.
42. L. Alberti, (1810), p 46.
43. A. Kropf and R. Godfrey, pp 56, 216. See also J.H. Soga (n.d.), Chapter 20. Each of the 12 months has a Xhosa name but Soga correctly points out that these might have been invented by the missionaries. The same could be said of the Xhosa names for the seasons.
44. There is a list of *iziganeko* in J.H. Soga (n.d.), pp 421 – 423; W.B. Rubusana (1966), pp 104 – 105.
45. W.B. Rubusana (1966), p 106.
46. The clearest accounts of the agricultural cycle are W. Shaw (1860), pp 413 – 415; J. Brownlee (1827), p 208; J. Maclean (1858), p 159.
47. J. Brownlee (1827), p 209; J. Campbell (1815), p 370; H. Lichtenstein (1812 – 1815); 1:334; S. Kay (1833), p 132; W. Shaw (1860), p 414.
48. F.G. Kayser, annual report, 3 July 1832. Kayser Papers, Cory Library, Grahamstown.
49. See, for instance, H. Lichtenstein (1812 – 1815), 1:316 – 317; W. Shaw (1860), pp 461 – 466; J. Backhouse (1844), p 278. The best description is in Andrew Smith's 'Kaffir Notes' manuscript in the South African Museum, Cape Town.
50. A. Kropf and R. Godfrey (1915), p 389.
51. H. Lichtenstein (1812 – 1815), 1:352, describing the great drought of 1804 – 1805.
52. J. Maclean (1858), pp 157 – 158; A. Kropf and R. Godfrey (1915), pp 37, 231; A. Smith of St Cyrus (1895), pp 174 – 175.
53. F.G. Kayser, Annual Report, 3 July 1832. Kayser Papers, Cory Library, Grahamstown.
54. L. Alberti (1810), pp 16 – 17n.
55. H. Lichtenstein (1812 – 1815), 1: 349; J. Backhouse (1844), p 241; W. Shaw (1860), p 403.
56. J.H. Soga (n.d.), p 123; Minutes of the Presbytery of Caffraria, q. D. Williams (1959), p 87; T.B. Soga q. E.M. Shaw and N. van Warmelo (1972), p 32.
57. Quoted by J.S. Marais (1944) p 17.
58. J. Barrow (1806), 1:144.
59. G. Stolz-J. Cuyler, 29 Dec. 1810, CO 2575.
60. A. Smith of St. Cyrus (1895), p 51; J.H. Soga (n.d.) p 382.
61. A. Smith of St. Cyrus (1895), pp 50, 140.
62. J. Backhouse (1844), p 249; H. Lichtenstein (1812 – 1815), 1:310 – 311; L. Alberti (1810), p 42. I identify the disease described by Lichtenstein and Alberti as anthrax through the skin 'eruptions'.
63. H. Lichtenstein (1812 – 1815), 1: 310 – 311.
64. L. Alberti (1810), p 70.
65. Interview with C. Phaphu, Grahamstown, 12 July 1975.
66. J. Brownlee (1827), p 209; Smith, 'Kaffir Notes'.
67. Cf. Vansina's comments on the traditional notion of migration, J. Van-

sina (1966), p 17 − 18.

CHAPTER II

1. See, for example, K.K. Ncwana (1963), and the fold-out genealogical tables in J. Maclean (1858) and A. Kropf (1889).
2. L.F. Maingard (1934), p 138; G. Harinck (1969), p 152n.
3. F. Brownlee (1923), p 111.
4. J.H. Soga (1930), pp 104 − 106.
5. William Kekale Kaye ('Native Interpreter'), MS n.d. (Nineteenth century), Grey collection 172c, South African Library, Cape Town. The MS has a translation attached, but I prefer my own. There are no differences in substance between the two translations.
6. The word 'clan' has had a somewhat chequered career in South African history and ethnology. A.T. Bryant, faithfully reflecting the implicit assumptions of oral tradition, thought that the basic principle of social organisation in pre-Shakan northern Nguniland was the clan, which he described as follows: 'Such single homestead (sic) popularly called a kraal was the basal unit of the old Zulu state, a microcosm of the whole clan system. The Zulu clan was but the multiplication of minor families thrown off from the common ancestral source still represented in the person of the reigning chieftain.' A.T. Bryant (1929), p 71. Bryant's views were subsequently challenged by Isaac Schapera, Monica Wilson and others, who pointed out that it was highly unlikely that particular localities were ever exclusively occupied by members of a single family, and that it was entirely possible that social stratification existed within the clan: for example, one lineage might be recognised as a chiefly lineage. A clear and sharp distinction was therefore drawn between the kinship unit, the 'clan' and the political unit, the 'chiefdom': 'A great deal of confusion has arisen because one writer after another has used *clan* both for the exogamous group claiming common descent, and for a local group under a subordinate leader. In this book *(The Oxford History)* it is used in the first sense only. By chiefdom is meant a political unit, occupying a defined area under an independent chief.' M. Wilson (1969a), p 118.

    The Xhosa themselves made no such distinction. The word *isizwe* (nation) is used for both clan and chiefdom. Hence one speaks of both *isizwe samaCira* (where the amaCira are an exogamous group, having no political functions) and *isizwe samaNdlambe* (where the amaNdlambe are a political unit, not practising exogamy). J.H. Soga, a native

Xhosa-speaker, epitomised the confusion by his complete inability to differentiate between the two. J.H. Soga (n.d.), pp 17 — 20. Clearly it is easier to distinguish between clan and chiefdom analytically than it is to do so historically.

7. AmaNgwevu — greybeards; amaMfene — people of the baboon; isiThathu — the three; amaNtshilibe — see J.H. Soga (1930), p 293.

8. 'Resurgam', 'Somana Hlanganise, late headman of Kentanie,' *Umteteli wa Bantu*, 4 Aug. 1932.

9. W.W. Gqoba, 'Umkhondo wamaGqunukhwebe' in W.B. Rubusana (1966), p 15.

10. Interview with P. Mqikela, Nqadu Great Place, Willowvale District, 31 Oct. 1974.

11. Interview with W. Nkabi, Bulembo Location, King Williams Town District, 24 Aug. 1975.

12. On the other hand, the clans were not so plastic that they could accommodate every political realignment. None of the chiefdoms ruled over by the descendants of Tshawe ever acquired any of the attributes normally associated with clanship. The Ntinde, for example, have existed as a chiefdom for over 300 years and are known to have absorbed many Khoi. Yet they have no common praises and they intermarry freely with one another. (One should note in passing that the hypothesis, recently put forward by R. Ross (1980), that the Ntinde are Khoi in origin is disproved by the journal of C.A. Haupt (1752), pp 294 — 299, which clearly identifies the Ntinde chief, Bange, as a Xhosa.) On one occasion, when commoner clans did unite in an attempt to recover lost influence, the result was not a new clan, but an association of councillors, the amaNdluntsha, who served an imaginary chieftainness.

13. Clan histories will be found in Appendix II. The incorporation of particularly important clans will be noticed at appropriate stages of the narrative.

14. Interview with R. Cakata, Xobo Location, Idutywa District, 5 Dec. 1975.

15. The only Iron Age archaeologist to work extensively in the area between the Fish and the Mbashe has been R.M. Derricourt. Unfortunately, the archaeological information presented in R. Derricourt (1977) is singularly uninformative. M. Cronin's excavation of an early Iron Age site at Mpame just east of the Mbashe has been dated to the seventh century A.D. (personal communication). There is still a great deal of uncertainty whether or not the early Iron Age people of the region were Khoi or Bantu-speaking.

16. For example, J.H. Soga (1930), pp 101 — 102; G. Harinck (1969), p 155n; M. Wilson (1969a), p 89.

17. J.B. Peires (1973).

18. They were however effectively used by M. Wilson (1959) in a famous

article which finally disposed of the idea that white and black arrived in South Africa simultaneously. Much of this is reprinted in M. Wilson (1969a), pp 78 – 85. See especially accounts of the *Santo Thome* and the *Santo Alberto*.

19. G. Harinck (1969), p 154n. There is however, much in this lengthy note which must be rejected. It is surprising that one who showed such acuteness in rejecting the date 1686 should have uncritically accepted the date 1702. (See Chapter IV, note 1. Harinck further follows J.K. Bokwe in confusing Gandowentshaba with Gwali. (See Chapter IV, note 2). Finally, his identification of 'Tokhe' with the Mpondo king Tahle is unsubstantiated, and in fact, unnecessary to his argument. 'Tokhe' must have been a subordinate chief for the *Stavenisse* survivors explicitly named 'Magamma' (unidentifiable) as the ruler of the Xhosa. For the full account of the *Stavenisse* shipwreck, see D. Moodie (1840), 1:426 – 428.

20. See Chapter IV (1).

21. See Chapter II (4).

22. The Thembu, Mpondo and Mpondomise, whose methods of transmitting oral history are identical to those of the Xhosa, all have genealogies of ten or more names between the myth which relates the founding of the kingdom and verifiable historical time, whereas the Xhosa have only three. See J.H. Soga (1930) for genealogies. This does suggest that the Xhosa kingdom was later than the others, and that the three names which survive denote different reigns. One is tempted to suggest a date of c. 1600, but 'before 1675' is less speculative.

23. Interview with Nombanjana Tyali, Kobonqaba 'B' Location, Kentani District, 12 Dec. 1975.

24. 'Vete' in F. Brownlee (1923), p 111. The question of the Dedesi is capably discussed by R. Derricourt in C. Saunders and R. Derricourt (1974), p 54.

25. Interview with N. Qeqe, Shixini Location, Willowvale District, Nov. 1975; F. Brownlee (1923), pp 111, 116; W.D. Hammond-Tooke (1968), p 87.

26. G.M. Theal (1897), 2: 111 – 112.

27. For the Qocwa, see Chapter II (4); for the Mfengu, S. Kay (1833), p 133; for the Khuma, S.E.K. Mqhayi (1939), p 2.

28. A certain chief Mjobi met one Grosvenor search party in 1783, and another in 1790. P. Kirby (1953), p 193; J. van Renen (1792), p 155. He told the first he was a Xhosa chief, and the second that he was a Thembu. The Ngqosini finally accepted Tshawe sovereignty. See Chapter II(4). For Mjobi, see J.H. Soga (1930), pp 194 – 198. The Ntshilibe clan also switched allegiance from Thembu to Xhosa. See M. Mbutuma, 'Ibali labaThembu', uncatalogued MS, Cory Library, Grahamstown.

29. For the Ngqosini, interview with S. Ndamase, Shixini Location, Willowvale District, 26 Nov. 1975. Information on the amaZangwa obtained

from informant at home of M. Sinkunzu, Nkomkoto, Kentani District, Dec. 1975.

30. Footnote to R. Collins (1809), p 9.

31. The social organisation of circumcision has changed considerably over time. This account is taken from L. Alberti (1810), pp 39 — 40; J. Brownlee (1827), pp 204 — 205; H. Dugmore (1858), pp 160 — 164; W. Shaw (1860) pp 455 — 460.

32. J. Backhouse (1844), p 232; Interview with M. Ranayi, Sholora Location, Elliotdale District, 18 Feb. 1976.

33. W. Shaw (1972), p 100.

34. L. Alberti (1810), p 84; H. Dugmore (1858), p 28.

35. H. Lichtenstein (1812 — 1815), 1:354.

36. Interview with M. Mnyanda, Mcotama Location, Kentani District, 21 Feb. 1976.

37. For the dispute between Siyolo and Mdushane, see S. Kay (1833), p 191. For the dispute between Sarhili and Hintsa, see MS 15,429 J. Ayliff — WMMS, Journal 14 July, 1835.

38. W.F. Xatasi, 'Ubukosi basexhibeni kwaNgqika,' *Izwi laBantu*, 27 May, 1902. The role played by Ngqika's age-mates is also noticed by J. Brownlee (1827), p 194.

39. W.Shaw (1860), pp 485 — 486.

40. Interview with M. Mnyanda, Mcotama Location, Kentani District, 21 Feb. 1976.

41. Interview with chief Meakin Phikisa (imiDushane), Nyumaka Location, Kentani District, 14 Jan. 1976.

42. H. Dugmore (1858), pp 12 — 13. For example of chiefs living with their senior brothers, see R. Collins (1809), pp 47 — 50.

43. R. Collins (1809), p 50; interview with Chief H. Dondashe, Kobonqaba Location, Kentani District, 14 April 1979.

44. See also G. Harinck (1969) and R. Ross (1980), both of which suffer from excessive reliance on isolated examples and lack a firm chronological framework.

45. 'Memorie van Jan van Riebeeck vir sy opvolger' in A.J. Boesëken (1966 — 1973), 1:34; D. Moodie (1840), 1:111. The Cape Khoi referred to any Bantu-speaker as Chobona. In this case, the geographical location near the Inqua rather than the Nama indicates that the reference is to the Xhosa rather than the Tswana.

46. D. Moodie (1840), pp 110 — 111.

47. Ibid., p 111.

48. Ibid., pp 152, 218, 225.

49. Ibid., p 110.

50. For a description of I. Schryver's visit to the Inqua, see D. Moodie (1840), 1: 433 — 440. The Inqua were living near the present town of Aberdeen (1689), which is described as five days journey from the Xhosa who were nearer the coast.

51. The full story is given by A. Kropf (1889), pp 5 – 11, who refers to Gwali as Gando throughout. (See Chapter IV, note 2.) It is quite clear from the clan-praises, that the Sukwini, Gqwashu and Nqarwane clans were formerly the Inqua. For example, 'Chwama', named in the tradition as Hinsati's son, is today one of the praises of the Sukwini clan. The Xhosa claim to Somerset East is based on the story of Gwali, and the mountains overlooking the town are believed to be named after Rharhabe's wife, Nojoli.

52. The fullest description of the battle against Hoho is by Juju (1880), which contradicts the claim of J.H. Soga (1930), p 130, that Hoho ceded the land peacefully.

53. Interview with W. Nkabi, Bulembo Location, King Williams Town District, 24 Aug. 1975.

54. C. Haupt (1752), p 292.

55. See Chapter IV (2).

56. C. Haupt (1752), pp 310 – 311.

57. See for example, W. Paterson (1789), p 85; D. Moodie (1840), 3:92; R. Collins (1809), p 12.

58. See L.W. Lanham (1964), pp 382 – 383.

59. L.F. Maingard (1934), pp 132 – 134.

60. C. Ehret (1967), pp 6 – 7.

61. J.A. Louw (1957), pp 3 – 5.

62. Ibid., pp 12 – 14.

63. R. Elphick (1977), p 60.

64. G. Harinck (1969), p 151.

65. For examples, see H. Lichtenstein (1812 – 1815), 1: 340 – 341; G. Thompson (1827), 2:7; A. Kropf (1889), p 34.

66. For rainmaking, see anonymous, undated manuscript, probably by William Shrewsbury, Wesleyan Methodist Missionary Archives, MS 15, 429. Cory Library, Rhodes University. For trade, see Chapter VII (1) below.

67. Nxele, the Xhosa diviner, had San wives. See extract from the diary of C.L. Stretch, copied by G.M. Theal, accession 378c, Cape Archives.

68. R. Collins (1809), p 44; J.V.B. Shrewsbury (1869), p 272; W.R. Thomson – J. Gregory, 30 April 1825, *RCC* XXI, p 174.

69. Interview with W. Nkabi, Bulembo Location, King Williams Town District, 24 Aug. 1975.

70. J. Massy – Major Forbes, 24 Aug. 1825, CO 234.

71. S.E.K. Mqhayi (1931), p 117.

72. M. Mzeni (Interview, Nqadu Location, Willowvale District, 19 Nov. 1975, amaMaya clan) and M. Mbutuma (MS 'Ibali labaThembu' – History of the Thembu, Cory Library, Rhodes University, Grahamstown) consider that the Maya exodus took place at the time of the dispute between Hlanga and Dhlomo, the Thembu equivalent of Cira and Tshawe, and therefore undateable. J.H. Soga (Thembu genealogy,

facing page 466 of [1930]) places it earlier. The Maya and the Hala (Thembu royal house) do not intermarry, which indicates that they are indeed related by blood. Members of the Qocwa clan interviewed do not remember arriving at the same time as the Maya, but seem to regard their sojourn in Thembuland as a waystation on their migration from further east. Interviews D.D.T. Mqhayi, Ngede Location, Kentani District, 28 Oct. 1975; A. Ndita, Ntlikwana Location, Willowvale District, 24 Oct. 1975; M. Kantolo Location, Kentani District, 27 Oct. 1975.

73.   J.H. Soga (1930), p 112. A. Kropf (1889), pp 5 — 11 confuses the story of Ziko with that of Gwali, as I argue below in Chapter IV note 2. G. Harinck (1969), following Kropf, thinks that the demotion of the Kwayi had a political motive.

74.   J.H. Soga (1930), pp 114 — 116. There is additional material on the Ndluntsha in Soga's unpublished uncatalogued version of *The South-Eastern Bantu*. M. Ranayi, interviewed Sholora Location, Elliotdale District, 18 Feb. 1976, the current head of the Ndluntsha, could add very little. The position of all the Great Councillors has lapsed since Transkei was brought under Colonial administration. After new land ceased to be available for the creation of new chiefdoms, junior branches of the royal house were awarded jurisdiction over land formerly administered by the Great Councillors.

75.   For the war between the Xhosa and the Ngqosini, see A. Kropf (1889) p 36; W.W. Gqoba, 'Umkhondo wamaGqunukhwebe' in W.B. Rubusana (1966), p 15.

76.   Among many Xhosa versions of the story of Khwane, see A.Z. Ngani (1947). For early English versions, see C. Rose (1829), pp 148 — 150; H. Dugmore (1858), pp 21 — 22.

CHAPTER III

1.   These are the terms in common use today, and it is possible to find them used similarly in the early nineteenth century. For example, Chungwa once referred to Xasa and Habana, chiefs inferior to him in power but not even members of his lineage, as his 'younger brothers'. J. Cuyler-Colonial Secretary, 7 July 1814, CO 2592.

2.   A. Kropf and R. Godfrey (1915), p 152; J.H. Soga (n.d.), pp 31 — 32; W.W. G(qoba), 'Umkhondo wamaGqunukhwebe' in W. Rubusana (1966), p 25. It is worth noting that all the chiefs were supposed to be present at important ceremonies involving one of their number.

For instance, the circumcision of Tyhali's eldest son was delayed because Maqoma was absent in Gcalekaland. C. Brownlee — G. Mackinnon, 9 Nov. 1849, BK 432.

3. The views expressed in this section differ radically from W.D. Hammond-Tooke (1965) which has been widely influential (M. Wilson (1969a), p 119n, for instance). There are two main points at issue. First, Hammond-Tooke argued that 'Cape Nguni' political units were inherently unstable and showed 'a strong tendency to split into two independent contraposed groups of co-ordinate status' (p 149). This fission was bilateral, each Right-Hand Son having a 'pre-emptive right to establish his own independent chiefdom' (p 152). In J.B. Peires (1975), I attempted to show that Hammond-Tooke's evidence did not support his conclusions, that segmentation was not bilateral but that all sons of chiefs became chiefs, and that fission was not sanctioned and expected, but occurred only in the case of Gcaleka and Rharhabe. Second, proceeding from the proposition that the Xhosa polity split every generation, Hammond-Tooke argued that it should be seen not as a single entity but as a 'cluster' of independent chiefdoms. This position derived partly from making territorial authority the sole criterion of political unity and partly from inadequate information concerning the tributary, military and judicial relationship between the king and the other chiefs. This question is also discussed in my article cited above. For the rest, I am happy to let the reader decide whether the evidence adduced in the following pages is compatible with Hammond-Tooke's hypotheses. This history could never have been written had I proceeded on the assumption that the Xhosa kingdom split mechanistically every generation and that its constituent chiefdoms had no closer relation to each other than they did to their Thembu neighbours.

4. For example, interviews with N. Qeqe, Shixini Location, Willowvale District, Oct. 1975. Cf J.H. Soga's explanation of the relationship between the king and the Ndluntsha, in the unpublished Xhosa MS of his *South-Eastern Bantu*, Cory Library Grahamstown, and S.E.K. Mqhayi's idealised picture of the happiness of Rharhabe's junior chiefs: 'Those little chiefs lived close together, and were set in a line to get the meat that was taken out of his pot, which they received still piping hot in all its broth!' 'URarabe' in W.G. Bennie (1935), p 133.

5. J.H. Soga (n.d.), pp 153 — 154.

6. For the Ngwane war of 1828, see W. Shaw (1972), p 138; F.G. Kayser, Diary, 27 July 1828. For war against the Mpondo, *Grahams Town Journal* (hereafter *GTJ*), 1 March 1838. Maqoma and Tyhali requested Hintsa's permission to begin the *Sixth Frontier War*. See, for example, 'Questions put by Colonel Smith to the Magistrate Tyali', 5 May 1836, 503 of 1837, p 79. Similarly, just before the *Eighth Frontier War*, 'Sandile has from the commencement of the Umlanjin affair been in

communication with Rili and flattering his vanity by reporting to him as a superior.' W. Fynn — G. Mackinnon, 18 Dec. 1850, BK 433. Even the much weaker Thembu King had the right to call out his subordinates. e.g. 'Ngubencuka called all the nations and small nations under him to come and fight against the Bhaca.' E.G. Sihele, 'Ibali laba-Thembu', uncatalogued MS, Cory Library, Grahamstown, p 15.

7. H. Dugmore (1858), p 32; Evidence of A. Smith, 635 of 1851, p 282; R. Godlonton (1835a), pp 217 — 218. King Sarhili's agreement was necessary before the chieftainness Sutu could be condemned for witchcraft. C. Stretch-Hall, 3 May 1842, 424 of 1851, p 118. For examples of intervention in succession disputes, see J.H. Soga (1930), pp 288 — 290; N.C. Mhala, 'Ukuvela kwamaNdlambe' in W. Bennie (1935), pp 147 — 148; W.W. G(qoba), 'Imbali yamaXhosa' in W. Rubusana (1966), pp 66 — 67.

8. When Ngqika abducted Ndlambe's wife, Thuthula, Ndlambe charged him at Hintsa's court. Hintsa decided in Ndlambe's favour and sent an army to assist him in obtaining compensation. Interviews with Chief E. Botomane, Ramntswana Location, Kentani District, 27 Oct. 1975; D. Runeyi, Shixini Location, Willowvale District, 25 Nov. 1975.

9. T.B. Soga (n.d.), p 115.

10. W. Gqoba in W. Rubusana (1966), pp 25 — 26. Cf. Evidence of John Tzatzoe, *Abo Com*, p 564, 'Although I am subject to the other chiefs, I could fight against the other chiefs.'

11. P.R. Kirby (1955), p 116. Cf. Sarhili in 1840, 'Hintza never trod on the Amararabi ground, and therefore I cannot, the Frontier chiefs have never come to see me, it will therefore not do for me to go and see them.' W. Fynn — G. Napier, 23 Dec. 1840, LG 404.

12. For instance, Ngqika consulted Ndlambe on whether to join the Slachters Nek rebels in 1815. H.C.V. Leibbrandt (1902), p 745.

13. Evidence of John Tzatzoe, *Abo Com*, p 567.

14. J.H. Soga (1930), p 190.

15. 'SoGwali kaNtaba' (S.M. Burns-Ncamashe), 'Ukuphala kukaPhalo uyise wamaXhosa', *Imvo Zabantsundu*, 23 Dec. 1961.

16. H. Dugmore (1858), p 33; S. Kay (1833), p 191.

17. C. Brownlee (1896), pp 185 — 186.

18. H. Dugmore (1858), p 28.

19. Bangela, chief of the Mdange, was deposed for 'cruelty' (Interview with B. Nqezo, Peelton Location, King Williams Town District, 24 Aug. 1975) or 'disobedience' ('Umkhondo kaMdange', in W. Rubusana (1966), p 70. Stinginess was the cause of the fall of Cira (Chapter II (1) and Thole, son of Langa (W. Gqoba in W. Rubusana (1966), p 66.) 'Stupidity' was the fault of Hleke (A. Kropf (1889), p 5.)

20. Interview with W. Nkabi, Bulembo Location, King Williams Town District, 24 Aug. 1975. Nkabi is not strictly correct historically, of course, but the point is that *ideally* chiefs of the same lineage do not

fight with each other. See also W. Shaw (1860), p 434.

21.   For Mdange, see A. Kropf (1889), p 5. For Mhala, see H. Dugmore (1858), pp 19 – 20.

22.   For the interference of Khawuta in Rharhabe affairs, see Chapter IV (2) below. For the interference of Hintsa in Mbede affairs, see Chapter IV (4) below.

23.   J.H. Soga (n.d.), pp 153 154.

24.   For instance, Hintsa was soon informed of the shooting of Chief Sigcawu by a commando in 1830. S. Kay (1833), p 302.

25.   All my best informants (Qeqe, Botomane, Melane) were agreed on this point. It is also evident from the actions of Maqoma, Tyhali, Mhala and Hintsa during the Frontier War of 1834 – 1835. See Chapter VI (3).

26.   S.E.K. Mqhayi (1931), p 115.

27.   See, for example, Hintsa in 1809, A. Stockenstrom (1887), 1:44. Sarhili in 1846, A. Stockenstrom-Cloete, 24 Aug. 1846, 912 of 1846, p 24.

28.   E. Botomane, 'Imvelaphi yamaRharhabe' in G. Nkonki (1968), p 110. Nkonki supplies an English translation, but this is my own.

29.   'Nzulu Lwazi' (S.E.K. Mqhayi), 'Umhala, A, Mbodla!', *Umteteli wa-Bantu*, 26 Sept. 1931. Mqhayi adds, 'There was nothing done at the Great Place of Sarhili which he [Mhala] did not follow after.'

30.   See the reaction of Phato in H.H. Dugmore (1958), p 86.

31.   Sandile is replying to his great councillor Tyhala, who is urging him not to take part in the war, Interview with Chief F. Mpangele, Mgwali Location, Stutterheim District, 26 Aug. 1975. For further evidence on this point see C. Rose (1829), pp 178 – 179; J.A. Chalmers (1877), p 379; F. Brownlee (1923), p 6.

32.   A. Kropf and R. Godfrey (1915), pp 219 ,481.

33.   For example, N. Qeqe, head of the Rudulu (Ngwevu clan): 'The Rudulu were dished out *(lawula)* as the amaJingqi, amaMali, amaVelelo were dished out ... It was said 'Qeqe is the Qawuka', that is the name of the ox from which we got our dish.' Interview, Shixini Location, Willowvale District, 20 Oct. 1975. See also note 4 above.

34.   J.V.B. Shrewsbury (1869), pp 175, 239; C. Rose (1829), p 179; W.K. Ntsikana, 'Imfazwe kaThuthula' in W. Rubusana (1966), p 53.

35.   W.D. Hammond-Tooke (1969), p 253.

36.   S. Kay (1833), p 77.

37.   J. Maclean (1858), p 128.

38.   J. Maclean (1858), p 116.

39.   P. Kirby (1955), p 118; S. Kay (1833), p 139; C. Rose (1829), p 167.

40.   This is clear from the speeches made at Sarhili's inauguration. See J. Ayliff-Wesleyan Methodist Missionary Society, 30 July 1835, MS 15, 429, Cory Library, Grahamstown. See also, H. Dugmore (1858), p 30.

41. Hintsa's speech at Sarhili's inauguration. See note 40 above.
42. Interview with Chief Thabatile Sigcawu, Jujura Location, Willowvale District, 4 Nov. 1975; A. Smith, 'Kaffir Notes'.
43. For example, during the cattle-killing of 1856 — 1857, Chief Oba led his followers to Thembuland in search of food. Interview with Chief Nqwiliso Tyhali, Middledrift, Ciskei, 17 Aug. 1975.
44. As W. Beinart (1980), has convincingly shown for the Mpondo.
45. See Chapter I (2).
46. Evidence of Tshuka, Cape of Good Hope, *Report and Proceedings of the Government Commission on Native Laws and Customs,* G4 of 1883, p 122.
47. There are thus obvious resemblances between the Xhosa social formation and the controversial 'Asiatic' mode of production. For a full discussion of the applicability of modes of production theory to precolonial Southern Africa, see P. Bonner (1980).
48. *'i-bandla:* the people of one chief, as distinguished from another . . . a division, cohort of an army, body of men.' A. Kropf and R. Godfrey (1915), p 23.
49. See note 58 below.
50. Interview with M. Kantolo, Kantolo Location, Kentani District, 27 Oct. 1975. The tradition is reproduced in full in Appendix I E.
51. J.T. van der Kemp (1804), p 436.
52. W.K. Ntsikana, 'Imfazwe kaThuthula' in W. Rubusana (1966), p 53.
53. H. Lichtenstein (1812 — 1815), 1:347; R. Collins (1809), pp 50 — 54.
54. S. Kay (1833), p 84.
55. Journal of F. Rawstorne, 23 May 1836, 1 Nov. 1836, LG 408.
56. J. Maclean-G. Mackinnon, 26 Feb. 1850, BK 74.
57. J. van der Kemp (1804), p 468; J. Campbell (1815), p 372.
58. J. Backhouse (1844), p 235; *Upundlo,* the sexual requisitioning of young women by the chief and his followers, often provoked resistance. Anonymous manuscript, probably by W. Shrewsbury, Chapter II. Wesleyan Methodist Missionary Society Archives, MS 15, 429, Cory Library, Grahamstown.
59. See Chapter II (1).
60. W.W. Gqoba in W. Rubusana (1966), p 66.
61. Mqhayi, Mxhamli, Dyani and Qasana. On the Ndlambe succession, see Chapter I (1).
62. Evidence of J. Read snr, *Abo Com,* p 603.
63. H. Dugmore (1858), p 16 — 17.
64. See the Dispatches of Mhala's Resident Agent, F. Rawstorne, LG 408. Also Journal of the Resident Agent, Fort Peddie, pp 10 — 11, Jan. 1845, GH 14/1; J. Maclean-G. Mackinnon, 26 Feb. 1850, BK 74.
65. N.J. Merriman (1957), p 103.
66. H. Dugmore (1858), pp 277 — 30; L. Alberti (1810), p 87; C. Rose (1829), p 142; S. Kay (1833), p 77; W. Shaw (1860), p 443.

67. W.K. Ntsikana in W. Rubusana (1966), p 53. One incident during the *War of the Axe* raised the interesting question of whether chiefship was inalienable. As a result of Mqhayi's treachery in two frontier wars, Sandile sent orders that the Xhosa 'were not to look upon Umgai's place as a Chief's place, nor upon his cattle as a Chief's cattle, but to treat them as a common man's.' Seeing that such a procedure undermined the basic principle that chiefship was an inherited quality, Mhala objected, saying, 'They were children of the same man, and how could a man be deprived of his chiefship.' J.W. Appleyard (1971), pp 57 — 58, 61. See also H. Lichtenstein (1812 — 1815), 1: 398.

68. E.G. Sihele, 'Ibali labaThembu', uncatalogued MS, Cory Library.

69. R. Collins (1809), p 16.

70. H. Lichtenstein (1812 — 1815), 1: 323.

71. H. Lichtenstein (1812 — 1815), 1: 353 — 354. For details of tribute, see W. Shaw (1860), pp 442 — 443; H. Dugmore (1858), pp 29 — 31; J. Maclean (1858), p 152; J.H. Soga (n.d.), pp 115 — 116; J. van der Kemp (1804), p 437; A. Kropf and R. Godfrey (1915), pp 9, 43, 298.

72. W.W. Gqoba in W. Rubusana (1966), pp 25 — 26.

73. J.K. Bokwe (1914), p 32.

74. 'Whenever a chief is circumcised some wealthy man is eaten up, so that they may get possession of the cattle.' Evidence of Dashe, Cape of Good Hope, *Report and Proceedings of the Government Commission on Native Laws and Customs*, G 4 of 1883, p 80. See also sources in note 71 above.

75. S. Kay (1833), pp 77, 81; J.W.D. Moodie (1835), 2: 275.

76. J. Brownlee (1827), p 201; R. Collins (1809), pp 16, 47.

77. S.E.K. Mqhayi, 'URharhabe' in W. Bennie (1935), p 132.

78. H. Dugmore (1858), p 38.

79. J. Solilo, 'Izinto zeKomkhulu lamaXhosa', in W. Bennie (1935), p 221.

80. Interview with M. Kantolo, Kantolo Location, Kentani District, 25 Oct. 1975. See Appendix I E.

81. For example, see W. Shaw (1972), p 109.

82. The case of one such unfortunate is recorded by S. Kay (1833), p 128n.

83. R. Niven-C.L. Stretch, 24 Aug. 1837, *Caffrarian Messenger,* Oct. 1837. Niven continues, 'Confiscation of cattle, and the facilities tacitly allowed the accused for escape, even when apprehended, diminish the list of its public executions. Within the last two years, none have been heard to suffer death by it, this side of the Great Kye.' In 1849, a year of mounting religious excitement, there were 27 witchcraft cases, involving 62 persons, of whom only eight were executed. H. Fynn-R. Southey, 14 Dec. 1849, Southey papers, Acc 611 (5), Cape Archives.

84. By P. Bonner at the Nguni workshop, Rhodes University, June 1979, on the basis of Swazi evidence.

85. R. Godlonton (1835 — 1836b), p 67.

86. J. Goldswain (1946 — 1949), 1: 135. See also R. Collins (1809), p 41, on Hintsa's residence.
87. H. Lichtenstein (1812 — 1815), 1: 331.
88. For example, J.W.D. Moodie (1835), 2: 244.
89. H. Dugmore (1858), p 28; C. Brownlee (1896), pp 178 — 179. M. Wilson and W.D. Hammond-Tooke have speculated that political authority might have derived from an extension of the *busa* system. See, for example, W.D. Hammond-Tooke (1975), pp 29 — 30. For an alternative explanation of the origin of political authority among the Xhosa, see Chapter II (1).
90. L. Alberti (1810), pp 77 — 78.
91. See Chapter II (3).
92. L. Alberti (1810), p 78.
93. See Chapter VI (2) and VIII (1).
94. I would like to thank Jacklyn Cock for discussions on this point. Needless to say she is not responsible for what follows.
95. For example, Hintsa: 'It was a fine thing to have nine wives, as they were of use working in the fields.' C. Rose (1829), p 185; a chief on first seeing a plough; 'This thing . . . is as good as ten wives,' W. Shaw (1860), pp 419 — 420.
96. R. Niven-C.L. Stretch, 24 Aug. 1837, *Caffrarian Messenger*, Oct 1838.
97. M. Molyneux 'Androcentrism in Marxist Anthropology', *Critique of Anthropology*, 3 (1977).
98. J.B. Wright (1979) is an excellent discussion of the material and ideological forms of control which men exercise over the productive labour of women in the Zulu kingdom. Most of it applies equally well to the Xhosa.
99. For example, the beads and copper rings worn by women were obtained through trade, and their bushbuck-skin caps through the hunt. L. Alberti (1810), pp 32 — 35.
100. Cf. Godelier on the Incas: 'The characteristic feature of this mechanism is that the mode of production positively *maintains* some of the former communal relations, takes advantage of them and utilises them for its *own* mode of reproduction; this results in the partial *destruction* of the former communal relations. In practice, therefore, both economically and politically, the Asiatic mode of production *prolongs and contradicts* former communal relations. On the ideological level, this inferior deformation of former communal relations *hides* the oppression and domination inherent in the Asiatic mode of production, because the old ideological forms, which now serve different ends, correspond to former more egalitarian relations of production.' M. Godelier (1977), pp 68 — 69. Emphases in the original.
101. This section is indirectly indebted to all the anthropologists since Mauss who have worked on reciprocity, but especially to M.D. Sahlins (1972).

102. W. Shaw-H. Rivers, 23 Aug. 1822, CO 2645.
103. W. Nel-J. Cuyler, 7 Feb. 1811, CO 2575. Ngqika also defended the killing of shipwreck survivors because 'they, being strangers, had nothing to do in the country any more than the wolves'. J.T. van der Kemp (1804), p 467.
104. Interview with N. Qeqe, Shixini Location, Willowvale District, Nov. 1975. The question in the middle of the passage is rhetorical: no question was asked by the interviewer at that point.
105. W. Fynn-G. Mackinnon, 7 Dec. 1850, BK 433.
106. See Chapter IV (1).
107. H. Lichtenstein (1812 – 1815), 1:402n.
108. Cory interview no 69, Tini Maqoma, Alice District.
109. C. Rose (1829), p 56. See also R. Collins (1809), p 51, for a similar attitude on the part of Ndlambe.
110. See J.H. Soga (1930), pp 131 – 132, 248 – 249.
111. For example see A.G. Bain (1949), p 92, and Chapter VII (2).
112. See for example, the rejection of Chungwa's attempts to become incorporated into Colonial society. Chapter IV (3). For attempts by Xhosa chiefs to marry white women, see Collins in Moodie, V., 48; J.E. Alexander (1837), 1: 400 – 401; Cory interview 125, Mrs. Waldek, Alice, 20 Jan. 1916.
113. A. Kropf and R. Godfrey (1915), p 139, 488. For example, Sarhili's message to Sandile during the *Ninth Frontier War:* 'This wild beast! These pale animals! I don't think we shall ever beat them!' Interview with S. Mgqala, Sittingbourne Location, King Williams Town District, 20 Aug. 1975. The most common term used by Xhosa (and many other speakers of southern Bantu laguages) for whites is *abelungu.*

CHAPTER IV

1. G.M. Theal gives 1702 as Phalo's date of birth through assuming that the Xhosa encountered by a party of European adventurers in that year were the Gwali. G.M. Theal (1897), 1: 391 – 392, 2: 124. But the fullest available account of this expedition gives no clear indication of who these 'Caffers' were, or where they were found. See H.C.V. Leibbrandt (1897), pp 133 – 149. Since Phalo was a reigning chief by 1736 (see note 4 below), it seems reasonable to assume that he was born no later than 1715.
2. The most straightforward version of the story of Gwali is that of Chief F. Mpangele, reproduced here as Appendix I D. This agrees in

substance with J.H. Soga (1930), pp 121 — 122, H. Dugmore (1858), pp 15 — 16, and G. Theal (1897) 2: 124. A second version is that of J.K. Bokwe, which appears in A. Kropf (1889), pp 5 — 11 and is summarised in English by G. Harinck (1969), pp 155 — 157. Here, the leading characters are Gandowentshaba and Tshiwo instead of Gwali and Phalo. The other figures — Mdange, Hinsati, Hleke and Ntinde — appear in both versions. The balance of probability is tipped towards the majority version by the factor that the Bokwe version leaves no room on the genealogy for Gwali at all. Indeed, Bokwe contradicts himself with regard to Gwali, calling him a brother of Ngconde on p 4 and a son of Ngconde on p 7. A third version, that of 'Sogwali kaNtaba' (S.M. Burns-Ncamashe), 'Ukuphala kukaPhalo, uyise wamaXhosa,' *Imvo Zabantsundu*, 23 Dec. 1961, is distorted by the fact that the amaGwali have accepted the seniority of the line of Phalo since the late eighteenth century, but nevertheless contains two features which seem to have descended from Gwali's claim to kingship: Phalo is not the son of a Tshawe, but of a commoner delegated by Mdange. Second Phalo's mother was put into the house of Gwali's mother, which suggests that she was not really the Great Wife.

3. 'Sogwali kaNtaba', 'EzobuRarabe Jikelele', *Imvo Zabantsundu*, 16 Sept. 1961. It is not clear who accompanied Gwali into exile. The Ntinde certainly did, and they were joined by the Hleke according to Mpangele but not according to A. Kropf (1889), p 5. According to A. Kropf (1889), p 110, the Gwali and Ntinde joined Mdange against Hinsati but according to J.H. Soga, 'UPalo', in W. Bennie (1935), p 113 they fled from him.

4. Phalo is best remembered in Colonial historiography as the king ruling at the time of the 1736 massacre of Hermanus Hubner, an ivory trader, and his party. The fullest account of this incident is H. de Vries and H. Scheffer, 'Relaas . . . weegens het voorgevallens op de Togt naar it land der Caffers,' Cape Archives, C 354, 10 July 1737, pp 313 — 324. Phalo was not personally involved, but it may account for his subsequent reluctance to meet European travellers.

5. Almost all my informants told me this story. An English version may be found in W.T. Brownlee, (1925), pp 5 — 6.

6. J.H. Soga (1930), pp 36 — 37. W.D. Hammond-Tooke (1965), p 159.

7. The best account of this is in J.H. Soga (1930), pp 142 — 144.

8. Cory interview no. 113, Mdandala, 26 Jan. 1910, Kentani.

9. S.E.K. Mqhayi, 'URarabe' in W. Bennie (1935), p 132. See also W.F. Xatasi, 'Inkosi zamaXhosa,' *Izwi Labantu*, 31 Dec. 1901; Interview with M. Mnyanda, Mcotama Location, Kentani District, 21 Feb. 1976.

10. This incident is very obscure and appears to be forgotten today. The only account of it is in A. Kropf (1889), pp 35 — 37. It is also referred to by W.W. Gqoba, 'UNxele' in W. Bennie (1935), p 196, and A. Smith

'Kaffir Notes' but unfortunately, they do not expand. It is not clear when it happened, but since only three years intervened between the deaths of Phalo and Gcaleka, I have assumed it took place before Phalo's death. At one time, Rharhabe also lived between the Tsomo and the White Kei, R. Collins (1809), p 9.

11. S. Mqhayi, 'URarabe,' in W. Bennie (1935), p 132.

12. A. Sparrman (1786), 2: 10 − 11; for Gcaleka's death, see R.J. Gordon-G. Fagel, Aug. 1779. VC 595, p 130.

13. F. von Winkelman (1789), p 90.

14. Interview with Chief J.M. Dinizulu Sigidi, Taleni Location, Idutywa District, 29 Oct. 1975.

15. Interview with Chief E. Botomane, Ramntswana Location, Kentani District, 16 Dec. 1975.

16. Winkelman, p 92.

17. The fullest description of Ruiter's career is given by A. Sparrman (1786) 2: 155 − 158. This appears to correspond to other references, although R.J. Gordon labelled it 'a chain of stupid lyes', VC 595, p 85.

18. Cory interview no. 114. Sijaxo (head of iNtshinga and Chief Councillor of Gwebinkumbi), Willowvale, Jan. 1910. Sijaxo confuses Hintsa with Khawuta. The story of the elevation of the Giqwa is given in J.H. Soga (1930), pp 145 − 146. However, whereas Soga's version says Nqwiliso was already Khawuta's pipebearer at the time of his elevation, Giqwa informants say that Khawuta had met him while hunting. This latter version would suit the incorporation hypothesis better than the former. Interview with M. Maki, Shixini Location, Willowvale District, 26 Nov. 1975. The possibility that the amaGiqwa were the Hoengiqua is strengthened by the fact that Ruiter was allied with the anti-Ndlambe faction which fled to Khawuta during the 1793 war. See P.J. van der Merwe (1940), p 57.

19. For the creation of the Qawuka, see Chapter II (1). J.H. Soga's accounts of the division between iNtshinga and iQawuka (1930), pp 145 − 146; (n.d.) pp 22, 101 − 104, are misleading. His main informant must have been Ntshinga, since he refers to them as the 'royal' division and to the Qawuka as the 'commoner' division, and accepts the Ntshinga version of Qawuka origin. Another source of confusion was his inability to differentiate between 'clan' and 'chiefdom'. His version is the only one previously published, as far as I am aware. My own version is derived from interviews with N. Qeqe, the religious head of the Qawuka division (Shixini Location, Willowvale District, 26 Nov. 1975), Mbhodleha Maki, descendant of Maki, the Giqwa circumcised with Sarhili (Shixini Location, Willowvale District, 26 Nov. 1975) and P. Mqikela who was a councillor of Ngangomhlaba, the last king in whose reign (1924 − 1933) this division had practical significance. (Nqadu Location, Willowvale District, 24 Nov. 1975).

20. Interview with M. Ranayi, Sholora Location, Elliotdale District,

18 Feb. 1976.

21. See Chapter II (3).

22. A. Kropf, (1889), p 34; S.E.K. Mqhayi, 'URarabe' in W. Bennie (1935), pp 34 – 35. C. Brownlee (1896), p 182.

23. Interview with B. Nqezo, Peelton Location, King Williams Town District, 24 Aug. 1975. Translated from the Xhosa. See also R. Collins (1809), p 9, J.H. Soga, (1930), p 130.

24. 'Vervolg van het Dagverhaal van de landreise daar den weledelen Gestrengen Heer Mr. Joachim Baron van Plettenburg' in E.C. Godee Molsbergen (1916 – 1932) 4: 47.

25. C.A. Haupt (1752), pp 297, 299.

26. W. Paterson (1789), p 92 – 93; R.J. Gordon-G. Fagel, Aug. 1779, VC 595, p 130.

27. The fullest account is in E.G. Sihele's fine uncatalogued Thembu history, 'Ibali labaThembu', Cory Library, Grahamstown. Rharhabe sided with his wife's people, the Ndungwana, against their overlord, the Thembu king, Ndaba. Ndaba took refuge with Gcaleka upon which, Rharhabe, to prevent a combination, persuaded him to move to his (Rharhabe's) place. After a while Ndaba left in fear of his life, taking some of Rharhabe's cattle with him. According to A. Kropf (1889), pp 38 – 40, the quarrel arose over the dowry owed to Rharhabe by the Qwathi. J.H. Soga (1930), pp 131 – 132, manages to combine the two stories, except that he wrongly asserts that Ndaba wanted Rharhabe's daughter for himself. The quotation is from A. Kropf (1889), p 40. By Jan. 1783 Ndlambe was the chief of the Rharhabe. H. Muller and J.A. Holtshausen, 'Rapport' in P.R. Kirby (1953), p 170.

28. J.H. Soga (1930), pp 128 – 129 makes out that Rharhabe was victorious in his war with Gcaleka, that he was loyal to Phalo and that he migrated willingly. This is contradicted by the contemporary evidence of Haupt, Gordon and Paterson. Ngqika, Rharhabe's grandson admitted on at least one occasion that the amaRharhabe had been defeated. See A. Stockenstrom (1887), 1: 45; R. Collins (1809), p 9. S. Mqhayi, 'URarabe' in W. Bennie (1935), pp 130 – 131, depicts Rharhabe as the leader of a great migration.

29. N.C. Mhala, 'Ukuvela kwamaNdlambe' in W. Bennie (1935), pp 146 – 149. N.C. Mhala was Ndlambe's grandson. According to J.H. Soga (n.d.), p 31, Langa, chief of the amaMbalu also assisted in installing Ngqika. The story is related by Sir George Cory (1910 – 1939), 1: 26n, but the decision seems purely arbitrary since Sir George was apparently not informed that the councillors and Ndlambe solicited Khawuta's recognition for their respective candidates.

30. 'Commandant A. van Jaarsveld's Report of the Expulsion of the Kafirs,' in D. Moodie (1840), 3: 110 – 112; R. Collins (1809), pp 9 – 10, 14; J. Brownlee (1827), p 193; Nqezo interview (see Note 23 above). Contemporary reports placed the blame on Gona Khoi employed by Boers

whom the Xhosa claimed stole their cattle. See D. Moodie (1840), 3: 91 — 92. But it appears quite clearly from the deposition of J.H. Potgieter (ibid, p 92) that not all the Xhosa chiefdoms were equally responsible, and that the Gona Khoi in question were refugees from Xhosaland.

31. J. Marais (1944), p 18; P.J. van der Merwe (1938), p 306.

32. J. Marais (1944), p 22; R. Collins (1809), p 12; J. van Renen (1792), p 152.

33. P. van der Merwe (1938), pp 280 — 282; D. Moodie (1840), 3: 96.

34. This account of the *Second Frontier War* is based on J. Marais (1944), Ch. IV; P.J. van der Merwe (1940); A.S. Faure, 'Dagregister, gehouden den ondergetekende Landdrost of desselfs rheis naar 't Cafferland' (10 Dec. 1793), VC 68, pp 483 — 532; H.D. Campagne, 'Berigt nopens den oorsprong, voortgang en ruptures der Kaffers' VC 76, pp 205 — 285.

35. N.C. Mhala, 'Ukuvela kwamaNdlambe' in W. Bennie (1935), W.F. Xatsai, 'Ubukosi basexhibeni kwaNgqika,' *Izwi Labantu*, 27 May 1902.

36. For accounts of the war itself, see N.C. Mhala in W. Bennie (1935); Juju (1880), pp 291 — 292; J. Brownlee (1827), pp 194 — 195; J.H. Soga (1930), pp 158 — 160; R. Collins (1809), pp 11 — 13; J. Barrow (1806), 1: 146 — 147. Some confusion surrounds the question of whether Ngqika's defeat of Ndlambe and of Hintsa were separate events. The evidence of Barrow who visited Ngqika shortly after the war would seem to be conclusive. Some authorities give the commencement of the war as 1797, but it was reported to the Colonial authorities as early as 7 May 1795. GR 1/2.

37. H. Lichtenstein (1812 — 1815), 1: 352 — 353, 355; J. Campbell (1815), p 368. R. Collins (1809), p 13, reports that Ngqika's punishments were very cruel, but it should be remembered that he had spoken to many of the latter's enemies.

38. J. Brownlee — (Bird), 19 Jan. 1821, CO 142; R. Collins (1809), pp 16, 47.

39. J.T. van der Kemp (1804), p 436.

40. W.F. Xatasi, 'Ubukosi basexhibeni kwa Ngqika' *Izwi Labantu*, 27 May 1902; H. Dugmore (1858), pp 12 — 14, 20. The imiNgxalasi of Peelton Location, King Williams Town District formerly claimed to being descended from Mlawu's councillors. See W.D. Hammond-Tooke (1958), pp 110 — 111. They now claim descent from Lutshaba, a brother of Rharhabe. Interview with Chief S. Komani and councillors, Peelton Location, King Williams Town District, 5 Sept. 1975. Yet another tradition states that Ntsusa, the daughter of Rharhabe, was appointed chief in place of Mlawu. See S. Kay (1833), p 152.

41. This is deduced from the fact that Nqeno was a Ngqika supporter in 1803, whereas Thole was a Ndlambe supporter, H. Lichtenstein (1812 — 1815), 1: 376, 392. Thole and his descendants are not heard of after

1809 (R. Collins [1809], p 50). There is also a tradition which ascribes the change in fortunes to the superior generosity of Nqeno's mother. See W. Rubusana (1966), pp65 – 67. The two explanations are by no means incompatible.

42. T. Lyndon-Major MacNab, 7 Oct. 1799, BO 68.

43. R. Collins (1809), p 12; J.T. van der Kemp (1804), pp 415 – 417.

44. T. Lyndon-Major MacNab, 7 Oct. 1799, BO 68. For Buys generally, see A.E. Schoeman (1938).

45. J. van der Kemp (1804), p 408; H. Lichtenstein (1812 – 1815), 1: 312, 356; J. Marais (1944), pp 115 – 116.

46. J. van der Kemp (1804), p 415.

47. For a perceptive discussion of frontier relations, see H. Giliomee, (1979), pp 296 – 299. Giliomee's chapter provides an excellent chronological narrative which I hope absolves me from attempting the same here.

48. P. van der Merwe (1930), pp 265 – 266, 269.

49. J. Marais (1944), pp 12, 24, 28; H. Lichtenstein (1812 – 1815), 1: 385, 409; H. Fynn (1950), p 180; T. Pringle (1835), p 285; F. Dundas-G. Yonge, 20 Feb. 1800, *RCC* III, p 55.

50. J. Campbell (1815), p 365.

51. J. Campbell (1815), p 367.

52. See Chapter IX (2).

53. See Chapter VII (3).

54. H. Lichtenstein (1812 – 1815), 1; 426; Diary of N. Hurter, Feb. 1792, GR 1/9.

55. T. Lyndon-Major MacNab, 7 Oct. 1799, BO 68. Ngqika must have had a vastly exaggerated idea of Buys's importance.

56. J. Cuyler-Colonial Secretary, 9 Dec. 1809, CO 2566; R. Collins (1809), p 51.

57. H. Lichtenstein (1812 – 1815), 1: 268 – 269.

58. J.S. Marais (1944), pp 5 – 6. Even Adriaan van Jaarsveld, who led the Boers in the *First Frontier War,* recognised that the Zuurveld 'had formerly been their own land.' J.S. Marais (1944), p 6. The Slachters Nek rebels of 1815 were prepared to return the Zuurveld to the Xhosa for the same reasons. H.C.V. Leibbrandt (1902), p 744.

59. Journal of R.J. Gordon, 9 Jan. 1778, VO 592, p 118. Van Plettenburg was also aware that the chiefs he dealt with were subject to Rharhabe, but he evaded the issue by sending Rharhabe presents via the Gwali chiefs. E.C. Godee-Molsbergen (1916 – 1932), 4: 47, 50 – 51. The chiefs who made the agreement believed they were about to be attacked by the Governor's party. R.J. Gordon-G. Fagel, n.d. (1799), VC 595.

60. J.S. Marais (1944), p 6; T. Pringle (1835), p 270; J. Brownlee (1827), p 192. There are numerous allusions to the second 'purchase' from the company official. A. Stockenstrom (1887), 1: 58; R. Collins (1809),

p 10; J. van der Kemp (1804), p 467; T. Philipps (1960), p 158; Diary of C.L. Stretch, MS 14, 588, Cory Library, Grahamstown.

61. S.D. Neumark (1957). See, for example, pp 102 – 103. Neumark's ideas were taken up by M. Legassick (1971). It is hoped that S. Newton-King's current research on frontier trade will do much to clear up the the questions raised by the Neumark thesis.

62. This was as true of the Boers as of the Xhosa. Cf. 'while it was not possible to subjugate the Xhosa by force of arms, it was easy to capture cattle.' H. Giliomee (1979), p 303.

63. For the return of cattle by chiefs, see P. van der Merwe (1938), p 282; D. Moodie (1840), 3:98; T. Pringle (1835), p 286. For restraint by the Boers, see J. Marais (1944), pp 11 – 12, 23; H. Lichtenstein (1812 – 1815), 1: 364.

64. M. Wilson (1969b), p 240.

65. See note 60 above.

66. All these points are covered in Diary of N. Hurter, 14 – 29 Feb. 1792, GR 1/9. For Xhosa assistance of Khoi against the San, see C. Haupt (1752), p 288.

67. J. Marais (1944), pp 28 – 29.

68. J. Marais (1944), p 18n; R. Collins (1809), pp 19, 42.

69. J. Marais (1944), p 98.

70. Deposition of H.J. van Rensburg, 3 Dec. 1797, BO 72.

71. J. Marais, (1944), pp 106 – 107, thought that Chungwa was mistaken when he apprehended a British attack. Giliomee, who has examined additional evidence, feels that the attempt was indeed made. H. Giliomee (1975), pp 283 – 285. Andrew Smith, 'Kaffir Notes', writing some twenty-five years later, reports a rumour that Van der Walt, leader of the Boer volunteers, attacked Chungwa independently of Vandeleur.

72. Examination of C. Botha. 15 Aug. 1800, *RCC*, III, p 213.

73. *Transactions of the London Missionary Society*, II, pp 83 – 85; J. van der Kemp-A. Barnard, 3 Aug. 1802, quoted in S. Bannister (1830), p clxxiv. H. Giliomee (1975), p 322, doubts Chungwa's innocence. The chief grounds for this appears to be that Chungwa led the Xhosa in the 1799 war. But it was precisely because Chungwa was successful then that he wished to keep the peace. Giliomee also cites a statement of R. Collins (1809), p 13. But Collins mixed up the confusion of 1786 with the war of 1793 (R. Collins [1809], p 10) and probably confused 1799 and 1801. In addition to the citation already given in this and the preceding note, the following also indicate Chungwa's innocence before he was attacked by the commando; J. Marais (1944), pp 106n, 132; G. Yonge-F. Dundas, 5 Jan. 1801, *RCC*, III, pp 370 – 371: 'Questions proposed to Mr. Maynier' 27 Aug. 1801, *RCC*, IV, p 61.

74. H. Lichtenstein (1812 – 1815), 1: 383 – 386.

75. R. Collins (1809), p 46.

76. J. Cuyler-A. Barnard, 26 Sept. 1807, CO 2561; R. Collins (1809), p 54; J. van der Kemp and J. Read, 'Annual Report of the London Missionary Society' in *Transactions of the LMS*, II, p 241.
77. See Table I.
78. J. Cuyler-A. Barnard, 26 Sept. 1807, CO 2561.
79. Transcript of a conversation between Cuyler and Ndlambe, 25 Feb, 1808, CO 2563.
80. J. Cuyler-Colonial Secretary, 9 Dec. 1809, CO 2566.
81. J. Cuyler-C. Bird, 4 Oct. 1810, CO 2572.
82. J. Cuyler-Colonel Secretary, 8 Jan. 1811, CO 2575.
83. This is not, of course, to suggest that only the British committed atrocities. Cf. The murder of Landdrost Stockenstrom: A. Stockenstrom (1887), 1: 59 – 60, 67.
84. H. Lichtenstein (1812 – 1815). 1: 365.
85. Ibid., 1: 397 – 404.
86. Ibid., 1: 376 – 377, 381, 399, 426.
87. Ibid., 1: 384 – 386.
88. Ibid., 1: 384, 438 – 439.
89. Ibid., 1: 405, 407 – 408.
90. Ibid., 1: 386.
91. Ibid., 1: Ch. 24.
92. CO 2559 'Information received from Captain Alberti' Enclosure in J. Cuyler-Captain Gordon, 6 March 1806; W.M. Freund (1972), p 637.
93. Most Xhosa see this as the sole reason for the quarrel between Ngqika and Ndlambe. There is a good account by W.K. Ntsikana, 'Imfazwe ka-Thuthula' in W. Rubusana (1966). The date of the incident is clear from R. Collins (1809), pp 15 – 16 and is confirmed by the fact that even the best of the earlier sources (Van der Kemp, Alberti, Lichtenstein) fail to mention so dramatic an incident. Since the abduction occurred in 1807, it cannot have been the cause of hostilities commencing in 1795.
94. J. Cuyler-A. Barnard, 26 Sept. 1807. CO 2561.
95. J. Cuyler-Governor Caledon, 25 Dec. 1809, CO 2572.
96. J. Cuyler-Colonial Secretary, 18 Feb. 1810, CO 2572.
97. CO 2577. See depredation reports for the first and third quarters; CO 2566 Memorial of P.J. du Toit. Enclosure in J. Cuyler-Colonial Secretary, 4 July 1809; CO 2575 J.A. van Niekerk-J. Cuyler, 13 Feb. 1811; CO 2576 A. Stockenstrom-C. Bird, 26 July 1811.
98. H. Lichtenstein (1812 – 1815), 1: 426.
99. H. Lichtenstein (1812 – 1815), 1: 402n; L. Alberti (1810), p 116; H. Maynier and A. Somerville-G. Yonge, 14 Aug. 1800, *RCC*, III p 212.
100. H. Lichtenstein (1812 – 1815), 1: 395.
101. 'Message from Lieutenant Colonel Graham to Gaika' (undated) *RCC*, XXI, p 349.
102. 'Uzugcine mna wena nam ndikugcine'. S.E.K. Mqhayi, 'Idabi lama-

Linde' in W. Bennie (1935), p 194.

103. Evidence of John Tzatoe (Dyani Tshatshu), *Abo Com*, p 569. Tshatshu was, of course, giving the sense of the exchange rather than the actual words used.

104. For Ngqika's participation in the proceeds of cattle-raiding, G. Fraser-C. Bird, 31 July 1818, CO 2613.

105. A. Stockenstrom (1887), 1: 158; Letters from Capt. Gethin-G. Fraser, 31 Oct. 1817, 3 Nov. 1817, 13 Nov. 1817, CO 2608. For the Colonial response, see C. Bird-J. Cuyler, 4 Dec. 1817, CO 4839.

106. Speech of Nxele's councillors, according to notes taken by Stockenstrom and reproduced in T. Pringle (1835), p 284. Even if Pringle 'doctored' this speech stylistically, there is no reason to believe that the sense differs from what was actually said. Stockenstrom approved of the version given. A. Stockenstrom (1887), 1: 120.

107. Ndlambe had quarreled with Mdushane's mother. J.H. Soga (1930), p 150.

108. See Chapter V.

109. Interview with Chief E. Botomane, Ramntswana Location, Kentani District, 16 Dec. 1975.

110. Curiously, this opinion was shared by Grahamstown politician and Cape M.P., George Wood, who started off as a trader in Hintsa's country, and thought him 'a marvelously clever man, the greatest black man I ever knew.' Cape of Good Hope *Report and Proceedings of the Government Commission on Native Laws and Customs*, G4 of 1883, For more on Hintsa, see the works of Kay, Shaw, Shrewsbury, Rose and especially, his conversations with Andrew Smith. P.R. Kirby (1955), pp 115 – 118.

111. J. Ayliff-Wesleyan Methodist Missionary Society, 30 July 1834. MS 15,429. Cory Library, Grahamstown.

112. C. Rose (1829), pp 142 – 143.

113. J.H. Soga (1930), pp 288 – 290, places the incident in the time of Sarhili, which is very unlikely, since the quarrel must have taken place shortly after Nqoko's death. Chief J.M. Dinizulu Sigidi (descendant of Mguntu) places the incident in the time of Hintsa, when the amaMbede were still living in the Ciskei. He says Mguntu and Kalashe (whom he calls Mahote) were twins, but 'the councillors preferred Mguntu'. (Interview, Taleni Location, Idutywa District, 29 Oct. 1975).

114. Interview with S. Ndamase, Shixini Location, Willowvale District, 20 Nov. 1975. Mr. Ndamase is the 'chief' of the Ngqosini, being descended from the chief mentioned in the tradition. It is impossible to date this and the preceding incident.

115. J. Brownlee-C. Bird, 26 Aug. 1822, CO 163.

116. Interview with D. Runeyi, Shixini Location, Willowvale District, 25 Nov. 1975.

117. A. Stockenstrom (1887), 1: 115. W. Shrewsbury-W.M.S.· Directors,

31 Mar. 1827, Wesleyan Missionary Society Archives MS 15, 429, Cory Library, Grahamstown.

118. This was Fraser's commando of Jan. 1818. See G. Fraser-C. Bird, 31 July 1818, CO 2613.

119. J. Williams-G. Fraser, 1 May 1818, CO 2613.

120. A. Kropf (1889), p 49.

121. T. Pringle (1835), p 278.

122. For an eyewitness account of the battle of Grahamstown, see C.L. Stretch (1876). For a discussion, see Chapter IX (2) below.

CHAPTER V

1. For a good example of this among a South African people see E.J. Krige, quoted in I.M. Lewis (1968), pp xviii — xix.

2. On the possibility of inferring history from ritual, see T.O. Ranger (1974), pp 26 — 33.

3. The best short discussion of Khoisan religion is in I. Schapera (1930), Chs. VII & XIII.

4. The word 'witches' as used in this thesis includes sorcerers.

5. For a full list of these, see L.F. Maingard (1934), p 135.

6. G. Harinck (1969), p 153.

7. J. Cradock-Graham, n.d. *RCC*, VIII, p 160.

8. Private communication from Graham, No addressee, 2 Jan. 1812, *RCC*, VIII, p 237.

9. Lieutenant Colonel Graham's answer to Gaika, n.d., *RCC*, XXI, p 350.

10. 'Justus' (1837), p 43 n.

11. J. Graham, no addressee, 26 Feb. 1812, *RCC* VIII, p 286.

12. T. Pringle (1835), p 174.

13. Cradock-Col. Vicars, 27 Nov. 1813, reprinted in *Report of the Trial Stockenstrom v. Campbell for Libel* (2nd ed., Cape Town, 1838), p 21.

14. See, for example, L. Alberti (1810), pp 87 — 93; J. Campbell (1815), pp 374 — 375); H. Lichtenstein (1812 — 1815) 1: 341 — 344.

15. 'A Native Minister' (I. Wauchope) (1908), p 34.

16. *Ukukafula*: see A. Kropf and R. Godfrey (1915), p 177. For a description of the ceremony see J.H. Soga (1930), pp 90 — 91.

17. The fullest accounts of Xhosa religion are J.H. Soga (n.d.) chs. VIII — X, and A. Kropf (1889), pp 186 — 209. Most of the early travellers and missionaries have useful descriptions. See, for example, L. Alberti (1810), ch XI; H. Lichtenstein (1812 — 1815), 1: 311 — 321; W. Shaw (1860) pp 444 — 466. The perspective adopted in thsi section owes

much to R. Horton (1967), and P. Worsley (1970).

18. Anonymous, undated manuscript (probably by William Shrewsbury), Wesleyan Methodist Missionary Society Archives, MS. 15,429, Cory Library, Grahamstown.

19. Interview with Mdandala, 26 Jan. 1910, Kentani. Cory interviews, Cory Library, Grahamstown.

20. I.M. Lewis (1971), ch. VII.

21. L. Alberti (1810), pp 93 − 94; H. Lichtenstein (1812 − 1815), 1: 319; J.W.D. Moodie (1835), 2: 271.

22. J. Campbell (1815), p 366.

23. The best accounts of Nxele are those by 'A Native Minister' (1908); an untitled, undated manuscript by William Kekale Kaye, 'A Native Interpreter', No. 172C, Grey Collection, South African Library, Cape Town; J.L. Döhne (1862), which is the basis for A. Kropf (1891); J. Read (1818). Other accounts include J. Brownlee, 'On the origins and rise of the prophet Nxele,' No 172C, Grey Collection, South African Library, Cape Town; extract from the diary of C.L. Stretch, copied by G.M. Theal, Accession 378c, Cape Archives; and T. Pringle (1835), Ch. XIV.

24. Döhne (1862), p 59. The concept of sin was, of course, borrowed from Christianity which Nxele seems to have adopted at an early age.

25. Kaye MS, 'Camagu' means 'Forgive and be pacified', and is usually addressed to an ancestor or a diviner.

26. Nxele subsequently told the missionary James Read that 'a large fire was presented before him, and that there were persons who had got hold of him to throw him into it, but that Taay came and delivered him.' J. Read (1818), p 284.

27. T. Pringle (1835), p 279.

28. We are indebted to Read's account for our knowledge of Nxele's early beliefs.

29. The most satisfactory account of how Nxele extricated himself from this difficulty is in W. Shaw (1972), p 103. 'Makanna ordered them all to enter the water and wash, with which the people complied, but as they entered the water *en masse* they could not refrain from bellowing forth the usual war yell. Makanna now informed them they ought not to have done so, and since they had thought proper to follow their own headstrong will, and not listened to his directions, all was now over, and every man might return to his own home.'

30. There is something of a problem in establishing the chronology of Nxele's actions and attitudes, as most accounts of Nxele were written after his death, and none of them traces the changes in his behaviour. The very exact account left by Read of Nxele's Christian phase enables us to infer such changes.

31. T. Pringle (1835), p 286.

32. 'A Native Minister' (1908), p 34. Wauchope's evidence may be regarded

as particularly interesting. His grandfather fought on the Ndlambe side at Amalinde and he knew several of Nxele's descendants.

33. G.M. Theal (1915), 3: 205.
34. These were particularly rife during the great drought of 1842. See *GTJ*, 4 Aug. 1842; *CFT*, 3 Jan. 1843.
35. For Mngqatsi, see D. Williams (1959), pp 301 — 302; J. Backhouse (1844), pp 217, 278; F.G. Kayser, Diary, 13 Nov. 1836, Kayser papers, Cory Library, Grahamstown.
36. There are very few contemporary European references to Ntsikana, and these are very brief. C. Rose (1829), pp 135 — 137, is a typical example. Fortunately there are several detailed accounts in Xhosa. J.K. Bokwe (1914), the only substantial description in English, purports to be a distillation of these, but he omits occurrences detrimental to Ntsikana's image. See note 39 below. The Xhosa accounts by W.K. Ntsikana (Ntsikana's son), M.N. Balfour (one of his converts) and Zaze Soga, which appeared in various nineteenth-century missionary publications, have been reprinted in W.G. Bennie (1935). Kaye, MS (cited in n. 23), contributes a valuable secular viewpoint.
37. 'Ntsikana rose up from his bed, and went to the door, and just as he came out, the ox walked on towards the gate of the kraal. Ntsikana followed and as he himself reached the gate, Hulushe [the ox] ... was already standing looking at him, as if wondering and in sorrow ... Ntsikana approached and, stretching forward his arms, Hulushe bent his neck. For a while Ntsikana leaned his body with outstretched arms between the horns and on the neck of the favourite ox.' J. Bokwe (1914), p 29.
38. 'Le nto indingeneyo, ithi makuthandazwe, makuguqe yonke into.' Ntsikana in W.G. Bennie (1935), p 10. The crucial verb here is 'guqa', To stoop, bend on or upon; to bend the knee, to kneel down' A. Kropf and R. Godfrey (1915), p 137.
39. This absolutely critical stage in Ntsikana's development is ignored by Bokwe, although he reprints Zaze Soga's Xhosa account, which mentions it (p 53). There is also a reference to Ntsikana's rejection by Ndlambe in N. Falati, 'The Story of Ntsikana', MS. 9063, Cory Library, Grahamstown, dated St Marks, 1895.
40. J. Bokwe (1914), p 12. I prefer my own translation.
41. Kaye MS.
42. J. Bokwe (1914), p 15.
43. Kaye MS.
44. The official version from which this is taken is printed in J. Bokwe (1914), p 26. I prefer my own translation. The earliest printed version of this hymn is in C. Rose (1829), pp 136 — 137. It is noteworthy that the specifically Christian lines of the official version do not appear in Rose's rendering, and are attributed (in another context) by Wauchope (whose grandmother was converted by missionary Van der Kemp)

to Van der Kemp. 'A Native Minister' (1908), p 21.

45.   J. Bokwe (1914), p 20.

46.   B. Wilson (1975), pp 236 – 237.

47.   Quoted by D. Williams (1959), p 331.

48.   W. Shaw (1860), p 471.

49.   J.W.D. Moodie (1835), 2:279.

50.   J.V.B. Shrewsbury (1869), pp 273 – 274; W. Shaw (1860), p 464. Missionary Young once told some Xhosa who were reluctant to leave their ploughing for his preaching that God would send a crop failure. (S. Young – *WMS*, 5 Jan. 1830, MS 15,429, Cory Library, Grahamstown). The threat succeeded.

51.   J.V.B. Shrewsbury (1869), p 383.

52.   A. Steedman (1835), 1: 27; W. Shaw (1860), p 331; J.W.D. Moodie (1835), 2: 255 – 256.

53.   For a very full discussion of this aspect, see D. Williams (1959), ch. IV.

54.   S. Kay (1833), pp 183, 272. For further examples of the missionaries being blamed for drought and disease, Shrewsbury, Journal entry for 23 June 1827, MS 15,429 Cory Library, Grahamstown; W.R. Thompson-R. Plasket, 13 April 1826, CO 291; H. Fynn (1950), p 196.

55.   W.R. Thompson-Colonial Secretary, 23 Feb. 1822, *RCC*, XIV, p 299; H. Somerset-J. Bell, 15 Jan. 1829, CO 366.

56.   Deposition of W.G. Atherstone, quoted in evidence of T.F. Wade, *Abo Com*, p 393.

57.   W. Macmillan (1963), pp 101n, 150.

58.   Quoted D. Williams (1959), p 165.

59.   Mrs. J. Ross – (sister), 13 Oct. 1829, q. U. Long (1947), p 231.

60.   Evidence of John Tzatzoe, *Abo Com*, p 572.

61.   J. Read (1818), p 283.

62.   J. Philip, q. W. Macmillan (1963), p 97.

63.   J.T. van der Kemp – (?), 3 Dec. 1806, CO 2559.

64.   There is a very full discussion in D. Williams (1959), Ch. VII.

65.   D. Williams (1959), Ch. VII, lays some stress on the 'ethnic' factor to the extent of suggesting that the Gqunukhwebe were more attentive to Christianity because they had so much Khoi 'admixture'. This proposition appears quite illogical. More Khoi converted because more Khoi were uprooted. Their ethnic origins had nothing to do with it.

66.   J. Backhouse (1844), p 239; J. Warner, q. D. Williams (1959), p 334.

67.   J. Campbell (1815), p 367. See also W. Macmillan (1963), p 97.

68.   J. Williams-G. Burder, 14 Apr. 1818, q. B. Holt (1956), p 80. Punctuation supplied.

69.   W. Shaw-G. Marley, 3 Dec. 1827, Cory Library, Grahamstown. For more on the relation between Christianity and European civilisation, see Chapter VII (4).

CHAPTER VI

1. A. Stockenstrom (1887), 1: 157 – 158.
2. Ibid., 1: 55.
3. C. Stretch (1876), p 302.
4. C. Somerset-Bathurst, 15 Oct. 1819, *RCC*, XII, p 339. For a description of the ceded territory, see Stocker in *RCC*, XIII, p 50.
5. C. Somerset's plan was never a neutral belt, pure and simple, although this is what he told Ngqika. See D. Williams (1961), p 26, n. 45; cf. D. Macmillan (1963), p 79, A.K. Millar (1965), pp 117 – 118, 125. Millar's comment that Somerset did 'so much to procure' peace on the frontier seems singularly inappropriate. Somerset was well aware of the agricultural potential of the territory (see note 4 above) and intended to settle a party of Highlanders in it, but they never arrived (H.K. Hockly [1949], p 85.) See also A. Stockenstrom (1887), pp 132, 167 – 168, 172 – 173, 237 – 238; J. Alexander (1837), 1: 373. As late as 1825, Somerset proposed to give away part of the Ceded Territory to win political support among the Boer farmers. M. Donaldson (1974), p 367. No record was made of the agreement, and the whites present at the time disagree as to what was actually said. C. Somerset-Bathurst, 15 Oct. 1819, *RCC*, XII, pp 337 – 345; C. Bird-Commissioners of Enquiry, 27 Dec. 1824, *RCC*, XIX, p 357; H. Somerset-Commissioners of Enquiry, 24 Oct. 1825, CO 323; Evidence of A. Stockenstrom, *Abo Com*, pp 46 – 49.
6. The Colonial assertion was made on the extremely dubious grounds that there were no Xhosa west of the Keiskamma at the time of Ngqika's birth. Evidence of Stockenstrom, *Abo Com*, p 46.
7. C. Rose (1829), p 75; J. Brownlee (1827), 2: 200.
8. J. Soga (n.d.), p 345.
9. 'Deposition of Ganya,' 503 of 1837, p 74; 'Questions put by Colonel Smith to the Magistrate Tyalie,' 5 May 1836, 503 of 1837, p 75; Evidence of J. Philip, *Abo Com*, p 679; S. Kay (1833), p 495.
10. S. Kay – *WMS*, 18 Feb. 1826; S. Young – *WMS*, 28 Mar. 1828. S. Young – *WMS*, 1 Jan. 1829; all in *WMS* archives MS 15,429, Cory Library, Grahamstown; W. Shaw (1860), pp 470 – 474; W. Shaw-H. Rivers, 8 Aug. 1823, CO 2653; W. Shaw-Officer Commanding Caffre Drift Post, 12 Aug. 1825, CO 283.
11. See Chapter IV (4).
12. H.M. Scott-Commissioners of Enquiry, 25 Jan. 1825, *RCC*, XIX, pp 476 – 478; T. Philipps, Letters, Vols. I and II, p 114. MS 14,264, Cory Library, Grahamstown, adds: 'He Ngqika, was however compelled, he fixed upon two very strong men each put a string around the man's neck and ran different ways but they failed (he was not dead). They were then forced to tread on him — too shocking to relate.' It is disturbing that this passage was omitted from the published edition of

Philipps' letters.

13. See for example, C. van der Nest-W. Harding, 7 Sept. 1823, CO 2649.

14. Somerset later denied that he had given any such order. But see C. Somerset-H.M. Scott, 14 Feb. 1822 and 22 Feb. 1822, *RCC*, XIV, pp 291, 295.

15. T. Philipps (1960), pp 149 — 150; H.M. Scott-Commissioner of Enquiry, 29 June 1824, *RCC*, XVIII, pp 37 — 43.

16. After the death of Xasa and the flight of Funa in the 1818 — 1819 Frontier War, Botomane had emerged as the leader of the imiDange on the frontier. Ntsusa was the daughter of Rharhabe. She was assisted in her administration by Nukwa, a full brother of Ndlambe.

17. W.R. Thomson-H.M. Scott, 10 June 1822, CO 165.

18. The Colonial authorities had a vague idea that Ngqika would be able to recompense himself for the loss of the Ceded Territory by taking land from Ndlambe. A. Stockenstrom (1887), 1: 159; J. Jones-Rogers, 13 Oct. 1821, *RCC*, XIV, p 143; Evidence of J.H. Rutherford, 50 of 1835, pp 205 — 206.

19. C. Trappes-C. Bird, 25 June 1821, CO 2637; J. Bell-Stockenstrom, 9 Apr. 1829, LG 1; W. Shaw (1972), p 152.

20. Mrs J. Ross — (father), 22 Dec. 1829 in U. Long (1947), p 235.

21. H. Somerset-R. Plasket, 31 Jan. 1826, CO 287. For more details on this commando, see Note 95 below.

22. H. Somerset-J. Bell, 3 Apr. 1828 and enclosures, CO 357.

23. H. Somerset-J. Bell, 6 Mar. 1829, CO 366.

24. H. Somerset-R. Bourke, 29 Aug. 1826, CO 287.

25. A. Steedman (1835), 1: 8 — 10.

26. W. Shaw-H. Rivers, 23 Aug. 1822, CO 2645.

27. Mrs. J. Ross — (father), 22 Dec. 1829 in U. Long (1947), p 235.

28. A. Steedman (1835), 1: 5 — 6.

29. C. Rose (1829), p 97; J.W.D. Moodie (1835), 2: 263.

30. Ibid.

31. Mrs. J. Ross — (father), 22 Dec. 1829 in U. Long (1947), p 235.

32.   S. Kay (1833), pp 45 — 46.

33. T. Philipps (1960), p 286.

34. W.R. Thomson-H.M. Scott, 10 June 1822, CO 165.

35. Evidence of J. Read Snr. *Abo Com*, p 603.

36. S. Kay (1833), pp 184 — 185; W.R. Thomson-J. Bell n.d., CO 362; *Cape Argus*, 30 Dec. 1857.

37. The sons of Ndlambe mentioned most often in early Colonial records are 'Guishee', 'Koetze', 'Maveechee' and Mxhamli. Three sons of Ndlambe are reported to have died in the battle of Grahamstown, G. Cory (1910 — 1939), 1: 390.

38. J. Bell-A. Stockenstrom, 9 Apr. 1829, LG 1; C. Rose (1829), pp 211 — 212. The Ndlambe and the Gqunukhwebe were themselves at odds, since the Gqunukhwebe were by their own admission, occupying

Ndlambe territory. See evidence of W. Shaw, *Abo Com*, pp 92 — 93; W. Shaw-R. Bourke, 6 Apr. 1826, *RCC*, XXVI, p 368; J. Brownlee-C. Bird, 1 May 1823, CO 184.

39. S. Kay (1833), p 191. Kay did not unfortunately give the name of the son, but it was probably not Siwani, the eventual successor, who was still a minor in 1835. See also H. Dugmore (1858), p 33.

40. S. Young — *WMS*, 26 June 1829, MS 15,429 Cory Library, Grahamstown; Stockenstrom (1887), 1: 313.

41. J.V.B. Shrewsbury (1867), p 244; W. Shrewsbury — *WMS*, 31 Dec. 1826, MS 15,429, Cory Library Grahamstown; C. Brownlee (1896), pp 185 — 186; J. Maclean (1858), p 132.

42. After the war of 1835, the imiDushane divided into 3 sections: that under Qasana, that under Siyolo (also hostile in the war) and that under Siwani. Siwani's mother, Nonibe, was made much of by Governor D'Urban, and this may be the reason why Siwani eventually emerged as Mdushane's heir.

43. Interview with W.M. Nkabi, Mbulembo Location, King Williams Town District, 24 Aug. 1975; W.D. Hammond-Tooke (1958), pp 83 — 84. Gasela's action may have been irregular, since his father Nukwa was still alive over twenty years later. J. Maclean (1858), p 134.

44. Two fine unpublished manuscripts on Thembu history by M. Mbutuma and E.G. Sihele, both entitled 'Ibali labaThembu', have been deposited in the Cory Library, Grahamstown. Other sources are J.H. Soga (1930), Ch. XXIV and W.D. Cingo (1927). The latter is not very helpful. Because of the continuing political importance of clans among the Thembu and because there is relatively little documentary information about their early history, Thembuland seems a particularly promising and important area for historical fieldwork. One can only hope that it will be undertaken as soon as possible.

45. J.H. Soga (1930), p 473; Sihele MS.

46. R. Collins (1809), p 46; S. Kay (1833), pp 151 — 152.

47. Sihele is very detailed here.

48. F. von Winkelman (1788 — 1789), pp 92 — 93.

49. R. Collins (1809), p 43; A. Stockenstrom (1887), 1:44; Mbutuma MS.

50. J.H. Soga (1930), p 186. Today the Nqabe consider themselves Thembu.

51. H. Lichtenstein (1812 — 1815), 1: 359; J. van der Kemp (1804), p 404.

52. Sihele MS.

53. For the continuation of this dispute, see Chapter VIII.

54. Sihele MS; A. Smith (1955), p 130.

55. This history of the Bomvana is taken entirely from J.H. Soga (1930), Ch. XX. Soga spent most of his life as a missionary among the Bomvana. Soga appears to have had trouble fitting the Bomvana *amabali* into a coherent chronological sequence, and I have rearranged the order so that Bomvana history is compatible with information on the period derived from other sources. It is difficult to date these occurrences,

but they must have occurred before 1809, since Hintsa was already
married to Nomsa at that date. Collins (1809), p 41.

56. The best account of Bhaca history available to me was an unpublished
     typescript by W. Power Leary, Resident Magistrate at Mt. Frere, dated
     22 May 1906, NA 623, Cape Archives. I am indebted to R. Moorsom
     for this reference. Other accounts of their history may be found in
     J.H. Soga (1930), pp 435 – 446; W.D. Hammond-Tooke (1955 –
     1956); A.T. Bryant (1929), *passim*. See also Cory interview no. 119,
     W.R.D. Fynn, Queenstown, April 1913.

57. For excellent Ngwane accounts of these events, see D.F. Ellenberger
     and J.C. MacGregor (1912), pp 186 – 188; Msebenzi (1938), Ch. 5 and
     pp 261, 262, 264. For extracts from various contemporary works, see
     evidence of F.T. Wade, *Abo Com*. pp 409 – 412. In addition to works
     there cited, see T. Philipps (1960), pp 350 – 353.

58. It is not clear to what extent Dundas was deliberately mislead by
     Ngubencuka. For his own account of events, see W. Dundas-
     H. Somerset, 1 Aug. 1828 and his report dated 15 Aug. 1828, quoted in
     Msebenzi (1938), pp 239 – 249.

59. See H. Somerset-R. Bourke, 26 Aug. 1828, quoted in Msebenzi (1938),
     pp 250 – 252.

60. For example, B. d'Urban-Hintsa, 29 Apr. 1835, 279 of 1836, p 33.

61. The only contemporary report of these hostilities is S. Kay's journal
     in S. Kay – *WMS*, 29 Apr. 1830. See also journal entry for 1 June 1830
     in S. Kay – *WMS* (date illegible); W. Boyce – *WMS* 11 May 1830;
     W. Shaw – *WMS*, 18 May 1830 (all references MS 15,429, Cory
     Library, Grahamstown); S. Kay (1833), p 299; 'Thembu History per
     chief Falo Mgudlwa at Qumanco, 18 June (19)35' in McLaughlin
     papers, Cory Library, Grahamstown.

62. J.H. Soga (1930), pp 365 – 366.

63. J. Orpen-W. Stanford, 11 June 1907. Cory accession no. 1242.

64. This is one of the 12 or so *amabali* that almost all informants knew.
     T.B. Soga explains the tradition in terms of a custom called *inyama
     yamahlwempu* (poor peoples' meat) which he says applies to poor
     Xhosa, as well as Mfengu. The idea is that the recipient should be
     provoked into earning his keep, rather than lazily accepting the genero-
     sity of others, T.B. Soga (n.d.), pp 100 – 103. J.H. Soga suggested that
     the tale might relate to a witchcraft ordeal. The Mfengu were much
     feared as sorcerers. J.H. Soga-W. Mears, 7 May 1928. Mears Papers,
     S.A. Library, Cape Town.

65. Journal of W. Shrewsbury 10 Dec. 1826 in Shrewsbury – *WMS*,
     31 Dec. 1826, MS 15,429 Cory Library, Grahamstown. The original is
     fuller than the version in J.V.B. Shrewsbury (1869), p 236, and is
     worth quoting in full since it was written before views of Xhosa-Mfengu
     relations were coloured by the political bias of the observer. 'The several
     Kaffer chiefs, ever anxious to augment their power and influence by an

increase of dependents, gave them a favourable reception. To some parties, they made grants of land and enriched them with cattle, permitting them to live by themselves, under a subordinate chief of their own country, while others were so distributed and mingled amongst the Kaffers, that in another generation they will be one people.' Apart from G. Cory (1910 – 19139) 3: 133, no historian, not even Theal, has believed Missionary Ayliff's politically motivated claim that the Mfengu were in any sense slaves of the Xhosa. The Mfengu themselves emphatically reject this view. For one especially spirited discussion among many, see the series of articles, headed 'The Fingo Slavery Myth' which appeared in the *South African Outlook* (June-Sept. 1935). The traditional view is set out in J. Ayliff and J. Whiteside (1912). The best Xhosa account is R.T. Kawa (1930). R. Moyer (1976) is the only detailed history which has yet appeared.

66. T. Makiwane – *South African Outlook* (1935), p 195.
67. One tradition says that the Zizi pointed out Njokweni, while hiding their real chief, Mhlambiso. R. Moyer (1976), pp 119 – 120. It seems equally possible that he was simply a nominee of Hintsa. See also R. Moyer (1976), p 184.
68. R. Kawa (1930), p 45.
69. A.B. Armstrong-H.G. Smith, 6 March 1835, 503 of 1837, p 220.
70. R. Kawa (1930), p 45.
71. J. Ayliff and J. Whiteside (1912), p 19.
72. 'The Fingoes,' undated unsigned manuscript, dictated by Veldman Bikitsha NA 623, Cape Archives.
73. H. Somerset-J. Bell, 27 Feb. 1829, CO 366.
74. It was widely suspected at the time that Maqoma was being removed to make way for the Khoi settlement which followed him. See, for example, Evidence of R. Aitchison, *Abo Com*, p 8. D. Campbell, the Civil Commisssioner of Grahamstown, seems to have had a personal dislike of Maqoma. See D. Campbell-J. Bell, 27 Mar. 1829, CO 2712. Stockenstrom was also a strong proponent of expulsion. See Stockenstrom (1887), 1: 305 – 311. Maqoma was a particular favourite of Colonel Henry Somerset and this may have prejudiced Somerset's many enemies against him.
75. Evidence of J. Philip, *Abo Com*, p 631. Maqoma told the missionary Ross, with whom he was on excellent terms, that he was intervening at Bawana's request. Mrs. J. Ross – (sister), 13 Oct. 1829, quoted U. Long (1947), p 231.
76. Interview with Chief Gladstone Maqoma, Ngqungqe Location, Kentani District, 19 Dec. 1975.
77. G.L. Cole-G. Murray, 2 Jan. 1830, 252 of 1835, pp 52 – 54. See also evidence of T.F. Wade, *Abo Com*, pp 372 – 373.
78. Mrs. J. Ross – (parents), 17 Apr. 1830 quoted by U. Long (1947), p 233.

79. Evidence of R. Aitchison, *Abo Com,* p 9. For a detailed description of the effects of the drought on the Xhosa, see letter from 'A Subscriber,' *GTJ,* 18 July 1833.

80. See A. Stockenstrom-Government Secretary, 12 May 1830, quoted in *Abo Com,* p 105.

81. W. Chalmers-C.L. Stretch, 21 Nov. 1835 in U. Long (1947), p 83.

82. 'Statement of the Frontier Caffres to Colonel Somerset and Governor Sir B. D'Urban,' 503 of 1837, p 49. This was dictated to the missionary Chalmers by Tyhali and his councillors on 31 Dec. 1834, at the time of the greatest Xhosa successes, and sets out the causes of the war as percieved by them. The second quotation is from the evidence of T.F. Wade, *Abo Com,* p 391.

83. Evidence of C. Bradford, *Abo Com,* p 160.

84. Quoted W. Macmillan (1963), p 91. See also evidence of C. Bradford, *Abo Com,* p 160.

85. Evidence of R. Aitchison, *Abo Com,* p 9.

86. Ibid., p 8.

87. Evidence of W. Gisborne, *Abo Com,* p 357.

88. Letter to *South African Commercial Advertiser,* quoted S. Bannister (1830), p 98. See also evidence of W. Shaw, *Abo Com,* pp 54 − 55; H. Fynn (1950), p 196. The Boers did want the Ceded Territory and the Xhosa must have been aware of this. See 'Afer' (1827), pp 11 − 13; Evidence of W. Cox, *Abo Com,* p 432; W. Chalmers-C.L. Stretch, 21 Nov. 1835, quoted U. Long (1947), p 83.

89. Evidence of W. Gisborne, *Abo Com,* p 357.

90. 'Deposition of Chief Botma', 503 of 1837, p 77.

91. At the time some emphasis was laid on the distinction between patrols and commandos. Patrols were composed of soldiers only and performed routine functions; commandos were far larger, included civilians, and were summoned for major punitive operations or when resistance was expected. The difference was one of degree rather than of kind, and 'commando' is used here to include patrols as well. See Evidence of T. Philipps and evidence of W. Dundas, *Abo Com,* pp 26, 134.

92. The commando system was severely criticised at the time, particularly by Stockenstrom. See A. Stockenstrom (1887), 1: 100 − 105; Evidence of A. Stockenstrom, *Abo Com,* pp 82 − 88. For examples of herders' negligence, see R. Collins (1809), p 21; *GTJ,* 12 Dec. 1839. S. Mitra (1911), pp 149 − 150 criticised carelessness in the very middle of a war. For more recent criticism see W. Macmillan (1963), pp 77 − 79; H.A. Reyburn, 'Studies in Frontier History: V: Reprisals,' *The Critic* (Cape Town), Oct. 1935.

93. That this was the usual procedure is evident from the report of a commando which was never accused of any impropriety. See H. Somerset-Plasket, 17 Jan. 1826. CO 287. See also R. Armstrong-H. Somerset, 6 Feb. 1826, CO 287; H. Somerset-T.F. Wade, 12 Aug. 1831 quoted

Abo Com, p 114; Evidence of W. Gisborne, *Abo Com,* p 358.

94. 'Statement of the Frontier Caffres' 503 of 1837, p 49; W. Chalmers-B. D'Urban, 6 Feb. 1835, 503 of 1837, p 82. Evidence of A. Stockenstrom, *Abo Com,* p 114; C. Rose (1829), pp 92 – 93.

95. The correspondence on this incident sheds an interesting light on the trustworthiness of official reports. Henry Somerset's almost comic attempts to justify himself involve, *inter alia*, the invention of a dying Xhosa whose blood marks the spoor all the way to the guilty homestead. See H. Somerset-R. Plasket, 26 Dec. 1825, CO 234; H. Somerset-R. Plasket, 20 Jan. 1826, CO 287; A. Armstrong-H. Somerset, 18 Jan. 1826, CO 287. For a hostile account, see T. Philipps (1960), pp 293 – 294, 219 – 298.

96. The commando which visisted the Ntsusa passed through Ngqika's country, but Xhosa as far away as the Ndlambe fled to Mt. Coke mission station to avoid it. S. Kay (1833), p 87.

97. 'Tyali-Editor,' *GTJ,* 10 Apr. 1834. See also S. Mqhayi (1931), p 102; 'Questions put by Col. Smith to the Magistrate Tyhalie,' 503 of 1837, p 75; J. Ross-J. Bell. 17 Aug. 1830, CO 381. 'A Kaffer' – Editor, *GTJ,* 17 Apr. 1834; Evidence of John Tzatzoe, *Abo Com,* p 572.

98. J. Philip, quoted W. Macmillan (1963), p 97.

99. See Chapter III (2).

100. L. Alberti (1810), pp 116 – 117.

101. R. Collins (1809), p 51; C. Rose (1829), p 56.

102. J. Campbell (1815), p 371.

103. T. Philipps (1960), p 175.

104. Evidence of T. Philipps, *Abo Com,* p 34; W.R. Thomson-H. Somerset, 29 June 1830, LG2.

105. Evidence of T. Philipps, *Abo Com,* p 34.

106. H. Somerset-Government Secretary, 24 Apr. 1834, CO 434; Evidence of T. Philipps, *Ab Com,* p 34.

107. For Ngqika see R. Collins (1809), p 48; for Tyhali, J. Alexander (1837), 1: 400; for Sandile, Cory interview no. 125, Mrs Waldek, Alice, 20 Jan. 1916.

108. *GTJ,* 17 Oct. 1833.

109. Evidence of J. Read, snr. *Abo Com,* pp 593 – 594.

110. See Chapter III (2).

111. See Chapter IV (4).

112. Evidence of W. Shaw, *Abo Com,* p 92.

113. The exact circumstances surrounding the death of Sigcawu was the subject of a heated debate between Wade and Stockenstrom at the Aborigines Committee. The consequences of the incident were determined by what the Xhosa believed had happened, namely that the commando had told Sigcawu 'to come near and lay down his assegaes; he did so, and the commando shot him dead.' 'Statement of the Frontier Caffres,' 503 of 1837, p 49.

114. S. Kay (1833), pp 302 — 303. Emphases in the original.

115. J. Ross — J. Philip, 31 Jan. 1836, quoted *Abo Com*, p 718.

116. Evidence of John Tzatzoe, *Abo Com*, pp 564, 567.

117. W. Chalmers-H. Somerset, 20 Dec. 1834, 252 of 1835, p 123. For further evidence on the initial hesitation of the chiefs see D. Campbell-Government Secretary, 23 Dec. 1834, 252 of 1835, p 124; F. Kayser — *South African Commercial Advertiser* quoted *Abo Com*, p 720.

118. J. Ayliff-B. D'Urban, 19 June 1835, 503 of 1837, p 229; 'Deposition of a great Chief (Name concealed),' 23 Apr. 1836, 503 of 1837, p 229.

119. Even the Sotho felt that the fate of the Xhosa prefigured their own. Evidence of J. Philip, *Abo Com*, p 629.

120. A.B. Armstrong-H.G. Smith, 6 Mar. 1835, 503 of 1837, p 220. See also Deposition of R. Walker, 9 Feb. 1835, 503 of 1837, p 214. J. Ayliff-B. D'Urban, 18 June 1835, 503 of 1837, p 220; Cory interview no. 116, Manxiwa, Willowvale, 29 Jan. 1910.

121. H.G. Smith-B. D'Urban, 29 Apr. 1835 and 31 Aug. 1835, G. Theal (1912), pp 138, 361. See also Chapter VIII (3).

122. S. Kay (1833), pp 304, 383.

123. 'Deposition of Tyalie' 4 May 1836, 503 of 1837, p 234; H.G. Smith-B. D'Urban, 30 Aug. 1835, G. Theal (1912), p 360. 'Deposition of Macomo,' 28 Apr. 1836, 503 of 1837, p 232; Hintsa attempted to make a separate peace with the Boers saying they 'should have restitution for their cattle in three days.' A. B. Armstrong — (?) H.G. Smith 21 Feb. 1835, 503 of 1837, pp 216 — 217. See also J. Backhouse (1844), p 299.

124. Enclosure 12 in B. D'Urban-Lord Glenelg, 9 June 1836, 503 of 1837, 'Constituting a chain of proofs . . . concerning the Conduct of Hintsa,' pp 210 — 244, proved this point conclusively. See for example pp 214, 216, 235.

125. Evidence of S. Young, *Abo Com*, p 659.

126. W.B. Boyce-H.G. Smith, 23 July 1836 and J.M. Bowker-H.G. Smith, 23 July 1836, 503 of 1837, pp 267 — 268.

CHAPTER VII

1. L. Alberti (1810), p 71.

2. Cf. the Mpondo who did trade for cattle to obtain subsistence after the Mfecane. W. Beinart (1980).

3. L. Alberti (1810), p 71; H. Lichtenstein (1812 — 1815), 1: 340; S. Kay

(1833), p 120.

4.   L. Alberti (1810), p 71.

5.   There was a large salt-pan on the Zwartkops River, and salt was easily obtainable from the sea. Van der Kemp found that the inland Xhosa did not use salt. J. van der Kemp (1804), p 438.

6.   H. Lichtenstein (1812 – 1815), 1: 338; J.V.B. Shrewsbury (1869), p 262.

7.   H. Lichtenstein (1812 – 1815), 1: 369.

8.   M. Wilson (1969a), pp 145, 152.

9.   H. Lichtenstein (1812 – 1815), 1: 338.

10.   J. Read (1818), p 285. Africans from Delagoa Bay visited Ngqika as early as 1805. L. Alberti (1810), pp 7 – 12.

11.   For Mpondo trade, see W. Beinart (1980), pp 128 – 129; M. Hunter (1961), p 134.

12.   The copper which the Xhosa are reported as supplying to the Thembu (R. Collins [1809], p 39) and the Mpondo (S. Kay [1833], p 374) may have come from the Colony. But since the trade in African copper continued as late as the 1820s (W. Shepstone, quoted in anonymous manuscript, probably by W.J. Shrewsbury, Wesleyan Methodist Missionary Archives, MS 15,429, Cory Library, Grahamstown), we may assume that Colonial copper supplemented an earlier trade.

13.   R.H. Elphick (1977), pp 62 – 67. G. Harinck (1969), pp 160 – 165; Journal of Isaq Schryver in D. Moodie (1840), 1: 437; H. Lichtenstein (1812 – 1815), 1: 367 – 368; 2: 409.

14.   H. Somerset–J. Bell, 27 Mar. 1828, Enclosure by W. Macdonald, CO 357.

15.   S.J.K. van Maaslandsluys, q. G. Harinck (1969), p 165.

16.   W. Paterson (1789), p 93.

17.   T. Philipps (1960), pp 179 – 182. Xhosa tobacco may even have reached as far north as the Kwena. See Livingstone, quoted by M. Wilson and L. Thompson (1969 – 1971) 1: 148.

18.   H. Lichtenstein (1812 – 1815), 1: 333, 338.

19.   J. van der Kemp (1804), p 472. On San desire for Xhosa dagga, see A. Kropf (1889), pp 32 – 33. San trade with the Mpondo is well documented, and trade between the San and the Xhosa may have followed a similar pattern. See A. Steedman (1835), 2: 280.

20.   J. van der Kemp (1804), p 472.

21.   J. Marais (1944), p 31.

22.   J. van der Kemp (1804), p 439.

23.   Interview with N.C. Melane, Qwaninga Location, Willowvale District, 17 Feb. 1976.

24.   The Hubner massacre of 1736. See Chapter IV, note 4.

25.   V.S. Forbes (1965), p 13.

26.   C. Haupt (1752), p 299.

27.   D. Moodie (1840). 3: 5. References to early Boer-Xhosa trade may be

found in D. Moodie (1840), 3: 2 — 6, 20 — 22, 24, 34, 39, 73, 76n. Harinck's statement that these expeditions were regulated by Xhosa chiefs is not supported by his references. G. Harinck (1969), p 165.

28. A. Sparrman (1786), 2: 155.

29. A. Hallema (1932), *passim*.

30. D. Moodie (1840), 3: 76n.

31. J. Marais (1944), p 24.

32. The notion of interaction, which is linked with the idea that contact with European 'civilisation' uplifts and modernises 'primitive' peoples, was first proposed by H.M. Robertson (1934), and is the dominant theme of M. Wilson and L. Thompson (1969 — 1971). The limitations of such an approach were sharply exposed in M. Legassick (1971). Legassick's recent (1979) attempt to elaborate a theory of dependence for the Cape's northern frontier fails, in my opinion, because (1) it overemphasises exchange, to the exclusion of production and labour relations, (2) it is situated at a point in time when capitalist penetration had not yet made a significant impact on indigenous social structures. For analogous reasons, it seems to me unwise to push the beginnings of 'underdevelopment' on the Cape eastern frontier as far back as the first exchange relations between white and black.

33. D. Moodie (1840), 3: 73.

34. H. Lichtenstein (1812 — 1815), 1: 386 — 387.

35. 'Minutes of the proceedings of a special and supreme Commission,' 27 Feb. 1801, *RCC*, IV, p 199.

36. The lack of any analytical account of settler trade with the Xhosa is a glaring hiatus in settler historiography. The best contemporary accounts are S. Bannister (1829), Ch. IV; R. Godlonton (1835 — 1836), Part II; Letter from 'An Emigrant of 1820' in *GTJ*, 6 Apr. 1932.

37. H.B. Giliomee (1966), p 326. For employment of Xhosa labour between 1812 and 1820, see T. Willshire-J. Cuyler, 6 Jan. 1820, CO 2926; J. Cuyler-C. Bird, 13 May 1820, CO 2626. For trade between Xhosa and Colony, see Bird-J. Brownlee, 30 Dec. 1818, *RCC*, XII, p 121; S. Bannister (1829), p 114.

38. R. Aitcheson-Commissioners of Enquiry, 19 Mar. 1824, *RCC*, XIV, p 153; M.J. Sparks-Colonial Secretary, 27 Jan. 1822, *RCC*, XIV, p 275; H. Rivers-C. Bird, 13 Feb. 1822, CO 2645. The remainder of the paragraph is taken from H. Somerset-R. Plasket, 1 Nov. 1825, CO 234. Trial of J. Stubbs Jnr. and T. Hood, enclosed in H. Rivers-C. Bird, 26 June 1823, CO 2653; Deposition of Peter Kettlehouse, 18 Feb. 1825, CO 233; T. Stubbs (1978), pp 84 — 85.

39. See Chapter III (3).

40. These were J. Stubbs, T. Mahony and J. Brown. G. Pigot-R. Wilmot, 20 June 1823, CO 2653; G.M. Theal (1915), 1: 384; Forbes-Plasket, 29 Aug. 1825, with enclosures by W. Shaw, CO 233; W. Dundas — (?), 9 Aug. 1825, CO 2671.

41. Trial of Stubbs and Hood, enclosed in H. Rivers-C. Bird, 26 June 1823, CO 2653; Khoi intermediaries were active in the illegal trade. See H. Rivers-C. Bird, 3 May 1824, CO 2662; T. Stubbs (1978), p 87.
42. C. Rose (1829), pp 211 — 212.
43. See 'Minutes . . . of a conference . . . at the Kat River,' *RCC*, XI, p 313.
44. For official accounts of these fairs, see T. Onkruyd-H. Rivers, 22 July 1822, CO 2645; Onkruyd-Rivers, 7 May 1823, CO 2653; Onkruyd-Rivers, 7 July 1823, CO 2653. Afer (1827), 12: 227, 13: 14, claims that the purpose of holding these fairs was to enable the officials to reap all the benefits.
45. W.R. Thomson-C. Bird, 16 Aug. 1822, *RCC*, XV, p 17.
46. Evidence of W. Dundas, *Abo Com*, p 132. See also evidence of W. Shaw, *Abo Com*, p 127; 'Report of Mr Whitworth,' 12 Feb. 1825, *Annual Report of the Wesleyan Methodist Missionary Society* (1825); S. Kay (1833), p 120; J.W.D. Moodie (1835), 2: 238.
47. W.R. Thomson-J. Gregory, 30 Apr. 1825, *RCC*, XXI, p 178.
48. For these regulations, see the Proclamation of 23 July 1824, *RCC*, XVIII, pp 179 — 181.
49. Evidence of Captain Spiller, *Abo Com*, p 71.
50. Andrew Smith, Kaffir Notes, S.A. Museum, Cape Town.
51. J. Bigge and W. Colebrooke-Earl Bathurst, 25 May 1825, *RCC*, XXI, p 320.
52. Descriptions of the fair include A. Steedman (1835), 1: 5 — 10; T. Philipps (1960), pp 293 — 294; H. Dugmore (1958), pp 34 — 36; Lieut. Rutherford-Commissioners of Enquiry, 14 Dec. 1824, *RCC*, XIX, pp 315 — 316; A good description from the viewpoint of a wholesale merchant is W. Fleming-Commissioners of Enquiry, 24 May 1825, *RCC*, XXI, pp 394 — 396. For licences issued see CO 2671.
53. T. Philipps (1960), p 293.
54. Andrew Smith, Kaffir Notes, S.A. Museum, Cape Town.
55. F.G. Kayser-Dr. Hesekiel, 15 May 1832, Kayser papers, Cory Library, Grahamstown.
56. H.S. Ormond-H. Somerset, 28 Apr. 1826, CO 287.
57. For these attempts see H. Somerset-R. Plasket, 6 Jan. 1826 and 31 Jan. 1826, CO 287. The fairs were held twice a week. The traders wanted them held four times a month.
58. H.S. Ormond-H. Somerset, 28 Apr. 1826, CO 287.
59. Mrs. J. Ross-Mrs. Blackwood, n.d. (late 1824 or early 1825) quoted in U. Long (1947), p 218.
60. See sources quoted in note 52 above, and H. Somerset-R. Bourke, 29 Aug. 1826, CO 287; W. Dundas-R. Plasket, 4 Apr. 1826, CO 2682.
61. W. Dundas-R. Plasket, 14 Nov. 1826, CO 2682.
62. II. Somerset-R. Plasket, 20 June 1826, CO 287; H. Somerset-R. Plasket, 23 Jan. 1827, CO 333; R. Godlonton (1835 — 1836a), pp 142 — 143.

63. The statement that the coastal belt east of the Fish River bush was not elephant country is based on the absence of euphorbia and spekboom trees, which attract elephants.

64. Ordinance 81 of 1830. For a full discussion of Colonial policy on the frontier trade before 1835, see M.E. Donaldson (1974), pp 309 − 332.

65. M. Donaldson (1974), p 313.

66. For criticism of traders, see S. Young − *WMS*, 18 Aug, 1831. MS. 15,429, Cory Library, Grahamstown; C. Stretch, 'Diary', MS 14,558, Cory Library, Grahamstown; Emigrant of 1820 in *GTJ*, 6 Apr. 1832; Evidence of T. Philipps, *Abo Com*, p 30; J. Backhouse (1844), pp 212, 219.

67. D. Campbell-J. Bell. 28 Jan. 1831, CO 2728; Memorial of E. Hanger, 17 Dec. 1830, CO 3947.

68. P. Kirby (1955), p 116.

69. Cf. *CFT*, 30 Jan. 1845: 'In hides there has been a decrease of about £7 000 − also in horns to the amount of more than £700. This has been caused by the abundance of corn and milk in Kafirland, which rendered it unnecessary for the Kafirs to slaughter any oxen for food. In short, the Kafir trade is greatly dependent upon the seasons in Kafirland − if they are favourable, the Kafirs give themselves less trouble to collect the articles they deal in than in times of scarcity.'

70. On one occasion, he asked, 'Who gave that man permission to go about my country showing the people his goods?' *GTJ*, 16 May 1833.

71. *GTJ*, 24 July 1834.

72. Evidence of T. Philipps, *Abo Com*, p 27; R. Godlonton (1835 − 1836a), p 149. *CFT*, 23 Apr. 1842 reported value of produce received in 1841 as £16 650. For effect of the war on frontier trade, T.H. Bowker (1970), p 132; *GTJ*, 13 Jan. 1842.

73. *CFT*, 21 Apr. 1842. Detailed lists of traders by area add up to even less than thirty. See T. Shepstone-H. Hudson, 3 Sept. 1839, LG 432; C.L. Stretch-H. Hudson, 9 Sept. 1839, LG 432; W.M. Fynn-H. Hudson, 19 Feb. 1838, LG 427.

74. T. Shepstone-H. Hudson, 3 Sept. 1839, LG 432.

75. *CFT* 30 June, 1 Sept. 1840; 21 Apr. 1842; C. Stretch-H. Hudson, 12 Oct. 1840, LG 399; W.M. Fynn-H. Hudson, 16 July 1838, LG 424. The first season of increased gum prices yielded 200 000 lb. *CFT*, 14 May 1845.

76. *CFT* 28 Nov. 1845; Journal of Resident Agent, Fort Peddie, 10 Sept. 1845, GH 14/1.

77. W.M. Fynn-H. Hudson, 8 May 1839, LG 430.

78. A.B. Armstrong-C.L. Stretch, 15 June 1841, LG 437; *CFT* 15 Feb. 1848.

79. W.M. Fynn-H. Hudson, 16 July 1838, LG 424.

80. C. Bundy (1979).

81. See Chapter III (2).

82. See Chapter II (3) and Chapter VI (2).
83. D. Moodie (1840), 3: 73.
84. For kidnapping, H. Lichtenstein (1812 — 1815), 1: 385, 409; H.F. Fynn (1950), p 80. For prisoners of war, H. Maynier-Commissioners of Inquiry, 25 Apr. 1825, *RCC*, XXI, p 387. The fullest description of Xhosa labour in the early period is Statement of Mrs. Gardner, 13 June 1825, 50 of 1835, p 174. See also, Mr. Moodie-J. Gregory, 6 Dec. 1823, 50 of 1835, p 176; R. Collins (1809), p 10; F. Winkelman (1788 — 1789), p 98; W. Macmillan (1963), p 79n; B. Jantjies, q. Giliomee in R. Elphick and H. Giliomee (1979), p 302.
85. Mr. Moodie-J. Gregory, 6 Dec. 1823, 50 of 1835, p 176; E.M. Cole-A. Hudson, 5 May 1839, LG 430.
86. R. Collins (1809), p 22.
87. Proclamations of 1797, 1812, 1817 and 1820 specifically prohibited the employment of Xhosa. M. Donaldson (1974), p 370. Batavian Governor Janssens attempted the same in 1803. H. Lichtenstein (1812 — 1815). 1: 389.
88. T. Stubbs (1978), p 162.
89. On black immigration into the Colony, see M. Donaldson (1974), pp 345 — 352; C.F.J. Muller (1974), Ch III.
90. For the provisions of Ordinance 49, see M. Donaldson (1974), pp 371 — 373.
91. CO 2712, Return of Registered Labourers shows 162 'Caffres' and only 14 other 'native foreigners'.
92. See, for example, the contracts given in C. Muller (1974), pp 120 — 121.
93. W.R. Thomson-J. Gregory, 30 Apr. 1825, 50 of 1835, p 188; *GTJ*, 24 June 1841.
94. W. Fynn-H. Hudson, 9 July 1840, LG 404.
95. J. Goldswain (1946 — 1949). 2: 8 — 9. For further discussion on squatting, see Chapter VIII (4).
96. Examinations of Caffres found in the Colony, 30 Sept. 1836, LG 396; C. Stretch-H. Hudson, 17 Oct. 1936, LG 396.
97. Xhosa attempted to rent pasturage from the Khoi who had been given their lands on the Kat River. C. Stretch-Capt. Sutton, 24 Nov. 1843, LG 445.
98. *CFT* 20 Jan. 1841.
99. J. Goldswain (1946 — 1949), 2: 10, 11, 13.
100. J. Hare-G. Napier, 30 Jan. 1840, 424 of 1851, p 52.
101. *CFT* 9, 16 Dec. 1840, 5 May 1841, 7 July 1841. Information runs out when the *CFT* stopped publishing the proceedings of the magistrate's court.
102. *CFT* 9, 16 Dec. 1840, 27 Jan. 1841.
103. *CFT* 10 March, 12 May, 23 Dec. 1841.
104. *CFT* 10 March, 1841; A. Berrange-Attorney-General, 14 Sept. 1849,

1288 of 1850, pp 22 – 23.

105. For example, Diary of C.L. Stretch 17, 28, 31 March 1845, GH 14/1.
106. 'Explanations by Sir Rufane Donkin,' *RCC*, XV, p 104.
107. D. Williams (1959), p 235. Surprisingly enough, Williams's thesis is the only detailed examination of the attitude of eastern Cape missionaries to the civilisation of which they formed part, although there are numerous studies of missionary activity elsewhere. See also M. Kaplan (1975), Ch. I (b). For an illuminating spectrum of missionary thought on 'civilising' the Xhosa, see BK 433, containing missionary responses to Smith's circular on this question. Cf. M. Wilson (1969b), p 239.
108. Diary of J. Ayliff, 22 Nov. 1841, MS 15,544, Cory Library, Grahamstown. A. Kropf went so far as to assert that the Xhosa 'must be encouraged to serve the farmers in the Colony, whence they usually bring back a good deal of knowledge about cultivation.' A. Kropf – High Commissioner, 8 May 1848, BK 433.
109. See, for example, Evidence of H. Hallbeck, *Abo Com*, p 339; W.R. Thomson-R. Plasket, 8 Feb. 1827; CO 323. Diary of C.L. Stretch 6 Nov. 1844; CO 323, C. Brownlee-G. Mackinnon, 26 Jan. 1849, BK 432.
110. There is a full discussion in D. Williams (1959), pp 230 – 232.
111. Simply scraping the hide clean was 'a hard day's work for two men'. MacLaren, q. E. Shaw and N. van Warmelo (1974), p 171.
112. *CFT*, 27 Nov. 1845.
113. Use of money was, for this reason strongly urged by W.R. Thomson (D. Williams (1959), pp 239 – 240) and Harry Smith (MS 2033 6 Oct. 1835), among others.
114. Interview with M. Mnyanda, Mcotama Location, Kentani District, 21 Feb. 1976.
115. Interview with M. Soga, conducted by A. Blow, Feni Location, Kentani District, 15 Jan. 1976. 'Soga was a seller of *izixhobo*, a certain type of spear. Soga kindled a fire with charcoal made of the willow tree. He smelted stones, and there came out on the one side iron which he then cut into *izixhobo*.'
116. R. Niven-C.L. Stretch, 24 Aug. 1837, *Caffrarian Messenger*, Oct. 1838.
117. J. Backhouse (1844), p 211.
118. A. Bain (1949), pp 188 – 189.

CHAPTER VIII

1. J. Ayliff-B. D'Urban, 19 June 1835, Deposition of a great chief,

23 Apr. 1836, 503 of 1837, pp 229, 231; Statement of April, a Bechuana, 19 Feb. 1835, LG 9.

2.   J. Ayliff — 'a brother missionary', 17 March 1835, 503 of 1837, p 223. Manxiwa, Hintsa's son, also stressed the kinship bond in his interview with Sir George Cory. He said Hintsa 'was related to Gaika and did not wish to help the English against him.' Interview 116, Willowvale, 19. Jan. 1910.

4.   Deposition of Louis Arnolus, 10 May 1836, 503 of 1837, p 235; *Grahams Town Journal,* 6 Feb. 1835.

5.   Acc. 983. Caesar Andrews, 'Reminiscences of the Kafir War of 1834 — 1835'. For the sequence of events see D'Urban-Aberdeen, 19 June 1835 and enclosures, 279 of 1836, pp 15 — 57. For reasons that will become obvious, all accounts must be treated with caution but especially those written after the event, for example, H. Smith (1903), J. Bisset (1875). I have made considerable use of diaries kept on a daily basis, although the diarists were generally not well placed to observe all the crucial transactions. See, for instance, T.H. Bowker (1970), W.F.A. Gilfillan (1970), J. Goldswain (1946 — 1949).

6.   W. Gilfillan (1970), p37.

7.   See Chapter VI (2); R. Moyer (1976), Ch. 2.

8.   Declaration of the Fingo Chiefs, 4 Sept. 1837, LG 406; W. Gilfillan (1970), pp 33 — 34; T.H. Bowker (1970), p 123.

9.   W.T. Brownlee (1936). A fuller text of Bikitsha's narrative may be found in NA 623, Cape Archives. I am indebted to Richard Moorsom for drawing this to my attention.

10.   Ayliff himself stresses the extent to which he was responsible for the Mfengu seeking British protection. See J. Ayliff, 'History of the Wars causing the dispersion of the Fingoes,' MS 15,544, Cory Library, Grahamstown.

11.   R. Kawa (1930), pp 46 — 47.

12.   B. D'Urban, Government Notice No. 14, 3 May 1835, quoted in J. Ayliff and J. Whiteside (1912), pp 28 — 30.

13.   W. Gilfillan (1970), p 37.

14.   J. Goldswain (1946 — 1949), 1: 106.

15.   H. Smith-Mrs Sargant, 7 May 1835, G. Theal (1912), p 154.

16.   H. Smith (1903), p 401.

17.   B. D'Urban-Aberdeen, 19 June 1835, 279 of 1836, p 21.

18.   MS 2033 B. D'Urban-H. Smith, 10 Nov. 1835.

19.   J. Bisset (1875), p 21.

20.   B. D'Urban-J. Bell, 18 May 1835, G. Theal (1912), p 171.

21.   Proclamation of 10 May 1835, quoted G. Theal (1912), p 156.

22.   G. Theal (1912), p 158 ff, passim.

23.   T.H. Bowker (1970), pp 137 — 165, esp. pp 155, 157. Bowker was stationed at Fort Wellington in Ndlambe territory. 'The Kaffirs have an idea and they are not mistaken, that we are desirous of peace. As for

ourselves at this place, though not afraid of the Kaffirs yet, we are not their equals in the field. If this was to continue our small force would be meeting with disaster at some time or other.'

24. G. Theal (1912), pp 241 – 294, esp. Smith-D'Urban, 25 July 1835, pp 277 – 280.

25. W. Macmillan (1963), p 168. D'Urban was obliged to accept the situation. G. Theal (1912), p 293.

26. Articles of a treaty of peace etc., 17 Sept. 1835, in G. Theal (1912), p 391.

27. MS 2033 B. D'Urban -J. Bell, 25 Sept. 1835.

28. Communication from his Brittanic Majesty's Governor to the Chiefs Macomo and Tyalie, 1 Sept. 1835, G. Theal (1912), p 362. See also J. Alexander (1837) 2: 276, 319, 341.

29. Articles of a Treaty of Peace etc., 17 Sept. 1835, G. Theal (1912), p 390.

30. J. Hare-G. Napier, 8 Sept. 1842, 424 of 1851; T.H. Bowker (1970), p 157.

31. Select Committee on the Kafir Tribes, 635 of 1851. Evidence of Dr. A. Smith, p 295.

32. W. Boyce-D'Urban, 28 July 1835, Journal of the Rev. Messrs. Shepstone, Palmer and Boyce, 21 Aug. 1835, G. Theal (1912), pp 286 – 288, 344 – 347. This is not the least sordid of the Wesleyans' activities over this period.

33. Smith's private correspondence with D'Urban is full of mechanical imagery such as 'I will, though, be assured, turn all these wheels to the progression of our machine.' MS 2033 H. Smith-B. D'Urban, 27 Oct. 1835.

34. H. Smith-B. D'Urban, 16 Aug. 1835, G. Theal (1912), p 328.

35. Smith's intentions are fully set out in MS 2033, H. Smith-B. D'Urban, 6 Oct. 1835.

36. MS 2033 B. D'Urban-H. Smith, 30 Sept. 1835.

37. For Smith's own account see H. Smith (1903), Ch. XXXVIII.

38. Letter from 'Miles', *GTJ*, 19 May 1836.

39. MS 2033 Smith-D'Urban, 28 Oct., 1 Nov., 3 Nov. 1835.

40. MS 2033 Smith-D'Urban, 26 Oct. 1835.

41. H. Smith (1903), p 431.

42. W. Macmillan (1963), p 168.

43. MS 2033 B. D'Urban-H. Smith, 28 Jan. 1836; H. Smith (1903), pp 446 – 447.

44. MS 2033 H. Smith-B. D'Urban, 5 Dec. 1835; H. Smith (1903), pp 428, 457.

45. Smith thought Mhala was very attached to him. H. Smith (1903), pp 441 – 445. But the journal of Mhala's agent shows otherwise. See LG 408.

46. Journal of F. Rawstorne, 1 – 2 Apr. 1836, LG 408.

47. MS 2033 H. Smith-B. D'Urban, 21 Dec. 1835.
48. See official records in LG 420.
49. J. Stanley-D. Campbell, 16 May 1836, W. Hartley-D. Campbell, 1 July 1836, LG 420; MS 2033; D'Urban-Smith, 28 Jan. 1836; F.G. Kayser, Diary, 27 March 1836, Uncatalogued, Cory Library, Grahamstown.
50. J. Hare-G. Napier, 13 Nov. 1843, 424 of 1851, p 183.
51. For very detailed accounts of the events leading up to Glenelg's decision to repudiate D'Urban's annexations, see J. Galbraith (1963), Ch. VII and W. Macmillan (1963), Ch. XI.
52. MS 15,429 Ayliff-Wesleyan Methodist Missionary Society, Journal, 14 July 1834.
53. MS 15,429 Ayliff-Wesleyan Methodist Missionary Society, Journal, 30 July 1834.
54. MS 14,254/13 A.W. Burton, 'Ninth Kaffir War,' Vol. I, p 5, quoting W.W. Fynn. For the role of the Great Councillors in Xhosa politics, see Chapter IV (2).
55. J.H. Soga (n.d.), pp 100 – 102.
56. *GTJ*, 21 July 1836.
57. MS 15,429 Shaw-Wesleyan Methodist Missionary Society, 25 July 1837.
58. MS 15,429 Ayliff-Wesleyan Methodist Missionary Society, 19 May 1837; T. Smith (1864), pp 111 – 112.
59. For example, *Grahams Town Journal*, 28 April 1836, 18 Jan. 1838; W. Fynn-Hudson, 12 July 1838, LG 424; W. Fynn-Hudson, 18 Oct. 1838, LG 426.
60. W.M. Fynn-Hudson, 17 Feb. 1838, LG 404.
61. *GTJ* 29 Sept. 1836; MS 15,544 Diary of J. Ayliff, 9 Dec 1836; *GTJ* 18 May 1837; LG 404 W.M. Fynn-Hudson, 17 Feb. 1836. For Gasela's expedition against the Sotho, see Chapter VIII (3).
62. *GTJ* 29 Sept. 1836; *GTJ* 1 March 1838; *GTJ* 20 Sept. 1838; W.M. Fynn-Hudson, 4 Dec. 1838, LG 427.
63. *CFT* 15 Feb., 7 Mar., 26 Dec. 1844.
64. H.F. Fynn-Hudson, 18 Aug. 1839, LG 431.
65. Fragmentary reports can be found in LG 404, which contains the letters from W.M. Fynn, the British Resident at Butterworth to Hudson, the Agent-General in Grahamstown.
66. *GTJ* 13 Feb. 1840.
67. *CFT* 23 Dec. 1841.
68. W.M. Fynn-Hudson, 5 July 1843, LG 404.
69. *CFT* 25 Jan., 15 Feb. 1844.
70. E.G. Sihele, 'Ibali labaThembu,' uncatalogued MS Cory Library pp 31, 33 – 34. Sihele stresses that it was the Gcina not the Thembu who were defeated. He is, however, very explicit as to the large tribute paid to the Gcaleka by Mtirara. This may or may not be the incident described by J.H. Soga (1931), pp 240 – 241.

71. *CFT* 21 Dec. 1843, 15 Feb. 1844.
72. *GTJ* 26 July 1838.
73. *GTJ* 10 Oct. 1846.
74. *CFT* 27 July 1847.
75. W. Rubusana (1906), p 228. A. Kropf and R. Godfrey (1915), p 299, give a slightly different version.
76. 'Kreili's Answer to the Governor's Message', enclosed in Maitland-Grey, 20 Jan. 1847, 912 of 1848, p 16.
77. It is interesting to note that right up to the final separation Sarhili asserted the essential unity of the Gcaleka and the Rharhabe. He told Stockenstrom that 'Kreili can rule, and be responsible for all Kafirland if the English will not interfere between himself and his subjects, and if the English acknowledge and countenance him as paramount chief, he will be responsible as such.' Stockenstrom-Cloete, 24 Aug. 1846, 912 of 1848, p 24.
78. On early Xhosa immigration to the north, see H. Lichtenstein (1812 − 1815), 1: 369 − 370 and M. Wilson (1969b), p 236. On the Xhosa of the Kareebergen and their subsequent history see P. Kallaway (1980).
79. A great deal of material on Nzwane was collected by J.M. Orpen. See Cory accession 112, J.M. Orpen-G. Cory, letters from 18 Aug. − 5 Oct. 1920.
80. Reminiscences of John Montgomery, *Cape Times*, 13 Apr. 1921.
81. R. Collins (1809), p 16.
82. H. Leibbrandt (1902), pp 278, 661.
83. For Tregardt's settlement in Hintsa's country, see C.F.J. Muller (1974), pp 339 − 365. Muller rejects the overwhelming evidence that Tregardt was involved in running guns to the Xhosa. See Smith-D'Urban, 17 Apr. 1835, G. Theal (1912), p 360; Deposition of Maqoma, 28 Apr. 1836, 503 of 1837, p 232; Deposition of Tyali, 4 May 1836, 503 of 1837, p 234; J. Alexander (1837), 2: 275; and the following, probably not known to Professor Muller: Evidence of W. Cox, 538 of 1836, p 352; Smith-D'Urban, 28 Dec. 1835, GH 19/4; C.L. Stretch 'Report,' 31 Dec. 1842, LG 402.
84. For Tregardt, see note 83 above. For Mnyaluza, see G. Theal (1912), pp 138, 361.
85. MS 2033 H. Smith-B. D'Urban, 6 March 1836.
86. See note 47 above.
87. P. Sanders (1975), p 51.
88. *GTJ*, 30 Aug. 1838; J.M. Bowker-Hudson, 11 Sept. 1838, LG 425; W.D. Hammond-Tooke (1958), p 85.
89. W. Fynn-G. Mackinnon, 21 Jan. 1850, BK 433; G. Mackinnon-H. Smith, 11 Feb. 1850, BK 371.
90. Far and away the best account of the treaty system and its collapse is in a neglected thesis by G.B. Crankshaw (1960). Both the standard authorities on the period, J. Galbraith (1963) and W. Macmillan (1963)

are too absorbed with other matters to give the problem of settler expansionism any attention. It has therefore been necessary for me to consider settler history in rather more detail than would otherwise be appropriate.

91. Through his action in expelling Maqoma from the Kat River in 1829, Stockenstrom became more responsible than any other single person for causing the *Sixth Frontier War*. His opponents, who viewed him as an unprincipled placehunter and landgrabber, insinuated that his motivation was to create a human barrier between the Xhosa and his own vast estate. *GTJ* 13 June 1839.

92. For the full text of Stockenstrom's treaties, see 424 of 1851, pp 2 − 7.

93. See the discussion of the old commando system, Chapter VI (3).

94. Undated, unsigned memorandum in Agent H.F. Fynn's handwriting addressed to Governor Maitland, GH 19/4. See also A. Stockenstrom (1887) 2: 118 − 119.

95. A. Stockenstrom-J. Philip, 25 Aug. 1842, q. W. Macmillan (1963), p 264. Emphasis in the original.

96. Acc. 1415 (77), Vol. 9, J. Hare-G. Napier, 12 Aug. 1842. There are numerous references in the sources to the difficulties of finding herdsmen. See for example 424 of 1851. pp 62, 63, 203.

97. For the development of sheep-farming in Albany district, see A.C.M. Webb (1975), pp 178 − 193. For a similar analysis to that developed here, but related to a later period, see T. Kirk (1980) and (1972).

98. A. Webb (1975), p 210.

99. Examination of Caffres found in Colony, 30 Sept, 1836, LG 396; C.L. Stretch-Hudson, 16 Aug. 1842, LG 441.

100. *GTJ*, 13 Jan. 1842.

101. C.L. Stretch, 'Memorandum on the Stockenstrom Treaty System' query 19, in G. Crankshaw (1960). Crankshaw has not numbered the pages but the memorandum is drawn up in the form of numbered queries, and references will be cited according to the query.

102. J. Goldswain (1946 − 1949), 2: 8 − 13; C.L. Stretch-Hudson, 18 June 1838, LG 424. Many farmers were too undercapitalised to pay their labourers, even in kind (*GTJ*, 21 Nov. 1839), and this must have encouraged them to allow squatters on their property.

103. W. Macmillan (1963), pp 266, 279 − 280; C.L. Stretch-Hudson, 30 Aug. 1841, LG 400; Undated unsigned memorandum (H.F. Fynn)-Maitland, GH 19/4.

104. *CFT*, 9 Dec. 1840.

105. *GTJ*, 19 Jan. 1837.

106. There is no satisfactory account of the changes made in the Cape as a result of the Commission of Enquiry into Somerset's administration. One aspect, Ordinance 50, has been illuminatingly discussed by S. Newton-King (1980).

107. S.D. Neumark (1957) has demonstrated that the Boers were not independent of the market. However, he does not seriously assess the extent to which the market affected production.

108. I am here referring to the distinction which Marx draws between the circuit M-C-M[1] as opposed to the circuit C-M-C[1] (where M equals Money and C equals commodity). See *Capital*, I, Chs. 3 and 4. I hope, however, that the text is intelligible to those who do not understand or agree with Marx.

109. This discussion on land policy begins from L.C. Duly (1968). Duly severely limits the usefulness of his book by failing to consider exchanges of land between settlers and by failing to consult the *Grahams Town Journal* or the *South African Commercial Advertiser* which contain much relevant information. The topic of land speculation at the Cape is wide open for future research. See Kirk's useful comments in T. Kirk (1980).

110. The settlers were given land on condition that they used it. The appointment of a commission to issue individual titles sent a number of those who had abandoned their locations scurrying back. See A. Webb (1975), pp 79 − 80.

111. *GTJ*, 22 Oct. 1835. Godlonton was arguing that the government should not give away land in the new province free. He was probably motivated less by a desire to stop speculation than by a desire to confine it to those who were already in possession of some capital. For Godlonton's alleged speculations, see *GTJ* 10 May 1838, replying to an attack in the *South African Commercial Advertiser*. The *Advertiser* sporadically published attacks on prominent frontier speculators, braving when it did so the Colony's severe libel laws.

112. Natal is the classic model of uncontrolled speculation. See H. Slater (1975).

113. For the rise in land values, see G. Napier-J. Russell, 10 July 1841, 424 of 1851, p 87; G. Cory (1910 − 1939), 4: 357n; W. Macmillan (1963), p 267; B. Le Cordeur (1979), p 15.

114. A. Webb (1975), p 175.

115. Ibid., p 177.

116. T.H. Bowker (1970), pp 115 − 116. One of Lord Glenelg's correspondents referred to Smith as 'blinded by T.C. White and his retinue of bloodthirsty settlers.' Letter from James Clark, no date, no addressee. ZP 1/1/89, p 120, Cape Archives microfilm of Colonial Office (London) file CO 48/165. Smith himself caught some of the speculative mania: 'At the source of the Buffalo . . . I am to have a grant of land, which at some future period, when I am no more, will be invaluable.' H. Smith-Mrs Sargant, 7 May 1835, G. Theal (1912), p 152. So did Gilfillan. See W. Gilfillan (1970), pp 45, 47, 48.

117. See, for example, *GTJ* 6 Jan. 1842; J. Alexander (1837), 2: 56.

118. J.M. Bowker (1864), p 125.

119. A. Webb (1975), pp 172 − 173; B. Le Cordeur (1979), p 17.
120. T. Stubbs (1978), p 136.
121. B. Le Cordeur (1979), p 17; W. Macmillan (1963), pp 270, 178; A. Stockenstrom (1887), 2: 97; T. Stubbs (1978), pp 135 − 136, 211, 214; T. Kirk (1972), p 186.
122. B. Le Cordeur (1979), p 10.
123. Q. Webb (1975), p 195; Stretch 'Diary' in G. Crankshaw (1960), p 343, estimates the cost of the *War of the Axe* as £1 500 000. Andrew Smith thought it was £2 000 000. 635 of 1851, p 75.
124. A. Webb (1975), pp 194 − 195; J. Freeman (1851), p 79.
125. *GTJ* 13 Jan. 1842; T.H. Bowker (1970), p 132. James Howse was killed in the *Eighth Frontier War.*
126. For details of war scares, see G. Crankshaw (1960), pp 121 − 125. The classic analysis of the psychology of war scares may be found in Chapter 6 of S. Marks (1970).
127. C.L. Stretch-Hudson, 15 Sept. 1840, LG 399. The sheepfarming Bowkers were specifically accused of spreading alarms to buy up cheap land on the Koonap River, *GTJ* 8 Aug. 1839.
128. G. Cory (1910 − 1939), 2: 313 − 314.
129. Among celebrated cases taken up by the *Grahams Town Journal* one may mention: (1) Rudman, a Colonist believed murdered by the Xhosa, actually shot himself by accident. M. West-Hudson, 25 June 1841, 424 of 1851, p 93; (2) A letter accusing Maqoma of entering the Colony illegally was discredited when one of the signatories revealed his landlord had threatened to evict him unless he signed it. *GTJ* 9 May, 6, 25 June, 18 July 1839; (3) Blatant falsehoods in the compensation claims of farmers named Niland and Van Aardt. See Crankshaw, pp 74 − 75. Lieutenant-Governor Hare warned Governor Napier not to believe one-twentieth of what he read in the *Journal.* Acc 1415 (77), Vol. 5, Hare-Napier, 31 May 1839.
130. W. Macmillan (1963), p 176. For the sequence of events in this and the following paragraph, see W. Macmillan (1963), Ch. XI, G. Crankshaw (1960), pp 33 − 50; A. Stockenstrom (1887), 2: Ch. XXI − XXIII.
131. It has been argued that D'Urban lifted martial law because of ambiguities in the legal status of Queen Adelaide. Since D'Urban showed no inclination to submit to a Secretary of State, he was hardly likely to have quailed before a couple of Cape Judges. It is extremely naive to believe that D'Urban, aware of the legal problems for over a month, was suddenly overwhelmed by them on precisely the day after Stockenstrom left for the frontier.
132. Much to the annoyance of the *Grahams Town Journal.* See issues of 3 and 10 Nov. 1836.
133. *Report of the trial, Stockenstrom v. Campbell for libel,* (Cape Town, 1838).
134. For full details of the way in which Stockenstrom was eased out of his

position, see Acc 1415 (77), Vol. 1.

135. J. Hare-G. Napier, 13 Nov. 1843, 424 of 1851, p 184.

136. 'I declined, for the sake of a few head of cattle, to run the risk of endangering the peace of the country.' G. Napier-J. Russell, 1 June 1841, 424 of 1851, p 85.

137. For details of Napier's modifications, see G. Napier-J. Russell, 11 Dec. 1840, 424 of 1851, pp 68 − 81.

138. From 1839, the chiefs were presented with the non-reclaimable list at Quarterly Meetings presided over by Hare. G. Napier-J. Hare, 9 Aug. 1839, 424 of 1851, p 56. On the non-reclaimable list, see G. Crankshaw (1960), pp 77 − 83 and Stretch 'Memorandum', queries 9 and 10.

139. This is the burden of Crankshaw's edition of Stretch's diary, which is a day to day account of Stretch's activities enforcing the reclaimable provisions of the treaty.

140. Stretch, 'Memorandum,' query 9.

141. *Colonial Times*, 26 Feb. 1840.

142. W. Macmillan (1963), p 265.

143. Ibid., p 278.

144. Mrs. J. Fairbairn-Mrs. G. Christie, 8 Sept. 1836, in U. Long (1947), p 129; Journal of J.M. Bowker, 21, 27 July 1836, LG 405; Hobson-Bowker, 3 Oct. 1836, LG 405; R. Southey-Stockenstrom, 3 Oct. 1836, LG 405.

145. Meeting of His Excellency with the Kafir chiefs (1840), 424 of 1851, pp 79, 81; Hudson-Stretch, 13 May 1841, LG 635; A. Cole-C. Stretch, 1 Oct. 1838, LG 426.

146. C. Stretch-Hudson, 24 Sept. 1838, LG 426; F. Kayser-Lieutenant Governor, 13 Apr. 1838, LG 422.

147. G. Napier-Glenelg, 25 May 1838, 424 of 1851, p 31; J. Hare-C. Napier, 21 Apr. 1842, 424 of 1851, pp 114 − 115; C. Stretch-Hudson, 15 Feb. 1842, LG 400.

148. As Stretch pointed out, see C. Stretch-Hudson, 22 June 1840, LG 398. Maqoma once said, 'There were thieves in the Colony as well as in Caffreland, and the Governor had no more power to destroy his thieves than the chiefs have theirs.' Statement by Maqoma, LG 432.

149. 'My word to the Government has been destroy the thieves with your army.' LG 432. Statement by Nqeno, C. Stretch-Hudson, 17 Oct. 1843 LG 401. Ngqika's attitude was more or less the same: 'If white man cross the river black man should kill him and if black cross white man should kill him.' Philipps's Letters, I and II, p 114. MS 14,264 Cory Library, Grahamstown.

150. C. Stretch-Hudson, 17 Oct. 1843, LG 401.

151. C. Stretch-Hudson, 7 Sept. 1841, 29 Jan. 1842, LG 400.

152. *Colonial Times*, 26 Feb. 1840.

153. Advertisement by Sandile in *Cape Frontier Times*, 20 Oct. 1842. Dugmore stuck to his allegations, enthusiastically backed by the

Grahams Town Journal. But they were dismissed by Theophilus Shep-stone. T. Shepstone-Hudson, 14 Apr. 1842, 424 of 1851, pp 112 – 114. I offer prospective researchers into the role of the Wesleyans in undermining the treaty system the following comments on mission-aries: William Boyce ('a bad one'), William Shaw ('such impudence'), William Shepstone ('not a bit better than the others'). Hare concludes 'They are a dishonest set, the whole brotherhood, and the whole press of England to back them.' Acc 1415 (77), Vol. 3, J. Hare-G. Napier, 4 Jan. 1839.

154. C. Stretch-Hudson, 6 Jan. 1839 (sic, in fact, 1840), LG 398.

155. J. Brownlee-C. Stretch, 16 Dec. 1839, LG 398.

156. J. Hare-G. Napier, 30 Jan. 1840, 424 of 1851, p 52. Hare thought that Stretch had engineered the demonstration himself. Acc 1415 (77) Vol. 6, J. Hare-G. Napier, 23 Jan. 1840. One is perhaps over-inclined to take Stretch at face value, so it might be as well to report Hare's warn-ing to Napier in *ibid.*, 20 Sept. 1839: 'Take my word for it that he is a great humbug.'

157. J. Hare-G. Napier, 6 Feb. 1840, Acc 1415, (77), Vol. 6.

158. C. Stretch-Hudson, 23 July 1838, LG 424.

159. C. Stretch-Hudson, 17 Oct. 1843, LG 401.

160 This statement is based on the *Grahams Town Journal* and *Cape Fron-tier Times* for the period, and by comparing the 'depredation' reports of 1841 month by month with the reports for 1842. See LG 599. Apart from the great increase in the number of robberies in 1842, they also differ in their nature. From 1842 accounts begin to appear of robberies by armed bands of Xhosa.

161. C. Stretch-Hudson, 22 Nov. 1842, 424 of 1851, p 143. See also C. Stretch-Hudson, 29 Jan. 1842, LG 400; C. Stretch-Hudson, 27 Dec. 1842, LG 401.

162. Hudson-R. Godlonton, 7 Feb. 1842, LG 636.

163. Declaration of the Gaika chiefs, 28 Jan. 1843, LG 401.

164. J. Hare-G. Napier, 6 June 1842, Acc 1415 (77), Vol. 5.

165. For details of the circumstances surrounding Tyhali's death, see Napier-Stanley, 30 May 1842 and enclosures, 424 of 1851, pp 116 – 123 and *Cape Frontier Times* 12 May 1842.

166. A letter from missionary A. M'Diarmid, *Grahams Town Journal,* 19 May 1842, defends Maqoma's behaviour but the balance of the evi-dence is on the other side, particularly because of the suspicions of Tyhali himself.

167. Statement of the Chief Tyhali, 14 Apr. 1842, 424 of 1851, p 116.

168. See Chapter III (1), VI (1).

169. There are references here and there in the obviously biased European sources to the drinking habits of the chiefs. But the number and detail of references to Maqoma's alleged alcoholism is quite exceptional and therefore somewhat persuasive. One example: 'He (Maqoma) is now

more or less deranged in his mind. Several medical men have declared him insane. He is certainly so occasionally . . . I believe his only desire is to get strong drink.' Memorandum by H. Calderwood, undated, (1847) GH 8/46. Tyhali also said, 'When my messengers went to him he was always drunk, and knew not what they said.' Statement by the chief Tyhali, 14 Apr. 1842, 424 of 1851, p 116. Maqoma's drinking habits are even mentioned in his praises. See Rubusana (1906), pp 257, 528. A certain degree of breakdown is also implied in his repeated attempts to settle quietly in the Colony, away from his political responsibilities. See for example 424 of 1851, pp 114 − 116.

On the other hand, one should consider that Maqoma was encouraged to drink by the Colonial authorities because it kept him quiet. He received a daily ration of liquor. H. Calderwood-R. Woosnam, 1 July, 1847, GH 8/46. Moreover, he was able to control his problem. He kept no liquor at his own place, but went to Fort Beaufort three or four times a week. A.W. Cole (1852), p 181. He presumably appeared intoxicated more often than he was. Finally, Stretch's 'Diary' provides firm evidence that Maqoma was usually able to carry out his duties as a chief.

170. A. Edgar-H. Hudson, 21 June 1841, 424 of 1851, p 92. For other references to the decline in the power of the chiefs see, for example, 424 of 1851, pp 57, 65, 85.

171. This is another subject which could be developed by further research. See, for example D. Campbell-J. Bell, 31 Aug. 1832, CO 2735 (Hermanus); Borcherds-Hudson, 14 June 1841, LG 437 (Sende); *GTJ* 4 Apr. 1842 (Xegwana).

172. J. Hare-G. Napier, 28 Dec. 1838, Acc 1415, (77), Vol. 3.

173. LG 400, C. Stretch-Hudson, 31 Aug. 1842; LG 403, Reply of the Chief Sandile, 19 Aug. 1844; J. Maclean (1858), p 136.

174. C. Stretch-Hudson, 17 Jan. 1843, LG 401.

175. There is much about this incident which remains obscure. The lengthy correspondence in 424 of 1851 is strongly biased against Sandile, and must be read in conjunction with Stretch's dispatches. See especially C. Stretch-Hudson, 10 July (six, it must have been June) 1843, LG 401.

176. A. Stockenstrom-D'Durban, 3 Aug. 1837, 424 of 1851, p 18.

177. The phrase is D'Urban's own. See J. Ayliff and J. Whiteside (1912), p 30. For the history of the Mfengu in this period see R. Moyer (1976), Ch. 5.

178. *GTJ*, 2 Nov., 4 Dec. 1937, 8 June 1838.

179. A. Stockenstrom-B. D'Urban, 9 Aug. 1837, 424 of 1851, p 21.

180. Article 28, 424 of 1851, p 6.

181. 'We are afraid the Governor will send us too far away, and give our father Gaika's country to the Fingos. He must not do so. The Fingoes are a bad people.' (Maqoma) Memorandum of a Conference with Caffer Chiefs, 15 Aug. 1835, G. Theal (1912), p 324.

182. The political motivation of such thefts is demonstrated by a case where the theives returned stolen property on finding it to be Xhosa rather than Mfengu property. T. Shepstone-Hudson, 14 Apr. 1842, 424 of 1851, p 113.
183. J.M. Bowker-B. D'Urban, 3 Aug. 1837, 424 of 1851, pp 17 − 18.
184. *GTJ*, 19 Jan. 1837.
185. J. Hare-G. Napier, 25 Jan. 1839 and enclosures 424 of 1851, pp 41 − 44.
186. MS 15,429 (Unsigned) − Wesleyan Methodist Missionary Society, 5 May 1837.
187. H. Ward (1948), 1: 167; S. Mqhayi (1931), p 108.
188. *GTJ*, 14 Apr. 1842; T. Shepstone-Hudson, 11 Apr. 1842, LG 407.
189. T. Shepstone-Hudson, 2 May 1843, LG 407.
190. T. Shepstone-Hudson, 14 May 1843, with marginal notes by Hare, LG 407.
191. R. Tainton-T. Shepstone, 15 Sept. 1845, GH 14/1; Journal of Shepstone, 30 Apr. 1845, GH 14/1; T. Shepstone-Hudson, 18 June 1845, LG 408.
192. G. Cory (1910 − 1939), 4: 10 − 11; Journal of T. Shepstone, 23 July 1845, GH 14/1.
193. *Berliner Missionberichte*, Sept. 1840, p 137.
194. For the official view of the dispute between Mhala and Gasela, see G. Napier-Stanley, 3 June 1843 and enclosures, 424 of 1851, pp 144 − 150; also H. Ward (1848), 1: 150 − 153.
195. *Berliner Missionberichte*, Nov. 1845, pp 181 − 182. Gasela died in 1845 and was succeeded by his son Toyise. There seems to have been some irregularity concerning his succession connected with the fact that Gasela's father, Nukwa, was still alive, and with the presence of a more highly born claimant, Ncanca. J. Maclean-G. Mackinnon, 12 Oct. 1849, BK 428; W.D. Hammond-Tooke (1958), p 84.
196. See, for example, Maitland-Stanley, 21 March 1846, 786 of 1847, p 22.
197. See Stretch's bitter 'Detailed account of the visit of his Excellency, Sir P. Maitland, in September 1844' in Stretch 'Memorandum'. For Maitland's own view, see P. Maitland-Stanley, 7 Dec. 1844, 424 of 1851, pp 227 − 237.
198. C. Stretch-H. Somerset, 18 Sept. 1844, GH 14/1.
199. C. Stretch-J. Montagu, 25 Sept. 1844, GH 14/1.
200. P. Maitland-Stanley, 6 Sept. 1844, 424 of 1851, pp 218 − 227.
201. C. Stretch-Hudson, 13 July 1845, LG 403.
202. Journal of H. Somerset, 1 July 1845, GH 14/1.
203. Diary of C.L. Stretch, 27 Sept. 1845, GH 14/1.
204. P. Maitland-Stanley, 21 March 1846 and numerous enclosures, 786 of 1847, pp 20 − 82 gives full details of the so-called 'Block Drift incident'.
205. For the axe incident and its aftermath, see P. Maitland-Stanley,

31 March 1846 and enclosures, 786 of 1847, pp 82 — 108.

206. Cory interview no. 112, Maseti, Kentani, Jan. 1910; no. 125, Yekele Vuyana, Middledrift, 19 Jan. 1916.

CHAPTER IX

1. I use 'heroic age' to refer to a period when individual bravery was more decisive than military technology and wars were regulated according to mutually agreed principles which minimised the loss of human life. Generally speaking, the term applies to all wars among the Xhosa and their African neighbours, except the San and the Mfecane invaders. The military conventions of the heroic age governed the conflict between Ngqika and Ndlambe around the turn of the nineteenth century, according to the contemporary reports of L. Alberti (1810) and H. Lichtenstein (1812 — 1815). They were witnessed some thirty years later by S. Kay (1833), missionary to Hintsa at the time of his struggle with the Thembu king, Ngubencuka, and J.H. Soga (n.d.) described them on the basis of his conversations with participants in the *War of Nongxakazelo* (1874) between Sarhili and Ngubencuka's grandson, Ngangelizwe. The sources on which this section is based are chronologically very diverse, but they all describe military values and techniques which persisted over a long period of time and differed radically from the new type of warfare introduced by the Colonists.

2. For a full description of the different types of spear, see J.H. Soga (n.d.), pp 77 — 78.

3. L. Alberti (1810), p 89; H. Lichtenstein (1812 — 1815), 1: 269.

4. *'Ukuzibula'*, literally 'to give birth to the first child'. See *'Nzulu Lwazi'* (S.E.K. Mqhayi), 'UTyala Nteyi,' *Umteteli waBantu*, 22 Nov. 1930.

5. Interviews with N. Qeqe and D. Runeyi, Shixini Location, Willowvale District, Oct. 1975.

6. S. Kay (1833), pp 214 — 215; L. Alberti (1810), p 90.

7. Interview with Mwezeni Mnyanda, Mcotama Location, Kentani District, 21 Feb. 1976. Cf. J. Brownlee (1827), p 197, where Ngqika's men seized the crane feathers of Hintsa's men.

8. J.H. Soga (1930), p 131.

9. A. Kropf (1889), p 36.

10. 'A Native Missionary' (1908), p 10.

11. L. Alberti (1810), p 90.

12. For the doctoring of the army, see J.H. Soga, (n.d.), pp 66 — 67, 173 — 175; A. Kropf and R. Godfrey (1915), p 163; J. Solilo in W. Bennie

(1935), p 221; J. Backhouse (1844), p 245.

13.   Interview with W. Nkabi, Bulembo Location, King Williams Town District, 24 Aug. 1975.

14.   Interview with N. Qeqe (see note 5 above).

15.   Interview with R. Cakata, Xobo Location, Idutywa District, 5 Dec. 1975. Mr. Cakata is a descendant of the man in question. Compare a report in the *Cape Frontier Times*, 31 July 1845, which describes how the Gcaleka royal family were doctored from the body of an enormous snake killed in their country. It concludes: 'On the animal's death it imparts its strength and power of excitement to him who killed it, and as no man can be allowed to possess greater power in the land than the king, he the king becomes possessed of that power by killing the slayer of the animal.'

16.   For tying up, J.H. Soga (n.d.), pp 173 – 175; A. Kropf and R. Godfrey (1915), p 177. For Sarhili's powers in this respect, interviews with Qeqe and Runeyi (note 5 above).

17.   J.H. Soga (n.d.), pp 198 – 201; A. Kropf and R. Godfrey (1915), p 113.

.18.   J.H. Soga (n.d.), pp 76 – 77; M. Hunter (1961), p 408. The Xhosa occasionally mutilated the bodies of European soldiers killed in the frontier wars for this reason which was not, of course, appreciated by other Europeans. The practice was, however, by no means universal. See, for instance, J. Alexander (1837), 1: 338, 415; 2: 249.

19.   L. Alberti (1810), p 90; Juju (1880), p 291; C.L. Stretch (1876), p 301.

20.   For a description of the ceremony at which crane-feathers were awarded, see T.B. Soga (n.d.), pp 140 – 141.

21.   C. Somerset-Bathurst, 22 May 1819, *RCC* XII, p 194.

22.   Ngqika was despised for his lack of bravery in battle. See R. Collins (1809), p 13. According to Wauchope, Ngqika was accompanied to the battle of Amalinde by Mtyingili, a famous coward, 'so that the chief might have the benefit of his cowardly instinct to fly in time should it be necessary to do so.' 'A Native Minister' (1908), p 29.

23.   L. Alberti (1810), p 92.

24.   'Nzulu Lwazi' (S.E.K. Mqhayi), 'Umhala, A. Mbodla!' *Umteteli wa-Bantu*, 10 Oct. 1931.

25.   See J.H. Soga (n.d.), Ch. IV for most of this paragraph. Soga's diagram on p 69 seems over-elaborate, and I have limited myself to what is confirmed by other sources. The Xhosa word *amaphiko*, like its English equivalent, is also used for 'the wings of a bird'.

26.   J. Bokwe (1914), pp 21 – 22.

27.   J. Campbell (1815), p 375; L. Alberti (1810), p 92. For the limited nature of wars in West Africa, see R.S. Smith (1976), p 53.

28.   For the deaths of Rharhabe and Mlawu, see S. Mqhayi, 'URarabe' in W. Bennie (1935), pp 136– 137; A. Kropf (1889), pp 38 – 40. The Qwathi are related to the Xesibe. Tshaka, chief of the Gqunukhwebe

was killed fighting Ndlambe.

29. N.C. Mhala in W. Bennie (1935), p 155; W.K. Ntsikana, 'Imfazwe kaThuthula' in W.B. Rubusana (1966), p 53.

30. G. Nkonki (1968), pp 166; J. Campbell (1815), p 375, says prisoners were killed but this is contradicted by his statement on the same page, that not more than one or two Xhosa died during a war. Aberti, who knew the Xhosa rather better, said that anyone who dropped his weapons would not be killed, but taken prisoner and ransomed. L. Alberti (1810), p 92.

31. H. Lichtenstein (1812 – 1815), 1: 343.

32. See Chapter I (3) and for example, A. Kropf (1889), p 37; H. Lichtenstein (1812 – 1815), 1: 340, ascribes the ferocity of the war against the San to the fact that the latter poisoned their weapons.

33. A. Kropf and R. Godfrey (1915), p 78.

34. A. Kropf and R. Godfrey (1915), p 138. Xhosa and Zulu war dances were variations on a common base, as is shown by their use of a single word (Xh. – guya; Z – giya) for 'to do a war dance'.

35. There is a discussion of war-cries in J.H. Soga (n.d.), p 74, who gives the impression that they were mainly instructions during battle, but this was not the case. T.B. Soga (n.d.), p 155, has the fullest description of songs and dances which deal with war.

36. J. Solilo in W. Bennie (1935), p 219.

37. There is a very full description in W.R. Thomson-C. Bird, 16 Aug. 1822, CO 163. Mqhayi gives very fine examples of the addresses of Ngqika and Ndlambe to their armies before *Amalinde* in W. Bennie (1935), p 195. These are translated and explained in J.H. Soga (n.d.), pp 80 – 81.

38. Evidence of W. Gisborne, *Abo Com.*, p 357.

39. J. Goldswain (1946 – 1949), 1: 92.

40. J. Alexander (1837), 1: 338. See also I. Stocker, 'Report upon Kaffraria,' March 1820, *RCC*, XIII, p 66.

41. 'Nzulu Lwazi' (S.E.K. Mqhayi), 'Umhala, A, Mbodla!' *Umteteli waBantu*, 10 Oct. 1931. J. Bisset (1875), pp 84 – 85 names Siyolo instead of Mxhamli, but I have preferred Mqhayi's version. For the official report of the *Battle of the Gwangqa*, see H. Somerset-Cloete, 8 June 1846, 786 of 1847, pp 151 – 152. For eye witness accounts, see J. Bisset (1875), Ch. XII; B. Adams (1941), Ch. XIII.

42. In addition, most of the available information comes from the official sources and this passes over much that we should like to know about. Two exceptions are H.D. Campagne's account of the *Second Frontier War* (VC 76), and Barrow's of the *Third* but neither are particularly detailed or reliable.

43. The best and most accessible primary source on the *First Frontier War* is 'Commandant A. van Jaarsveld's Report of the Expulsion of the Kafirs,' 20 July 1781, in D. Moodie (1840), 3: 110 – 112. For secondary accounts see P.J. van der Merwe (1938), Ch. VII and

J. Marais (1944), pp 7 — 10.

44. On the *Second Frontier War*, see P.J. van der Merwe (1940). J.S. Marais (1944), Ch IV.

45. For the *Third Frontier War*, see J.S. Marais (1944), Ch. VIII and XI and H. Giliomee (1975), Ch. XI and XII. The most accessible primary sources are in *RCC*, Vols. II and III.

46. Dundas-Ross, 23 Aug. 1799, *RCC*, II, p 276.

47. J.S. Marais (1944), p 108.

48. L. Alberti (1810), p 99.

49. A. van Jaarsveld in D. Moodie (1840), 3: 110 — 111.

50. Ibid., p 111.

51. R. Collins (1809), p 14.

52. Vandeleur-Dundas, 13 Aug. 1799, *RCC*, II, p 467.

53. J. Campbell (1815), p 99.

54. P.J. van der Merwe (1940), pp 43 — 44, 52.

55. Ibid., pp 42 — 43.

56. A. van Jaarsveld in D. Moodie (1840), 3: 110.

57. J. Barrow (1806), 1: 414 — 415.

58. Vandeleur-Dundas, 13 Aug. 1799, *RCC*, II, pp 467 — 468.

59. A. van Jaarsveld in D. Moodie (1840), 3: 110; J. Brownlee (1827), p 193.

60. P.J. van der Merwe (1940), p 43; J. Barrow (1806), 1: 149, 421.

61. P.J. van der Merwe (1938), p 270; D. Moodie (1840), 3: 91, De Jager-Bresler, 27 July 1799, *RCC*, II, p 445.

62. See, for example, R. Collins (1809), p 17; J. Marais (1944), p 12.

63. J. Campbell (1815), p 99.

64. A. van Jaarsveld in D. Moodie (1840), 3: 110; P.J. van der Merwe (1938), p 274.

65. P.J. van der Merwe (1940), p 49.

66. MIC 158 (1), Cory Library, (Copy of Graham papers in Rhodes House, Oxford), Graham-Lyster, 15 Oct. 1811. There is no good secondary account of this war, but a selection of official dispatches may be found in *RCC*, VIII.

67. J. Graham, no addressee, 2 Jan. 1812, *RCC*, VIII, p 235.

68. For the *Fifth Frontier War*, see C. Stretch (1876); T. Pringle (1835), pp 277 — 287; A. Stockenstrom (1887), 1: Chs. VII — VIII; *RCC*, XII; *GTJ*, 26 Sept. 1846, containing the dispatches of Colonel Willshire, commanding Grahamstown during the *Battle of Grahamstown*.

69. G. Fraser-Landdrost of Uitenhage, 4 Feb 1819, *RCC*, XII, p 135.

70. A. Stockenstrom (1887), 1: 350 — 351; *GTJ* 26 Sept. 1846; J. Alexander (1837), 1: 350 — 351.

71. If one excepts the so-called *Battle of the Gwangqa* (1846), in which the Xhosa were taken by surprise and gave little resistance. For the *Battle of Grahamstown*, see C.L. Stretch (1876), and *GTJ*, 26 Sept. 1846.

72. *GTJ* 26 Sept. 1846.
73. For the last phase of the war, see A. Stockenstrom (1887), 1: 153 — 163.
74. J. Brownlee (1827), p 200.
75. A. Stockenstrom (1887), 1: 155 — 156.
76. The War of 1834 — 1835 is exceptionally well documented. Apart from the official bluebooks, 279 of 1836 and 503 of 1837, G.M. Theal published the unofficial correspondence of D'Urban and Smith in *The Kafir War of 1835*. (London, 1912). In addition to the sources cited in Chapter VIII, note 5 above, see J. Alexander (1837) and R. Godlonton (1835 — 1836b).
77. 'Statement of April, a Bechuana,' 18 Feb. 1835, LG 9 is a unique account of the Xhosa invasion from the viewpoint of an ordinary participant on the Xhosa side.
78. 'Statement of the Frontier Caffres to the Commandant and to His Excellency the Governor,' 31 Dec. 1834, 503 of 1827, p 49; also printed in Godlonton (1835 — 1836a), pp 52 — 57.
79. The Colonial authorities were not interested in negotiating; indeed it is questionable if they understood the purpose of Tyhali's statement. For a typical reaction, see J. Alexander (1837), 1: 423.
80. 'Statement of April, a Bechuana,' 19 Feb. 1835, LG 9; MS 15,544 Diary of J. Ayliff, 8 Sept. 1840.
81. *GTJ*, 15 Aug. 1846; *CFT* 18 Aug. 1846.
82. MS 15,429 S. Young-WMS Directors, Wesleyville, 10 Aug. 1830.
83. R. Godlonton (1835 — 1836b), p 115. Another newspaper editor commented, 'They are as nimble as bucks and as cunning as foxes. You never know what they are driving at until they are down on you.' *CFT*, 18 Aug. 1846.
84. J. Bisset (1875), p 109; *GTJ* 1 Aug. 1846; *CFT* 4 Aug. 1846.
85. T.H. Bowker (1970), pp 143 — 144; W.F.A. Gilfillan (1970), p 50.
86. T. Stubbs (1978), pp 125 — 126.
87. J. Goldswain (1946 — 1949), 1: 92; T.H. Bowker (1970), pp 98 — 99. For further examples of Xhosa taunting, see J. Bisset (1875), p 109; W. Munro (1887), 1: 153.
88. *GTJ* 29 Aug. 1846.
89. J. Goldswain, (1946 — 1949), 1: 93; W. Gilfillan (1970), pp 26, 28; *GTJ* 29 Aug. 1846.
90. T.H. Bowker (1970), pp 98, 102, 104.
91. For a vivid, if one-sided account of the fighting in lower Albany during the *War of the Axe*, see J. Bisset (1875), Ch. X.
92. One sure sign of approaching war was when Xhosa employed in the Colony, slipped away to join their people. See, for example, *GTJ*, 31 Jan., 14 Feb., 28 March 1846.
93. T.H. Bowker (1970), p 155.
94. J. Appleyard (1971), p 65; *GTJ* 16 May 1846.

95. J. Appleyard (1971), p 70.
96. *GTJ* 30 May 1846. For other chiefs riding horses into battle, see T.H. Bowker (1970), p 157; R. Godlonton (1835 — 1836b), p 214; *GTJ* 9 May 1846.
97. Melville-Size, 24 June 1846, 786 of 1847, p 163.
98. *GTJ* 16 May 1846; T.H. Bowker (1970), p 156.
99. W. Southey in *GTJ*, 29 Aug. 1846.
100. Cory interview 116, Manxiwa ('Lindinxura'), Willowvale, 29 Jan. 1910.
101. Among numerous references to Xhosa spies, see J. Alexander (1837), 2: 221; W. Gilfillan (1970), p 27; T.H. Bowker (1970), pp 116, 150. For a fascinating description of one of Shaka Zulu's spies, see C. Webb and J. Wright (1976), pp 192 — 194.
102. See, for example, J. Appleyard (1971), p 70.
103. See, for example, T.H. Bowker (1970), pp 114, 213 — 214; W. Gilfillan (1970), pp 25 — 26; *GTJ* 27 June 1846.
104. J. Alexander (1837), 1: 213 — 214.
105. For example, *CFT* 6 Oct. 1846: 'British troops are quite out of their element in fighting Kafirs . . . It is of no use collecting a large force and making combined movements upon rocks, mountains, ravines and jungles where the enemy can elude the vigilance and laugh at the useless efforts of the troops to get at them.'
106. F. Rex — sister, 7 May 1835 in U. Long (1947), p 169. There is not unfortunately an adequate account of the Khoi regiments.
107. For an overall view of Mfengu participation in the *Frontier Wars*, see R. Moyer, 'The Mfengu, Self-Defence and the Cape Frontier Wars' in C. Saunders and R. Derricourt (1974), pp 101 — 126.
108. *GTJ* 5 Sept. 1846. The only difference in physical appearance between the Xhosa and the Mfengu was the Mfengu custom of piercing their ears. Thus on 20 June 1846, the *GTJ* records the case of an alarmed Mfengu clapping his hands to his ears and shouting out 'Fingo! Fingo!'
109. Cory interviews, 112, Maseti, Kentani , January 1910.
110. The sources on the *Seventh Frontier War* are not nearly as good as those on the *Sixth*, and I have relied heavily on the weekly reports in the *Grahams Town Journal* and *Cape Frontier Times*. The official dispatches may be found in 786 of 1847 and 912 of 1848. The best of an indifferent crop of memoirs is J. Bisset (1847). See also, B. Adams (1941); J.W. Appleyard (1971); S.M. Mitra (1911); A. Stockenstrom (1887), 2: Chs. XXVI — XXVII; T. Stubbs (1978), Ch. VII.
111. P. Maitland-Stanley, 15 May 1846, 786 of 1847, p 125.
112. Maitland was forced to slaughter his draught oxen for food. He had hoped to subsist on Xhosa cattle, but was never able to capture any. *CFT*, 21 July 1846.
113. For the *Battle of the Gwangqa*, see note 41 above.
114. The official accounts of the interview are 'Statement of Conference on 21 Aug. 1846', 786 of 1847, pp 178 — 180. Controversy raged over

whether or not Colonel Johnstone, the ranking British officer, had shaken hands with Sarhili. Maitland was later forced to publish Stockenstrom's account of the meeting which he had mysteriously omitted from his earlier dispatches. See P. Maitland-Grey, 26 Jan. 1847, 912 of 1848, pp 23 – 25.

115. T. Stubbs (1978), pp 735 – 736; *CFT* 20, 27 Oct. 1846; 23 March 1847. T. Kirk (1972), pp 135, 183.

116. *CFT*, 27 Oct. 1846.

117. *GTJ*, 16, 23 Jan. 1847.

118. *GTJ*, 19 Sept. 1846.

119 *CFT*, 26 May 1846; *GTJ*, 23 May, 6 June 1846.

120. *GTJ*, 14 Feb., 28 March 1846; C. Stretch-Major Smith, 12 Apr. 1846, LG 403.

121. *CFT*, 26 March, 7 July, 4, 25 Aug. 1846.

122. H. Calderwood-B. Maitland, 3 Oct. 1846, 786 of 1847, p 188.

123. *GTJ*, 7 Nov. 1846. See also *CFT* 3 Nov. 1846.

124. P. Maitland-Grey, 26 Nov. 1846, 786 of 1847, p 195. See also, *GTJ* 3, 10, 31 Oct. 1846.

125. *GTJ*, 3 Oct. 1846.

126. See, for example, J. Bisset (1875), p 1. Guy has stressed the importance of seasons and supplies in J. Guy (1971), pp 563 – 565. Similar considerations applied to war in precolonial West Africa. R.S. Smith (1976), p 42.

127. P. Maitland-W. Gladstone, 11 June 1846, 786 of 1847, p 141. *CFT* 7 July 1846 published a Xhosa war plan, elicited from survivors of the Gwangqa charge. Mhala was to take possession of the Fish River bush and starve out Fort Peddie; Sandile was to cut communication between Fort Beaufort and Peddie; Maqoma was to hold the Addo Bush and cut the supply route between Port Elizabeth and Grahamstown. The plan was never executed, but it shows that the Xhosa appreciated the importance of supplies in the Colonial war effort.

128. *CFT*, 13 Oct. 1846; P. Maitland-W. Gladstone, 11 June 1846, 786 of 1847, p 140.

129. For the Burns Hill wagon train, see J. Bisset (1875), Ch. IX; enclosures in J. Hare-P. Maitland, 20 Apr. 1846, 786 of 1847, pp 118 – 120. For Fort Peddie wagon train, see Richardson – Quarter-Master General 8 May 1846, 786 of 1847, p 135; D. Campbell-Cloete, 21 May 1846, 786 of 1847, pp 149 – 150.

130. *GTJ* 22 Aug. 1846; W. Munro (1887), 1: 154 – 155; M. Johnstone-Cloete, 15 Sept. 1846, 786 of 1847, p 174.

131. P. Maitland-W. Gladstone, 18 Sept 1846, 786 of 1847, p 153.

132. H. Pottinger-Grey, 20 Feb. 1847, 912 of 1848, p 27.

133. P. Maitland-Stanley, 24 Apr. 1846, 786 of 1847, p 115.

134. Cf. J. Guy (1971), p 564.

135. Cf. *CFT* 22 Sept 1846. 'His Excellency has dismissed the whole of the

Burgher forces — not because the war is over — not because their services are no longer required — but because their domestic affairs, and the agricultural necessities of the country require their presence at home.'

136. As the financial reformers discovered when they tried to block funds for the *War of the Axe*. See T. Kirk (1972), pp 177 – 178, 137.

137. *GTJ*, 25 Dec. 1847.

138. *GTJ*, 21 Aug. 1847; 4 Sept. 1847.

139. W. Gilfillan (1970), p 26; T.H. Bowker (1970), p 118.

140. P. Maitland-Grey, 14 Oct. 1846, 786 of 1847, p 181.

141. *GTJ*, 12 Dec. 1846.

142. *CFT*, 29 Dec. 1846.

143. For Maitland's registration scheme, see P. Maitland-Grey, 20 Jan. 1847, 912 of 1848, pp 8 – 9; For settler criticism of it, *CFT* 26 Jan. 1847; *GTJ* 6 Feb. 1847; and Pottinger's opinion, H. Pottinger-Grey, 14 Apr. 1847, 912 of 1848, p 80.

144. *GTJ* 15 May 1847.

145. *GTJ* 28 Aug. 1847.

146. *CFT* 6 Sept. 1847; See also *GTJ* 10 Apr. 1847.

147. S. Mitra (1911), p 197.

148. Bisset, the officer responsible, denied that there had been any deception (see J. Bisset [1875] Ch. XVI), but see Chapter VIII, for his general untruthfulness. Governor Pottinger certainly believed that Sandile had been tricked. Berkeley-Pottinger, 27 Nov. 1847, MSB 40 SA Library, Cape Town. Sandile always maintained afterwards that he had been unjustly dealt with, and his refusal to trust his person to the Colonial authorities partly contributed to the outbreak of the *Eighth Frontier War* in 1850. See C. Brownlee (1896), pp 293 – 295.

149. For a general overview of firearms in South Africa, see S. Marks and A. Atmore (1971).

150. J.H. Soga (n.d.), p 77.

151. Cory interview 72, S.R. Ralph, 18 Apr. 1909. The Xhosa did make some use of horses in war outside of the battle itself. For chiefs on horses, see note 96 above; for Xhosa sending spies and messengers, T.H. Bowker (1970), p 150; *CFT* 26 Jan. 1847. Sir Harry Smith shared Xhosa opinions on the general unsuitability of horses for frontier warfare. H. Smith, 'Notes on the Kafir war,' 912 of 1848, p 111.

152. C. Somerset-Bathurst, 22 May 1819, *RCC* XII, p 201.

153. For my remarks on the Zulu, I am indebted to Dr. Guy's modestly titled article (see note 126 above), which is far ahead of anything else written on the subject.

154. See Chapter VII (2).

155. For an overview of the firearms trade, see G. Cory (1910 – 1939), 4: 336 ff. For some of the names involved, see T.H. Bowker (1970), p 106; Acc 1415 (77), Vol. IV, J. Hare-G. Napier, 22 Feb. 1839;

T. Shepstone-H. Hudson, 13 July 1840, LG 406.

156. G. Napier-Glenelg, 12 July 1838, 424 of 1851, pp 32 — 33. See also *GTJ* 29 July 1841.

157. For the mechanics of the trade, which worked largely through Khoi intermediaries, see Deposition of David Slinger, 5 Feb. 1841, 424 of 1851, p 101; W. Fynn-H. Hudson, 17 Feb. 1838, LG 404; J. Bowker-H. Hudson, 5 June 1838, LG 423; *GTJ* 10 May 1838.

158. B. Adams (1941), p 117; *GTJ* 16 May 1846, 9 Jan. 1847.

159. Evidence of Captain H.C.C. Owen, 635 of 1851, pp 318 — 319. For ammunition running out during the war, see *GTJ* 6 June 1846.

160. J. Bisset (1875), pp 79, 87; B. Adams (1941), pp 133, 181, 182.

161. B. Adams (1941), p 181.

162. *CFT* 17 Feb. 1841.

163. Interview with S. Mgqala, imiQhayi Location, King Williams Town District, Aug. 1975.

164. For firearms in South Africa in this period, see F. Lategan (1974), esp. pp 99 — 100; various articles in *Journal of the Historical Firearms Society of South Africa*, (1958), Vol. I. (1958).

165. G. Tylden (1956 — 1957), p 207.

166. J. Bisset (1875), p 92. Emphasis in the original.

167. B.Adams (1941), p 153.

168. *GTJ* 6 June 1846.

169. P. Maitland-Stanley, 24 Apr. 1846, 786 of 1847, p 115.

170. H. Pottinger-Grey, 26 June 1847, 912 of 1848, p 87.

171. Complaints that the Boers killed women and children date back to the *Second Frontier War*. See note 60 above. Khoi and Mfengu auxiliaries thought that Xhosa women were fair game. See J. Alexander (1837), 2: 120. Even the Colonists commented on the fact that Xhosa spared women and children, but here too there were exceptions. See e.g. *CFT* 2 June 1846.

172. Interview with W. Nkabi, Bulembo Location, King Williams Town District, 24 Aug. 1975; Appleyard (1971), pp 81 — 82; Alexander (1837), 2: 60 — 61; *CFT*, 6 Oct. 1846.

173. *GTJ*, 8, 22 Aug. 1847. *CFT* 6 Sept. 1847; B. Adams, (1941), p 150.

174. J. Bisset (1875), Ch. III.

175. B. D'Urban-Glenelg, 7 Nov. 1835, 279 of 1836, p 89.

176. W. Boyce (1838), p xii.

177. *GTJ* 29 Aug. 1846.

178. Many of the sources refer to the Xhosa carrying away their wounded. R. Godlonton (1835 — 1836b), p 117, mentions an instance when three Xhosa were killed 'endeavouring to drag away their slain.' J. Bisset (1875), p 108, says that the Xhosa carried off their dead while their bodies were still warm, but not when they had gone cold and rigid.

179. For the debate on the number of dead at the Gwangqa, see *GTJ* 29 Aug., 5 Sept., 26 Sept. 1846.

180. L. Alberti (1810), pp 92 – 93.
181. J. Bisset (1875), p 11. See also B. Adams (1941), p 152; T. Stubbs (1978), p 169.
182. J. Bisset (1875), pp 91, 95 – 96.
183. R. Godlonton (1835 – 1836b), p 61; W. Gilfillan (1970), pp 34 – 35.
184. C. Stretch-H. Hudson, 17 Oct. 1836, LG 396.
185. 'Examinations of Caffres found in the colony,' 30 Sept. 1836, LG 396.
186. G. Mackinnon-High Commissioner, 20 Dec. 1848, 1056 of 1849, p 37.
187. In view of the Governor's declared intention to expel them from the Ceded Territory, many of the Ngqika chiefs thought they might win concessions by abandoning Sandile when Pottinger moved against him in August 1847. See H. Calderwood, Memorandum, 13 July 1847, 912 of 1848, p 114; *GTJ* 25 Sept. 1847.

CHAPTER X

1. The last of the important Ngqika chiefs to set up his own great place was Anta who had lived with his brother Sandile, during the latter's minority. After the *War of the Axe*, Anta moved up to the Windvogel-berg (later Cathcart). Toyise, son of Gasela, also claimed the country. J. Maclean-J. Mackinnon, 12 Oct. 1849, BK 428.
2. See J. Maclean (1858), p 116.
3. J. Maclean (1858), p 153; Evidence of J. Freeman, 635 of 1851, p 28. Freeman estimated that 100 people were now living in a village.
4. M. Wilson (1969b), p 254; Evidence of Sir P. Maitland, 635 of 1851, p 361; J.W.D. Moodie (1835), 2: 269.
5. W. Rubusana (1966), p 104.
6. T.H. Bowker (1970), p 115.
7. See Chapter VII (3).
8. *CFT* 29 Jan. 1841.
9. See Chapter VII (4).
10. See Chapters IV (1) and VI (1).
11. Smith thought that by abolishing judicial fines and *upundlo* he could win the support of commoners against their chiefs. MS 2033 H. Smith-B. D'Urban, 20 Dec. 1835, 14 Feb. 1835.
12. The Kaffir Police were established by Smith during his reign over the Province of Queen Adelaide to provide him with an executive machinery independent of the chiefs. They were taken over by the Diplomatic Agents under the treaty system and employed as messengers and thief-takers. They were distrusted by the Colonists, and many

joined the Xhosa during the War of 1850 — 1853. There is constant reference to the Kaffir Police in the correspondence of the Diplomatic Agents (LG file) and they deserve a closer examination than I have been able to give them.

13. See Chapter VII (3). This alliance was to assume tangible form when the Kat River Khoi joined the Xhosa in the War of 1850 — 1853. See T. Kirk (1973).

14. See Chapter VII (4).

15. See, for example, *CFT* 28 Dec. 1843; H.G. Smith-Earl Grey, 7 Jan. 1850, 1288 of 1850, p 24.

16. The most recent biographies are J. Lehmann (1977) and A. Harington (1977). Smith's own official dispatches for the period may be found in 969 of 1848, 1056 of 1849 and 1288 of 1850.

17. See, for example, H. Smith-Earl Grey, 23 Dec. 1847, 969 of 1848, p 24; A. Harington (1977), pp 213, 223; G. Cory (1910 — 1939), 5: 105.

18. 'Meeting of Kafir Chiefs,' 7 Oct. 1848, 1056 of 1849, p 33.

19. S.E.K. Mqhayi (1931), p 109.

20. From Smith's address at his first public meeting with the Xhosa chiefs, H. Smith-Grey, 7 Jan. 1848, 949 of 1848, p 51.

21. 'The settlers in the eastern districts are very desirous of becoming proprietors, by purchase, of a considerable portion of the tract of country lately added to the colony,' explained Smith, 'and having, generally speaking, acquired large fortunes by the war expenditure, they are prepared to pay large prices for these lands.' H. Smith-Grey, 23 March 1848, 1056 of 1849, p 7. See also T. Kirk (1972), pp 301 — 304; G. Theal (1915), 3: 67 — 69.

22. Evidence of H. Renton, 635 of 1851, p 385.

23. R. Niven-Secretary to Government, 2 Oct. 1848, BK 433; A. Mac-Diarmid-R. Southey, 17 May 1848, BK 433. Nqeno's successor, Stokwe, did not have a single ox.

24. T. Kirk (1972), p 288.

25. The idea of taxation was born together with annexation, and was mooted by Earl Grey to Pottinger as a 'stimulus to industry'. T. Kirk (1972), pp 170, 178. G. Mackinnon-H. Smith, 2 July 1848, 1056 of 1849, p 19.

26. *CFT* 19 Nov. 1850.

27. H. Calderwood-R. Woosnam, 18 Nov. 1847, GH 8/46. The destitute labourers included Sandile's brother, Matwa. Calderwood's representations on the labour question date back to March 1847.

28. This was mentioned at Smith's first big public meeting (see note 20 above) and was finally embodied in Ordinance 3 of 1848, enclosed in H. Smith-Grey, 29 July 1848, 1056 of 1849, pp 26 — 28.

29. These are preserved as CO 4487.

30. W. Edye-J. Maclean, 2 Feb. 1849, BK 433.

31. See Chapter VII (3).
32. The official form of indenture did provide for the wages to be specified but cf. C. Brownlee-G. Mackinnon, 29 Oct. 1849, BK 432. Brownlee who was responsible for issuing indentures in Ngqika country thought that it was unnecessary to specify wages since the Xhosa 'would expect to receive the ordinary rate of wages given under ordinary circumstances, to persons employed as they would be on their arrival in the western districts.'
33. We know of this through the protests of Xhosa who refused to proceed further once they discovered what had happened. H. Hudson-Resident Agent, Fort Peddie, 17 July 1848, BK 58; J.L. Brown-W.M. Edye, 5 June 1848, BK 433.
34. C. Brownlee-G. Mackinnon, 7 Sept., 13 Sept., 5 Oct., 15 Oct. 1849, BK 432.
35. G. Mackinnon-H. Smith, 22 April 1848, BK 371; C. Brownlee-G. Mackinnon, 29 Oct. 1849, BK 432.
36. G. Mackinnon-H. Smith, 31 Dec. 1849, 1288 of 1850, p 25.
37. G. Mackinnon-High Commissioner, 20 Dec. 1848, 1056 of 1849, p 37.
38. C. Brownlee-G. Mackinnon, 3 Sept., 29 Oct. 1849, BK 432.
39. J. Maclean-G. Mackinnon, 26 Aug. 1850, BK 74.

APPENDIX I A

1. During my fieldwork, when an official meeting was called to 'give the history', I often found that this consisted of only the genealogy, and had to recommence my explanations of what it was that I wanted.
2. See Chapter II (1).
3. The duplication of certain praise-names in the praises of different clans raises intriguing possibilities in tracing relationships, but there are too many documented coincidences of names to permit hypotheses on these lines. See Chapter II, note C.
4. J. Opland, 'Praise Poems as Historical Sources' in Saunders and Derricourt (1974), pp 1 – 37.
5. W. Rubusana (1906).
6. I regularly questioned informants concerning allusions in praise-poems given by Rubusana, but in no case was I able to get an explanation of a point I did not already understand.
7. See, for example, A. Mafeje (1967).
8. S.E.K. Mqhayi; 'URarabe' in W. Bennie (1935), p 139.
9. Nkonki differentiates between *amavo* (semi-mythical legends) and

amabali (historical narratives). This distinction has now lost its force. I found *amavo* used only as an occasional synonym for *amabali*. Nkonki himself classifies 'The origins of the amaRharhabe' and 'The quarrel between Ngqika and Ndlambe' as *amavo* although they are unquestionably historical narratives, G. Nkonki (1968), pp 42 − 48.

10.   For a discussion of the effect of the means of transmission on the tradition, see J. Vansina (1965), pp 31 − 45.

11.   Functionalist anthropologists such as Malinowski and Radcliffe-Brown used to argue that since all myth was functional to the present, oral societies could transmit no valid information about the past. See J. Vansina (1965), p 12. Recently, symbolists have adopted a similar position. See, for example L. de Heusch (1975). These anthropologists seem to have ignored mnemonic devices, institutionalised means of transmission, and survivals of the past in the present, all of which lend some certainty to diachronic myth-interpretation.

12.   Similar arguments have recently been put forward for the Tswana by J.L. Comaroff (1974).

13.   Vansina defines a cliché, which he calls a *wandersagen* or complex stereotype, as follows: 'a literary device for explaining a historical fact which is already known, for adding colour to a narrative, or for describing a disagreeable past event without upsetting existing cultural values.' J. Vansina (1965), p 74.

14.   Ibid., pp 62 − 63.

15.   A. Roberts (1974), p 45.

16.   Interview with Thabevu Monayi, Jujura Location, Willowvale District, 3 Nov. 1975.

17.   Interview with Bomvane Fikile Anta, Teko Location, Kentani District, 8 Jan. 1976; 'Umfi uOba Ngonyama Tyali,' *Izwi la Bantu*, 23 Apr. 1907.

18.   For instance, one informant asserted that Maqoma had refused to kill his cattle in 1857. Subsequent investigation showed that Maqoma's son, Kona, from whom the informant was descended, had indeed refused to kill. Interview with Chief Gladstone Maqoma, Ngqungqe Location, Kentani District, 19 Jan. 1976.

19.   Interview with Mrs. Elizabeth Mpanga, Thwecu Location, King Williams Town District, 19 Aug. 1975.

20.   See H. Scheub (1976).

21.   The informant was N. Qeqe. The incident occurred at Shixini Location, Willowvale District on 30 Nov. 1975.

22.   Interview with Wallace Sukutu, Urban Location, Alexandria, 27 Feb. 1976.

23.   For a list of these, see Appendix ID.

24.   For the history of Xhosa literature, see A.C. Jordan (1973) and D.P. Kunene and R.A. Kirsch (1967). These deal with some of the authors mentioned, as does A.S. Gerard (1971), which is however

occasionally inaccurate, and not particularly helpful.

25. For detailed information on Xhosa newspapers, see L. Switzer and D. Switzer (1979).

26. For a detailed discussion of the Lovedale Press in the time of Shepherd, see J.B. Peires (1979).

27. R.H.W. Shepherd (1945), p 15.

28. *Imvo ZabaNtsundu*, 23 Dec. 1961.

29. The most complete treatment of Mqhayi as a literary figure is W. Kuse (1977). In addition to the general works cited in Note 24 above, see Mqhayi's autobiography, S.E.K. Mqhayi (1939).

30. S.E.K. Mqhayi (1931).

31. S.E.K. Mqhayi (1931), p 134.

32. This phrase was used by the Lovedale Press when they decided to reject the manuscript. J. Peires (1979) p 167.

33. There has been no full-scale study of Soga. See D. Kunene and R. Kirsch (1967), p 12, and R.F.A. Hoernle's biographical note in J.H. Soga (1930), pp xi – xv.

34. For J.H. Soga's grandfather, Soga, see Chapter VII (4).

35. This manuscript has now been deposited in the Cory Library, Rhodes University.

36. For example, Khawuta's reign was dated 1792 – 1820, rather than 1778 – 1794. This mistake causes Soga to confuse the capture of young Hintsa in c. 1795 with the *Battle of Amalinde* (1818). See J.H. Soga (1930), pp 145, 157 – 159.

37. Consider for instance, the way he dismisses the story of the origin of the Right-Hand House, and the invention of a law regarding the killing off of the sons of a chief in order to explain the presence of only one chief per generation in the early part of the genealogy. J.H. Soga (1930), pp 36 – 37, 103 – 104.

38. See Chapter IV, note 19.

39. A. Wilmot and J.C. Chase (1869).

40. G.M. Theal (1877), p iv.

41. Ibid.

42. G.M. Theal (1897), 2: Ch. XVIII.

43. NA 623, Cape Archives, I would like to thank R. Moorsom for drawing these to my attention.

44. For example J. Marais (1944), J.S. Galbraith (1963); and especially W.M. Macmillan (1963).

45. M. Wilson and L.M. Thompson (1969 – 1971).

46. L.M. Thompson, (London, 1969).

47. C. Saunders and R. Derricourt, (1974).

48. Wilson does cite a number of Xhosa written sources (1969a), pp 85 – 86, but she hardly uses them. For the exceptions, see pp 92 – 93, 122.

Bibliography

A. ORAL SOURCES

Tapes of the fieldwork, conducted between August 1975 and February 1976, are in my personal possession. A selection of transcripts and translations have been deposited at the Memorial Library, University of Wisconsin-Madison, and the Cory Library, Rhodes University, Grahamstown. Full reference to interviews referred to in the text may be found in the footnotes. A list of important informants is given in Appendix I C. As explained in Appendix I B, an attempt was made to visit every important chiefdom. A list of chiefs approached is given below. The willingness and ability of the chiefs to help varied considerably, but none refused altogether.

I.   CISKEI

    EAST LONDON DISTRICT
    amaNdlambe (Mhala)
    amaGqunukhwebe (Phato)

    HEWU DISTRICT
    amaHlubi (Zimema)

    KING WILLIAM'S TOWN DISTRICT
    imiDushane (Siwani)
    imiDange
    amaGasela (amaNtsusa)
    amaHleke
    imiNgqalasi
    amaNtinde
    imiQhayi

MIDDLEDRIFT DISTRICT
amaGqunukhwebe (Kama)

STUTTERHEIM DISTRICT
amaZibula (Sandile)

VICTORIA EAST DISTRICT
imiNgcangatelo (Oba kaTyali)

II   TRANSKEI

ELLIOTDALE DISTRICT
amaGcaleka (Dimanda)
amaVelelo (Mdabuka)

IDUTYWA
amaMbede (Nqoko) (two segments)

KENTANI
imiDushane (Qasana)
amaGwali
amaGwelane (Anta)
amaJingqi (Maqoma)
amaKweleshe (Mcotama)
amaMbalu (Nqeno)
amaMbombo (Mnyango kaSandile)
imiNgcangetelo (Feni kaTyali)
imiNgcangatelo (Oba kaTyali)
iTsonyana (Bhurhu)

WILLOWVALE DISTRICT
amaGojela (Manxiwa) (two segments)
amaJingqi (Ncaphayi kaHintsa)
amaMali (Xelinkunzi kaSigcawu)
amaMbede (Mithi)
amaTshayelo (Lutshaba kaPhalo)
amaVelelo (two segments)
Gcaleka Great Place at Nqadu

B.   ARCHIVES AND MANUSCRIPT COLLECTIONS

I.   GOVERNMENT ARCHIVES, CAPE TOWN.

BK 425-33	British Kaffraria, Letters received, 1848 — 1850.
BO 68-75	British Occupation. Letters received from Graaff-Reinet; Disturbances in the Interior of the Colony.
CO 122-434	Letters received from Sundry Military and Naval Officers, Churches, Commandant of the Frontier, Agents and Missionaries in the Interior, and Commissioner-General.
CO 2559-2619	Letters received from Landdrosts of Graaff-Reinet and Uitenhage, 1806 — 1834.
CO 2625-2750	Letters received from Landdrosts of Graaff-Reinet, Bathurst, Albany and Somerset, 1820 — 1834.
GH 8/23	Chief Commissioner, British Kaffraria. Letters, 1848 — 1852.
GH 8/46	H. Calderwood. Letters, 1847 — 1848.
GH 14/1	Border Tribes and Agents, 1836 — 1846.
GH 19/4	Border Tribe Treaties and Misc. Papers, 1835 — 1845.
GR 1/1 — 1/9	Graaff-Reinet. Minutes of Meetings of Landdrost and Heemraden, 1786 — 1795.
GR 12/1 — 12/2	Graaff-Reinet. Letters and Reports from Field-Cornets, Veld Wagtmeesters, Veld Kommandants and private individuals, 1781 — 1794.
LG 1-9	Commissioner-General for the Eastern Districts, 1823 — 1832. Lieutenant-Governor of the Eastern Cape, 1835 — 1846.
LG 420-59	Agent General. Letters received from various officials and private individuals regarding Kaffirs, Fingoes etc.
NA 623	Information collected for and by South African Native Affairs Commission, 1903 — 1906.
VC 68	(A.S. Faure) Dagregister gehouden den ondergetekende Landdrost op deselfde rheis naar t'Cafferland, 10 Dec. 1793.
VC 76	(H.D. Campagne). Berigt Nopens den oorsprong voortgang en ruptures der Kaffers.
VC 592-8	R.J. Gordon, Dagboek.
ZP 1/1/89	Microfilm of Colonial Office (London) CO 48/165.
Acc. 378c	Diary of C.L. Stretch as copied by G.M. Theal.
Acc. 519 (5)	B. D'Urban papers.
Acc. 611 (5)	R. Southey papers.
Acc. 983	C. Andrews, Reminiscences of the Kafir War of 1834 — 1835.

Acc. 1415 (77)   Sir G. Napier papers.

II   SOUTH AFRICAN LIBRARY, CAPE TOWN

Andrews, Caeser. Original Field Diary (1835).
Berkeley, George. Papers.
Grey Collection. Africa-South (Kafir) No. 158. 172. incluidng Wm
    Kekale Kaye, Interpreter. 'Kafir Legends and History' and 'Gexesha
    lika Shiwo Yama Xosa', and J. Brownlee. 'The Origins or Rise of the
    prophet Nxele'.
Mears, W.G.A. 'Papers'.

III   SOUTH AFRICAN MUSEUM, CAPE TOWN

Smith, Andrew. Kaffir Notes.

IV   CORY LIBRARY, RHODES UNIVERSITY, GRAHAMSTOWN

Ayliff, John. 'History of the Wars causing the dispersion of the
    Fingoes'. MS 15,544.
Burton, Alfred W. Notebooks. MS 14,264.
Cory, George. Accessions. MS 791-1241.
D'Urban, Benjamin. Correspondence, copies of letters and other docu-
    ments, collected by G.M. Theal. MS 2033.
Kayser, Frederick G. Papers, on loan to Cory Library.
Mbutuma, M. Ibali labaThembu. Uncatalogued.
Philipps, Thomas. Letters to My Kinsfolk. MS 14,264.
Sihele, E.G. Ibali labaThembu. Uncatalogued.
Soga, J.H. 'Kwa SaBantsundu'. MS 14,254.
Stretch, C.L. Diary. MS 14,588.
Wesleyan Methodist Missionary Society. Microfilm of London Archives.
    MS 15,429.

C. BLUE BOOKS

50 of 1835; 252 of 1835. Papers relative to the condition and Treatment of
    the Native Inhabitants of Southern Africa.

538 of 1836; 425 of 1837. Report of the Select Committee on Aborigines (British Settlements).

279 of 1836. Cape of Good Hope; Caffre War and Death of Hintza.

503 of 1837. Copies of extracts of any further despatches.

786 of 1847. Correspondence re State of the Kaffirs on the Eastern Frontier.

912 of 1848; 969 of 1848; 1056 of 1849; 1288 of 1850. Correspondence re State of the Kaffir Tribes on the Eastern Frontier.

424 of 1851. Papers re Kafir Tribes 1837 — 1845.

635 of 1851. Report from the Select Committee on relations with the kaffir tribes.

Cape of Good Hope, *Report and Proceedings of the Government Commission on Native Laws and Customs,* G4 of 1883.

D. NEWSPAPERS AND PERIODICALS

Annual Reports of the Wesleyan Methodist Missionary Society, 1822 — 1850.
Berliner Missionberichte, 1837 — 1850.
Caffrarian Messenger, 1838 — 1845.
Cape Frontier Times, 1840 — 1850.
Grahams Town Journal, 1831 — 1850.
Imvo Zabantsundu, 1959 — 1965.
Izwi laBantu, 1901 — 1902, 1906 — 1909.
Transactions of the London Missionary Society, 4 vols., 1800 — 1818.
Umteteli waBantu, 1926 — 1939.

E. PUBLISHED WORKS

'A Native Minister', (1908). (I. Wauchope). *The Natives and their Mission-aries.* Lovedale: The Lovedale Press, (1908).

Acocks, J.P.H. (1975). *Veld Types of South Africa.* 2nd ed. Memoirs of the Botanical Survey of South Africa, no. 40. Pretoria: Department of Agricultural Technical Services, (1975).

Adams, Buck. (1941). *The Narrative of Private Buck Adams.* Edited by A. Gordon-Brown. Cape Town: Van Riebeeck Society, 1941.

'Afer'. (1827). 'The Caffre Frontier'. *Oriental Herald.* 12 — 13 (1827), 12: 11

— 21, 225 — 236; 13: 13 — 17.

Alberti, Ludwig. (1810). *Alberti's Account of the Xhosa in 1807.* 1810; translated by W. Fehr. Cape Town: Balkema, 1968.

Alexander, James. (1837). *Narrative of a voyage of observation among the colonies of western Africa . . . and a campaign in Kafferland.* 2 vols. London: Colburn, 1837.

Appleyard, John W. (1971). *The War of the Axe and the Xhosa Bible.* Ed. J. Frye. Cape Town: Struik, 1971.

Ayliff, John and Whiteside, J. (1912). *History of the Abambo, generally known as the Fingos.* Butterworth: Gazette, 1912.

Backhouse, James (1844). *Narrative of a visit to the Mauritius and South Africa.* London: Hamilton Adams, 1844.

Bain, Andrew G. (1949). *Journals of Andrew Geddes Bain.* Edited by M. Lister. Cape Town: Van Riebeeck Society, 1949.

Bannister, Saxe. (1830). *Humane Policy.* 1830; reprint ed., London: Dawson, 1968.

Barrow, John. (1806). *Travels into the Interior of South Africa.* 2nd ed. 2 vols., London: Cadell and Davies, 1806.

Beinart, William J. (1980). 'Production and the material basis of chieftainship: Pondoland, c. 1830 — 1880'. In *Economy and Society in Pre-industrial South Africa,* pp 120 — 147. Edited by S. Marks and A. Atmore. London: Longman, 1980.

Bennie, William Govan. (1935). *Imibengo.* Lovedale: The Lovedale Press, 1935.

Bisset, John. (1875). *Sport and War in Africa.* London: Murray, 1875.

Boëseken, Anna J. (1966 — 1973). *Suid-Afrikaanse Argiefstukke: Belangrike Kaapse Dokumente.* 2 vols. Cape Town: Direkteur van Argiewe, 1966 — 1973.

Bokwe, John Knox. (1914). *Ntsikana.* Lovedale: The Lovedale Press, 1914.

Boniface, C.E. (1829). *Relation du naufrage du navire francais l'Eole sur le cote de la Caffrerie.* Cape Town: Bridekirk, 1829.

Bonner, Philip. (1980). 'Classes, the mode of production and the state in pre-colonial Swaziland.' In *Economy and Society in Pre-industrial South Africa,* pp 80 — 101. Edited by S. Marks and A. Atmore. London: Longman, 1980.

Botha, C. Graham. (1927). *The Wreck of the Grosvenor.* Cape Town: Van Riebeeck Society, 1927.

Bowker, John M. (1864). *Speeches, Letters and Selections from Important Papers.* Grahamstown: Godlonton and Richards, 1864.

Bowker, T. Holden. (1970). 'War Journal'. In *Comdt. Holden Bowker,* pp 97 — 165. Edited by I. Mitford-Barberton. Cape Town: Human and Rousseau, 1970.

Boyce, William. (1838). *Notes on South African Affairs.* Grahamstown:

Aldum and Harvey, 1838.

Brownlee, Charles. (1896). *Reminiscences of Kaffir Life and History*. 2nd ed. Lovedale: The Lovedale Press, 1896.

Brownlee, Frank. (1923). *The Transkeian Native Territories: Historical Records*. Lovedale: Lovedale Press, 1923.

Brownlee, John. (1827). 'Account of the Amakosae, or Southern Caffres.' In George Thompson, *Travels and Adventures in Southern Africa*. 2 vols., 1827; reprinted Cape Town: Van Riebeeck Society, 1967 – 1968. 2: 191 – 219.

Brownlee, William T. (1925). *The Progress of the Bantu*. Lovedale: The Lovedale Press, 1925.

Brownlee, William T. (1936). 'D'Urban, Hintsa and the Fingoes.' *The Critic* (Cape Town), 4 (1936), 157 – 163.

Bryant, A.T. (1929). *Olden Times in Natal and Zululand*. London: Longman, 1929.

Bunbury, C.F.J. (1848). *Journal of a residence at the Cape of Good Hope*. London: Murray, 1848.

Bundy, Colin. (1979). *The Rise and Fall of the South African Peasantry*. London: Heineman, 1979.

Campbell, John. (1815). *Travels in South Africa*. London: Black, Parry, 1815.

Chalmers, J.A. (1878). *Tiyo Soga*. 2nd ed. Edinburgh: Elliot, 1878.

Cingo, W.D. (1927). *Ibali labaThembu*. Emfundisweni: Mission Press, 1927.

Coetzer, P.J. (1879). *Gebeurtenisse uit di Kaffer-oorloge fan 1834, 1835, 1846, 1850 tot 1853*. 1897; reprint ed., Cape Town: Struik, 1963.

Cole, A.W. (1852). *The Cape and the Kafirs*. London: Bentley, 1852.

Collins, Richard. (1809). 'Journal of a Tour of the North-Eastern Boundary, the Orange River and the Storm Mountains.' In *The Record*, ed. D. Moodie. 1840; reprint ed. Balkema: Cape Town and Amsterdam: 1960, Part V.

Comaroff, John, L. (1974). 'Chiefship in a South African Homeland.' *Journal of Southern African Studies*. 1 (1974): 36 – 51.

Cory, George. (1910 – 1939). *The Rise of South Africa*. 6 vols. 1910 – 1939; reprint ed., Cape Town: Struik, 1965.

De Heusch, Luc. (1975). 'What Shall we do with the drunken King?' *Africa* 45 (1975): 363 – 372.

Derricourt, Robin M. (1977). *Prehistoric Man in the Ciskei and Transkei*. Cape Town : Struik, 1977.

Döhne, J.L. (1862). *Das Kafferland und Seine Bewohner*. Berlin: Berliner Evangelisches Missionshaus, 1862.

Dugmore, Henry H. (1858). 'Rev, H.H. Dugmore's Papers.' In *A Compendium of Kafir Laws and Customs*, pp 1 – 56; 160 – 168; Edited by J. Maclean, 1858; reprint ed., Grahamstown: J. Slater, 1906.

Dugmore, Henry H. (1958). *Reminiscences of an Albany Settler.* Edited by F.G. van der Riet and L.A. Hewson. Grahamstown: Grocott and Sherry, 1958.

Duly, Leslie C. (1968). *British Land Policy at the Cape, 1795 – 1844.* Durham: Duke University Press, 1968.

Ehret, Christopher. (1967). 'Cattle-Keeping and milking in eastern and southern African history: the linguistic evidence.' *Journal of African History* 8 (1967): 1 – 17.

Ellenberger, D.F. and MacGregor, J.C. (1912). *History of the Basuto.* London: 1912.

Elphick, Richard H. (1977). *Kraal and Castle: Khoikhoi and the making of White South Africa.* New Haven: Yale University Press, 1977.

Elphick, R. and Giliomee H. (1979). *The Shaping of South African Society, 1652 – 1820.* London: Longman, 1979.

Forbes, Vernon S. (1965). *Pioneer Travellers in South Africa.* Cape Town: Balkema, 1965.

Freeman, John. (1851). *A Tour in South Africa.* London: Snow, 1851.

Freund, William M. (1972). 'The Eastern Frontier of the Cape Colony during the Batavian Period, 1803 – 1806.' *Journal of African History* 13 (1972): 631 – 645.

Fynn, Henry F. (1950). *The Diary of Henry Francis Fynn.* Eds. J. Stuart and D.M. Malcolm. Pietermaritzburg: Shuter and Shooter, 1950.

Galbraith, John S. (1963). *Reluctant Empire.* Berkeley and Los Angeles: University of California Press, 1963.

Gerard, A.S. (1971) *Four African Literatures.* Berkeley: University of California Press, 1971.

Gilfillan, W.F.A. (1970). 'Diary.' in *The Story of One Branch of the Gilfillan Family in South Africa.* Edited by M. Gilfillan. Johannesburg: privately printed, 1970.

Giliomee, Hermann B. (1966). 'Die Administrasietydperk van Lord Caledon, 1807 – 1811.' *Archives Year Book for South African History,* 1966.

Giliomee, Hermann B. (1975). *Die Kaap tydens die Eerste Britse Bewind.* Cape Town: HAUM, 1975.

Giliomee, Hermann. (1979). 'The Eastern Frontier, 1770 – 1812.' in Elphick, R. and Giliomee, H, *The Shaping of South African Society,* (1979), pp 291 – 337.

Godee-Molsbergen, E.C. (1916 – 1932). *Reizen in Zuid-Afrika in de Hollandse Tijd.* 4 vols. The Hague and s'Gravenhage: Marthinus Nijhoff, 1916 – 1932.

Godelier, M. (1977). *Perspectives in Marxist Anthropology.* Translated by R. Brain. Cambridge: University Press, 1977.

Godlonton, Robert. (1836a). *Introductory Remarks to a Narrative of the*

Irruption of the Kafir Hordes. Grahamstown: Meurant and Godlonton, 1836.

Godlonton, Robert. (1836b) *A Narrative of the Irruption of the Kafir Hordes.* Grahamstown: Meurant and Godlonton, 1836.

Goldswain, Jeremiah. (1946 – 1949). *The Chronicle of Jeremiah Goldswain.* Ed. U. Long. 2 vols. Cape Town: Van Riebeeck Society, 1946 – 1949.

Guy, J.J. (1971). 'A Note on Firearms in the Zulu Kingdom with special reference to the Anglo-Zulu war, 1879.' *Journal of African History* 12 (1971): 557 – 570.

Guy, J.J. (1978). 'Production and Exchange in the Zulu Kingdom.' *Mohlomi.* 2 (1978): 96 – 106.

Hallema, A. (1932). 'Een bezoek van Mnr. Hendrik Swellengrebel aan den Kaffir-Kapitein Jeramba.' *Zuid-Afrika* 9 (1932): 131 – 137.

Hammond-Tooke, W.D. (1955 – 1956). *The Tribes of Mount Frere District.* Ethnological Publications No. 33. Pretoria: Government Printer, 1955 1956.

Hammond-Tooke, W.D. (1958). *The Tribes of King Williams Town District.* Ethnological Publications, no. 41. Pretoria: Government Printer, 1958.

Hammond-Tooke, W.D. (1965). 'Segmentation and Fission in Cape Nguni Political Units.' *Africa* 35 (1965): 143 – 166.

Hammond-Tooke, W.D. (1968). 'Descent Group Scatter in a Mpondomise Ward.' *African Studies* 27 (1968): 83 – 94.

Hammond-Tooke, W.D. (1969). 'The 'other side' of frontier history.' In *African societies in Southern Africa,* pp 230 – 258. Edited by L.M. Thompson. London: Heinemann, 1969.

Hammond-Tooke, W.D. (1975). *Command or Consensus: the development of Transkeian Local Government.* Cape Town: David Philip, 1975.

Harinck, Gerrit. (1969). 'Interaction between Xhosa and Khoi: emphasis on the period 1620 – 1750.' *In African Societies in Southern Africa,* pp 145 – 169. Edited by L.M. Thompson. London: Heinemann, 1969.

Haupt, C.A. (1752). 'Journal . . . op de togt door den vaandrig August Frederik Beutler.' In *Reizen in Zuid-Afrika in de HollandseTijd,* 3: 265 – 336. Edited by E.C. Godee-Molsbergen. s'Gravenhage: Martinus Nijhoff, 1922.

Hockly, Harold K. (1949). *The Story of the British Settlers of 1820 in South Africa.* Cape Town and Johannesburg: Juta, 1949.

Holt, Basil. (1954). *Joseph Williams and the Pioneer Mission to the South-eastern Bantu.* Lovedale: The Lovedale Press, 1954.

Horton, Robin. (1967). 'African Traditional Thought and Western Science.' *Africa* 37 (1967): 158 – 187.

Hunter, Monica. (1961). *Reaction to Conquest.* 2nd ed. Oxford: University Press, 1961.

Jabavu, D.D.T. *et al.* (1953). 'The Fingo Slavery Myth.' *South African Out-*

look 65 (1935): 123 – 124, 134 – 135, 195 – 196.

Jabavu, D.D.T. (1952). *Imbumba YamaNyama*. Lovedale: Privately Printed 1952.

Jordan, Archibald C. (1973). *Towards an African Literature*. Berkeley and Los Angeles: University of California Press, 1973.

Juju. (1880). 'Reminiscences of an Old Kaffir.' *Cape Monthly Magazine*, 3rd series, 3 (1880): 289 – 294.

'Justus' (1837) (A.G. Campbell). *The Wrongs of the Caffre Nation*. London: Duncan, 1837.

Kawa, Richard Tainton. (1930). *Ibali lamaMfengu*. Lovedale: Lovedale Press, 1930.

Kay, Stephen. (1833). *Travels and Researches in Caffraria*. London: John Mason, 1833.

Kirby, Percival R. (1953). *Source Book on the Wreck of the Grosvenor*. Cape Town: Van Riebeeck Society, 1953.

Kirby, Percival R. (1955). *Andrew Smith and Natal*. Cape Town: Van Riebeeck Society, 1955.

Kirk, Tony. (1973). 'Progress and decline in the Kat River Settlement.' *Journal of African History* 14 (1973): 411 – 428.

Kirk, Tony. (1980). 'The Cape economy and the expropriation of the Kat River Settlement.' In *Economy and Society in Pre-industrial South Africa*, pp 226 – 246. Edited by S. Marks and A. Atmore. London: Longman, 1980.

Kropf, Albert. (1889). *Das Volk der Xosa-Kaffern*. Berlin: Berliner Evangelichen Mission-Gesellschaft, 1889.

Kropf, Albert. (1891). *Der Lugenprofeten Kafferlands*. Berlin: Berliner Evangelischen Missions-Gesellschaft, 1891.

Kropf, A. and Godfrey R. (1915). *A Kafir – English Dictionary*. 2nd ed. Lovedale: The Lovedale Press, 1915.

Kunene, D.P. and Kirsch, R.A. (1967). *The Beginnings of South African Vernacular Literature*. Los Angeles: University of California, 1967.

Lanham, L.W. (1964). 'The Proliferation and Extension of Bantu Phonemic Systems influenced by Bushman and Hottentot.' *Proceedings of the Ninth International Congress of Linguists* Cambridge, Mass. 1962, pp 382 – 391; The Hague: Martinus Nijhoff, 1964.

Lategan, Felix. (1974). *Die Boer se Roer*. Cape Town: Tafelberg, 1974.

Legassick, Martin. (1971). 'The Frontier Tradition in South African Historiography.' *ICS Collected Seminar Papers* 2 (1971): 1 – 33.

Lehmann, Joseph. (1977). *Remember you are an Englishman*. London: Jonathan Cape, 1977.

Leibbrandt, H.C.V. (1897). *Precis of the Archives of the Cape of Good Hope: The Defence of Willem Adriaan van der Stel*. Cape Town: Richards, 1898.

Leibbrandt, H.C.V. (1902). *The Rebellion of 1815, generally known as*

Slachter's Nek. Cape Town: Richards, 1902.

Lewis, I.M. (1968). *History and Social Anthropology.* London: Tavistock, 1968.

Lewis, I.M. (1971). *Ecstatic Religion.* Harmondsworth: Penguin, 1971.

Lichtenstein, H. (1812 — 1815). *Travels in Southern Africa in the Years 1803, 1804, 1805 and 1806.* Translated by A. Plumptre. 2 vols. 1812 — 1815; Reprint ed., Cape Town: Van Riebeeck Society, 1928 — 1930.

Long, Una. (1947). *An index to authors of unofficial privately-owned manuscripts relating to the history of South Africa, 1812 — 1920.* London: Lund Humphries, 1947.

Louw, J.A. (1957). 'The Nomenclature of Cattle in the South-Eastern Bantu Languages.' *Communications of the University of South Africa,* C2 (1957), pp 1 — 19.

Maclean, John. (1858). *A Compendium of Kafir Laws and Customs.* 1858; Reprint ed., Grahamstown: J. Slater, 1906.

Macmillan, William M. (1963). *Bantu, Boer and Briton.* 2nd ed., Oxford: University Press, 1963.

Mafeje, A. (1967). 'The role of a Bard in a Contemporary African Community.' *Journal of African Languages* 6 (1967): 193 — 223.

Maggs, T.M.O'C. (1980). 'The Iron Age Sequence South of the Vaal and Pongola Rivers: Some historical implications.' *Journal of African History* 21 (1980): 1 — 15.

Maingard, L.F. (1934). 'The Linguistic Approach to South African Prehistory and Ethnology.' *South African Journal of Science* 31 (1934): 117 — 143.

Majeke, Nosipho. (1954). *The Role of the Missionaries in Conquest.* Johannesburg: Society of Young Africa, 1954.

Marais, J.S. (1944). *Maynier and the First Boer Republic.* Cape Town: Maskew Miller, 1944.

Marks, Shula. (1970). *Reluctant Rebellion.* Oxford: University Press, 1970.

Marks, S. and Atmore, A. (1971). 'Firearms in Southern Africa: a Survey.' *Journal of African History* 12 (1971): 517 — 130.

Meintjies, J. (1971). *Sandile: The Fall of the Xhosa Nation.* Cape Town: T.V. Bulpin, 1971.

Merriman, N.J. (1957). *The Cape Journals of Archdeacon N.J. Merriman.* Edited by D.H. Varley and H.M. Mathew. Cape Town: Van Riebeeck Society, 1957.

Minutes of the Proceedings of the Court of Inquiry . . . on the fate of the Caffer chief Hintza. Cape Town: Zuid-Afrikaan, 1837.

Millar, Anthony K. (1965). *Plantagenet in South Africa.* Cape Town: Oxford University Press, 1965.

Mitra, S.M. (1911). *Life and Letters of Sir John Hall.* London: Longmans, 1911.

Moodie, Donald. (1840). *The Record: or a series of Official Papers relative*

to the Condition and Treatment of the Native Tribes of South Africa.
1840; reprint ed., Amsterdam and Cape Town: Balkema, 1960.

Moodie, J.W.D. (1835). *Ten Years in South Africa.* 2 vols. London: Bentley,
1835.

Morgan, N. (1833). 'An Account of the Amakosae.' *South African Quarterly
Journal* 1 (1833), 1 − 12, 33 − 48, 65 − 71.

Mqhayi, S.E.K. (1931). *Ityala lamaWele.* 7th ed. Lovedale: Lovedale Press;
1931.

Mqhayi, Samuel E.K. (1934). *UMqhayi waseNtab'ozuko.* Lovedale; Lovedale
Press, 1939.

Msebenzi. (1938). *History of Matiwane and the AmaNgwane Tribe.* Ed.
N.J. van Warmelo. Ethnological Publications No 7. Pretoria: Government Printer, 1938.

Muller, C.F.J. (1974). *Die Oorsprong van die Groot Trek.* Cape Town and
Johannesburg: Tafelberg, 1974.

Munro, W. (1887). *Records of service and campaigning in many lands.* 2 vols.
London: Hurst and Blackett, 1887.

Neumark, S.D. (1957). *Economic Influences on the South African Frontier,
1652 − 1836.* Stanford: University Press, 1957.

Newton-King, S. (1980). 'The labour market of the Cape Colony, 1807 −
1828.' In *Economy and Society in Pre-industrial South Africa,* pp 171
207. Edited by S. Marks and A. Atmore. London: Longman, 1980.

Ngani, A.Z. (1947). *Ibali lamaGqunukhwebe.* Lovedale: Lovedale Press,
1947.

Paravicini di Capelli, W.B.E. (1965). *Reize in de Binnenlanden van Zuid-
Afrika.* Ed. W.J. de Kock. Cape Town: Van Riebeeck Society, 1965.

Paterson, William. (1789). *A Narrative of Four Journeys into the Country
of the Hottentots and Caffraria.* London: Johnson, 1789.

Peires. J.B. (1975). 'The Rise of the Right-Hand House in the History and
Historiography of the Xhosa.' *History in Africa.* 2 (1975): 155 − 175.

Peires, J.B. (1979). 'The Lovedale Press: Literature for the Bantu Revisited.'
History in Africa. 6 (1979): 155 − 175.

Philipps, Thomas. (1960). *Philipps, 1820 Settler.* Ed. A. Keppel-Jones.
Pietermaritzburg: Shuter and Shooter, 1960.

Poulantzas, Nicos. (1973). *Political Power and Social Classes.* London:
New Left Books, 1973.

Pringle, Thomas. (1835) *Narrative of a Residence in South Africa.* 1835;
Reprint ed., Cape Town: Struik, 1966.

Ranger, T.O. (1974). 'Report on the Conference for the Historical Study of
East African Religion, Limuru, June 1874.' *African Religious Research*
4 (1974): 6 − 46.

Read, James. (1818). 'Narrative of the journey of Mr. Read and others to

Caffraria.' *Transactions of the London Missionary Society* 4 (1818): 280 – 293.

Reyburn, H. (1934 – 1935) 'Studies in Frontier History.' *The Critic* (Cape Town) 3 – 4 (1934 – 1935); 3: 40 – 55, 101 – 109, 148 – 163. 204 – 209; 4: 46 – 59, 105 – 116.

Roberts, Andrew. (1974). *A History of the Bemba.* London: Longman, 1974.

Robertson, H.M. (1934). '150 years of economic contact between White and Black.' *South African Journal of Economics* 2 (1934): 403 – 425.

Rose, Cowper. (1829). *Four Years in Southern Africa.* London: Colburn and Bentley, 1829.

Ross, Robert. (1880). 'Ethnic Identity, Demographic Crises and Xhosa-Khoi Interaction.' *History in Africa*, 7 (1980): 259 – 271.

Rubusana, Walter B. (1906). *Zemk'iinkomo Magwalandini.* London: Butler and Tanner, 1906.

Rubusana, Walter B. (1966). *Zemk'iinkomo Magwalandini.* Abridged ed. Lovedale: Lovedale Press, 1966.

Sahlins, Marshall D. (1972). *Stone Age Economics.* Chicago: Aldine, 1972.

Sanders, P. (1975). *Moshoeshoe.* Cape Town: David Philip, 1975.

Saunders, C. and Derricourt. R. (1974). *Beyond the Cape Frontier: Studies in the History of the Transkei and Ciskei.* London: Longman, 1974.

Schapera, Issac. (1930). *The Khoisan Peoples of South Africa.* London: Routledge, 1930.

Scheub, Harold. (1976). *The Xhosa Ntsomi.* Oxford: University Press, 1976.

Schoeman, A.E. (1938). *Coenraad de Buys.* Pretoria: De Bussy, 1938.

Shaw, Barnabas. (1840). *Memorials of South Africa.* 1840; reprint ed., Cape Town: Struik, 1970.

Shaw, E.M. and Van Warmelo, N.J. (1972). 'The Material Culture of the Cape Nguni: Part 1, Settlement.' *Annals of the South African Museum* 58 (1972): 1 – 102.

Shaw, E.M. and Van Warmelo, N.J. (1974). 'The Material Culture of the Cape Nguni: Part 2, Technology.' *Annals of the South African Museum* 58 (1974): 103 – 214.

Shaw, William. (1860). *The Story of my Mission in South-eastern Africa.* London: Hamilton Adams, 1860.

Shaw, William. (1972). *The Journal of William Shaw.* Edited by W.D. Hammond-Tooke. Cape Town: Balkema, 1972.

Shepherd, Robert H.W. (1945). *Lovedale and Literature for the Bantu.* Lovedale: Lovedale Press, 1945.

Shrewsbury, J.V.B. (1867). *Memorials of the Reverend William J. Shrewsbury.* London: Hamilton Adams, 1867.

Slater, Henry. (1975). 'Land, labour and capital in Natal: The Natal Land and Colonisation Company.' *Journal of African History* 16 (1975): 257 – 283.

Smith, Harry. (1903). *Autobiography of Sir Harry Smith.* Ed. G.C. Moore

Smith. London: Murray, 1903.

Smith, Robert S. (1976). *Warfare and Diplomacy in Pre-Colonial West Africa*. London: Methuen, 1976.

Smith, Thornley. (1864). *The Earnest Missionary: a memoir of the Rev. Horatio Pearse*. London: Adams, 1864.

Smith of St. Cyrus, Andrew. (1895). *A Contribution to South African Materia Medica*. 3rd ed. Lovedale: Lovedale Press, 1895.

Soga, John Henderson. (n.d.) *The Ama-Xosa: Life and Customs*. Lovedale: Lovedale Press, n.d. (1931?).

Soga, John Henderson. (1930). *The South-Eastern Bantu*. Johannesburg: Witwatersrand University Press, 1930.

Soga, Tiyo Burnside. (n.d.) *Intlalo kaXhosa*. Lovedale: Lovedale Press, n.d. (1938?).

Somerville, W. (1979). *William Somerville's Narrative of his Journeys to the Eastern Cape Frontier and to Lattakoe, 1799 – 1802*. Edited by E. and F. Bradlow. Cape Town: Van Riebeeck Society, 1979.

Sparrman, Anders. (1786). *A Voyage to the Cape of Good Hope*. 2nd ed., 2 vols. London: Robinson, 1786.

Steedman, Andrew. (1835). *Wanderings and adventures in the Interior of Africa*. 2 vols. London: Longmans, 1835.

Stockenstrom, Andries. (1887). *The Autobiography of the late Sir Andries Stockenstrom*. Edited by C.W. Hutton. 2 vols. Cape Town: Juta, 1887.

Stout, Benjamin. (1975). *Narrative of the Loss of the Ship Hercules*. 1798; reprint. ed. by A. Porter. Port Elizabeth: Historical Society of Port Elizabeth, 1975.

Stretch, Charles Lennox. (1876). 'Makana and the attack on Graham's Town.' *Cape Monthly Magazine* New Series 12 (1876): 297 – 303.

Stubbs, Thomas. (1978). *The Reminiscences of Thomas Stubbs*. Eds. W.A. Maxwell and R.T. McGeogh. Cape Town: Balkema, 1978.

Switzer, L. and D. (1979). *The Black Press in South Africa and Lesotho*. Boston: G.E. Hall, 1979.

Theal, George M. (1877). *Compendium of South African History and Geography*. 3rd ed. Lovedale: Lovedale Press, 1877.

Theal, George M. (1897). *History of South Africa under the Dutch East India Company*. 2 vols. London: Sonnenschein, 1897.

Theal, George M. (1912). *Documents relating to the Kaffir War of 1835*. London: Cowes, 1912.

Theal, George M. (1915). *History of South Africa from 1795 to 1872*. 4th ed. 5 vols. London: Allen and Unwin, 1915.

Thompson, George. (1827). *Travels and Adventures in Southern Africa*. 2 vols. 1827; reprint ed. Cape Town: Van Riebeeck Society, 1967 – 1968.

Tylden, G. (1956 – 1957). 'Shoulder Firearms in Southern Africa, 1652 – 1952.' *Africana Notes and News* 12 (1956 – 1957): 198 – 219.

Van der Kemp, Johannes T. (1804). 'An account of . . . Caffraria.' *Trans-actions of the London Missionary Society.* 1 (1804): 349 — 505.

Van der Merwe, P.J. (1938). *Die Trekboer in die Geskiedenis van die Kaap-kolonie.* Cape Town: Nasionale Pers, 1938.

Van der Merwe, P.J. (1940). *Die Kafferoorlog van 1793.* Cape Town: Nasio-nale Pers, 1940.

Van Reenen, D.G. (1937). *Die Joernaal van Dirk Gysbert van Reenen, 1803.* Eds. W. Blommaert and J.A. Wiid. Cape Town: Van Riebeeck Society, 1937.

Van Reenen, Jacob. (1792). 'A journey from the Cape of Good Hope under-taken in 1790 and 1791.' Ed. and trans. E. Riou, 1792. In *The Wreck of the Grosvenor.* Edited by C.G. Botha. Cape Town: Van Riebeeck Society, 1927.

Vansina, Jan. (1965). *Oral Tradition.* Translated by H.M. Wright. Chicago: Aldine Press, 1965.

Vansina, Jan. (1966). *Kingdoms of the Savannah.* Madison: University of Wisconsin Press, 1966.

Von Winkelman, F. (1888 — 1889). 'Reisaantekeningen.' In *Reizen in Zuid-Afrika in de Hollandse Tijd,* 4: 63 — 99. Edited by E.C. Godee-Molsbergen. Gravenhage: Martinus Nijhoff, 1932.

Ward, Harriet. (1848). *Five Years in Kaffirland.* 2 vols. London: Colburn, 1848.

Webb, C. and Wright, J.B. (1976). *The James Stuart Archives: Volume I.* Pietermaritzburg and Durban: University of Natal Press, 1976.

Williams, Donovan. (1961). *Where Races Meet.* Johannesburg: A.P.B., 1961.

Wilmot, A.C. and Chase, J.C. (1869). *History of the Colony of the Cape of Good Hope.* Cape Town: J.C. Juta, 1869.

Wilson, Bryan. (1975). *Magic and the Millennium.* St. Albans: Paladin, 1975.

Wilson, Monica. (1959). 'The Early History of the Transkei and Ciskei.' *African Studies* 18 (1959): 167 — 179.

Wilson, Monica. (1969a). 'The Nguni People.' In *The Oxford History of South Africa.* Edited by M. Wilson and L. Thompson. 2 vols. Oxford: University Press, 1969 — 1971; 1: 75 — 130.

Wilson, Monica. (1969b). 'Co-operation and Conflicts: The Eastern Cape Frontier.' In *The Oxford History of South Africa.* Edited by M. Wilson and L. Thompson. 2 vols. Oxford: University Press, 1969 — 1971; 1: 233 — 271.

Wilson, Monica. (1969c). 'Changes in social structure in Southern Africa.' In *African Societies in Southern Africa,* pp 71 — 85. Edited by L.M. Thompson. London: Heinemann Educational Books, 1969.

Wilson, Monica and Thompson, Leonard. (1969 — 1971). *The Oxford History of South Africa.* 2 vols. Oxford: University Press, 1969 — 1971.

Worsley, Peter. (1970). *The Trumpet Shall Sound.* 2nd ed. St. Albans: Paladin, 1970.

F. UNPUBLISHED PAPERS AND DISSERTATIONS

Crankshaw, G.B. (1960). 'The Diary of C.L. Stretch: a Critical Edition and Appraisal.' M.A. thesis, Rhodes University, 1960.

Donaldson, Margaret. (1974). 'The Council of Advice at the Cape of Good Hope, 1825 – 1834.' Ph.D. dissertation, Rhodes University, 1974.

Harington, Anthony. (1977). 'Sir Harry Smith in South Africa.' Ph.D. dissertation, University of South Africa, 1977.

Kallaway, Peter, (1980). 'The Xhosa of the Karreebergen.' Conference on Class Formation, Culture and Consciousness: the Making of Modern South Africa. Anglican Regional Management Centre, January 1980.

Kaplan, Mark J. (1975). 'Aspects concerning British administration in the Cape Eastern Frontier with special reference to the origins of the War of 1846.' BA (honours) research essay, University of Cape Town, 1975.

Kirk, Tony. (1972). 'Self-Government and Self-Defence in South Africa: the Interrelations between British and Cape Politics, 1846 – 1854.' D.Phil dissertation, Oxford University 1972.

Kuse, Wandile. (1977). 'The Form and Themes of Mqhayi's Poetry and Prose.' Ph.D dissertation, University of Wisconsin, 1977.

Le Cordeur, Basil. (1979). 'The Politics of Eastern Cape Separatism, 1820 – 1836.' Paper presented to the conference of the South African Historical Association. February 1979.

Moyer, Richard A. (1976). 'A History of the Mfengu of the Eastern Cape.' Ph.D. dissertation, University of London, 1976.

Nkonki, Garvey. (1968). 'The Traditional Prose Literature of the Ngqika.' M.A. thesis, University of South Africa, 1968.

Peires, J.B. (1973). 'Chronology of the Cape Nguni till 1900.' M.A. thesis, Universty of Wisconsin, 1973.

Webb, A.C.M. (1975). 'The Agricultural Development of the 1820 Settlement down to 1846.' M.A. thesis, Rhodes University, 1975.

Williams, Donovan. (1959). 'The Missionaries on the Eastern Frontier of the Cape Colony, 1799 – 1853.' Ph.D. dissertation, University of the Witwatersrand, 1959.

Wright, John B. (1979). 'Women and Production in the Zulu Kingdom.' Paper presented to the Nguni History Workshop, Rhodes University, June 1979.

Index